WHAT IS THE FAMILY OF LAW?

This book argues that the legal understanding of 'family' in the UK continues to be underpinned by the idealised image of the 'nuclear family', premised upon the traditional, gendered roles of 'father as breadwinner' and 'mother as homemaker'. This examination of the law's model of the 'family' has been prompted by the substantial reforms that have taken place in family law in recent decades, and the significant evolution in social attitudes and familial practices that has occurred in parallel.

Throughout the book, the influence of the nuclear family is noted in several different contexts: various specific legal definitions of 'family', the legal regulation of adult, conjugal relationships, the attribution of legal parenthood and the construction of the role of the 'parent' within the law. Ultimately, this book argues that while these reforms have resulted in additional categories of relationship coming to be situated within the nuclear family model, there has not, as yet, been any fundamental alteration of the underpinning concept of the nuclear family itself.

This book concludes by considering the possibilities offered beyond the 'nuclear family'; exploring the reconceptualising of the legal understanding of 'family' around alternative and potentially 'radical' models of 'family'.

What is the Family of Law?

The Influence of the Nuclear Family

Alan Brown

•HART•
OXFORD • LONDON • NEW YORK • NEW DELHI • SYDNEY

HART PUBLISHING

Bloomsbury Publishing Plc

Kemp House, Chawley Park, Cumnor Hill, Oxford, OX2 9PH, UK

HART PUBLISHING, the Hart/Stag logo, BLOOMSBURY and the Diana logo are trademarks of Bloomsbury Publishing Plc

First published in Great Britain 2019

A catalogue record for this book is available from the British Library.

Library of Congress Cataloging-in-Publication data

Names: Brown, Alan (Law teacher), author.

Title: What is the family of law? : the influence of the nuclear family / Alan Brown.

Description: Oxford, UK ; Portland, Oregon : Hart Publishing, 2019. | Based on author's thesis (doctoral – University of Strathclyde, 2016). | Includes bibliographical references.

Identifiers: LCCN 2018040272 (print) | LCCN 2018041416 (ebook) | ISBN 9781509919598 (Epub) | ISBN 9781509919581 (hardback : alk. paper)

Subjects: LCSH: Domestic relations—Great Britain. | Parent and child (Law)—Great Britain. | Husband and wife—Great Britain. | Nuclear families—Great Britain.

Classification: LCC KD750 (ebook) | LCC KD750 .B76 2019 (print) | DDC 346.4101/5—dc23

LC record available at https://lccn.loc.gov/2018040272

ISBN: HB: 978-1-50991-958-1
ePDF: 978-1-50991-960-4
ePub: 978-1-50991-959-8

Typeset by Compuscript Ltd, Shannon
Printed and bound in Great Britain by TJ International Ltd, Padstow, Cornwall

To find out more about our authors and books visit www.hartpublishing.co.uk. Here you will find extracts, author information, details of forthcoming events and the option to sign up for our newsletters.

ACKNOWLEDGEMENTS

This book was based upon my PhD thesis and I want to thank both of my supervisors, Dr Mary Neal and Professor Kenneth Norrie, for their invaluable help and support both while completing the thesis (which at times seemed an impossible task) and afterwards when approaching the revision of that thesis into this book. Moreover, I am immensely grateful to the examiners of my thesis, Professor Jonathan Herring and Professor Nicole Busby, who provided me with substantial insight and assistance when I embarked upon this book project, as well as for their advice throughout the revisions. To all my family, friends and colleagues (from both during and after my PhD) who have helped and supported me in various ways throughout the time that this project has been ongoing. Particularly, I want to thank my mum for believing in me, for reading drafts of this work on far more occasions than she would have believed possible over the past several years and for noticing all those errant commas. Finally, to Lynsey, for her patience, for listening to another 'philosophical question' and for being there through the ups and downs of this entire process, I could not have done it without you.

TABLE OF CONTENTS

PART IV
THE FUTURE

TABLE OF CASES

TABLE OF LEGISLATION

Domestic Legislation

International Legislation

> what happens when the old certainties (rooted in religion, tradition, biology, etc.) lose much of their force without actually disappearing and new options redraw the areas for personal choice, not in a free space outside society but in one that involves new social regulations, pressures and controls.

Elisabeth Beck-Gernsheim, *Reinventing the Family: In Search of New Lifestyles*, (Cambridge, Polity Press, 2002) 7

Introduction

There are certain tensions inherent to the legal regulation of the 'family' and family life. Some of these relate to the dominant, orthodox understanding of what law is and how it functions. Consequently, such tensions are focused around the idea that in considering the 'family', the law is straying into 'private' areas that it is unsuited to addressing. While other tensions reflect the complexity of how 'family' is socially understood and the role that families play in the lives of individuals. These tensions are therefore centred upon whether the law can properly recognise and regulate this complexity. As well as this, as O'Donovan comments:

> Myths are not an obvious source of law but where relationships of women and men are talked of, myths inform the discourse. The classical tradition records universal themes in human lives: conception, birth, childhood, sexual union, love, betrayal, error. These find an expression in family law although their mythical origins are not acknowledged.[1]

The concepts of the law and the family do not seamlessly interact with one another.[2] With that said, there have been significant changes in the familial demographics of UK society throughout the twentieth and early twenty-first centuries: fewer marriages,[3] a rise in divorce,[4] an increase in cohabitation outside

[1] Katherine O'Donovan, *Family Law Matters* (London, Pluto Press, 1993) 9.

[2] See eg Rt Hon Mrs Justice Hale, 'Private Lives and Public Duties: What is Family Law For?' (1998) 20(2) *Journal of Social Welfare and Family Law* 125, 133, who commented that 'We may have spent far too long concentrating on things that the law cannot do at the expense of things that it could. The law is not good at enforcing personal relationships.'

[3] Office for National Statistics (ONS), 'Marriages in England and Wales: 2015', (February 2018) 4, shows a significant decline in marriages since the late 1960s (from over 400,000 per year to under 250,000 per year); in 2015 there were 239,020 marriages of opposite-sex couples and 6,493 between same-sex couples, available at: www.ons.gov.uk/peoplepopulationandcommunity/birthsdeathsandmarriages/marriagecohabitationandcivilpartnerships/bulletins/marriagesinenglandandwalesprovisional/2015. Similar statistics are available for Scotland, which show a decline from over 40,000 marriages per year in the 1960–70s to under 30,000 per year in recent years, National Records of Scotland, 'Marriage and Civil Partnership Time Series Data', (August 2017), available at: www.nrscotland.gov.uk/statistics-and-data/statistics/statistics-by-theme/vital-events/marriages-and-civil-partnerships/marriages-and-civil-partnership-time-series-data.

[4] ONS, 'Divorces in England and Wales, 2012', (February 2014) 2, shows a substantial increase in divorce both generally from the 1930s onwards (in 1931 there were only 3,764 instances of divorce) but also specifically in the period from the late 1960s to the 1980s, after the reform of the divorce regime (from under 24,000 divorces in 1960 compared with a peak of around 160,000 in 1985), available at: www.ons.gov.uk/ons/dcp171778_351693.pdf. Similar statistics are available for Scotland, showing a general increase from only 468 divorces in 1934, with a similar peak of 13,365 in 1985, National Records of Scotland, 'Divorces Time Series Data', (March 2013), available at: www.nrscotland.gov.uk/statistics-and-data/statistics/statistics-by-theme/vital-events/vital-events-divorces-and-dissolutions/divorces-time-series-data.

marriage[5] and a higher number of single parent families.[6] Alongside these social changes, there have been substantial and diverse reforms to various aspects of English and Scots family law,[7] including: the liberalisation of the divorce regime,[8] legislation governing assisted reproduction,[9] increasing legal recognition of unmarried cohabiting couples,[10] reform of the adoption regime,[11] the introduction of civil partnership[12] and the subsequent extension of marriage to same-sex couples.[13] Writing extra-judicially, the President of the Family Division Sir James Munby has observed that 'Perhaps in no other area of law have there been such changes in recent decades as in family law'.[14]

However, as Kaganas and Day Sclater have commented 'it has long been recognised that law is a clumsy tool for managing complex family problems, let alone intimate relationships or emotional trauma. The law is clumsy because it deals in generalities and is ill-equipped to take full account of the subtleties of emotion and motivation'.[15] Thus, the complexity and variability of 'family' structures and

[5] ONS, 'Short Report: Cohabitation in the UK, 2012', (November 2012) 1, shows that there were 5.9 million people cohabiting in the UK in 2012, which is around double the figure from 1996, available at: http://webarchive.nationalarchives.gov.uk/20160107161903/http://www.ons.gov.uk/ons/dcp171776_284888.pdf. See further ONS, 'Families and Households: 2017', (November 2017) 5, which shows in 2017 there were just under 3.3 million cohabiting couple families in the UK, representing 17.3% of total families, available at: www.ons.gov.uk/peoplepopulationandcommunity/birthsdeathsandmarriages/families/bulletins/familiesandhouseholds/2017.

[6] ONS, 'Social Trends: Households and Families', (No. 41, February 2011) 7, shows that between 2001–2010 the percentage of people in 'Married Couple Families' has fallen from 72.4% to 68% and that there has been a corresponding increase in 'Cohabiting Couple Families' (12.5% to 15.3%) and 'Lone Parent Families' (14.8% to 16.2%) during that period, available at: http://webarchive.nationalarchives.gov.uk/20160107023650/http://www.ons.gov.uk/ons/rel/social-trends-rd/social-trends/social-trends-41/index.html.

[7] It is worth being clear, at this stage, that the law interacts with the family in a variety of contexts beyond what is traditionally understood as 'family law'. This book will consider some of those contexts, eg some aspects of the law regulating landlord and tenant in ch 1, s II, 'The Law's "Definition(s)" of "Family"'. However, the book will generally confine itself to considering those issues that are traditionally thought of as 'family law' – the legal regulation of the conjugal relationship and the 'parent/child' relationship. Consequently, for example, there will be no consideration of the role of the 'family' in the context of immigration law, see eg the definition of 'relevant family association' contained in s 40 of the Borders, Citizenship and Immigration Act 2009, or of the influence of family and family relationships within the legal regime governing social welfare in the UK.

[8] Divorce Reform Act 1969 and Divorce (Scotland) Act 1976.

[9] Human Fertilisation and Embryology Act 2008, which amended the Human Fertilisation and Embryology Act 1990.

[10] Through both the specific statutory regime in ss 25–30 Family Law (Scotland) Act 2006 and the ad hoc inclusion of cohabitants within other statutory provisions, eg the Child Support Act 1991.

[11] Adoption and Children Act 2002 and Adoption and Children (Scotland) Act 2007.

[12] Civil Partnership Act 2004, also notable is the Gender Recognition Act 2004, which provided the means for legal recognition of a change of gender, subsequent to the decision in *Bellinger v Bellinger* [2003] UKHL 21, [2003] 2 AC 467.

[13] Marriage (Same Sex Couples) Act 2013 and the Marriage and Civil Partnership (Scotland) Act 2014.

[14] Sir James Munby, 'Years of Change: Family Law in 1987, 2012 and 2037' [2013] 43(3) *Fam Law* 278, 278. See further eg John Eekelaar, 'Then and Now – Family Law's Direction of Travel' (2013) 35(4) *Journal of Social Welfare and Family Law* 415.

[15] Felicity Kaganas and Shelley Day Sclater, 'Contact Disputes: Narrative Constructions of "Good" Parents' (2004) 12(1) *Feminist Legal Studies* 1, 6.

forms in twenty-first century society clashes with the law's desire for clarity and certainty and this ongoing tension underpins the arguments advanced within this book. As a result of this tension, as Chan observes 'it is clear that what counts as a family, for legal purposes, is itself a legal construct'.[16] It is that construct, the legal understanding of the 'family', which this book examines.[17] I argue that the law in the UK continues to be underpinned by the idealised image of the traditional nuclear family and that this is problematic for the regulation of the diversity of family forms and practices within twenty-first century UK society.

This book argues that the legal understanding of 'family' in the United Kingdom continues to default to this traditional 'nuclear family', which comprises the nexus of the conjugal relationship and the 'parent/child' relationship, and that this traditional archetype sits uneasily against the diversity and complexity of family forms, structures and practices in contemporary UK society. The traditional nuclear family model retains significant normative and rhetorical power and authority, in spite of the seemingly progressive legal reforms of recent decades, the vast changes in societal demographics, and the resultant prevalence and acceptance of a greater variety of family forms.[18] Moreover, the values upon which that idealised image of family is premised are perpetuated; in particular, the separation of gender roles ('man as breadwinner' and 'woman as homemaker') which is intrinsic to the traditional nuclear family. Indeed, while the nuclear family model now encompasses relationships (same-sex couples and unmarried opposite-sex cohabitants) which were previously located outside its boundaries, the values and assumptions of the archetypical, nuclear family have not been displaced or significantly altered in the process. In this regard, Gittins observes that:

> Central to ideologies about 'the family' have been beliefs about gender and age relations – in fact, the two cannot really be separated. Ideals and statements about what

[16] Winnie Chan, 'Cohabitation, Civil Partnership, Marriage and the Equal Sharing Principle' (2013) 33(1) *Legal Studies* 46, 46.

[17] There are a variety of significant recent legislative developments that affect families and family life in the UK, but which are not directly related to the legal understanding of the 'family' and are therefore outside the scope of this book's consideration. The foremost example is the Legal Aid, Sentencing and Punishment of Offenders Act 2012, which has resulted in the availability of legal aid in family cases in England and Wales being drastically reduced; it is now not available unless there is evidence of domestic violence (Sch, 1 para 12) or harm to the child (Sch, 1 para 13). The impact of these reforms is ongoing, but it is already clear that the reforms have had an effect on the operation of the family court process, with a significant increase in self-representation. Indeed, it is apparent that this reduction in the availability of legal aid will have a substantial influence upon the legal approach to regulating the 'family' in the future. See further eg Stephen Cobb, 'Legal Aid Reform: Its Impact on Family Law' (2013) 35(1) *Journal of Social Welfare and Family Law* 3, Chris Bevan, 'Self-Represented Litigants: The Overlooked and Unintended Consequence of Legal Aid Reform' (2013) 35(1) *Journal of Social Welfare and Family Law* 43, David Emmerson and John Platt, 'Legal Aid, Sentencing and Punishment of Offenders Act 2012: LASPO Reviewed' [2014] 44(4) *Fam Law* 515 and Kirsteen Mackay, 'A Plea from Scotland: Preserving Access to Courts in Private Law Child Contact Disputes' [2013] 25(3) *Child and Family Law Quarterly* 294.

[18] Eekelaar, 'Then and Now – Family Law's Direction of Travel' 420, has argued that 'one might say that the earlier law was based on a constructed vision of the world, one in which people lived, or were expected to live, according to neat moral and behavioural categories imagined by law'.

> a family should be are comprised of statements about the roles and behaviour deemed appropriate for men, women and children within families and society generally.[19]

Ultimately, I will argue that regardless of substantive legislative reforms, changes in social demographics and the growing diversity of familial practices, the legal understanding of the 'family' continues to be centred around the idealised image of the traditional 'nuclear family', consisting in the nexus of the conjugal relationship and the parent/child relationship, and that despite the acceptance of a greater diversity of family forms the legal system continues to conceptualise all families through the prism of the nuclear family. The book will conclude by considering various normative concepts, ideals and values; ranging from 'care' to 'vulnerability' to 'autonomy', that could potentially underpin an alternative image or model of the 'family' within legal understanding. However, I will argue that it is the very focus upon images and models of family that should be rejected; instead the diversity of the lived reality of families and contemporary family life should be embraced.

In order to evidence my overarching argument, I will consider how the law defines and understands the 'family'. This book will demonstrate that there is no single, overarching *definition* of the 'family' within the law, but that instead there is a determinate and archetypical *idealised image* of the 'family' which underpins and influences legal regulation of familial relationships and is employed by the law across different contexts. This idealised image is that of the traditional 'nuclear family', consisting in the nexus of the conjugal relationship and the parent/child relationship. The elements of the nuclear family image will be examined throughout this book, in order to reveal the underlying assumptions and values which underpin the law's construction and understanding of 'family.' A number of contexts in which there is a specific legal definition of 'family' will be examined,[20] in order to illustrate how the idealised image of the nuclear family has influenced the judicial interpretation of these definitions, drawing the boundary of 'family' around adult conjugal relationships and (at least de facto) parent/child relationships, and excluding all other forms of long-term, interdependent and 'caring' relationships from the law's understanding of 'family'.

Subsequently, I will consider the legal understanding and regulation of the core familial relationships that comprise the central nexus of the nuclear family.

[19] Diana Gittins, *The Family in Question: Changing Households and Familiar Ideologies*, 2nd edn (Basingstoke, MacMillan, 1993) 4.

[20] There are a range of legislative provisions which give legal rights or obligations to individuals on the basis of familial relationships or connections, but which do not utilise the terminology of 'family', see eg s 1(3) of the Fatal Accidents Act 1976 which uses the term 'dependant' to set out the various categories of people who are able to raise actions for 'wrongful act causing death', s 1(1) of the Inheritance (Provision for Family and Dependants) Act 1975, which lists the groups of people who are able to bring claims in English law in cases of intestacy, s 2(1) of the Succession (Scotland) Act 1964, which sets out the equivalent Scottish provisions for intestate succession and s 1(1) of the Family Law (Scotland) Act 1985, which sets out the relationships in which the obligation of aliment is owed. These provisions, and their interpretation, will not be considered in any detail in the book, because they do not refer to statutory definitions of the concept of 'family' itself.

This will involve detailed consideration of both: (i) the law's approach to recognising and regulating adult personal relationships, and (ii) the legal understanding of parenthood and parenting. I will observe that legal regulation of adult personal relationships remains centred on 'marriage-like' conjugality, with traditional, heterosexual marriage still the law's model or 'gold standard'. Non-marital relationships (those between same-sex couples and unmarried opposite-sex cohabitants) are recognised and regulated by the law insofar as they share sufficient features and characteristics in common with marriage to be considered capable of performing similar societal functions. Since relationships between same-sex partners and unmarried heterosexual cohabitants can also be located within the central nexus of the nuclear family model (the conjugal relationship and the parent/child relationship), their recognition and regulation does not alter the fundamental reliance upon that idealised image, nor affect its normative power in shaping the legal understanding of the 'family'.

I will also illustrate the continuing centrality of the nuclear family model by examining the legal regulation of the parent/child relationship and showing how, despite the increasing use of the gender-neutral language of the 'parent', the law still deploys a gendered, binary model of parenting and parenthood wherein the gendered parenting roles of the mother and the father are understood and constructed differently. This will be demonstrated via a consideration of two distinct aspects of the legal regulation of the parent/child relationship: the attribution of legal parenthood, and the legal understanding of the role of the 'parent'. Regarding the former, I will observe that the law's approach to the attribution of legal parenthood is premised upon a binary, two-parent model, ideally consisting of one mother and one father. It will be shown that in determining parenthood, the law continues to attach significance to marriage and thereby to be influenced by the traditional, nuclear family model. This is particularly apparent in the contexts of assisted reproduction and surrogacy, where more complex, 'alternative' forms of reproduction are disruptive to traditional understandings and thus are potentially transformative, but are nevertheless forced within the confines of the binary, two-parent model of the nuclear family. I will build on this in considering the construction of the parental role, arguing that in spite of the appearance of the usage of the gender-neutral language of 'parent', the law continues to rely upon the traditional, gendered constructions of 'mother as natural carer' and 'father as breadwinner' associated with the nuclear family model, in its understanding of the parental role. I will illustrate this by exploring judicial understandings of the parental role and showing the continued normative influence of the gendered parenting roles upon these understandings.

Finally, I will consider the potential normative role of the theoretical concepts of 'care', 'relationality', 'vulnerability', 'choice' and 'autonomy' in providing an alternative 'model' to underpin the legal understanding of the 'family'. However, I will conclude that the legal understanding of 'family' should not be premised upon any image or model, instead this conceptual focus upon modelling the 'family' should be replaced by an approach based upon more appropriately recognising the diversity of family structures and the growth of non-traditional family forms within contemporary UK society. Ultimately, I will conclude that, in spite of the substantial volume of family law reform over the past several decades, and the significant developments in social and familial demographics within UK society, the legal understanding of the 'family' continues to be underpinned by the idealised image of the traditional nuclear family, comprising the nexus of the conjugal relationship and the parent/child relationship.

I. Theoretical Context

Recent reforms in family law have created the space within which this book situates its argument, because this book considers the legal meaning of 'family' in light of the considerable reform undertaken within family law in recent years. The overarching conclusion is that, despite radical shifts in family profiles and a considerable volume of legal reforms responding to these shifts, there has *not* been the radical shift that might appear at first sight in the law's understanding of 'family', since the latter remains firmly premised upon the nuclear family model.

To that end, this book builds upon the critical examinations of the legal understanding of 'the family' in the work of earlier writers, including Boyd,[21] Dewar,[22] Glennon[23] and Millbank.[24] The consideration of the 'family' in this work has been particularly influenced by two works which pre-date much of the aforementioned legislative reform; Diduck's, *Law's Families*[25] and O'Donovan's, *Family Law Matters*.[26] In *Law's Families*, Diduck observed that 'The family on which family law and policy is based bears only slight resemblance to the way we do family inside and outside the home on a day-to-day basis'.[27] This tension between the legal construct of the 'family' and the everyday reality of family life and familial practices continues to be apparent. In *Family Law Matters*, O'Donovan comments that 'Family law is dynamic, it is in flux. But it is embedded in the legal tradition from which it springs'.[28] This statement remains as pertinent now

[21] Susan Boyd, 'What is a "Normal" Family? *C v C (A Minor) (Custody: Appeal)*' (1992) 55(2) *Modern Law Review* 269.

[22] John Dewar, 'The Normal Chaos of Family Law' (1998) 61(4) *Modern Law Review* 467.

[23] Lisa Glennon, '*Fitzpatrick v Sterling Housing Association Ltd* – An Endorsement of the Functional Family?' (2000) 14(3) *International Journal of Law, Policy and the Family* 226.

[24] Jenni Millbank, 'The Limits of Functional Family: Lesbian Mother Litigation in the Era of the Eternal Biological Family' (2008) 22(2) *International Journal of Law, Policy and the Family* 149.

[25] Alison Diduck, *Law's Families*, (London, Markham, 2003), see also eg Alison Diduck, 'If Only we can Find the Appropriate Terms to Use the Issue Will Be Solved: Law, Identity and Parenthood' [2007] 19(4) *Child and Family Law Quarterly* 458, Alison Diduck, 'Shifting Familiarity' (2005) 58(1) *Current Legal Problems* 235 and Alison Diduck, 'What is Family Law For?' (2011) 64(1) *Current Legal Problems* 287.

[26] O'Donovan, *Family Law Matters*, see also Alison Diduck and Katherine O'Donovan (eds), *Feminist Perspectives on Family Law* (Abingdon, Routledge-Cavendish, 2006).

[27] Diduck, *Law's Families* 212.

[28] O'Donovan, *Family Law Matters* xiv.

as it was 25 years ago, and this book explores the contradiction between the need for family law to respond dynamically to changes in family forms and practices and the continuing dominance of traditional ideals and values about the nature and structure of the 'family'. My central argument is that different types of relationship have been subsumed into the existing, dominant model of family: the nuclear family, comprising the nexus of the conjugal relationship and the parent/child relationship. As such, this work is firmly grounded in the existing literature, but it also develops and builds upon the insights of earlier authors given the changing context of legislative reform, societal demographics and family forms and practices. Indeed, as O'Donovan observes:

> For me the greatest significance of law is that it addresses the ineluctable problems of what people are and how they live, and it prescribes answers. These answers reveal a great deal about the kind of society prescribed. Law is not autonomous. It is part of the social order whose functions it serves. But it is also symbolic. We need to know what it means in people's lives.[29]

The recent reforms in family law are an example of the law providing such 'answers' and in this book, I argue that those answers illustrate the continuing normative dominance of the traditional, nuclear family model.

As well as the aforementioned literature which considers the 'family' as an overarching legal concept, my work relies upon and is situated within the literature which identifies and critiques the gendered nature of the dominant legal and cultural understanding of parenthood.[30] My exploration of the legal construction of parenthood in chapters four and five is underpinned by the work of various writers who examine the legal understanding of the gendered parenting roles of 'mother'[31] and 'father'[32] and explore the continuing influence of these traditional roles on the way the role of the 'parent' is currently understood within the law. Moreover, when considering the legal understanding of 'motherhood', I join the critical literature which challenges the dominant construction of motherhood as a 'natural', indivisible status, fundamentally linked to the process of gestation.[33]

[29] Katherine O'Donovan, *Sexual Divisions in Law* (London, Weidenfeld and Nicholson, 1985) 20.

[30] See eg Emily Jackson, 'What is a Parent?', in Diduck and O'Donovan (eds), *Feminist Perspectives on Family Law*, Kim Everett and Lucy Yeatman, 'Are Some Parents More Natural Than Others?' [2010] 22(3) *Child and Family Law Quarterly* 290, Susan Boyd, 'Gendering Legal Parenthood: Bio-Genetic Ties, Intentionality and Responsibility' (2007) 25 *Windsor Yearbook of Access to Justice* 63 and Kaganas and Day Sclater, 'Contact Disputes: Narrative Constructions of "Good" Parents'.

[31] See eg Katherine O'Donovan, 'Constructions of Maternity and Motherhood in Stories of Lost Children' in Jo Bridgeman and Daniel Monk (eds), *Feminist Perspectives on Child Law* (London, Routledge-Cavendish, 2000).

[32] See eg Sally Sheldon and Richard Collier, *Fragmenting Fatherhood: A Socio-Legal Study* (Oxford, Hart Publishing, 2008).

[33] See eg Katherine O'Donovan and Jill Marshall, 'After Birth: Decisions about Becoming a Mother' in Diduck and O'Donovan (eds), *Feminist Perspectives on Family Law*, Gillian Douglas, 'The Intention to Be a Parent and the Making of Mothers' (1994) 57(4) *Modern Law Review* 636 and O'Donovan, 'Constructions of Maternity and Motherhood in Stories of Lost Children' in Bridgeman and Monk (eds), *Feminist Perspectives on Child Law*.

I also engage with the body of work which explores the legal understanding of lesbian parenthood[34] in order to consider the continuing influence of the dominant, 'natural', indivisible construction of the role of the 'mother'[35] despite recent legislative reforms which enable the recognition of a non-gestational female 'parent' in lesbian couples.[36] Similarly, my discussion of the legal understanding of 'fatherhood' draws upon the developing body of literature[37] which has identified the 'fragmentation of fatherhood';[38] this literature observes the tension within the law between the traditional construction of the 'father', based upon the public, 'breadwinner' role, and the developing construction of a private, caring 'fatherhood', based around greater involvement in day-to-day parenting.[39]

The theoretical framework of this book draws on the work of feminist writers who have critiqued the gendered and patriarchal nature of law itself, including the works of Pateman,[40] Moller Okin,[41] Boyd[42] and O'Donovan.[43] In discussing the underpinning values of the nuclear family in chapter two, I focus upon those feminist theorists who have critiqued the dominant, orthodox, liberal construction

[34] See eg Sarah Beresford, 'Get Over Your (Legal) "Self": A Brief History of Lesbians, Motherhood and the Law' (2008) 30(2) *Journal of Social Welfare and Family Law* 95, Fiona Kelly, '(Re)Forming Parenthood: The Assignment of Legal Parentage Within Planned Lesbian Families' (2009) 40(2) *Ottawa Law Review* 185, Robert Leckey, 'Law Reform, Lesbian Parenting, and the Reflective Claim' (2011) 20(3) *Social and Legal Studies* 331 and Leanne Smith, 'Tangling the Web of Legal Parenthood: Legal Responses to the Use of Known Donors in Lesbian Parenting Arrangements' (2013) 33(3) *Legal Studies* 355.

[35] Within this, the book engages with the empirical literature on the parenting of lesbian couples, see eg Gillian Dunne, 'Opting into Motherhood: Lesbians Blurring the Boundaries and Transforming the Meaning of Parenthood and Kinship' (2000) 14(1) *Gender and Society* 11, Jacqui Gabb, 'Lesbian M/Otherhood: Strategies of Familial-linguistic Management in Lesbian Parent Families' (2005) 39(4) *Sociology* 585 and Leanne Smith, 'Is Three a Crowd? Lesbian Mothers Perspectives on Parental Status in Law' [2006] 18(2) *Child and Family Law Quarterly* 231.

[36] Under the 'status provisions' for parenthood in cases of assisted reproduction in the Human Fertilisation and Embryology Act 2008, ss 42–48.

[37] See eg Richard Collier, *Masculinity, Law and the Family* (London, Routledge, 1995), Deborah Lupton and Lesley Barclay, *Constructing Fatherhood: Discourses and Experiences* (Thousand Oaks, SAGE, 1997), Sally Sheldon, 'Fragmenting Fatherhood: The Regulation of Reproductive Technologies' (2005) 68(4) *Modern Law Review* 523 and Leanne Smith, 'Clashing Symbols? Reconciling Support for Fathers and Fatherless Families After the Human Fertilisation and Embryology Act 2008' [2010] 22(1) *Child and Family Law Quarterly* 46.

[38] See Sheldon and Collier, *Fragmenting Fatherhood: A Socio-Legal Study*.

[39] See eg Felicity Kaganas, 'A Presumption that "Involvement" of Both Parents is Best: Deciphering Law's Messages' [2013] 25(3) *Child and Family Law Quarterly* 270, Scott Coltrane, *Family Man: Fatherhood, Housework and Gender Equality* (New York, Oxford University Press, 1996), Anna Dienhart, *Reshaping Fatherhood: The Social Construction of Shared Parenting* (London, SAGE, 1998) and Barbara Hodson (ed), *Making Men into Fathers: Men, Masculinities and the Social Politics of Fatherhood* (Cambridge, Cambridge University Press, 2002).

[40] Carole Pateman, *The Sexual Contract* (Cambridge, Polity Press, 1988).

[41] Susan Moller Okin, *Women in Western Political Thought* (London, Virago, 1980).

[42] Susan Boyd (ed), *Challenging the Public/Private Divide: Feminism, Law and Public Policy* (Toronto, Toronto University Press, 1997).

[43] O'Donovan, *Sexual Divisions in Law* and O'Donovan, *Family Law Matters*.

of the 'legal subject' as intrinsically 'masculine'.[44] Naffine,[45] for example, has extensively critiqued the orthodox construction of the legal subject and who has characterised that subject as the 'man of law'.[46]

The consideration of the legal and social understanding of the 'family' within this work is also influenced by the growing body of literature on the moral and ethical significance of 'care',[47] particularly the work of Held,[48] Tronto[49] and Noddings.[50] This literature is premised upon recognition of the 'relational subject', as Held describes, 'The ethics of care … characteristically sees persons as relational and interdependent, morally and epistemologically'[51] and consequently this literature focuses on the centrality of relationships and interdependence.[52] Most relevantly for the analysis here, the literature on 'care' has been developed by Herring, in *Caring and the Law*,[53] toward an alternative normative approach[54] which seeks

[44] See eg Susan James and Stephanie Palmer (eds), *Visible Women: Essays on Feminist Legal Theory and Political Philosophy* (Oxford, Hart Publishing, 2002) and Nicola Lacey, *Unspeakable Subjects: Feminist Essays in Legal and Social Theory* (Oxford, Hart Publishing, 1998). This book also engages with the more general critique of the orthodox, liberal construction of the legal subject, see eg Costas Douzinas and Adam Geary, *Critical Jurisprudence: The Political Philosophy of Justice* (Oxford, Hart Publishing, 2005), Anthony Carty (ed), *Post-Modern Law: Enlightenment, Revolution and the Death of Man* (Edinburgh, Edinburgh University Press, 1990), Costas Douzinas and Ronnie Warrington, *Justice Miscarried: Ethics, Aesthetics and the Law* (New York, Harvester Wheatsheaf, 1994) and Zygmunt Bauman, *Postmodern Ethics* (Oxford, Blackwell, 1993).

[45] See eg Ngaire Naffine, *Law and the Sexes: Explorations of Feminist Jurisprudence* (Sydney, Allen and Unwin, 1990), Ngaire Naffine and Rosemary J Owens (eds), *Sexing the Subject of Law* (North Ryde, LBC Information Services, 1997), Ngaire Naffine, *Law's Meaning of Life: Philosophy, Religion, Darwin and the Legal Person* (Oxford, Hart Publishing, 2009), Ngaire Naffine, 'Who are Law's Persons: From Cheshire Cats to Responsible Subjects' (2003) 66(3) *Modern Law Review* 346 and Ngaire Naffine, 'Can Women Be Legal Persons?' in James and Palmer (eds), *Visible Women: Essays on Feminist Legal Theory and Political Philosophy*.

[46] Naffine, *Law and the Sexes: Explorations of Feminist Jurisprudence*, states, at 100 'The legal model of the person, it will be argued, is a man, not a woman. He is a successful middle-class man, not a working class male. And he is a middle-class man who demonstrates what one writer has termed a form of "emphasised" middle-class masculinity. In short, he is a man; he is a middle class man; and he evinces the style of masculinity of the middle class.'

[47] See eg Carol Gilligan, *In a Different Voice: Psychological Theory and Women's Development* (Cambridge, MA, Harvard University Press, 1982), Marilyn Friedman, *Liberating Care* (Ithaca, Cornell University Press, 1993) and Ruth Groenhout, *Connected Lives: Human Nature and an Ethics of Care* (Lanham, Rowman and Littlefield, 2004).

[48] Virginia Held, *The Ethics of Care* (New York, Oxford University Press, 2006).

[49] Joan Tronto, *Moral Boundaries: A Political Argument for an Ethic of Care* (New York, Routledge, 1993).

[50] See eg Nel Noddings, *Caring: A Feminine Approach to Ethics and Moral Education* (Berkeley, University of California Press, 1984) and Nel Noddings, *Starting at Home: Caring and Social Policy* (Berkeley, University of California Press, 2002).

[51] Held, *The Ethics of Care* 13.

[52] Jonathan Herring, 'The Disability Critique of Care' (2014) 8 *Elder Law Review* 1, observes, at 3, that 'Ethics of care is based on the belief that people are relational. People understand themselves in terms of their relationships'.

[53] Jonathan Herring, *Caring and the Law* (Oxford, Hart Publishing, 2013).

[54] Jonathan Herring, 'The Legal Duties of Carers' (2010) 18(2) *Medical Law Review* 248, 254, states, 'Relying on an ethic of care, I would promote a vision of the law which sees people with interdependent relationships as the norm around which legal and ethical responses should be built.'

to diminish the law's reliance on the abstract, individualised subject.[55] Herring suggests that this understanding of the law 'starts with a norm of interlocking mutually dependent relationships, rather than an individualised version of rights'.[56] I will engage with this literature throughout my consideration of the legal understanding of the 'family' in chapter one, my exploration of the legal regulation of the conjugal relationship in chapter three and my examination of the legal understanding of the parental role in chapter five. Finally, the book will conclude in chapter six with a detailed, critical exploration of the potential of this literature to underpin alternative 'models' of the family, rather than the idealised image of the traditional nuclear family.[57] As well as the literature on 'care', chapter six also considers the literature on 'vulnerability'[58] and 'autonomy',[59] particularly the work of Fineman,[60] and therefore my work engages with these theoretical and conceptual perspectives.

II. Outline

The book is structured in four parts, the first three of which explores a different familial relationship, before the final part considers the possibilities offered by reconceptualising the legal understanding of 'family' around alternative and radical models of family.

Part One, which consists of chapters one and two, considers the 'family' as a legal concept. To begin with, chapter one briefly considers 'family' as a wider social concept, noting the lack of consensus as to its meaning. Subsequently the chapter observes that the law in the United Kingdom similarly lacks a single overarching definition of the 'family', either in statute or under common law. However, the chapter will identify three specific contexts in which legal definitions of family have apparently been developed: succession by 'family members' to private sector tenancies under the Rent Acts; the right to 'family life' in Article 8 of the European

[55] The relationship between the literature on 'care' and the orthodox construction of the 'legal subject' as rational, autonomous and self-interested will be considered below at ch 2, s II, 'Critiquing the Orthodox Construction of the Legal Subject'.

[56] Herring, *Caring and the Law* 46.

[57] However, it is not my aim in this work to develop an alternative normative approach to understanding the 'family', but rather first to elucidate and demonstrate the continuity of, the law's preference for the 'nuclear family' form, and secondly to explore the possibilities raised by such a shift in normative approach.

[58] See eg Julie Wallbank and Jonathan Herring (eds), *Vulnerabilities, Care and Family Law* (London, Routledge, 2013) and Martha Fineman and Anna Grear (eds), *Vulnerability: Reflections on a New Ethical Foundation for Law and Politics* (New York, Routledge, 2014).

[59] Mortimer Sellers (ed), *Autonomy in the Law*, (Aa Dordrecht, Springer, 2007) and Jonathan Herring, *Relational Autonomy and Family Law* (Springer, 2014).

[60] See eg Martha Fineman, *The Autonomy Myth: A Theory of Dependency* (New York, The New Press, 2004).

Convention on Human Rights; and the free movement of 'family members' under the EU 'Citizenship Directive'. The chapter will show that, in each of these contexts, the idealised image of the traditional, nuclear family (comprising the nexus of the conjugal relationship and the parent/child relationship) is central to how these definitions are interpreted and understood by the judiciary.

Chapter two builds upon chapter one by exploring why this idealised image of the nuclear family has come to exert such significant influence upon the legal understanding of the family. The chapter will argue that the combination of the following factors; the historical recurrence and dominance of the nuclear family form, the orthodox, liberal construction of the 'legal subject' and the continuing influence of the separate and distinct gender roles of male 'breadwinner' and female 'homemaker' of the 'public/private' divide, has resulted in the traditional, nuclear family being positioned as the 'natural' and 'common sense' construction of the 'family' within social and cultural discourse. Consequently, I will argue that this positioning has resulted in the nuclear family coming to underpin the law's definitions and understanding of the 'family'.

Part Two, which consists solely of chapter three, examines one of the core relationships within the central nexus of the nuclear family: the conjugal relationship. This chapter shows how the legal regulation of adult personal relationships is premised around marriage and 'marriage-like' conjugal relationships. The chapter considers the continuing centrality of marriage within the law, suggesting that the historical judicial definition retains significant influence upon contemporary judicial understandings of marriage, in spite of the recent legislation extending marriage to same-sex couples. Subsequently, the chapter explores the centrality of conjugality to the legal regulation of adult relationships. I will argue that the law privileges the conjugal couple form because it is constructed as performing important social functions, both for its members themselves and in relation to the upbringing of children. Within this, I will focus upon the legal regulation of cohabitation and note the extension of the marriage model to other relationships. I will argue that this extension has occurred on the basis that such relationships are understood as being sufficiently 'marriage-like'; they share characteristics and features (with particular emphasis given to their conjugality) with traditional, heterosexual marriage such that they are positioned within the idealised image of the nuclear family.

Part Three, comprising chapters four and five, examines the other core relationship within the central nexus of the nuclear family: the 'parent/child' relationship. These chapters explore the law's approach to parenthood and parenting, focusing upon the attribution of legal parenthood and the legal understanding of the parental role. Chapter four considers how legal parenthood is determined and assigned in a variety of contexts: natural reproduction, medically assisted reproduction and surrogacy. Although the chapter will set out the substantive differences between the regimes which determine legal parenthood in cases of natural reproduction and assisted reproduction, I will argue that across these diverse contexts legal parenthood is consistently premised upon a binary, two-parent model, which ideally envisages one mother and one father as the legal parents.

Chapter five builds upon this and explores the legal construction of the role of the 'parent'. The chapter will argue that the law has a relatively opaque understanding of the role of the 'parent'. As a result of this the legal understanding of parenthood continues to rely upon the archetypical gendered parenting roles of 'mother' and 'father', which are understood as representing the 'natural' and 'common-sense' parental roles. The chapter also examines the legal interpretation of the welfare of the child, arguing that this interpretation provides evidence of the influence of these gendered parenting roles. Additionally, the chapter will consider the legal understanding of the role of the non-gestational female parent in lesbian couples. I will observe that there has been limited legislative or judicial engagement with the nature of this parental role because it lacks the readily understood 'natural' construction possessed by the gendered parenting roles. This will be taken to support the conclusion that the legal understanding of the role of the 'parent' is premised upon the distinct, gendered parenting roles of 'mother' and 'father' of the nuclear family.

Part Four, solely comprising chapter six, will involve a detailed critical exploration of the alternative models of 'family', including approaches centred on 'care', 'relationality' and 'vulnerability', as well as models based upon autonomy and choice, which are present throughout the multi-disciplinary literature on the construction of 'family'. This chapter will consider the potential impact of these alternative models upon the legal regulation of the 'family' and possible family law reform. To that end, this chapter briefly considers the developing literature on these various conceptual factors, as well as how these alternative approaches develop the earlier critiques of the orthodox construction of the liberal, legal subject (as set out in chapter two). The chapter sets out the ambiguity and vagueness inherent to the concepts of 'care' and 'vulnerability' and explores whether this impacts upon the ability of these concepts to underpin the legal understanding of the 'family'. It concludes by arguing that the uncertainty of 'family' should be embraced and consequently that any conceptual model of 'family' (based upon any of these conceptual values) should be rejected. The resultant approach to the legal understanding of the 'family' would be situated within the lived reality of contemporary family life and therefore would be able to recognise and regulate the diversity of relationships and family forms present within twenty-first century UK society.

Finally, the book will conclude by arguing that the legal understanding of 'family' in the United Kingdom continues, notwithstanding radical law reform over the past four decades, to be premised upon the idealised image of the traditional 'nuclear family', comprising the nexus of the conjugal relationship and the 'parent/child' relationship. The normative power of the idealised image of the nuclear family is evident in the fact that legal regulation of adult relationships is centred upon the conjugal relationship. Moreover, the gendered parenting roles of 'mother' and 'father', which are embedded in the nuclear family, continue to possess normative influence in the judicial and legislative understanding of the role of the 'parent'. Accordingly, the overall conclusion of this book will be that despite legislative reforms and changes in familial demographics, the traditional nuclear family remains the idealised image upon which the legal understanding of the 'family' is based.

PART I

The Family

> An unprecedented fluidity, fragility and in-built transience (the famed 'flexibility') mark all sorts of social bonds which but a few dozen years ago combined into a durable, reliable framework inside which a web of human interactions could be securely woven.

Zygmunt Bauman, *Liquid Love: On the Frailty of Human Bonds* (Cambridge, Polity Press, 2003) 91

1

What is the Law's 'Family'?

Diduck has observed that '"The Family" has almost iconic status in popular and "official" discourses, even though there is no official or universal definition of it. It means different things to different people, and meets different needs for different people.'[1] Indeed, social and cultural understandings of 'family' are shifting and twenty-first century UK society comprises a greater diversity of family structures and forms than at any time previously.[2] The sociologist Chambers has commented that, 'What we define as "family" is now more flexible and dynamic, and embraces new kinds of intimacies that were once ignored or condemned.'[3]

These shifts are reflected in the language used by both the government and the judiciary when they consider and discuss families.[4] The foundational document of the previous coalition government stated that, 'The Government believes that strong and stable families *of all kinds* are the bedrock of a strong and stable society.'[5] Similar rhetoric appears within judicial language; in *Fitzpatrick v Sterling Housing Association Ltd.*[6] Lord Clyde observed that 'The concept of the family has undergone significant development during recent years, both in the United Kingdom and overseas … Social groupings have come to take a number of different forms',[7] and in *Ghaidan v Godin-Mendoza*,[8] where Lord Millett observed 'times change, and with them society's perceptions change also'.[9] More recently in *Re G (Children) (Shared Residence Order: Biological Non-Birth Mother)*,[10]

[1] Diduck, *Law's Families* 1.

[2] See eg ONS, 'Families and Households: 2017' (November 2017); ONS, 'Marriages in England and Wales: 2015' (February 2018) and ONS, 'Short Report: Cohabitation in the UK, 2012' (November 2012), for evidence of the shifts in demographics within UK society.

[3] Deborah Chambers, *A Sociology of Family Life: Change and Diversity in Intimate Relationships* (Cambridge, Polity Press, 2012) 54.

[4] This is especially notable when compared to the 'family values' rhetoric of the Conservative governments of the late 1980s and early 1990s.

[5] 'The Coalition: Our Programme for Government' (HM Government, May 2010) 19, emphasis mine, available at: www.gov.uk/government/uploads/system/uploads/attachment_data/file/78977/coalition_programme_for_government.pdf.

[6] *Fitzpatrick v Sterling Housing Association Ltd* [2001] 1 AC 27.

[7] ibid, per Lord Clyde at 51.

[8] *Ghaidan v Godin-Mendoza* [2004] UKHL 30, [2004] 2 AC 557.

[9] ibid, per Lord Millett at 583. See further eg the language of the House of Lords in *Re G (Children) (Residence: Same-Sex Partner)* [2006] UKHL 43, [2006] 2 FLR 629 and *Re P (Adoption: Unmarried Couples)* [2008] UKHL 38, [2008] 2 FLR 1084.

[10] [2014] 2 FLR 897.

Black LJ observed that 'Families are formed in different ways these days and the law must attempt to keep up and to respond to developments'.[11] Thus, both the government and the judiciary now acknowledge a greater variety of relationships as 'family'.

However, in spite of this apparent shift in the understanding of 'family' and the range of recent legislation concerning various aspects of the 'family',[12] there are relatively few statutes which utilise the term – at least as a concept activating legal consequences[13] – and the law in the United Kingdom lacks a single, overarching definition. In *Fitzpatrick*[14] Lord Nicholls observed that:

> Family is a word with several different meanings. In some contexts family means children ('when shall we start a family?') In other contexts it means parents and child ('accommodation suitable for families'). It may mean all persons connected however remotely by birth, marriage or adoption ('family tree').[15]

Because of the variability and indeterminacy inherent in the concept of 'family', I will argue that the judiciary – and the law itself – draws upon an archetypical, but determinate image of 'family'; the traditional, nuclear family. In this way, I argue that relationships and family forms are considered by law in light of this idealised image of the nuclear family and are granted recognition as 'family' based upon the extent to which they are understood as resembling that archetypical family. Consequently, I suggest that relationships are examined on the basis of whether they can be located within the boundaries of the nuclear family model or whether they can be constructed as performing the same functions as the nuclear family. To understand how and why the law relies upon this idealised image of 'family',[16] it is necessary to first consider the meaning of 'family' as a wider social concept.

Accordingly, this chapter will begin in section I, by considering 'family' as a social concept, observing the lack of an overarching definition within the literature and the apparent difficulty of producing such a definition. In section II, I will consider three legal definitions of 'family' which exist within specific contexts. I will argue that, in spite of the legal recognition of diverse family forms, these legal definitions of 'family' remain predominantly based around the idealised image of the traditional, heterosexual, nuclear family: the nexus of the conjugal relationship and the parent/child relationship.

[11] ibid, per Black LJ at 904. The effectiveness of the law's response to such developments in family forms and structures will be considered in ch 3 (in the context of adult personal relationships), as well as chs 4 and 5 (in the context of the relationship between parents and children).

[12] eg Adoption and Children Act 2002, Civil Partnership Act 2004, Human Fertilisation and Embryology Act 2008, Marriage (Same Sex Couples) Act 2013 and Children and Families Act 2014.

[13] Although s II 'Law's "Definition(s)" of "Family"' identifies and considers three areas where 'family' is used in that way.

[14] [2001] 1 AC 27.

[15] ibid, per Lord Nicholls at 41.

[16] Chapter 2, 'The Historical and Philosophical Underpinnings of the "Nuclear Family" Model', will further consider how this model of family came to be positioned as the idealised image of 'family'.

I. 'Family' as a Social Concept

'Family' is central to our understanding and experience of human existence. As Bernardes states 'Most people in Western industrialised societies, and probably most people worldwide, consider family living as the most important aspect of their lives'.[17] However, in spite of this importance of our families in shaping our identity, it is apparent from the sociological literature that the term 'family' is not easily definable; as Coltrane observes 'we can never be quite sure what family means unless we can understand the context in which it is used'.[18] This reflects the evolving nature of the cultural understanding of family;[19] Leeder has commented:

> The family has been around since the beginning of humankind and clearly will exist in some form forever … The family in the world is in process: resilient, the family copes with the forces acting on it and adapts in an ongoing manner that makes it a highly elastic and changeable form.[20]

The suggestion from the literature is that 'family' is not a fixed concept with a readily identifiable, simple definition. In this section, I will consider sociologists' attempts to understand the meaning of 'family' and conclude that the lack of a fixed meaning has resulted in the law lacking a readily available and identifiable social construction of 'family' to underpin its understanding. Moreover, I will argue subsequently that this absence of a simple definition has created the conceptual space which is filled by the idealised image of the traditional nuclear family.[21]

Given the lack of a readily apparent and straightforward definition of 'family',[22] some theorists have sought to understand and illuminate the meaning of family by reference to a variety of characteristics, features and connections which are said to be consistent across different family forms. Morgan suggests that the term 'family' should be employed 'to refer to sets of practices which deal in some way with ideas of parenthood, kinship and marriage and the expectations and obligations which are associated with these practices'.[23] Such theoretical understandings of the 'family' are often premised upon the emotional bonds between individuals, with these connections being articulated using a variety of terms; for example,

[17] Jon Bernardes, *Family Studies: An Introduction* (London, Routledge, 1997) 1.

[18] Scott L Coltrane, *Gender and Families* (Lanham, Rowman and Littlefield, 1998) 5. This reference to 'context' reflects the language of Lord Nicholls from *Fitzpatrick v Sterling Housing Association* [2001] 1 AC 27, at 41, quoted above, particularly the notion that 'Family is a word with several different meanings'.

[19] Gittins, *The Family in Question: Changing Households and Familiar Ideologies* at 3, has observed that 'an amalgam of discourses combine to create a dominant representation of what a family should be like. This representation changes over time, but nonetheless is presented as something universal'.

[20] Elaine Leeder, *The Family in Global Perspective: A Gendered Journey* (Thousand Oaks, SAGE, 2003) 2.

[21] This argument will be developed below in s II 'Law's "Definition(s)" of "Family"' and in more detail throughout ch 2 'The Historical and Philosophical Underpinnings of the "Nuclear Family" Model'.

[22] See eg Charles B Hennon and Stephan M Wilson, *Families in a Global Context* (New York, Routledge, 2008) for an exploration of the differences and similarities between families across different countries and cultures.

[23] David Morgan, *Family Connections: An Introduction to Family Studies* (Cambridge, Polity Press, 1996) 11.

intimacy,[24] love[25] or trust.[26] In this regard, Cheal suggests that 'a family is considered to be any group which consists of people in intimate relationships which are believed to endure over time and across generations'.[27] These statements illustrate the nebulousness that is seemingly inherent to such conceptual understandings of 'family', which necessarily cannot be simply rendered as descriptions that would readily identify those relationships which are included and those which are excluded from 'family'.

Other writers have attempted to provide a slightly more detailed description of the shared characteristics of families. McKie and Callan, for example, identify three 'principles and ideas'[28] which families are constructed as sharing: 'values', 'memories' and 'spaces and places'.[29] These understandings of 'family' propose that it is the shared experiences and the quality of the relationships involved that are the significant, defining features of the 'family'. Moreover, McKie and Callan attempt to provide greater clarity, identifying five 'common characteristics' of families, these are 'a common identity', 'economic co-operation and ownership', 'reproduction of the next generation', 'care work and domestic labour' and 'co-residence'.[30] However, it is suggested that these chosen characteristics are illustrative of the problems involved in attempting to provide greater detail, beyond reference to 'values' or 'principles and ideals', because these characteristics (particularly 'reproduction of the next generation') involve choices and judgements which would exclude some family forms from this framework for understanding the 'family'.

Related to this emphasis on characteristics, experiences and relationships, some theorists have also attempted to understand the 'family' by focusing upon the social role performed by families and identifying the core functions of families.[31] Silva and Smart suggest that the 'family' is not underpinned by a specific structure or form, but instead 'In this context of fluid and changing definitions of families, a basic core remains which refers to the sharing of resources, caring, responsibilities and obligations. What a family is appears intrinsically related to what it does.'[32] Moreover, there is a growing and developing body of work which seeks to ground a definition of 'family' within the literature on the moral and ethical significance

[24] Diduck, 'What is Family Law For?' 289, suggests that: 'What makes a relationship familial to me then is not necessarily a biological, legal or conjugal connection, rather it is what people do in it, it is a relationship characterized by some degree of intimacy, interdependence, and care.'

[25] Herring, 'The Disability Critique of Care' equates 'love' and 'care', stating, at 2 'Care is the manifestation of that most basic moral value: love. It involves meeting the needs of others, which is a primary good.'

[26] Trudy Govier, *Dilemmas of Trust* (Montreal, McGill's-Queen's University Press, 1998) 68, emphasises that 'Good enough families are founded, not on heterosexuality and stereotypical gender roles, not on male providers, not on biological reproduction, but on trust between people who live together in a home, trust each other, and are committed to building a life together.'

[27] David Cheal, *Sociology of Family Life* (Basingstoke, Palgrave, 2002) 4.

[28] Linda McKie and Samantha Callan, *Understanding Families: A Global Introduction* (London, SAGE, 2012) 23.

[29] ibid, at 23–24.

[30] ibid, at 21–23.

[31] The use of a 'function-based definition' of 'family' within the law will be considered below in s II, 'The Law's "Definition(s)" of "Family"'.

[32] Elizabeth B Silva and Carol Smart, 'The "New" Practices and Politics of Family Life' in Elizabeth B Silva and Carol Smart (eds), *The New Family?* (London, SAGE, 1999) 7.

of 'care';[33] Held has commented that 'An ethic of care focuses on attentiveness, trust, responsiveness to need, narrative nuance, and cultivating caring relations.'[34] On this basis, Herring provides a definition of 'family' that is premised upon the centrality of 'care', as 'People providing each other with a substantial amount of care in a relationship marked by commitment.'[35] Young similarly suggests that 'family' should be understood 'as people who live together and/or share resources necessary to the means for life and comfort; who are committed to caring for one another's physical and emotional needs to the best of their ability.'[36] These definitions combine references to the emotional connections within relationships with the identification of core characteristics that are understood as being central to all familial relationships. In this way, such understandings all involve elements of the same overlapping and related concepts, but with differing focuses. Moreover, all of these different theoretical approaches are united by their attempts to define 'family' without emphasising specific family forms or valorising particular categories of relationship.[37]

However, I argue that the various theoretical attempts to define the 'family' set out in this section, whether based on 'care', on identifying the social role of families, or on articulating shared familial characteristics and experiences, face similar problems in the context of defining 'family', since all of these approaches result in an ambiguous understanding of the 'family' and do not provide a simple, easily understandable definition. I suggest that this is due to the absence of consensus regarding which functions or characteristics are fundamental to all families,[38] and due to the vagueness which is seemingly inherent in definitions based upon 'care', experiences, or emotional connections. Noddings acknowledges this ambiguity in the context of care, observing that, 'Most people agree that the world would be a better place if we all cared more for one another, but despite that initial agreement we find it hard to say exactly what we mean by *caring*.'[39]

[33] As discussed above in the Introduction, see further eg Herring, *Caring and the Law*, who suggests, at 11, 'Caring is a most basic human need'.

[34] Held, *The Ethics of Care* 15.

[35] Herring, *Caring and the Law* 194.

[36] Iris Marion Young, *Intersecting Voices* (Princeton, Princeton University Press, 1997) 106.

[37] These issues will be considered subsequently in ch 6 'The Possibilities Offered by Alternative Models of the "Family"', which will explore the normative significance granted to particular relationship forms and consider whether moving beyond the dominant conceptual framework may provide an alternative understanding of the 'family' that better reflects UK society in the 21st century.

[38] While some of the central functions of a family may be apparent, I suggest that the boundaries of family functions are less clear. In this regard, compare the description given by Cheal, *Sociology of Family Life* 7, who comments 'The things that family members do are easy to identify. They give and lend money, they get children ready to go to school, they prepare and share food, they have sex and express love in other ways, and so on', and that of McKie and Callan, *Understanding Families: A Global Introduction* 23, who refer to 'Further characteristics and issues that come to mind when we think of families include childcare and working parents, solo childrearing, care for sick or older relatives, the legal and social implications of cohabitation, life after divorce for parents and children, and home-based care for the terminally ill.' These two descriptions illustrate the wide diversity of characteristics and functions that are potentially identifiable as being central to 'family' and therefore the difficulties of using these approaches to provide a precise, overarching, definition of 'family' as a social concept.

[39] Noddings, *Starting at Home: Caring and Social Policy* 11. See further eg Herring, *Caring and the Law* 13, who similarly notes that 'Producing a definition of care is far from straightforward.'

Nevertheless, my argument should not be understood as suggesting that the ambiguity associated with understanding the 'family' in terms of 'care', common characteristics or core functions is necessarily any more normatively problematic[40] than the 'nuclear family' model which I will discuss subsequently. Instead, my suggestion is that embracing such ambiguity does not provide a simple, unified definition of 'family' as a social concept and thus does little to further our understanding of the law's underlying model of family, which this chapter aims to elucidate. The normative claims made within the literature will be considered in more detail in chapter six; which will explore the possibilities offered by reconceptualising the legal understanding of 'family' around these alternative models of 'family' and suggest that a radical re-imagining of the 'family' may be necessary to reflect the diversity of families and the complexity and variability of family life in twenty-first century society.

With that said, from this overview of the literature, it is apparent that 'family' lacks a precise definition as a social concept.[41] As Cheal observes 'There is no single concept of the family which is true for all historical periods and in all places.'[42] Consequently the law does not have a simple, unified definition of the 'family' as a social concept to underpin its approach to defining and understanding family,[43] which creates the conceptual space that is subsequently filled by the idealised image of the traditional nuclear family.

II. The Law's 'Definition(s)' of 'Family'

The lack of a single, unified definition of 'family' as a social concept is reflected within legal understanding; Diduck and Kaganas have observed that 'There is no statutory definition of family, and there is really no common law definition either. How can law, which depends on certainty, cope with this lacuna?'[44]

Given this apparent absence of an overarching definition, how then does the law understand and define 'family'? In his textbook, *Family Law*,[45] Herring suggests five possible approaches the law could adopt: (1) 'The person in the street's definition', which he describes as being based on 'common usage' of the term 'family';[46] (2) 'An idealised definition', of which he states 'In our society many would see

[40] Ch 6, s II 'Abstract Models and Real Families' will explore whether ambiguity and uncertainty themselves are necessarily normatively problematic in the context of understanding and defining 'family'.

[41] See eg Carol Smart, *Personal Life: New Directions in Sociological Thinking* (Cambridge, Polity Press, 2007) for an attempt to escape from the problems caused by the conceptual category of the 'family'.

[42] Cheal, *Sociology of Family Life* 4.

[43] O'Donovan, *Family Law Matters* 11, argues that 'the lack of definition of the notion of family allows a subtext of values, such as those derived from patriarchy, to control'.

[44] Alison Diduck and Felicity Kaganas, *Family Law, Gender and the State*, 3rd edn (Oxford, Hart Publishing, 2012) 21.

[45] Jonathan Herring, *Family Law*, 7th edn (Harlow, Pearson Longman, 2015).

[46] ibid, at 3.

this as a married couple with children';[47] (3) 'A function-based definition', which 'examines the functions of families in our society' and determines family based upon whether relationships perform those functions;[48] (4) 'A formalistic definition', which is based upon 'whether the group of individuals in question has certain observable traits that can be objectively proved';[49] (5) 'A self-definition approach', which 'would state "you are a family if you say you are"'.[50]

The fact that these substantively different approaches are all intellectually sustainable illustrates the complexities of attempting to provide a legal definition of 'family'.[51] Herring observes that 'The law … in defining families uses a combination of a formalist and function-based approach.'[52] However, in the consideration of the law's attempts to define 'family' which follows, I will observe that in addition to these two approaches there has been significant reference to 'the person in the street's definition' of 'family'. I will argue that within this approach there is evidence of an 'idealised definition' of 'family', based upon the traditional, nuclear family, which has exerted significant influence on the law's definitions of 'family'.[53] Herring has observed that 'Many people have a stereotypical image of what the "ideal family" is like – a mother, a father and two children.'[54] Indeed, Bernardes describes this archetype of the 'nuclear family' in the following terms:

> [A] common and popular image of 'the nuclear family' portrays a young, similarly aged, white, married heterosexual couple with a small number of healthy children living in an adequate home. There is a clear division of responsibilities in which the male is primarily the full-time breadwinner and the female primarily the caregiver and perhaps a part-time or occasional income earner.[55]

The nuclear family is an idealised image of family, which provides a normative vision of family life;[56] Muncie and Sapsford comment that 'the idea of the nuclear family clearly retains a potency such that all other forms tend to be defined with reference to it'.[57] Boyd has previously claimed that the 'normal

[47] ibid, at 4.
[48] ibid, at 3.
[49] ibid.
[50] ibid, at 4.
[51] The impact of the inherent complexities involved in providing a legal definition of the 'family' will be further considered in ch 6, subs II(A) 'The Inherent Complexity of "Family" and the Potential of Uncertainty', in the context of the prospect of a radical re-imagining of the legal understanding of 'family'.
[52] Herring, *Family Law* 6.
[53] Therefore, I suggest that of Herring's five approaches, only the 'self-definition approach' has not exerted influence on the legal attempts to define 'family'. Arguably, this reflects the difficulties of giving legislative effect to such a self-definition approach.
[54] Herring, *Family Law* 2.
[55] Bernardes, *Family Studies: An Introduction* 2–3.
[56] Fiona Williams, *Rethinking Families* (London, Calouste Gulbenkian Foundation, 2004) 18, has observed 'The nuclear family of the post-war world, with its male breadwinner, was a construction of what family life *should* look like.'
[57] John Muncie and Roger Sapsford, 'Issues in the Study of "The Family"' in John Muncie, et all (eds), *Understanding the Family*, 2nd edn (London, SAGE, 1997) 10, see further Bernardes, *Family Studies: An Introduction* 3, who similarly observes, 'the idea of the "nuclear family" is remarkably powerful'.

family' of law 'is heterosexual, nuclear, generally white and middle class, and usually involves a dependent role for the women who has more responsibility for home and childcare than the man, and who preferably remains outside the workforce'.[58] Thus, I will argue that the 'idealised definition' of 'family', within legal understanding, is premised upon the traditional, nuclear family, which comprises the nexus of the conjugal relationship and the parent/child relationship.[59]

To that end, this section considers three different contexts in which there exists a legal definition of 'family': succession by 'family members' to private sector tenancies under the Rent Acts (subsection A), the right to respect for 'family life' under Article 8 of the European Convention on Human Rights (subsection B) and free movement for the 'family members' of EU citizens under Directive 2004/38/EC ('the Citizenship Directive') (subsection C). Of these contexts, two (the Rent Acts and ECHR, Article 8) leave family undefined, which has resulted in the definition being developed through judicial decisions, while the other (the EU Citizenship Directive) provide a formalistic definition of 'family', by specifying a fixed list of relationships. An examination of how the case law under the Rent Acts, has considered and expanded the definition of 'family', will reveal consistent reference to Herring's 'person in the street's definition' of 'family'.[60] Within this case law and those decisions considering 'family life' under Article 8 of the ECHR, as well as the Citizenship Directive's definition of 'family member', I will contend that there is substantial influence of, in Herring's terms, an 'idealised definition' of 'family'.[61] I will argue that this 'idealised definition' of 'family' is based around the traditional, heterosexual, nuclear family model; comprising the nexus of the conjugal relationship and the parent/child relationship. Moreover, in the following sections it will be shown how additional categories of relationship (unmarried cohabitants and same-sex couples) have been brought within these two judicial definitions of 'family' on the basis that those relationships share sufficient similarities and functions with this idealised, nuclear family. This shows that even where, in Herring's terms, a 'function-based definition' of 'family' is utilised, the functions which are considered significant reflect the idealised image of the traditional nuclear family.

[58] Boyd, 'What is a "Normal" Family? *C v C (A Minor) (Custody: Appeal)*' 276. It is worth noting that this description was expressed over 25 years ago and it is suggested that there have been some shifts in this 'normal family' of law in the time since.

[59] See eg Carol Smart, Bren Neale and Amanda Wade, *The Changing Experience of Childhood: Families and Divorce* (Cambridge, Polity Press, 2001) who observe, at 10 'children have been fused with their parents into an idealised, inseparable family unit. In the process, the diverse identities and interests of individual family members have been concealed'.

[60] See eg *Brock v Wollams* [1949] 2 KB 388.

[61] For examples of the influence of such a definition under the Rent Acts, see *Ross v Collins* [1964] 1 WLR 425 and *Joram Developments Ltd v Sharratt* [1979] 1 WLR 928, under ECHR, Art 8, see *Karner v Austria* (2004) 38 EHRR 24 and in European Court of Justice jurisprudence, see *D and Sweden v Council of the European Union* [2003] 3 CMLR 9 (Joined Cases C-122/99P and C-125/99P).

A. The Definition of 'Family' Under the Rent Acts

To begin, the foremost example within domestic law of the courts explicitly considering and interpreting the definition of 'family' at various points throughout the twentieth century was under the Rent Acts.[62] These Acts contained the statutory regime that governed the area of 'private sector' tenancies, prior to 1989.[63] The most recent legislation in England and Wales, the Rent Act 1977, provides that, 'a person who was a member of the original tenant's family'[64] will be 'entitled to an assured tenancy'[65] upon the original tenant's death;[66] this exists in combination with provision being made available for a 'surviving spouse'.[67] Crucially, there is no guidance within the Rent Acts themselves as to the meaning of 'family', which is not limited to specific categories of relationship. Wikeley has observed that 'since the early days of the Rent Acts the concept of "family", as a means of delineating the framework for defining succession to statutory tenancies, has proved to be remarkably problematic'.[68] This lack of legislative clarity as to the precise definition of 'family' has necessarily led to significant judicial consideration of the definition since the original statutory provision was enacted.[69] As a consequence the definition of 'family', under the Rent Acts, has been developed through judicial decisions.

The judgments in the cases which consider the definition of 'family' under the Rent Acts invariably make clear that the discussion of the definition of 'family' is specific to this particular statutory context.[70] This approach is encapsulated by

[62] Rent Act 1977 (as amended by Housing Act 1988) being the most recent. Since the Increase of Rent and Mortgage Interest (Restrictions) Act 1920, s 12(1)(g) some form of statutory protection was provided for a 'member of the tenant's family' under these Acts.

[63] Housing Act 1988 replaced the regime of 'protected tenancies' and 'statutory tenancies' under the Rent Acts with those of 'assured tenancies', which provide a much more limited regime of statutory protection for tenants. The provisions of the Rent Acts will still apply to tenancies created prior to the commencement of these Acts.

[64] Rent Act 1977, Sch 1, para 3(1).

[65] ibid, this is an 'assured tenancy' subject to the new tenancy regime of Housing Act 1988. Prior to that Act, the surviving family member would have been entitled to succeed to the 'statutory tenancy', Rent Act 1977, s 2(1)(b).

[66] Subject to the requirement that they were 'residing with him [in the dwelling-house] at the time of and for the [period of 2 years] immediately before his death'.

[67] Sch 1, para 2. The two major distinctions are that the 'spouse' does not require to have been resident for the 2-year period and that they are entitled to a 'statutory tenancy' as opposed to an 'assured tenancy', which is advantageous to the spouse because it continues under the more favourable Rent Act regime.

[68] Nick Wikeley, '*Fitzpatrick v Sterling Housing Association Ltd*: Same-Sex Partners and Succession to Rent Act Tenancies' [1998] 10(2) *Child and Family Law Quarterly* 191, 191.

[69] An early example of this need for clarity is provided in *Price v Gould* [1930] All ER 389, in which it was held that brothers and sisters of the tenant were included within 'family'.

[70] It is notable that the limited cases considering 'family' under the Housing Act 1985, s 87 (a statute concerning succession to public sector tenancies, which employs a formalistic definition, specifying a fixed list of relationships) also stress that the definition only applies to that specific context, see eg Ward LJ in *Sheffield City Council v Personal Representatives of Wall* [2010] EWCA Civ 922, [2011] 1 WLR 1342, at 1350.

the statement of Lord Slynn in *Fitzpatrick v Sterling Housing Association Ltd*[71] that 'In other statutes, in other contexts, the words may have a wider or narrower meaning.'[72] Notably, this statutory entitlement for 'family members' to succeed to a private sector tenancy no longer exists for tenancies created after January 1989.[73] However, in spite of these factors, I argue that the development throughout the cases of this definition of 'family' is illustrative of the law's understanding of 'family' more generally, particularly given the paucity of consideration of this concept otherwise within the law. Cretney and Reynolds have argued that, 'The interpretation of this expression … has caused the courts difficulty over the years, and the decisions were not easy to reconcile.'[74] However, through the development of the definition of 'family' in these decisions, I will argue that it is possible to see repeated reference to, in Herring's terms 'the person in the street's definition' of 'family'. I will also argue that this definition contains within it, in Herring's terms, an 'idealised definition' of 'family', based around the traditional, heterosexual, nuclear family; comprising the 'nexus' of the conjugal relationship and the parent/child relationship. I will further suggest that there is evidence within the judicial decisions of the usage of, in Herring's terms, a 'function-based definition' of 'family', which is based upon replicating the functions of this idealised image of the nuclear family, rather than upon reflecting an alternative understanding of 'family', premised upon the centrality of 'care', mutuality and interdependence.

i. 'Family' as Defined by the 'Ordinary Man' Test

From the initial reported cases it is apparent that 'family', in this context, is to be given its 'popular meaning'[75] and determined on the basis of the understanding of the 'ordinary man',[76] or as Herring has expressed it 'the person in the street's definition' of family'. In *Brock v Wollams*,[77] Cohen LJ formulated the test as 'Would an ordinary man, addressing his mind to the question whether Mrs. Wollams was a member of the family or not, have answered "yes" or "no"?'[78] This test was

[71] [2001] 1 AC 27.

[72] ibid, per Lord Slynn, at 32.

[73] Although the Housing Act 1988, s 17 retains an entitlement to succession of the 'assured tenancy' for the 'surviving spouse', which is now defined in both Acts to include civil partners and both opposite-sex and same-sex cohabitants.

[74] Stephen M Cretney and FMB Reynolds, 'Limits of the Judicial Function' (2000) 116 (Apr) *Law Quarterly Review* 181, 182.

[75] *Gammans v Ekins* [1950] 2 KB 328, at 331, per Asquith LJ, or as Evershed MR expressed it in *Langdon v Horton* [1951] 1 KB 666, at 669, quoting Shakespeare, 'the word "family" is used here, to borrow the words used of the soldier in King Henry V, in a sense "base, common, and popular"'.

[76] As Lord Denning MR put it in *Dyson Holdings Ltd v Fox* [1976] QB 503, at 508 'It is not used in the sense in which it would be used by a studious and unworldly lawyer'.

[77] *Brock v Wollams* [1949] 2 KB 388.

[78] ibid, per Cohen LJ, at 395.

thereafter consistently referred to and affirmed in subsequent cases.[79] However, O'Donovan has pointed out that the 'ordinary man' test is problematic because it:

> [D]oes not require a careful sampling of public opinion. Nor even is a jury polled for its opinion. Not only does it assume that the judiciary is in touch with public opinion, but it leaves open to the discretion of the judge the definition of popular morality, which may be confused with personal morality.[80]

Reliance on 'the person in the street's' understanding of family has allowed the judiciary to obscure the influence of an 'idealised definition', based upon the nuclear family, because this definition is presented as 'natural' and 'common sense' through the usage of the 'ordinary man' test. As Diduck and Kaganas comment:

> Law's normative vision of 'the family' with marriage as the benchmark, is reproduced each time a court is called upon to decide whether a particular living arrangement is 'familial' or not, but this vision is said to be that of the 'ordinary public' rather than that of the court.[81]

Nevertheless, over the course of the second half of the twentieth century, the 'common sense' definition was extended by the courts to cover a wider variety of relationships than under the original interpretation, as the common sense understanding of 'family' has been held to have changed over time.[82] The types of relationships that have been held to be 'family', together with those relationships that have not, establish the boundaries of the courts' understanding of 'family', as well as identifying the characteristics which are viewed as fundamental to a familial relationship. From these cases, it is possible to ascertain the factors and characteristics that have been granted the most significance within the judicial understanding of the 'ordinary man' test.

Initially, based on the understanding of the 'ordinary man' test, the definition of 'family' under the Rent Acts was interpreted narrowly by the courts. However, in spite of the repeated references to this 'ordinary man' test, there was additional judicial elaboration as to the scope of 'family' under this provision. The understanding of 'family' of these cases is summarised by Asquith LJ in *Gammans v Ekins*[83] where he stated:

> [T]he material decisions limit the membership of the same 'family' to three relationships: first, that of children; secondly, those constituted by way of legitimate marriage, like that between husband and wife; thirdly, relationships whereby one person becomes *in loco parentis* to another.[84]

[79] See eg Lord Diplock in *Joram Developments Ltd v Sharratt* [1979] 1 WLR 928, at 931 'This test, which does no more than say that "family" where it is used in the Rent Acts is not a term of art but is used in its ordinary popular meaning, has been repeatedly referred to and applied in subsequent cases.'

[80] O'Donovan, *Family Law Matters* 35.

[81] Diduck and Kaganas, *Family Law, Gender and the State* 27.

[82] This will be considered below at subs (II)(A)(iii), 'Unmarried Cohabitants', particularly the decision in *Dyson Holdings Ltd v Fox* [1976] QB 503, and subs (II)(A)(iv), 'Same-Sex Cohabitants', focusing on the decision in *Fitzpatrick v Sterling Housing Association Ltd* [2001] 1 AC 27.

[83] *Gammans v Ekins* [1950] 2 KB 328.

[84] ibid, per Asquith LJ, at 331.

It should be noted that at this point in history only surviving 'widows' were specifically referred to as a separate category within the applicable statutory provision[85] and thus surviving male spouses were considered 'family' at that time.[86] Therefore, this judicial statement seems to limit 'family' to that situation of 'widowers' and to parent/child relationships,[87] which is viewed as including de facto parent/child relationships.[88] I observe that, under the judicial interpretation of 'the person in the street's' understanding, the definition of 'family' was limited to the two relationships (the conjugal and the parent/child) which comprise the central nexus of the idealised nuclear family, identified above.

ii. The Role of the 'De Facto Familial Nexus'

The limits of the 'ordinary man' definition of 'family' were explored by Russell LJ nearly 15 years after *Gammans*, in *Ross v Collins*,[89] when he stated that:

> It still requires, it seems to me, at least a broadly recognisable de facto familial nexus. This may be capable of being formed and recognised as such by the ordinary man where the link would be strictly familial had there been a marriage, or where the link is through adoption of a minor, de jure or de facto, or where the link is 'step', or where the link is 'in-law' or by marriage.[90]

In *Ross* it was held that a non-sexual relationship between an elderly man and a much younger woman, who were unrelated by blood and who had lived together for around 22 years,[91] could not be considered 'family' under this definition.[92] This passage was quoted in full and affirmed by the House of Lords in *Joram Developments Ltd v Sharratt*,[93] which concerned relatively similar facts to *Ross*, except that *Joram Developments* involved an elderly woman and a significantly younger man: they too were not considered 'family' under this definition. Lord Diplock was explicit in his affirmation of the *Ross* reasoning, stating 'As for my reason for dismissing the instant appeal, I would not seek to improve upon what was said

[85] Increase of Rent and Mortgage Interest (Restrictions) Act 1920, s 12(g).

[86] As decided in *Salter v Lask* [1925] 1 KB 584. Surviving male spouses were not given equivalent protection to surviving female spouses until the definition was amended by the Housing Act 1980, s 76(1).

[87] *Jones v Trueman* [1949] EGD 277, having held that 'illegitimate children' were to be included within the definition of 'family'.

[88] *Brock v Wollams* [1949] 2 KB 388, having held that if a child was adopted in fact, but not in law, this would be considered 'family'.

[89] *Ross v Collins* [1964] 1 WLR 425.

[90] ibid, per Russell LJ, at 432.

[91] Miss Collins having originally sublet a room, before later becoming an unpaid 'housekeeper' in lieu of rent and subsequently acting as the tenant's primary carer after the death of his wife.

[92] This was the first of a series of cases concerning non-conjugal 'care'-based relationships where there was also no pre-existing familial relationship between those who had shared the home. In each of these cases such relationships were held to be outside the scope of the definition of 'family' under the Rent Acts.

[93] *Joram Developments Ltd v Sharratt* [1979] 1 WLR 928, the House of Lords limited this judgment to its own specific facts, per Lord Diplock, at 930.

there by my noble and learned friend (then Russell LJ).'[94] Taken together, these two cases seem to suggest that this 'broadly recognisable de facto familial nexus' is the boundary beyond which the judicial definition of 'family', based upon 'the person in the street's' understanding, will not go; given the refusal of the courts to apply the term 'family' to these two relatively similar factual situations. In *Ross* it is expressly stated that:

> [T]wo strangers cannot, it seems to me, ever establish artificially for the purposes of this section a familial nexus by acting as brothers or as sisters, even if they call each other such and consider their relationship to be tantamount to that.[95]

In this way, the boundaries of the 'ordinary man' test, which represents the 'common sense' understanding of 'family', are set by this 'de facto familial nexus'. I argue that the positioning of this boundary and the sharp contrast between the language of 'family' and the language of 'strangers', in the decisions in *Ross* and *Joram Developments*, illustrates the intertwining, within judicial reasoning, of 'the person in the street's' understanding and the idealised image of the nuclear family.

Moreover, Russell LJ's statement in *Ross*, quoted above, suggests that this 'de facto familial nexus' seems to be premised upon the existence of a marriage and/or a parent/child or de facto parent/child relationship. In other words, the 'de facto familial nexus' reflects the traditional, nuclear family, comprising the conjugal relationship (originally limited to married couples) and the parent/child relationship (widely defined to include 'de facto' relationships). Thus, I argue that it is the presence of these particular relationships that is central to establishing the existence of the 'de facto familial nexus', rather than either a 'function-based definition' or a definition premised around examining the interdependence and 'care' involved in any individual relationship.[96] Herring has recognised the primacy of conjugal relationships to the law's understanding of 'family', observing 'Care is at the centre of family life. Yet it is sexual relationships which have, for a long time, dominated family law and been regarded as the focus of the definition of a family and the marker for legal intervention.'[97] Indeed, the distinction between conjugal relationships and non-conjugal relationships is inherent to the judicial interpretation of the concept of the 'de facto familial nexus'.

Thus, I suggest that within the judicial consideration of 'family' under the Rent Acts, which is consistently asserted as being based upon the understanding of the 'person in the street', the 'de facto familial nexus' represented an 'idealised definition' of 'family' and this had as its basis the nuclear family.[98] An examination of the cases which have fallen outside the boundaries of the 'de facto familial nexus', as

[94] ibid, at 931.

[95] *Ross v Collins* [1964] 1 WLR 425, per Russell LJ, at 432.

[96] This approach therefore draws the boundary around the conjugal couple and the parent-child relationship. Subsequently, in ch 6, s I 'Exploring the Conceptual Influences', I will consider the radical possibilities offered by alternative understandings of 'family' that are not premised on particular relationships, family forms or structures.

[97] Herring, *Caring and the Law* 187.

[98] See eg the description, quoted above, given by Bernardes, *Family Studies: An Introduction* 2–3.

well as some cases which have extended the definition of 'family' under the Rent Acts, illustrates more clearly the centrality of this idealised image of the nuclear family.

a The Boundaries of the 'De Facto Familial Nexus'

The case of *Sefton Holdings v Cairns*[99] illustrates how strictly the boundary of the 'de facto familial nexus' and thus 'the person in the street's' understanding of family is interpreted. In this case a woman (then aged 23) had moved in with the family of a friend after the death of her boyfriend in World War II (her own parents both having predeceased her). Forty-five years later the daughter of the family died. The court determined that the defendant was not a member of the tenant's family, because the requisite 'de facto familial nexus' was not present in this case. Comparison was drawn with the factual circumstances in *Ross* and *Joram Developments*, with Lloyd LJ stating:

> But the fact remains that when the defendant was taken in nearly 50 years ago she was taken in, to use the language of Russell L.J., as a stranger; and however long she may have lived with the family and however kindly they may have treated her, and however close their friendship may have become, the defendant did not, and in my judgment could not, have become a member of Ada's family.[100]

This case makes clear that without the presence of either a conjugal relationship or a de facto parental relationship (as the defendant was an adult when she began residing in the household) the 'de facto familial nexus' could not be established and therefore there cannot be 'family' between adults who are unrelated by blood, who are instead referred to using Russell LJ's language of mere 'strangers'. The presence of these *relationships* appears to be the decisive criterion and the absence of such relationships removes the claim to the term 'family' under the Rent Acts' definition. This applies regardless of the mutuality and interdependence of the relationship itself, starkly illustrating the boundary of the 'de facto familial nexus' and the significance within this definition of the idealised image of the nuclear family.

The two contrasting decisions of *Jones v Whitehill*[101] and *Langdon v Horton*[102] further demonstrate the extent to which the courts have interpreted 'family' as being based around the existence of this 'de facto familial nexus'. In *Jones* it was held that a niece who had lived with her aunt and uncle for around the last two years of their lives was part of their 'family', whereas in *Langdon* it was held that first cousins who had lived together for around 30 years were not 'family', with Singleton LJ stating that 'I do not see that it is possible to say that a cousin is a member of another cousin's family merely because she is a cousin.'[103] While on

[99] *Sefton Holdings v Cairns* [1988] 2 FLR 109.
[100] ibid, per Lloyd LJ, at 111.
[101] *Jones v Whitehill* [1950] 2 KB 204.
[102] *Langdon v Horton* [1951] 1 KB 666.
[103] ibid, per Singleton LJ, at 672.

first glance these cases appear to have somewhat contradictory results, I argue that they both support the idea of the 'de facto familial nexus' as consisting of the nexus of the conjugal relationship and the parent/child relationship. In *Jones* the court was able to view the relationship between a niece and her uncle and aunt as suitably analogous to a 'parent/child' relationship and thus capable of falling within the boundaries of the 'de facto familial nexus'. In his short judgment, Evershed MR placed considerable significance on the fact that the defendant assumed, 'out of natural love and affection, the duties and offices peculiarly attributable to members of a family of going to live with her uncle and aunt to look after them in their declining years'.[104] It is submitted that the court treated these 'duties and offices'[105] as equivalent to those performed by children for their ageing parents and effectively constructed a de facto parent/child relationship on this basis.[106] Thus, I observe that only once the existence of the relationship had been established, the 'caring' provided within that relationship then appeared to take on significance within judicial reasoning.

In *Langdon*, on the other hand, the absence of this de facto parental relationship[107] meant that while the parties were related, they were not considered 'family'.[108] I suggest that this case was effectively treated as analogous with the factual circumstances in *Ross*, *Joram Developments* and *Sefton Holdings*. This construction of the relationship between the cousins is made explicit in the brief judgment of Danckwerts J, who stated:

> There were three persons in this case living together who were of the same sex, of the same generation, and of approximately the same age ... They were living together more for reasons of convenience, in which respect this case resembles ... the case of two old cronies or friends sharing a residence for purposes of convenience.[109]

This understanding of the relationship considered the existence of the extended familial relationship (that of first cousins) to be irrelevant and, as a consequence the relationship was considered to fall outside the boundary of the 'de facto familial nexus'. Therefore, any interdependence or 'care' that existed within the relationship was not understood to be a relevant consideration; as Singleton LJ commented 'in the present case the question to be asked is, whether the two sisters

[104] *Jones v Whitehill* [1950] 2 KB 204, per Evershed MR, at 207.

[105] Interestingly, this reference to 'love and affection' reflects the literature discussed above in s I, '"Family" as a Social Concept', but the significance granted to this factor within judicial reasoning is limited to the boundaries of a relationship considered suitably analogous to the parent/child relationship within the nuclear family model.

[106] In his subsequent judgment *in Langdon v Horton* [1951] 1 KB 666, Evershed MR, at 669, made clear that his judgment in *Jones v Whitehill*, 'should be read as meaning that I was not expressing any view on the general question whether nephews and nieces as such were within the compass of the formula'.

[107] As well as the absence of a conjugal relationship, which is not applicable in these factual circumstances due to the blood relationship of first cousins.

[108] *Langdon v Horton* [1951] 1 KB 666, at 671, Singleton LJ commented that 'the question is not whether all three were members of the same family, but whether the two sisters were members of the tenant's family. Prima facie, I should not have regarded a cousin as a member of the family of another cousin'.

[109] ibid, per Danckwerts J, at 673.

were members of their cousin's family. If they were not, they did not become so by living in her house for twenty-nine years'.[110] This statement shows that without the existence of the 'de facto familial nexus' the factual reality of the 'care', mutuality and interdependence of a relationship cannot render that relationship 'family' under this definition.

I suggest that these three cases demonstrate how the court's interpretation of this 'de facto familial nexus', within 'the person in the street's' understanding of family, reflects an 'idealised definition' of family, based upon the traditional nuclear family. In his judgment in *Langdon*, Evershed MR, in holding that the cousins were not 'family', states that the alternative result, 'would mean that we were substituting for the word "family" … the word "relations"'.[111] This approach illustrates that those relationships which are viewed as capable of being located within the boundaries of this 'de facto familial nexus' are those which the courts consider to share sufficient similarities and characteristics with the archetypical nuclear family, either through the presence of a conjugal relationship[112] or through the existence of a de facto parent/child relationship.

iii. Unmarried Cohabitants

The evolution in the judicial treatment of unmarried cohabiting couples shows how the definition of 'family' has been extended, by reference to 'the person in the street's' understanding, while still relying on the 'de facto familial nexus', which itself is unaltered by the extension of 'family'. There has been a clear development since the decision in *Gammans v Ekins*,[113] where it was held that a childless unmarried couple who had lived together for a significant period of time were not 'family'. The court believed that it would 'be an abuse of the English language'[114] to describe such a couple as a 'family', due to the fact that they were 'living in sin'.[115] However, relatively soon after the *Gammans* decision the definition of 'family' was extended in *Hawes v Evenden*[116] to include the survivor of an unmarried couple of 12–13 years, who had two children.[117] The existence of a connected parent/child relationship, completing the central nexus of the nuclear family, seems to have been important in influencing the judicial view of the 'familial' character of the unmarried cohabitants, with Somervell LJ stating, 'in a case where the evidence

[110] ibid, per Singleton LJ, at 672.
[111] ibid, per Evershed MR, at 670.
[112] The role of conjugality in regulating adult, personal relationships will be explored further below in ch 3, s II 'The Centrality of Conjugality'.
[113] [1950] 2 KB 328.
[114] ibid, per Asquith LJ, at 331.
[115] ibid, the moralistic determination of the judgment in this case is apparent, with Evershed MR going on to state, at 334 'It may not be a bad thing that by this decision it is shown that, in the Christian society in which we live, one, at any rate, of the privileges which may be derived from marriage is not equally enjoyed by those who are living together as man and wife but who are not married.'
[116] *Hawes v Evenden* [1953] 1 WLR 1169.
[117] Or as she was described by Somervell LJ, ibid, at 1170 'his mistress'.

justifies a finding that they all lived together as a family, then ... I think that the mother is a member of the family'.[118] This statement suggests that the presence of children was the decisive factor which led to the expansion of the definition of 'family' in this case.[119] The importance placed upon the parent/child relationship as foundational to the definition of 'family' in the initial decisions is shown by the statement of Bucknill LJ in *Brock v Wollams*[120] that, 'The primary meaning of the word "family" therefore is "children"'.[121]

The position of unmarried cohabitants without children was reconsidered by the Court of Appeal around 25 years after these cases in *Dyson Holdings Ltd v Fox*.[122] As in *Gammans*, this case concerned an unmarried cohabiting couple who had no children and here they had lived together for around 40 years. In *Dyson Holdings*, however, the court determined that this cohabiting couple were 'family'. This was done on the basis that the operation of the 'ordinary man' test allowed for changes in social attitudes to be reflected in this definition of 'family'.[123] James LJ stated that, 'The popular meaning given to the word "family" is not fixed once and for all time. I have no doubt that with the passage of years it has changed'[124] and Bridge LJ added 'it is, I think, not putting it too high to say that between 1950 and 1975 there has been a complete revolution in society's attitude to unmarried partnerships of the kind under consideration'.[125] Although there was some initial judicial hesitance about the scope of this extension of the definition,[126] it was accepted in subsequent cases[127] and relationships of significantly shorter length were subsequently held to be 'family',[128] until finally cohabiting couples were brought within the statutory definition of 'spouse' for the purposes of the legislation at issue in these cases.[129]

None of these decisions subsequent to *Dyson Holdings* altered the basic 'de facto familial nexus' described above in *Ross*; nor did they shatter the nuclear family paradigm. This line of authority simply lessens the significance that had previously been attached to marriage within judicial reasoning. The extension of the

[118] ibid, at 1171.

[119] Notably only 2 years earlier the court had decided that a male survivor of a cohabiting couple with a child was not 'family' in *Perry v Dembrowski* [1951] 2 KB 420. Although the judgment of Somervell LJ, at 422–423, left open the possibility that in different factual circumstances a surviving 'illegitimate father' may be capable of being considered 'family'.

[120] [1949] 2 KB 388.

[121] ibid, per Bucknill LJ, at 349.

[122] *Dyson Holdings Ltd v Fox* [1976] QB 503.

[123] Lord Denning MR went further in his judgment, ibid, stating at 509 'it appears to me that *Gammans v Ekins* [1950] 2 KB 328 was wrongly decided'.

[124] ibid, per James LJ, at 511.

[125] ibid, per Bridge LJ, at 512.

[126] *Helby v Rafferty* [1979] 1 WLR 13, where a cohabitation of five years was held to lack the 'permanence and stability', per Stamp LJ, at 18, required to be considered 'family'.

[127] *Watson v Lucas* [1980] 1 WLR 1493, where one of the parties to a 19-year long cohabitation was, in fact, married to another woman throughout this relationship, the couple were still considered 'family'.

[128] *Chios Property Investment Co Ltd v Lopez* (1988) 20 HLR 120 held that a relationship of only around two years' duration was enough to be considered 'family'.

[129] Housing Act 1988, s 39(2) and Sch 4, para 1(2), inserted Sch 1, para 2(2) into the Rent Act 1977.

definition of 'family' in these cases reflects, in Herring's terms, a 'function-based' approach to defining 'family', in that a clear analogy is drawn between marriage and those 'marriage-like' cohabiting relationships which had previously been refused recognition by the courts.[130] The extension is based upon the functions that those cohabiting relationships are seen to share with marriage, which remains understood as the archetypical conjugal relationship within the idealised image of the nuclear family. However, the existence of a conjugal relationship remains the decisive factor within the case law; thus the engagement with Herring's 'function-based definition' does not extend beyond the boundaries of the 'de facto familial nexus', which reflects the approach described above in *Jones v Whitehill*[131] and *Langdon v Horton*.[132] Consequently, those individuals in the factual circumstances exemplified by *Ross v Collins*[133] and *Joram Development Ltd v Sharratt*[134] remain situated outside the boundaries of that 'de facto familial nexus' and therefore are not considered to be 'family'.

iv. Same-Sex Cohabitants

In *Fitzpatrick v Sterling Housing Association Ltd*,[135] the House of Lords held that a same-sex couple who had cohabited for 18 years came within the definition of 'family'.[136] The decision emphasised the changing social attitudes that had occurred throughout the twentieth century.[137] In his judgment, Lord Clyde stated that:

> [T]he meaning of the word family in its sense of a group united by some tie or bond such as blood, marriage or personal affection may not have, as a matter of language, altered. What has changed are the precise personal associations to which the concept may now be applied.[138]

[130] The legal approach towards cohabitation more generally will be considered below in ch 3, subs II(A) 'The Legal Regulation of Cohabitation'.

[131] [1950] 2 KB 204.

[132] [1951] 1 KB 666.

[133] [1964] 1 WLR 425.

[134] [1979] 1 WLR 928.

[135] [2001] 1 AC 27. Prior to this decision, in a different statutory context (involving public sector tenancies under the Housing Act 1980) in *Harrogate Borough Council v Simpson* (1985) 17 HLR 205, it was held that the survivor of a same-sex female couple could not be described as having been 'living together as husband and wife' (one of the statutory definitions of 'family' under s 50(3)(b) of the Housing Act 1980) with their deceased partner and therefore they could not be considered 'family' under that definition.

[136] Prior to Sch 8, para 13 of the Civil Partnership Act 2004, which amended the Rent Act 1977, Sch 1, para 2 to expressly include both surviving civil partners and surviving same-sex cohabitees alongside surviving spouses. This followed on from the House of Lords decision in *Ghaidan v Godin-Mendoza* [2004] UKHL 30, [2004] 2 AC 557, decided prior to the 2004 Act coming into force; which held that due to s 3 of the Human Rights Act 1998, Sch 1, para 2(2) of the Rent Act should be read in such a way as to include same-sex cohabiting couples under the definition of 'spouse'. As the distinction between same-sex and opposite-sex couples in this context was considered to be a violation of ECHR, Art 14 in conjunction with Art 8.

[137] However, see Ralph Sandland, 'Not "Social Justice": The Housing Association, The Judges, The Tenant and His Lover' (2000) 8(2) *Feminist Legal Studies* 227, who observes, at 227, 'it is a case with, to say the least, a mixed message'.

[138] *Fitzpatrick v Sterling Housing Association Ltd* [2001] 1 AC 27, per Lord Clyde, at 50.

In other words, the 'de facto familial nexus' was still determining which relationships were considered 'family', but, in the same way as opposite-sex cohabitants, same-sex cohabitants were now regarded as capable of forming part of that nexus, due to developments in 'the person in the street's' understanding of 'family'. This decision can be seen as a further extension of what is considered an acceptable form of conjugal relationship within the 'de facto familial nexus'. As Lord Slynn stated 'I prefer to say that it is not the meaning which has changed but that those who are capable of falling within the words have changed.'[139] Moreover, his lordship sought to describe some of the features or characteristics of a relationship that would give rise to it being considered as familial when he observed that 'The hallmarks of the relationship were essentially that there should be a degree of mutual interdependence, of the sharing of lives, of caring and love, of commitment and support.'[140] The language in this judgment reflects the language of the literature on 'function-based' models of 'family'.[141] Indeed, in bringing same-sex conjugal relationships within the definition of 'family' on the basis that they share many of the core characteristics of marriage,[142] which remains the 'gold standard' of conjugal relationships, the court seemed to have adopted, in Herring's terms, a 'function-based' approach to defining 'family'.[143] Thus, the development of the definition of 'family' in *Fitzpatrick* shows that neither marriage nor heterosexuality is a prerequisite for the existence of the 'de facto familial nexus'.

However, regardless of the judicial reference to 'mutual interdependence' and 'caring and love', I contend that the existence of a conjugal relationship remains the crucial factor in determining whether a relationship is considered 'family' under the Rent Acts.[144] First, the examination of the development of the definition of 'family' throughout the case law, set out above, has established the centrality of the presence of the 'de facto familial nexus' to that definition[145] and has illustrated how strictly the boundary of that 'nexus' is drawn.[146] Secondly, in his judgment in *Fitzpatrick*,[147] Lord Clyde refers to 'the common bond in a partnership of two adult persons which may entitle the one to be in the common judgment of society a member of the other's family',[148] which reflects the emphasis on 'common sense'

[139] ibid, per Lord Slynn, at 39.
[140] ibid, at 38.
[141] As briefly set out above within s I, '"Family" as a Social Concept'.
[142] This will be considered further below in ch 3, subs I(C) 'Same-Sex Marriage and the Understanding of Marriage'.
[143] See eg Glennon, '*Fitzpatrick v Sterling Housing Association Ltd* – An Endorsement of the Functional Family?'
[144] Or in different factual circumstances the existence of a 'de facto' parent/child relationship.
[145] Described by Russell LJ in *Ross v Collins* [1964] 1 WLR 425, at 432.
[146] As shows by the decisions in *Langdon v Horton* [1951] 1 KB 666, *Joram Developments Ltd v Sharratt* [1979] 1 WLR 928 and *Sefton Holdings v Cairns* [1988] 2 FLR 109.
[147] *Fitzpatrick v Sterling Housing Association Ltd* [2001] 1 AC 27.
[148] ibid, per Lord Clyde, at 51.

understandings and Herring's 'the person in the street's definition' of family. His lordship continues, by stating that:

> It would be difficult to establish such a bond unless the couple were living together in the same house. It would also be difficult to establish it without an active sexual relationship between them or at least the potentiality of such a relationship. If they have or are caring for children whom they regard as their own they would make the family designation more immediately obvious, but the existence of children is not a necessary element.[149]

This shows the emphasis on the existence (or at least the potential existence) of a conjugal relationship, as well as the significance of a connected parent/child relationship, within the language of the judgment. I argue that it follows from this that any significance being granted to the mutuality and interdependence within relationships is secondary to those relationships being capable of being located within the central nexus of the idealised nuclear family.[150]

Moreover, the importance of the traditional nuclear family was reaffirmed by Lord Nicholls in *Fitzpatrick*, when he stated that 'the paradigm family unit was, and still is, a husband and wife and their children'.[151] As Glennon observes 'the term "family" was not updated as such or given a different meaning to accommodate changing social parameters. Instead, acknowledgment of changed social conditions enlarged the category of person entitled to be included within the definition of the family'.[152] I endorse this observation and argue that the nuclear family, based around a heterosexual marriage, remains the idealised image of 'family', within the judicial definition under the Rent Acts, but same-sex conjugal couples are being brought within the boundaries of this idealised image, in much the same way as unmarried heterosexual couples were in the *Dyson Holdings* decision.

B. The Definition of 'Family Life' under Article 8 of the European Convention on Human Rights

Another context where there has been significant judicial consideration of the definition of 'family' has been under Article 8 of the European Convention on

[149] ibid.

[150] ibid, at 44, Lord Nicholls states 'Where sexual partners are involved, whether heterosexual or homosexual, there is scope for the intimate mutual love and affection and long-term commitment that typically characterise the relationship of husband and wife.' The implication of this statement being that such scope for 'mutual love and affection' does not exist to the same extent outside the boundaries of relationships between 'sexual partners'.

[151] ibid, per Lord Nicholls, at 42. Furthermore, given how much it is relied on in the early cases, it is notable that his lordship criticises the usage of the 'ordinary man' test, stating, at 45 'This oft-quoted test has tended to bedevil this area of law … Contrary to what seems implicit in this form of question, the expression family does not have a single, readily recognisable meaning.'

[152] Glennon, '*Fitzpatrick v Sterling Housing Association Ltd* – An Endorsement of the Functional Family?' 235.

Human Rights (ECHR), which provides that: 'Everyone has the right to respect for his private and family life, his home and his correspondence.'[153] As with the Rent Acts, the term 'family life' is not defined in the convention and instead has been judicially interpreted over time by the European Court of Human Rights.

This understanding of 'family life' under Article 8 has been held to encompass various close familial relationships, including those between siblings,[154] grandparents and grandchildren[155] and even uncle and nephew.[156] The meaning and scope of 'family life' under Article 8 has undergone a development across the case law which broadly parallels that visible in the Rent Acts cases described above; beginning with an understanding of 'family life' primarily based around marriage and the traditional nuclear family in the early cases, the Court has gradually moved toward a broader and more inclusive understanding in the later cases. The Court has noted that 'the notion of the "family" in this provision is not confined solely to marriage-based relationships and may encompass other *de facto* "family" ties where the parties are living together outside of marriage'.[157] The 'illegitimate family'[158] of mother and child, unmarried cohabitants with children,[159] fathers who did not reside with their children,[160] childless unmarried cohabitants,[161] the relationship between a female to male transsexual and a child born to his female partner through artificial insemination[162] and most recently same-sex couples[163] have all been brought within the meaning of 'family life' under Article 8.

Despite these developments, 'de facto' relationships (those that are not registered formally with the state) do not *automatically* amount to 'family life', and the court has made clear that 'a number of factors may be relevant, including

[153] Article 8(1) of the European Convention on Human Rights. For a comparison of the approaches of the European Court of Justice and the European Court of Human Rights, see Helen Stafford, 'Concepts of Family Under EU Law – Lessons from the ECHR' (2002) 16(3) *International Journal of Law Policy and the Family* 410.

[154] *Moustaquim v Belgium* (1991) 13 EHRR 802, at 813, para 36.

[155] *Marckx v Belgium* (1979) 2 EHRR 330, at 348, para 45, see also *Vermeire v Belgium* (1993) 15 EHRR 488.

[156] *Boyle v UK* (1995) 19 EHRR 179.

[157] *Keegan v Ireland* (1994) 18 EHRR 342, at 360, para 44, this principle has consistently been reaffirmed. Strikingly similar words were used in the more recent case of *Schalk and Kopf v Austria* (2011) 53 EHRR 20, at 701, para 90.

[158] *Marckx v Belgium* (1979) 2 EHRR 330, at 346, para 40.

[159] *Johnston v Ireland* (1987) 9 EHRR 203.

[160] First, when there had previously been a marriage between mother and father in *Berrehab v Netherlands* (1989) 11 EHRR 322 and subsequently in all circumstances eg *Boughameni v France* (1996) 22 EHRR 228.

[161] *Keegan v Ireland* (1994) 18 EHRR 342.

[162] *X, Y and Z v UK* (1997) 24 EHRR 143.

[163] *Schalk and Kopf v Austria* (2011) 53 EHRR 20 at 702, para 94 'In view of this evolution the Court considers it artificial to maintain the view that, in contrast to a different-sex couple, a same-sex couple cannot enjoy "family life" for the purposes of art. 8.' It is notable that the Court and the Commission had previously rejected several opportunities to bring same-sex couples within the definition of 'family life', see eg *Karner v Austria* (2004) 38 EHRR 24, *Mata Estevez v Spain* [2001] ECHR 896 and *Simpson v United Kingdom* (1986) 47 D&R 274.

whether the couple live together, the length of their relationship and whether they have demonstrated their commitment to each other by having children together or by any other means'.[164] First, the significance given to the existence of children (as providing evidence of 'commitment') within this definition illustrates the importance of the central nexus of the conjugal relationship and the parent/child relationship within the nuclear family model. Secondly, in this context the use of, in Herring's terms, a 'function-based definition' of 'family' can only act negatively to exclude some conjugal relationships from the definition of 'family life', it cannot be employed to transform non-conjugal interdependent 'caring' relationships into 'family'. This approach is similar to that taken under the Rent Acts described above,[165] drawing the boundary around the conjugal relationship and the nuclear family. Nevertheless, one textbook on the ECHR[166] has observed that 'Family life is now understood as extending beyond formal relationships and the family based on marriage … The Court has taken into account increasingly the substance and reality of relationships, acknowledging developments in social practices and the law in European states.'[167]

Despite the trend of gradual extension, the Court has continually acknowledged, throughout this development, 'that protection of the family in the traditional sense is, in principle, a weighty and legitimate reason which might justify a difference in treatment'.[168] The repeated restatement of this principle suggests that the idealised image of the traditional nuclear family continues to exert significant influence on the manner in which the definition of 'family life' has evolved under Article 8. As White and Ovey have observed 'The core family within the case-law of the Strasburg Court is very much a man and a woman with children of whom they are the parents';[169] in other words, the central nexus of the conjugal relationship and the parent/child relationship. Thus, in spite of the appearance within the ECHR jurisprudence of some elements of Herring's 'function-based definition' of 'family', I contend that in defining 'family life' within this jurisprudence there continues to be reliance upon an 'idealised definition' of 'family', based around the traditional, nuclear family.

[164] *X, Y and Z v UK*, at 166, para 36.

[165] Throughout subs II(A) 'The Definition of "Family" Under the Rent Acts', but particularly at subs II(A)(iii), 'Unmarried Cohabitants' and II(A)(iv), 'Same-Sex Cohabitants'.

[166] DJ Harris, M O'Boyle, EP Bates and M Buckley, *Law of the European Convention on Human Rights* (Oxford, Oxford University Press, 2009).

[167] ibid, at 371.

[168] *Karner v Austria* (2004) 38 EHRR 24, at 537, para 40, this reflects the judgment 25 years previously in *Marckx*, where it was stated, at 346, para 40 'The Court recognises that support and encouragement of the traditional family is in itself legitimate or even praiseworthy.'

[169] Robin CA White and Clare Ovey, *Jacobs, White and Ovey: The European Convention on Human Rights*, 5th edn (Oxford, Oxford University Press, 2010) 337.

C. The 'Formalistic' Definition of 'Family Member' in EU Law

European Union law provides for certain rights in relation to freedom of movement and residence.[170] Directive 2004/38/EC ('the Citizenship Directive') provides, in Article 1(a) for 'the right of free movement and residence within the territory of the Member States by Union citizens and their family members'.[171] Article 2(2) of the directive contains a formalistic definition of 'family member' as follows: '(a) the spouse, (b) the partner with whom the Union citizen has contracted a registered partnership,[172] (c) the direct descendants who are under the age of 21 or are dependants,[173] (d) the dependent direct relatives in the ascending line'.[174] Therefore 'family member' under this definition is essentially restricted to registered conjugal relationships and parent/child relationships,[175] which reflects the central nexus of relationships that constitutes the nuclear family. It is notable that the relatively strict approach of this directive actually widened, if only very slightly, the original definition of 'family member' contained within the previous regulation governing freedom of movement for workers,[176] which did not include the category of 'registered partnerships'.[177]

The case of *Netherlands v Reed*,[178] which considered the previous definition, illustrates how rigidly the preceding provision was interpreted by the European Court of Justice (ECJ). In this case an unmarried cohabitant was not considered a 'family member' because such relationships are not specifically mentioned in the definition and the court stated 'it must be held that the term "spouse" in Article 10 of the regulation refers to a marital relationship only'.[179] The formalistic approach

[170] As a consequence of the result of the referendum on British membership of the European Union, it would appear that these rights will no longer be part of UK law in the future. This will occur either upon the expiration of the two-year period for negotiations under Art 50 of the Treaty on the European Union, on 29 March 2019, or after the completion of a transitional arrangement prior to the implementation of a new relationship between the UK and EU. However, there remains continuing uncertainty regarding the outcome of the negotiation and the precise time scale for the British exit from the EU. Moreover, these rights will remain part of UK law, at least until 29 March 2019 and possibly longer, until the end of any transitional arrangement.

[171] Directive 2004/38/EC, Article 1(b) additionally provides, 'the right of permanent residence in the territory of the Member States for Union citizens and their family members'.

[172] Subject to the further requirement in Art 2(2)(b) that the 'registered partnership' must be, 'on the basis of the legislation of a Member State, if the legislation of the host Member State treats registered partnerships as equivalent to marriage and in accordance with the conditions laid down in the relevant legislation of the host Member State'.

[173] Art 2(2)(c) also specifies that this category includes, 'those of the spouse or partner as defined in point (b)'.

[174] Art 2(2)(d) specifies similar provision for 'those of the spouse or partner as defined in point (b)'. The meaning of 'dependency' was explored in *Jia v Migrationsverket* [2007] QB 545 (Case C-1/05).

[175] Category (d) is dealing with a version of the parent/child relationship, where the elderly 'parent' has become a dependant of the 'child'.

[176] Regulation 1662/68/EEC, 'On Freedom of Movement for Workers within the Community'.

[177] ibid, Art 10(1).

[178] *Netherlands v Reed* [1987] 2 CMLR 448 (Case 59/85).

[179] ibid, para 15, at 465.

of the ECJ to the term 'spouse'[180] was also evident, in a different context, in *D and Sweden v Council of the European Union*,[181] where it was held that a registered same-sex partnership could not be considered equivalent to a marriage, with the court stating clearly, 'that concept is distinct from marriage'.[182] Gaffney-Rhys has noted that 'the European Court of Justice has adopted a very traditional interpretation of the terms spouse and marriage'.[183] Given the ECJ's strict approach to defining 'spouse'[184] and the fact that there is no specific provision for unmarried cohabitants within the definition, such relationships are not covered by this formalistic definition of 'family member'.

However, the 'Citizenship Directive' does provide for the right of entry and residence for 'the partner with whom the Union citizen has a durable relationship',[185] but crucially this is qualified on the basis that, 'The host Member State shall undertake an extensive examination of the personal circumstances'.[186] The factual circumstances of a cohabiting couple will be examined to determine whether their relationship is 'durable' before the right is granted, whereas if they were deemed to be 'family members' the right would apply automatically, as a result of that status. Therefore, a 'function-based definition', which considers the 'durability' of relationships is only utilised as a means of excluding some non-marital conjugal relationships. Consequently, under the 'Citizenship Directive' any consideration of the characteristics or the mutuality and 'caring' within individual relationships is limited to conjugal couples and therefore is subordinate to the existence of relationships situated within the central nexus of the nuclear family. It is notable that this approach shares similarities with that taken in the interpretation of 'family life' under Article 8 of the ECHR described above.[187]

On the basis of the definition of 'family member' prior to the 'Citizenship Directive', McGlynn suggested that, 'This "model European family" is a reproduction of the traditional "nuclear" family: that of the heterosexual married union, in which the husband is head of the family and principal breadwinner and the wife is

[180] This is also shown by the case of *Diatta v Land Berlin* [1986] 2 CMLR 164 (Case 267/83), where a married couple were separated and expecting to divorce but were still considered 'spouses' because their marriage had not been formally dissolved.

[181] *D and Sweden v Council of the European Union* [2003] 3 CMLR 9 (Joined Cases C-122/99P and C-125/99P).

[182] ibid, para 31, at 260.

[183] Ruth Gaffney-Rhys, 'EU Directive on Freedom of Movement' (2006) *International Family Law* 65, 66.

[184] However, in the recent decision of *Coman and Others v Inspectoratul General Pentru Imigrări and Others* (Case C-673/16), the ECJ held, at para 15 'that the term "spouse" within the meaning of Directive 2004/38 is gender-neutral and may therefore cover the same-sex spouse of the Union citizen concerned'. This dispute arose in the context of the recognition of a same-sex spouse under Art 2 of the Citizenship Directive in Romania, a country that does not allow for same-sex marriage.

[185] Directive 2004/38/EC Article 3(2)(b).

[186] ibid.

[187] See above at subs II(B) 'The Definition of "Family Life" under Article 8 of the European Convention on Human Rights'.

the primary childcarer.'[188] Thus, the extension of the definition of 'family member' in the 'Citizenship Directive' has been limited and the definition continues to be based around registered conjugal relationships and related parent/child relationships. We can see, therefore, that the nuclear family, comprising the nexus of the conjugal relationship and the parent/child relationship, remains the 'idealised definition' of 'family' that underpins the 'formalistic definition' of 'family member' in EU Law.

III. The Influence of the Nuclear Family Model within the Definitions of 'Family'

This chapter considered how 'family' is understood and defined within the law. The chapter began by exploring 'family' as a social and cultural concept, observing from the relevant literature that there is no consensus as to its meaning and no single, universally applicable definition of 'family'. Relatedly, I noted that the nature of the concept of 'family' results in inherent difficulty in providing such a universal definition. I observed that this lack of overarching definition is reflected in the law. However, this chapter identified and examined three specific legal contexts in which 'family' is defined, which spanned both domestic and European law. Within these definitions, I noted two contrasting approaches: a formalistic approach, under the Citizenship Directive, which limits 'family' to a list of particular relationships and excludes all other relationships from the definition; and an alternative approach, under the Rent Acts and Article 8 of the ECHR, which provides no specific guidance as to the extent of 'family' and instead allows the definition to be interpreted and developed judicially.

The judicial development of the definitions of 'family' under the Rent Acts and 'family life' under Article 8 followed a similar pattern. Both began with a fairly restrictive definition, based around traditional understandings of marriage and the nuclear family.[189] This archetype of 'family' subsequently became an idealised image within these definitions. Thereafter, both approaches extended their understanding of 'family' gradually[190] and ended up encompassing a much wider variety of relationships and family forms,[191] seemingly through the use of elements of Herring's 'function-based' approach to defining the 'family'. However, in spite of

[188] Clare McGlynn, 'The Europeanisation of Family Law' [2001] 13(1) *Child and Family Law Quarterly* 35, 47, see also eg Lorna Woods, 'Family Rights in the EU – Disadvantaging the Disadvantaged?' [1999] 11(1) *Child and Family Law Quarterly* 17.

[189] See eg the decisions regarding the Rent Acts in *Brock v Wollams* [1949] 2 KB 388 and *Gammans v Ekins* [1950] 2 KB 328.

[190] Illustrated by the inclusion of unmarried cohabitants, initial limited to those with children in *Hawes v Evenden* [1953] 1 WLR 1169 and *Johnston v Ireland* (1987) 9 EHRR 203, before subsequently including those without children in *Dyson Holdings Ltd v Fox* [1976] QB 503 and *Keegan v Ireland* (1994) 18 EHRR 342.

[191] Culminating in the inclusion of same-sex couples within the definitions in *Fitzpatrick v Sterling Housing Association Ltd* [2001] 1 AC 27 and *Schalk and Kopf v Austria* (2011) 53 EHRR 20.

this process of extension, within both approaches it is possible to identify a hierarchy of family forms, as Herring observes:

> Despite these developments recognising a variety of family forms it can be argued that there is a hierarchy of families in family law: with the top position being taken by married couples, with civil partners, then unmarried heterosexual couples and then unpartnered same-sex couples below them. Certainly the closer the relationship is to the 'ideal' of marriage the more likely it is to be recognised as a family.[192]

In the absence of a precise or detailed definition of 'family' in either the Rent Acts or ECHR Article, the courts have turned to the 'ordinary' understanding of the 'person in the street', represented through the 'de facto familial nexus'[193] or 'de facto family ties',[194] to fill the gap. This chapter has showed that these definitions reflect an idealised image of the traditional, heterosexual, nuclear family.[195] The approach taken to 'family member' under the Citizenship Directive provides additional evidence that it is the existence of the central nexus of the conjugal relationship and the parent/child relationship that is the decisive factor in granting the label of 'family' within the law.

The influence of this idealised image is illustrated by the way that definitions of 'family' and 'family life' have been expanded, by the judiciary, to include relationships which are viewed as sufficiently resembling the archetypical nuclear family. On the basis of their similarities such relationships can be situated within the parameters of the legal definitions of 'family'.[196] Consequently, relationships possessing 'marriage-like conjugality' (same-sex and opposite-sex cohabitants) are now considered 'family', whereas other interdependent and 'caring' relationships, that are non-conjugal, remain outside the boundaries of these definitions. Therefore, I argue that Herring's 'function-based definition' of 'family', as well as any alternative approach to defining 'family' premised upon caring, mutuality and interdependence, are subordinate to the idealised image of the nuclear family. Thus, any consideration of functions only occurs for conjugal relationships and consequently, the 'care' and interdependence of relationships cannot transform those relationships outside the central nexus of the nuclear family into 'family' under these legal definitions.[197]

Overall, this chapter has illustrated the continuing influence of the traditional nuclear family, characterised by the central nexus of the conjugal relationship and the parent/child relationship, upon the legal understanding of the 'family'. Given this conclusion, the next chapter explores why the 'nuclear family' has been positioned as the idealised image of the 'family' within legal understanding, by considering the historical and theoretical context that shaped that archetypical model of 'family'.

[192] Herring, *Family Law* 6.

[193] See eg *Ross v Collins* [1964] 1 WLR 425.

[194] See eg *Schalk and Kopf v Austria* (2011) 53 EHRR 20, at 701, para 90.

[195] See eg the description, quoted above, given by Bernardes, *Family Studies: An Introduction* 2–3.

[196] As is shown, under the Rent Act definition, by the contrasting approaches taken by the decisions in *Jones v Whitehill* [1950] 2 KB 204 and *Langdon v Horton* [1951] 1 KB 666.

[197] Subsequently, in ch 6 'The Possibilities Offered by Alternative Models of the "Family"', I will return to the alternative constructions of 'family' and consider whether such models provide a sounder normative framework, as well as whether those models would better reflect the diversity of family forms and structures within 21st century family life in the UK.

2

The Historical and Philosophical Underpinnings of the 'Nuclear Family' Model

In chapter one, I argued that the legal understanding of the 'family' was underpinned by an idealised image of 'family':[1] the traditional nuclear family, comprising the nexus of the conjugal relationship and the parent/child relationship. This chapter will explore the reasons for the nuclear family being positioned as the 'natural' or 'normal' family of law. It will consider both the nature of historical family forms and the values which underpin western society and the legal system: the divide between the public and private spheres of society and the orthodox construction of the rational and autonomous legal subject. Considering the 'public/private divide', Boyd has observed 'This divide, which has long informed dominant Western ways of knowing and being, denotes the ideological division of life into apparently opposing spheres of public and private activities, and public and private responsibilities.'[2] In regard to the orthodox construction of the legal subject, Bottomley and Bronitt have suggested that 'Liberalism at its heart posits the view of rational person or legal subject – perhaps famously embodied in the standards imposed by the "reasonable person" that inhabits the law of negligence and criminal law doctrine.'[3] This chapter will consider the construction of both of these central concepts and I will argue that the nuclear family model's significance inevitably arises from the intersection of these values and the historical prevalence of the nuclear family form.[4]

In section I, I will describe how the nuclear family has been a recurrent and dominant form of family throughout history, and how the image of the nuclear family aligns with the law's image of the individual – the 'legal subject'. Relatedly,

[1] See ch 1, s II 'The Law's "Definition(s)" of "Family"'.

[2] Susan Boyd, 'Challenging the Public/Private Divide: An Overview' in Boyd (ed), *Challenging the Public/Private Divide: Feminism, Law and Public Policy* 8.

[3] Stephen Bottomley and Simon Bronitt, *Law in Context*, 4th edn (Annandale, Federation Press, 2012) 1.

[4] See eg Richard Grassby, *Kinship and Capitalism: Marriage, Family and Business in the English-Speaking World, 1580–1740* (New York, Cambridge University Press, 2001) who notes, at 2 'Family historians have emphasized the continuity of communal forms, that the nuclear family had a long history and co-existed with kinship'.

I will argue that the delineation of the male and female gender roles within the 'public/private divide' has contributed to the gendered roles (the man as 'breadwinner' and the woman as 'homemaker') embodied within the traditional nuclear family. In section II, I will consider some of the theoretical critique of the orthodox construction of the legal subject that questions its supposed objectivity and self-evidence, as well as relying upon the feminist literature which examines the nature of its underpinning values. I will use this critique to illustrate some of the issues caused by the application of this orthodox construction of the legal subject. In section III, I will argue that the combination of the historical recurrence and dominance of the nuclear family form, the influence of the gendered roles of the public/private divide and the values of the orthodox legal subject, have resulted in the idealised image of the nuclear family being positioned and understood as the 'natural' and 'common-sense' understandings of 'family', which has in turn influenced the *legal* understanding of 'family' as described in chapter one.

I. The 'Family' and the 'Legal Subject'

In this section, I will explore how the idealised image of the nuclear family has come to exert significant gravitational force upon the law by considering the recurrence of the nuclear family form throughout history and examining the values and ideals which underpin this archetype of 'family'. To that end, this section will consider the orthodox construction of the 'legal subject'.[5] The characteristics that are encapsulated within the 'person' of law determine how individuals are understood by the law, and I will argue that this construction exerts significant influence upon the legal understanding of the 'family' composed of such individuals. As Naffine and Owens observe 'The legal person, or legal subject, plays an absolutely critical role in law. The attributes accorded by law to its subject serve to justify and rationalise law's very forms and practices.'[6] The orthodox understanding is that law employs a neutral and objective approach to its subject.[7] However this claim of

[5] Richard Tur, 'The "Person" in Law' in Arthur Peacocke and Grant Gillett (eds), *Persons and Personality in Contemporary Inquiry* (Oxford, Basil Blackwell, 1987) suggests at 123, that 'There is no general law of persons, but rather, a series of rules concerning relationships and liabilities.' Therefore, it is argued that the 'legal subject' is not necessarily a simple, unitary ideal, but rather that there exist various constructions of the subject throughout the law, employed in different areas and contexts. However, these 'subjects' share many similarities and are representative of the same underlying values and ideals, which are reinforced throughout law. Consequently for the purposes of this chapter the generic term 'legal subject' will be used.

[6] Ngaire Naffine and Rosemary J Owens, 'Introduction: Sexing Law' in Naffine and Owens (eds), *Sexing the Subject of Law* 7.

[7] For examples of the orthodox construction of the subject, see Bryant Smith, 'Legal Personality' (1928) 37(3) *Yale Law Journal* 283; DP Derham, 'Theories of Legal Personality' in Leicester Webb (ed), *Legal Personality and Political Pluralism* (Carlton, Melbourne University Press, 1958) and Peter Cane, *Responsibility in Law and Morality* (Oxford, Hart Publishing, 2002).

impartiality obscures the fact that law has in mind a particular type of individual with particular characteristics when it constructs the legal subject. I will argue that the values and ideals privileged by law as it conceptualises and defines its subject support the dominant understanding of the nuclear family and its positioning as the common-sense and 'natural' image of family within the law's definitions of 'family'.[8]

To begin, I will trace the historical conceptions of 'family', from classical societies through the Middle Ages and into the Enlightenment, observing that the nuclear family form is evident across these different historical contexts (subsection A). I will explore how the recurrence of this idealised image throughout history reflects the persisting notion of a division between the public and private spheres of society (subsection B). I will then consider how these historical family forms are influenced by the dominant, orthodox construction of the legal subject (subsection C).

A. 'Family' and the Subject in Historical Societies

The roots of the philosophical, political and legal systems of western society are found in the ideas and systems of Ancient Greece and Rome. Consequently, the family forms and structures, as well as the cultural values of those societies, possess a continuing relevance upon our understandings of the traditional and the 'natural'. On that basis, regarding the 'family' in Ancient Greece, the historian Lacey states that:

> The smallest unit of the state is the family, the oikos, which is comprised of the three elements, the male, the female and the servant … Male and female have a natural instinct to procreate themselves successors says Aristotle … and this introduces into the family a fourth element, the children.[9]

This basic family structure is not radically different from contemporary constructions, with its principal nuclear core. However, it is noteworthy that the central familial unit of Greek society was understood to include servants. The Greek conception of family ('the oikos') may more accurately be viewed as having encompassed the entirety of those living within a household. Moreover, regarding the conception of the relationship between husbands and wives, Harrison observed:

> There can be no doubt that a woman remained under some sort of tutelage during the whole of her life. She could not enter into any but the most trifling contract, she could not engage her own hand in marriage, and, she could not plead her own case in court.[10]

[8] As set out above in ch 1, s II, 'The Law's "Definition(s)" of "Family"'.

[9] WK Lacey, *The Family in Classical Greece* (Ithaca, Cornell University Press, 1984) 15.

[10] AW Harrison, *The Law of Athens: The Family and Property* (New York, Oxford University Press, 1968) 108.

Historians have observed that the legal status of men and women was substantively different in Ancient Greece,[11] it was the case that 'only adult male citizens could exercise the privileges of membership in the community to their full extent'.[12] It is apparent that this was a society which was characterised by male dominance of public office and affairs. Consequently, this was a society which employed a rigid division between the 'public' sphere (for men) and the 'private' sphere (for women). Indeed, it was engagement with the public sphere, which was limited to men, that was viewed as giving rise to the rights and duties associated with being a full legal subject.[13] On this basis, Dickenson has argued that the nature of the division between the genders in Ancient Greece went further than splitting society into separate public and private realms for men and women respectively, commenting 'In Aristotle women's absence from the public sphere is mirrored by their subordination in the private realm … I think Aristotle's male is the "symbol" of norm in both private and public arenas. In both realms women are less than full subjects.'[14] Thus, in Ancient Greece the female role was characterised by a dual subordination in both the public and private spheres.

The Roman conception of the 'family' followed a similar basic structure to that of the Greeks, which the historian Rawson details as follows:

> The nuclear family was small, but what the Romans meant as *familia* could be much larger. The Roman *familia* consisted of the conjugal family plus dependants (i.e. a man, his wife, and their unmarried children), together with the slaves and sometimes freedmen and foster-children who lived in the same household.[15]

It is apparent that this Roman *familia* had a central core, based around the nuclear family, which resembles the twenty-first century understandings of 'family'. However, like the Greek 'oikos', the Roman *familia* represented a family structure which was wider in scope than our twenty-first century conception including, as it did, all dependants, freedmen and slaves.[16] This Roman *familia*

[11] Much of the material written about the family of Ancient Greece primarily concerns the Athenian perspective (due to the extensive writings of Aristotle). While there would have been unifying themes and ideals across the city states, there would also evidently have been specific differences. While Lacey, *The Family in Classical Greece*, focuses primarily on Athens, she considers the significant differences of the Spartan model at 194–208.

[12] Raphael Sealey, *The Justice of the Greeks* (Ann Arbor, University of Michigan Press, 1994) 133.

[13] The presence of slavery was a fundamental feature of Ancient Greek society and therefore the Greeks had little difficulty with the notion that people could be considered as non-subjects or as mere property. Harrison, *The Law of Athens: The Family and Property* states at 163 'From many points of view slaves in fourth century Athens were chattels. Aristotle describes a slave as "a live possession" or "a live tool"'.

[14] Donna Dickenson, *Property, Women and Politics: Subjects or Objects?* (Cambridge, Polity Press, 1997) 46.

[15] Beryl Rawson, 'The Roman Family' in Beryl Rawson (ed), *The Family in Ancient Rome: New Perspectives* (London, Croom Helm, 1986) 7.

[16] Similar to Ancient Greece, Roman society was premised on the existence of widespread slavery, Gaius in his *Institutes of Gaius*, Francis de Zulueta (ed), (Oxford, Clarendon Press, 1946–53), wrote, 'Certainly, the great divide in the law of persons is this: all men are either free men or slaves', (D.1.5.2) (cf. Inst.Gai. 1. 9).

was underpinned by the concept of the *pater familias*, who exercised effective control over the behaviour and property of all other members of that family; Du Plessis describes the *pater familias* as, 'the eldest male ancestor of a specific family. He had in his power (potestas) all descendants traced through the male line. The paterfamilias was *sui inuri*, i.e. legally independent – he could not be in anyone else's power.'[17] This legal framework, based around the almost absolute power of the (male) *pater familias*, determined the relationship between husbands and wives in Roman society. The nineteenth-century scholar De Colquhoun stated:

> The Old Roman law conferred on the husband an almost absolute power over the wife by the *conventio in manum*; all she acquired vested in him, and he acquired the same rights over her person and property as if she had been his natural daughter.[18]

Women were therefore legally subordinate to both their husbands and (as with all other dependants) to their *pater familias*. The structuring of the Roman *familia* around the authority of the *pater familias* acted as a clear limit on women's participation in the public sphere, so that, as Frier and McGinn describe 'In the early Roman Empire … women were citizens but were nonetheless legally barred from voting, holding magistracies, serving as jurors, and generally performing what were thought of as public duties.'[19] This limited public role combined with the ultimate authority of the *pater familias* in the private realm reflects the dual subordination of women described above by Dickenson in relation to Ancient Greek society and this illustrates the gendered nature of legal subjecthood in the classical societies. While the political and legal systems in the UK emerged later, independently of the Greek and Roman empires and thus reflected different cultural norms, it is contended that the notion of delineated gendered roles remained a constant feature of Western philosophical and social understanding.[20] Indeed, this distinction continues to be reflected in the understanding of the 'natural' gender roles within the nuclear family.[21]

It has been observed by family historians[22] that by the end of the medieval period the nuclear family form had come to possess an even more central role

[17] Paul du Plessis, *Borkowski's Textbook on Roman Law*, 4th edn (Oxford, Oxford University Press, 2010) 110.

[18] Patrick Mac Chombaich De Colquhoun, *A Summary of the Roman Civil Law*, Volume 1, (London, V. and R. Stevens and Sons, 1849) 501.

[19] Bruce W Frier and Thomas AJ McGinn, *A Casebook on Roman Family Law* (Oxford University Press, 2004) 453.

[20] The influence will be shown in the examination of nineteenth and early twentieth century judicial attitudes in subs II(C), '"The Persons Cases": The Rejection of Women as Legal Subjects'.

[21] The significance of these gendered roles within the legal understanding of the parental role will be considered below in ch 5, s II, 'The Gendered Parenting Roles of the Nuclear Family'.

[22] See eg the works of anthropologist and historian Alan MacFarlane, *The Origins of English Individualism: The Family, Property and Social Transition* (Oxford, Blackwell, 1978) and *Marriage and Love in England: Modes of Reproduction, 1300–1840* (Oxford, Blackwell, 1986).

in English society[23] than it had enjoyed in the classical societies.[24] The historian Houlbrooke states that 'Between the fifteenth and eighteenth centuries there was little change in familial forms and functions. The nuclear family was dominant and wider ties of kinship were relatively weak.'[25] The significance of the nuclear family form is observed to have continued throughout the Renaissance, and Houlbrooke further observes that 'the momentous developments of this period, though certainly affecting family life, brought no fundamental change in familial forms, functions and ideals.'[26] Thus, the nuclear family continued to represent the dominant form of family, in England, in spite of significant cultural and societal changes.

The division between the public and private spheres of society and the associated view of women as lacking full legal subjecthood is also evident throughout medieval history, as Perkin has argued 'The subjection of women was enshrined in English law and custom for nine hundred years. Common Law reflected rather than caused that subjection.'[27] The division gained legal expression in England through the common law doctrine of coverture,[28] which was summarised by the writer Blackstone as follows: 'By marriage, the husband and wife are one person in law: that is, the very being or legal existence of the woman is suspended during the marriage, or at least is incorporated and consolidated into that of the husband.'[29] This gendered division dominated throughout Christendom in the medieval period and it also subsequently survived the cultural upheaval of the Renaissance; as the early twentieth century historian Goodsell observed:

> If the social position of the more favoured women was raised during the Renaissance, if they were educated and held in higher esteem, it yet remains true that little

[23] Some historians subscribe to an alternative narrative of far greater change in family forms, which views the dominance of the nuclear family form as occurring more recently and describes the 'family' of the medieval period as being based on a wider kinship structure. A leading example of this approach is presented by Lawrence Stone in *The Family, Sex and Marriage in England 1500–1800* (London, Penguin, 1979). Although it is worth noting that Stone's work has been the subject of significant academic criticism, eg Alan MacFarlane, 'Review of Stone' (1979) 18(1) *History and Theory* 103, where he stated, at 106 'His massive effort to fit the material into an inadequate scheme provides a compendium of the distortions produced when a tenacious but false paradigm blinds the historian.'

[24] However, the writing of notable seventeenth century philosopher Thomas Hobbes reflected the Greek and Roman construction and understanding of family. In his seminal work, *Leviathan* (first published 1651, reprinted by Cambridge University Press, 1991) 172, he described a family as consisting of, 'a man and his children, or of a man and his servants; or of a man, and his children, and servants together: wherein the Father or Master is the sovereign.'

[25] Ralph A Houlbrooke, *The English Family: 1450–1700* (London, Longman, 1984) 253.

[26] ibid, at 16. See further eg Grassby, *Kinship and Capitalism: Marriage, Family and Business in the English-Speaking World, 1580–1740.*

[27] Joan Perkin, *Women and Marriage in Nineteenth-Century England* (London, Routledge, 1988) 1.

[28] The gradual elimination of the doctrine of coverture and the wider evolution of the legal understanding of marriage will be considered in more detail in ch 3, subs I(A), 'The Legal Definition of Marriage.'

[29] Sir William Blackstone, *Commentaries on the Laws of England*, Vol 1, 4th edn (Oxford, J Exshaw, 1771) 442.

advancement was made in freeing them from the financial and legal disabilities of the Middle Ages.[30]

Therefore, both the nuclear family form and a gendered division of social roles were evident throughout the medieval and renaissance periods. The historical significance of the nuclear family form is illustrated by its consistent recurrence across different societies and time periods.

B. The Development of the 'Public/Private' Divide

While the notion of a division between the public and private spheres of society had existed throughout history,[31] and persisted throughout the supposedly 'transformative' developments that took place during the Enlightenment period;[32] Bottomley and Bronitt have noted that:

> From the earliest liberal philosophers there came the belief that social life was to be seen as divided into public and private spheres. The private, or domestic, sphere was an area that should be none of 'law's business' where 'the King's writ did not run'.[33]

This divide was adopted as a key tenet of liberal philosophy, with John Stuart Mill writing in *On Liberty*, that 'In England … there is considerable jealousy of direct interference, by the legislative or the executive power, with private conduct'.[34] Therefore, this particularly liberal understanding of the 'public/private' divide has been a crucial feature in the subsequent development of western society.[35] O'Donovan describes this liberal construction of the division between public and private spheres as referring:

> [T]o two distinct social realms constituted within liberal social philosophy divided from one another by legal regulation. The public realm is presented as that of state, market and politics, and is the world of men; the private realm, associated primarily

[30] Willystine Goodsell, *A History of Marriage and the Family*, 2nd edn (New York, The MacMillan Company, 1934) 257.

[31] The role of the liberal understanding of the public/private divide in shaping the nuclear family will be discussed further throughout the remaining sections of this chapter.

[32] Peter Gay, *The Enlightenment: An Interpretation – The Rise of Modern Paganism*, 4th edn (New York, WW Norton, 1995), states at 3 'The men of the Enlightenment united on a vastly ambitious program, a program of secularism, humanity, cosmopolitanism, and freedom, above all, freedom in its many forms – freedom from arbitrary power, freedom of speech, freedom of trade, freedom to realise one's talents, freedom of aesthetic response, freedom in a world of moral men to make his own way in the world.'

[33] Bottomley and Bronitt, *Law in Context* 8.

[34] John Stuart Mill, *On Liberty and Other Writings*, Stefan Collins (ed), (Cambridge, Cambridge University Press, 1989) 12.

[35] Boyd, 'Challenging the Public/Private Divide: An Overview' in Boyd (ed), *Challenging the Public/Private Divide: Feminism, Law and Public Policy* 8, states of the public/private divide, 'It has prevailed particularly over the past two centuries, as with the industrialisation of Western capitalist societies, people's lives were increasingly divided into public and private spheres at both material and ideological level.'

> with women, is the world of family. The values prevalent in the former are those of individualism; in the latter self-sacrifice and altruism are idealised.[36]

The onset of the enlightenment was heralded by some as the 'age of reason'[37] and it concerned itself with the freedom and liberty of man[38] but it did little, at least initially, for the legal or social position of women.[39] In England and Wales, the historical doctrine of coverture was not reformed until the various Married Women's Property Acts of the late nineteenth century.[40] These Acts granted women the capacity to exercise legal personhood separate from that of their husbands, allowing them to own and control their own property.[41] However, even this reform did not alter the legal reliance on the 'public/private' divide nor did it reduce its social power and it was not until further social and legal developments during the twentieth century[42] that women began to be seen as having social roles outside of the domestic context.[43] As Moller Okin argues 'As most present-day feminists agree, the political emancipation of women brought with it very little of substance with respect to their economic and social position, and their actual life experience.'[44]

I suggest that the allocation of gender roles within the idealised image of the nuclear family is premised upon the ideals derived from the particularly liberal understanding of the 'public/private' divide.[45] O'Donovan has noted that 'The division of labour whereby one spouse works for earnings and the other for love

[36] O'Donovan, *Family Law Matters* 23.

[37] Ernst Cassirer, *The Philosophy of the Enlightenment* (Boston, Beacon Press, 1955, translated from the original German edition, 1932), states at 6 'The eighteenth century is imbued with a belief in the unity and immutability of reason. Reason is the same for all thinking subjects, all nations, all epochs and all cultures.'

[38] See eg the much quoted words of Jean-Jacques Rousseau 'Man is born free, and everywhere he is in chains. Those who think themselves the masters of others are indeed greater slaves than they.' In *Of the Social Contract, Or Principles of Political Right* (first published 1762, reprinted by Dent, 1973).

[39] The historical lack of legal subjecthood granted to women is considered below at subs II(C) '"The Persons Cases": The Rejection of Women as Legal Subjects'.

[40] The Married Women's Property Acts 1870, 1882, 1884 and 1893. See also the Married Women's Property (Scotland) Acts 1881 and 1920.

[41] However, Albie Sachs and Joan Hoff Wilson, *Sexism and the Law: A Study of Male Beliefs and Legal Bias in Britain and the United States* (Oxford, Martin Robertson, 1978) 137, suggest that 'The Married Women's Property Act 1882, is often held out as a milestone in the march of women to equality, but in reality it did little more than save wealthy women from the irksome restraints of holding property through trustees.'

[42] See eg the extension of the franchise, through the Representation of the People Act 1918 (granted the right to vote to some women over 30) and Representation of the People (Equal Franchise) Act 1928 (granted women the same voting rights as men), the Guardianship of Infants Act 1925, which introduced the 'welfare principle' and therefore removed the power of legal guardianship from the father and the reform of Divorce, through the Divorce Reform Act 1969 and Divorce (Scotland) Act 1976.

[43] The contemporary understanding of the roles of men and women within the family and society is considered further below at ch 5, s II 'The Gendered Parenting Roles of the Nuclear Family'.

[44] Moller Okin, *Women in Western Political Thought* 290.

[45] This connection will be explored further below at subs III(A), 'The Legal Subject and the Nuclear Family'.

encapsulates the public/private split.'[46] This particular division of labour is reflected in the delineation between 'breadwinner' and 'homemaker' within the traditional nuclear family model.[47] Moller Okin expands upon this, commenting that:

> [T]he existence of a distinct sphere of private, family life, separated off from the realm of public life, leads to the exaggeration of women's biological differences from men, to the perception of women as primarily suited to fulfil special 'female' functions within the home, and consequently to the justification of the monopoly by men of the whole outside world.[48]

The separation of gender roles within the archetype of the traditional nuclear family reflects the historical significance of the 'public/private' divide, because as Boyd observes 'The public/private divide is intrinsically connected to the familial ideology that dominates capitalist societies.'[49] In this way, the symbiotic relationship between the liberal construction of the 'public/private' divide and the idealised image of the traditional nuclear family is illustrated.

Historically, the law has embraced the idea of a public/private divide, distinguishing between areas that were thought to be appropriate for legal regulation ('the public') and those that were not ('the private'), as O'Donovan observes:

> This division is not confined to distinguishing relations between individual and state from relations between individuals. It also draws a line dividing the law's business from what is called private. Although the boundary between the private and public shifts over time, the existence of the distinction and the notion of boundary are rarely questioned.[50]

The idea of a clear division between the public and private realms was encapsulated, in the early seventeenth century, by the seminal statement in *Semayne's Case*[51] that 'the house of every one is to him as his castle and fortress',[52] which came to be expressed in the maxim, 'an Englishman's home is his castle'. This clear separation of the public and private spheres continued to be reflected in judicial language over 250 years later in *Re Agar-Ellis*,[53] where Bowen LJ stated 'Both as regards the conduct of private affairs, and of domestic life, the rule is that Courts of Law should not intervene except upon occasion. It is far better that people should be left free'.[54] As recently as 40 years ago, the House of Lords stated in *Charter v Race Relations Board*[55] 'the natural antithesis to "public" is "private"'.[56]

[46] O'Donovan, *Sexual Divisions in Law* 9.
[47] See the description of the nuclear family above in ch 1, s II, 'The Law's "Definition(s)" of "Family"'.
[48] Moller Okin, *Women in Western Political Thought* 275.
[49] Boyd, 'Challenging the Public/Private Divide: An Overview' in Boyd (ed), *Challenging the Public/Private Divide: Feminism, Law and Public Policy* 17.
[50] O'Donovan, *Sexual Divisions in Law* 8.
[51] *Semayne's Case* (1604) 77 ER 194.
[52] ibid, at 196.
[53] *Re Agar-Ellis* (1883) 24 Ch 317.
[54] ibid, per Bowen LJ, at 335.
[55] *Charter v Race Relations Board* [1973] AC 868.
[56] ibid, per Lord Cross, at 906, see also the judgment of Lord Hodson, at 897.

O'Donovan has observed that 'The view is that the ongoing family and marriage should be left alone, so long as conflict does not cause breakdown.'[57] Indeed, the law's reluctance to interfere in the private realm results in the logical consequence that the regulation of the home and the family is understood as being inherently out-with the law's concern.

The significance of the public/private divide in historical judicial reasoning is illustrated again in the early twentieth century decision in *Balfour v Balfour*,[58] which concerned whether an agreement between a husband and wife regarding the payment of ongoing maintenance should be considered contractual. Atkin LJ clearly stated of such arrangements that 'they are not contracts, and they are not contracts because the parties did not intend that they should attend legal consequences'.[59] Subsequently such arrangements between husbands and wives have been described judicially as 'merely a matter of convenience'[60] and the House of Lords has stated that 'the court will be slow to infer legal obligations from transactions between husband and wife in the ordinary course of their domestic life'.[61] This presumption of a lack of intention to create legal relations[62] has been held to include similar agreements between those in other close familial relationships,[63] including mother and daughter in *Jones v Padavatton*.[64] Salmon LJ went on to state that this general presumption 'derives from experience of life and human nature which shows that in such circumstances men and women usually do not intend to create legal rights and obligations, but intend to rely solely on family ties of mutual trust and affection'.[65] In his judgment in *Balfour v Balfour*,[66] Atkin LJ essentially framed the decision in terms of recognising the divide between the public and private spheres, stating 'In respect of these promises each house is a domain into which the King's writ does not seek to run, and to which his officers do not seek to be admitted.'[67] Arrangements between husband and wife (or parents and children) are considered to be firmly within the 'private sphere' and therefore not

[57] O'Donovan, *Sexual Divisions in Law* 13.

[58] *Balfour v Balfour* [1919] 2 KB 571.

[59] ibid, per Atkin LJ, at 579.

[60] *Spellman v Spellman* [1961] 1 WLR 921, per Danckwerts LJ, at 926.

[61] *Pettitt v Pettitt* [1969] 2 WLR 966.

[62] The basic principle was repeatedly upheld by the Court of Appeal, see eg *Gould v Gould* [1970] 1 QB 275 and *Merritt v Merritt* [1970] 1 WLR 1211, two cases which considered whether the principle could be applied to married couples who were separated. The principle was referenced by Baroness Hale more recently in *MacLeod v MacLeod* [2008] UKPC 64, [2010] 1 AC 298, at 315. It may be noted that this presumption against the enforceability of agreements between family members is not made by Scots law.

[63] Notably the presumption was held not to apply to a 'man and his mistress' in *Diwell v Farnes* [1959] 1 WLR 624, showing the power of traditional marriage at that point in time.

[64] *Jones v Padavatton* [1969] 1 WLR 328, in his judgment Danckwerts LJ states, at 332 'there is no doubt that the same principles apply to dealings between other relations, such as father and son'.

[65] ibid, at 332.

[66] [1919] 2 KB 571.

[67] ibid, at 579.

subject to legal interference unless this presumption can be overturned.[68] These cases illustrate the influence exerted historically upon English judicial reasoning by the idea of a division between the public and private spheres, and by the understanding that the private sphere should not be subject to legal regulation or scrutiny.

C. The Orthodox Understanding of the 'Legal Subject'

The orthodox understanding holds that the legal subject represents a neutral and abstract standard[69] and consequently that the 'person' of law is not directly relatable to the physical human being.[70] The mid-twentieth century scholar Nekam commented that 'There is nothing in the notion of the subject of rights which in itself, would necessarily, connect it with human personality.'[71] Similarly, the positivist legal philosopher Kelsen observed that 'The person exists only insofar as he "has" duties and rights; apart from them the person has no existence whatsoever.'[72] The critical theorist Naffine, who has written extensively on the construction of the legal subject, has observed that:

> It is the conventional legal view, supported by many learned treatises, which asserts that law does not operate with a specific individual in mind, that it favours no one type of person. In its purported objectivity and neutrality, law is supposed to adopt a common approach to all.[73]

Under this dominant conception of the legal subject, the view is that law is not actually engaged in an ongoing process of constructing the subject, but rather that the 'legal subject' amounts to an objective and fixed standard,[74] which is based upon logical and rational principles.[75] Building on this conception, in a subsequent

[68] *Parker v Clark* [1960] 1 WLR 286 and *Collier v Hollinshead* (1984) 272 EG 941, provide examples of cases where the court departed from this general presumption, on the basis that in the particular factual circumstances the actions of the parties suggested an intention to create legal relations.

[69] Naffine, *Law and the Sexes: Explorations of Feminist Jurisprudence* 64–84.

[70] Arguably this lack of connection between the legal subject and an embodied human being is most clearly illustrated by the doctrine of 'separate legal personality' of corporations, associated with the case of *Salomon v Salomon & Co Ltd* [1897] AC 22, which endows a corporation with legal personality distinct from the individuals who control it, see eg Nicholas James, 'Separate Legal Personality: Legal Reality and Metaphor' (1993) 5(2) *Bond Law Review* 217.

[71] Alexander Nekam, *The Personality Conception of the Legal Entity* (Cambridge, MA, Harvard University Press, 1938) 26.

[72] Hans Kelsen, *General Theory of Law and State* (New York, Russell and Russell, 1945) 94.

[73] Naffine, *Law and the Sexes: Explorations of Feminist Jurisprudence* ix.

[74] The orthodox construction of the legal subject is described as the 'individuating, abstract form' of law, by David Sugarman and G.R Rubin, 'Introduction: Towards a New History of Law and Material Society in England 1750–1914' in GR Rubin and David Sugarman (eds), *Law, Economy and Society, 1750–1914: Essays in the History of English Law* (Abingdon, Professional Books, 1984) 49.

[75] Naffine, *Law and the Sexes: Explorations of Feminist Jurisprudence* at 24–29, see also eg Roger Cotterrell, *The Sociology of Law: An Introduction* (London, Butterworths, 1992) and Alison Jaggar, *Feminist Politics and Human Nature* (Lanham, Rowman and Littlefield, 1988).

work, Naffine went on to describe how this orthodox view of the nature of the legal subject is premised on the belief that:

> The construct of the legal person and its legal personality is purely a matter of legal expediency. The legal person has no moral or empirical content, thus defined. It relies neither on biological or psychological predicates; nor does it refer back to any particular social or moral idea of a person and it is completely distinguished from these philosophical conceptions of the person which emphasise the importance of reason or intrinsic human value.[76]

The orthodox construction views the legal subject as 'an abstraction'[77] and a necessary (legal) fiction,[78] whose existence allows the law to operate effectively and efficiently.[79] Kelsen famously describes the legal subject as being 'not a natural reality but a social construction created by the science of law'.[80] The subject is conceptualised as a purely legal standard which does not, and should not, visibly promote or preference any moral or ethical ideals or values in its application,[81] because, as Naffine comments, 'There is no moral essence to the legal person, in this view, and those who have sought to find one are misguided.'[82] Therefore, it is valuable to consider the values of the orthodox legal subject because the construction of the individual within the law can influence the legal understanding of the 'family'.

As has already been observed, the development of the law has been significantly influenced by the values of Enlightenment liberalism.[83] Similarly, I argue that the characteristics of the legal subject reflect the values that are privileged by construction of the individual within that same liberal philosophical tradition, which has underpinned the subsequent development of western society.[84] The historical strength of the ideology of liberalism, premised upon the centrality of reason, reflects a time in history when much of the world was beyond the explanation and comprehension of man; Douzinas and Geary suggest that 'The belief in reason's power to explain the world and the assumption that law

[76] Naffine, *Law's Meaning of Life: Philosophy, Religion, Darwin and the Legal Person* 35.

[77] Smith, 'Legal Personality' 293.

[78] Derham, 'Theories of Legal Personality' in Webb (ed), *Legal Personality and Political Pluralism*, described the legal subject as, 'artificial, fictional', at 6.

[79] FH Lawson, 'The Creative Use of Legal Concepts' (1957) 32(5) *New York University Law Review* 909, stated at 913, that it was 'created to serve certain purposes' and 'to conform to predetermined definitions'.

[80] Hans Kelsen, *Pure Theory of Law* (Berkeley, University of California Press, 1967) 174.

[81] The possibility of moral character of the legal subject has been considered in the context of corporate personality by Peter French, 'The Corporation as a Moral Person' (1979) 16(3) *American Philosophical Quarterly* 207.

[82] Naffine, *Law's Meaning of Life: Philosophy, Religion, Darwin and the Legal Person* 37.

[83] See above in subs I(B), 'The Development of the "Public/Private" Divide'.

[84] Bottomley and Bronitt, *Law in Context*, describe liberalism as 'the dominant ideology of modern western society dating from about the 17th century', at 5, see also Andrew Vincent, *Modern Political Ideologies*, 3rd edn (Chichester, Wiley-Blackwell, 2009) 23–83 and CB McPherson, *The Political Theory of Possessive Individualism: Hobbes to Locke* (Oxford, Clarendon Press, 1962).

can regulate our lives are psychological defences against the horrors of chaotic existence.'[85] The certainty provided by the values of reason, logic and rationality, transferred from the sciences through the growth of analytical legal positivism,[86] helped endow the law with a renewed sense of fundamental authority, after the decline of the once dominant natural law tradition.[87] Despite its purported and self-avowed neutrality and objectivity, the legal subject is constituted in a form that reflects the subject of the dominant philosophical theory of western capitalist society.[88]

Different writers have suggested a range of features as being essential to the conception of the liberal subject. Lukes has observed that 'The idea of the independent, rational citizen is a central presupposition of classical liberal democratic theory.'[89] Moller Okin notes that 'the liberal tradition assumes that the behaviour of its political actors will be based on self-interest',[90] while Dietz has suggested that 'the liberal individual might be understood as the competitive entrepreneur'.[91] O'Donovan has provided the following description of the liberal legal subject:

> The ideal legal subject in liberal theory is a rational, choosing person, capable of decision, an autonomous individual. This individual is without particularities of identity such as gender. Such a figure of neutrality is a deliberate legal creation to overcome differences – whether of cultural origin, race, gender, or other particularities.[92]

[85] Douzinas and Geary, *Critical Jurisprudence: The Political Philosophy of Justice* 43.

[86] Associated with the legal philosopher John Austin, see eg *Lectures on Jurisprudence or the Philosophy of Positive Law*, revised and edited by Robert Campbell, 3rd edn (London, John Murray, 1869).

[87] In the face of the decline of the power of the Church to control knowledge during the Enlightenment and the work of philosophers such as Thomas Hobbes, *Leviathan*, on the nature of state power and David Hume, *A Treatise of Human Nature*, (first published 1739, reprinted by Clarendon Press, 1896), on the 'is/ought distinction', who had questioned some of Natural Law's core assumptions.

[88] This reflection of capitalist values is illustrated by the aforementioned doctrine of 'separate legal personality'. In essence, under this doctrine, corporations are considered capable of possessing the characteristics of the 'legal subject'. On the issue of the subjecthood of corporations more generally, see eg Nicola Lacey, '"Philosophical Foundations of the Common Law": Social not Metaphysical' in Jeremy Horder (ed), *Oxford Essays in Jurisprudence*, 4th series (Oxford, Oxford University Press, 2000). However, some critical theorists would argue that some of the values supported by the orthodox 'legal subject' can actually be traced back to a much earlier point in history than the Enlightenment and the development of liberalism. See eg Mark C Taylor, *Deconstruction in Context: Literature and Philosophy* (Chicago, University of Chicago Press, 1986) 4, who argued that 'From its inception in Greece, Western philosophy has, for the most part, privileged oneness and unity at the expense of manyness and plurality. Accordingly the Western philosophical project can be understood as the repeated effort to overcome plurality and establish unity by reducing the many to the one.'

[89] Steven Lukes, *Individualism* (Oxford, Blackwell, 1973) 139, who additionally writes, at 56, 'autonomy is a value that has always been central to liberalism'.

[90] Moller Okin, *Women in Western Political Thought* 284.

[91] Mary Dietz, 'Context is All: Feminism and Theories of Citizenship' (1987) 116(4) *Daedalus* 1, 5.

[92] Katherine O'Donovan, 'With Sense, Consent, or Just a Con?: Legal Subjects in the Discourse of Autonomy' in Naffine and Owens (eds), *Sexing the Subject of Law* 47.

Thus, the liberal individual is typically characterised as a rational, autonomous,[93] self-determining and self-interested being[94] and the orthodox understanding of the legal subject reflects these values.[95] Moreover, the particular 'individual' envisaged by this construction exerts significant impact upon the traditional nuclear family model.[96]

II. Critiquing the Orthodox Construction of the Legal Subject

The orthodox understanding of the legal subject has not been universally accepted by theorists; instead it has been subjected to significant critique.[97] This critique questions the claims of the inherent objectivity and neutrality of the subject, as well as criticising the liberal values upon which the subject is premised;[98] it also involves a rejection of the notion that the legal subject amounts to an abstract standard that applies equally and fairly to all individuals. This critique serves to unpick the assumptions of the legal subject; and thus the assumptions from which the 'natural' understanding of the nuclear family derives. In this section I will consider some of the critical scholarship which disputes the orthodox construction's claims to objectivity and self-evidence and questions the applicability of the values that it is premised upon (subsection A). I will then explore the feminist critique that the legal subject is based upon and privileges, characteristics and values historically associated with men and an idealised form of masculinity (subsection B). To conclude, I will focus upon the historical 'persons' cases to illustrate some of the issues caused by the values and ideals of the orthodox construction of the legal subject (subsection C).

[93] The normative importance of the concept of 'autonomy' will be explored in further detail in ch 6, subs I(C), 'Autonomy and Choice'.

[94] When this liberal individual is translated into the legal subject, it finds expression as the 'reasonable man' of the common law; eg, the 'reasonable man' is used to determine the standard of care expected within the law of negligence, see eg *Blyth v Birmingham Waterworks Co* (1856) 11 Ex. 781.

[95] Alan Hunt and Gary Wickham, *Foucault and Law: Towards a Sociology of Law as Governance* (Boulder, Pluto Press, 1994) 114, comment that 'What is important is that the law helps guide/coerce/encourage/induce individuals towards certain ways of doing right and away from certain ways of doing wrong … and this helps bind them into a society.'

[96] This connection will be considered below at subs III(A), 'The Legal Subject and the Nuclear Family'.

[97] The orthodox construction of the legal subject has undergone significant and varied critique, the consideration of which here will be necessarily brief, for a fuller exploration of this critique; see eg Naffine, *Law's Meaning of Life: Philosophy, Religion, Darwin and the Legal Person.*

[98] See eg Fineman, *The Autonomy Myth: A Theory of Dependency*, for a critique of 'autonomy', one of the central values of the orthodox construction of the legal subject. The concept of 'autonomy' and its critique will be considered in more detail below at ch 6, subs I(C), 'Autonomy and Choice'.

A. The Legal Subject Favours Specific Individuals

It is argued that the orthodox construction's claim as to its own inherent objectivity and neutrality allows that construction of the legal subject to justify its own particular values, choices and assumptions on the basis that they amount to self-evident truths,[99] Naffine has observed:

> The legal person's very abstractness, his paradigm quality, serves to show that the legal approach is not even an approach in fact but an inherently neutral way of organising and arbitrating relations between human beings. By his any-personess, the legal man of law demonstrates the appropriateness and essential rightness of the law's particular approach to the world – the way that is not a way.[100]

I suggest that the continued influence of the orthodox construction derives, to a significant extent, from this abstractness. The apparent objectivity of the legal subject has been a significant contributor in helping to sustain the dominance of the orthodox construction of the legal subject. As Laster and Ranan put it 'The strength of the "reasonable man" ideology lies in its universalism.'[101] The portrayal of the subject as inherently neutral and objective obscures its basis in contested values which reflect the dominant, liberal philosophical traditions of western society.[102]

The consistent privileging of these specific characteristics and values within the conceptualisation of the legal subject has led to the perception that the ideals embodied by the orthodox understanding are fundamental and inherent to the idea of the subject itself, rather than the result of a choice between competing values.[103] These liberal values can be seen to recur throughout law itself; Davies has observed that, 'the idea of a unified actor who is independent and rational forms the basis not only of many areas of substantive law, but also of the idea of law itself, as it has been traditionally presented'.[104] Consequently, the legal subject's strong association with the liberal values of rationality, autonomy and self-interest is presented by the orthodox construction as an inescapable feature of

[99] Naffine, *Law and the Sexes: Explorations of Feminist Jurisprudence* 44–47.

[100] ibid, at 123.

[101] Kathy Laster and Padma Ranan, 'Law for One and One for All? An Intersectional Legal Subject' in Naffine and Owens, *Sexing the Subject of Law* 197. The authors go on to further comment that, 'The "reasonable man" test is a convenient ruse. It allows the common law to pretend that its standard of judgement is based on the "rationality" of Western Enlightenment philosophy, while still allowing realistic concessions to human frailty.'

[102] For a critique of these dominant moral and ethical values and traditions, see eg Bauman, *Postmodern Ethics* and the work of Emmanuel Levinas, eg *Alterity and Transcendence*, (Athlone, Linton, 1999), *Totality and Infinity*, (Pittsburgh, Duquesne University Press, 1999) and *The Levinas Reader*, Sean Hand (ed) (Oxford, Blackwell, 1989).

[103] Margaret Davies, *Asking the Law Question*, 3rd edn (Sydney, Lawbook Co, 2008) 357, describes these notions as amounting to, 'an assumption, or even a dogmatic assertion, which cannot be demonstrated'.

[104] ibid, at 330.

law itself, rather than as the outcome of any kind of value judgement.[105] Herring has observed that, 'Much of the law is based on the assumption that we are competent, detached, independent people who are entitled to have our rights of self-determination and autonomy fiercely protected.'[106] Going further, Naffine and Owens have contended that:

> Law has always assumed and constituted a subject who is deemed to act in certain ways, to wield certain rights and to assume certain responsibilities. And law has engaged in this act of creation quite self-consciously, fully aware that it is constituting a subject.[107]

Thus, the legal subject has been explicitly and consciously constituted and therefore it could be reconstituted with radically different underpinning values; critical literature has posited the possibilities of the 'relational subject'[108] or the 'vulnerable subject',[109] which reject the abstract and individuating conception of the orthodox legal subject.[110] While under the orthodox construction the subject is presented as an abstract standard, lacking in any moral content,[111] critics argue that the reality of its construction is that it favours a certain type of individual, who possesses specific characteristics.[112] Lukes observes that such privileging of a specific ideal type is unsurprising given that the '"individuals" involved here – whether natural, or utilitarian or economic men – always turn out on inspection to be social and indeed historically specific. "Human nature" always in reality belongs to a particular kind of social man.'[113] As described above, the legal subject is based upon the ideal of the liberal individual; a rational and

[105] Michael Gardiner, 'Alterity and Ethics: A Dialogical Perspective' (1996) 13(2) *Theory, Culture & Society* 121, argues, at 133, that due to the nature of the orthodox construction of the legal subject 'the state cannot be genuinely pluralistic; it cannot register and protect difference'.

[106] Herring, 'The Disability Critique of Care' 2.

[107] Naffine and Owens, 'Introduction: Sexing Law' in Naffine and Owens (eds), *Sexing the Subject of Law* 7.

[108] See eg Charles Foster and Jonathan Herring, *Identity, Personhood and the Law*, (Springer, 2017), who comment at 35 'The human self is profoundly relational. People are in the very nature independent and vulnerable. It follows from this that the basic moral value of humans is not found in their individual capabilities or in their membership of the species, but rather in their relationships.'

[109] See eg Martha Fineman, '"Elderly" as Vulnerable: Rethinking the Nature of Individual and Societal Responsibility' (2012) 20(1) *Elder Law Journal* 71 and Catriona Mackenzie, Wendy Rogers and Susan Dodds (eds), *Vulnerability: New Essays in Ethics and Feminist Philosophy* (Oxford, Oxford University Press, 2014).

[110] These alternative constructions of the legal subject will be explored in more detail below in ch 6, subss I(A), 'Care and Relationality' and I(B), 'Vulnerability'.

[111] See further eg Helen Stacey, *Postmodernism and Law: Jurisprudence in a Fragmenting World* (Burlington, Ashgate, 2001), who argues, at 179, 'morality is inherently laden with contradictions that cannot be overcome and with aporia that cannot be resolved. Morality is bound to be irrational because there is no such thing as a universal morality.'

[112] It has been suggested that the orthodox subject possesses characteristics typically associated with men and 'masculinity', see below at subs II(B), 'The Masculinity of the "Legal Subject" Masks Inequality'.

[113] Lukes, *Individualism* 75.

autonomous being.[114] Consequently, the construction of the subject is presented as neutral and self-evident, because it is based upon dominant cultural ideals that are presented as being 'natural' or 'common sense'. Indeed, on a similar basis the nuclear family is subsequently positioned as the 'natural' and 'common sense' understanding of family.[115] Building upon this critique, Bauman observes that, 'The morality of the moral subject does not, therefore, have the character of a rule. One may say that the moral is what resists codification, formalization, socialization, universalization.'[116] The literature on 'care'[117] suggests that the focus on the abstract 'individual' itself is normatively problematic, because it diminishes the importance of relationships between individuals to the notion of subjecthood;[118] as Herring argues:

> One of the most attractive aspects of an ethic of care approach is that it seeks to move away from an atomistic picture of individuals, with rights that compete against each other, to a model that emphasises the responsibilities of people towards each other in mutually supporting relations.[119]

This results in normative and theoretical attempts to move beyond the orthodox construction of the autonomous and liberal subject and construct an alternative subjecthood, premised upon the idea that as Herring and Foster suggest 'it is impossible to speak atomistically about an "individual". We are such quintessentially relational creatures that we should (and for all practical purposes do) abandon the legal fiction of a person who is an island unto herself.'[120] These potential alternative conceptual understandings of the subject, based upon 'care', 'relationality', 'vulnerability', or indeed a combination of these ethical values,[121] will be considered in more detail below in chapter six.[122]

[114] See above in subs I(C), 'The Orthodox Understanding of the "Legal Subject"'.

[115] See further below at s III, 'The Nuclear Family as the Natural Model of "Family"'.

[116] Bauman, *Postmodern Ethics* 54.

[117] This literature will be considered in more detail subsequently in ch 6, subs I(A), 'Care and Relationality'.

[118] Herring, 'The Disability Critique of Care' 3, presents a normative critique of this construction of the individual, arguing that, 'Ethics of care is based on the belief that people are relational. People understand themselves in terms of their relationships. They do not seek to promote only their own interests, not because they are "selfless", but because their interests are tied up with the interests of others.'

[119] Jonathan Herring, 'Where are the Carers in Healthcare Law and Ethics?' (2007) 27(1) *Legal Studies* 51, 68.

[120] Jonathan Herring and Charles Foster, 'Welfare Means Relationality, Virtue and Altruism' (2012) 32(3) *Legal Studies* 480, 497.

[121] This will also involve considering the attempts to reconceptualise 'autonomy' as 'relational autonomy'; see eg Rosie Harding, 'Legal Constructions of Dementia: Discourses of Autonomy at the Margins of Capacity' (2012) 34(4) *Journal of Social Welfare and Family Law* 425, 427, who states 'Relational autonomy … is an alternative approach to autonomy, predominantly expounded by feminist scholars, which rejects the liberalism of individual autonomy, and requires that attention is paid to the ways the individuals exist within relations of social support and community.'

[122] See below in ch 6, s I, 'Exploring the Conceptual Influences'.

Nevertheless, the orthodox presentation of the subject as abstract and objective has the consequence of measuring all individuals against the same standard. It is submitted that this is problematic because, as Sugarman and Rubin suggest 'this "individuality" is an abstraction, shorn of its particular context – and its relative position and power in society. As a result, substantial differences between relevant actors are obscured and ignored'.[123] Thus the standard of the legal subject acts to remove or conceal the actual differences between people; the subject is disinterested in the particular characteristics of individuals. As Barron observes 'Within a formally rational legal order, the legal subject is an abstract entity, stripped of contingent empirical determinations and thereby revealed as the essential sameness which characterises all human beings.'[124] Under the orthodox construction, the legal subject amounts to a totalising standard within which the particular behaviours, circumstances and characteristics of specific individuals are flattened out and judged in terms of the 'objective' standard of the (fictitious) rational, autonomous and self-interested liberal individual. Consequently 'Children, married women, bankrupts, lunatics, Jews and foreigners have all been assigned a distinct legal status within the history of the common law, distinguishing their legal position from that of the adult male, solvent, sane, Christian citizen.'[125] Throughout history, then, various different categories of person have been excluded from the status of 'legal subject',[126] illustrating that regardless of its claims to objectivity and abstraction, the legal subject has consistently acted with particular individuals in mind.

B. The Masculinity of the 'Legal Subject' Masks Inequality

This aspect of the orthodox construction of the legal subject – that it almost completely reduces differences between individuals to abstract sameness – allows law to ignore the substantial inequalities of circumstance of those individuals that come before it.[127] The paradox of the orthodox construction of the legal subject is that while it is traditionally presented as an objective standard, it is in reality laden with the subjective values of the philosophical, political and economic systems

[123] Sugarman and Rubin, 'Introduction: Towards a New History of Law and Material Society in England 1750–1914' in Rubin and Sugarman (eds), *Law, Economy and Society, 1750–1914: Essays in the History of English Law* 49.

[124] Anne Barron, 'Legal Discourse and the Colonisation of the Self in the Modern State', in Carty (ed), *Post-Modern Law: Enlightenment, Revolution and the Death of Man* 113.

[125] John Dawson, 'The Changing Legal Status of Mentally Disabled People' (1994) 2 *Journal of Law and Medicine* 38, 41.

[126] The example of the historical exclusion of women from full legal subjecthood is considered below at subs II(C), '"The Persons Cases": The Rejection of Women as Legal Subjects'.

[127] Douzinas and Warrington, *Justice Miscarried: Ethics, Aesthetics and the Law* 165, suggest that 'Equality is not equality but absolute dissymmetry'.

which underpin western society.[128] Within the standard of the legal subject, Douzinas and Warrington observe:

> The suffering face of the outsider is 'translated' into the reasonable man of the common law and on this basis is found not to be suffering at all, not to be in need of the very protection that the law is supposed to provide for the weak and the disadvantaged.[129]

The values of the legal subject are not impartial, but rather are premised upon a liberal vision of human nature which is contested.[130] Naffine has observed that the subject can be 'described as an undesirable caricature of a human being: impossibly self-possessed and self-reliant, will-driven, clinically rational and individualistic'.[131] By subjecting all people to this abstract standard and holding that all people are equal before the law, the reality of difference between rich and poor, man and woman, black and white, young and old, is concealed within the apparent 'objectivity' of the legal subject. This approach evokes the oft-quoted line of Anatole France, that the poor must 'labour in the face of the majestic equality of the law, which forbids the rich as well as the poor to sleep under bridges, to beg in the streets and to steal bread'.[132] The formal equality provided by the legal subject benefits those who conform to its characteristics and share its values;[133] however those individuals who do not fit within the ideal type of the liberal individual are significantly disadvantaged by the application of this standard.[134]

The type of individual envisaged by the dominant conception of the legal subject has been critiqued[135] on the basis that this individual is endowed with characteristics which are traditionally associated with men, and more precisely, with a particular idealised form of masculinity.[136] The denial of subjecthood to women in the 'persons cases', considered below, reflects the fact that historically in the UK, the dominant, orthodox construction of the legal subject was understood

[128] As described above at subs I(C), 'The Orthodox Understanding of the "Legal Subject"'.

[129] Douzinas and Warrington, *Justice Miscarried: Ethics, Aesthetics and the Law* 23.

[130] For the Marxist critique of the subject and of law generally see eg Evgenii Pashukanis, *Law and Marxism: A General Theory*, Chris Arthur (ed) (London, Pluto Press, 1989) and Hugh Collins, *Marxism and Law* (Oxford, Oxford University Press, 1982).

[131] Naffine, 'Who are Law's Persons: From Cheshire Cats to Responsible Subjects' 365.

[132] Anatole France, *Le Lys Rouge*, (Paris, Calmann-Levy, 1894).

[133] Below in ch 6, subs I(B), 'Vulnerability', I will consider the normative potential of radically reconstructing the legal subject around the universal vulnerability of human beings.

[134] The 'persons' cases described below at subs II(C), '"The Persons Cases": The Rejection of Women as Legal Subjects', illustrate how this applied in relation to women in the nineteenth and early twentieth century. Additionally, Douzinas and Warrington, *Justice Miscarried: Ethics, Aesthetics and the Law* 218–232, provide the example of the 'objective' test for the construction of 'refugee', from the cases of *R v Secretary of State for the Home Department, Ex p. Sivakumaran and Conjoined Appeals* [1988] AC 958 and *R v Secretary of State for the Home Department, Ex p. Bugdaycay* [1987] AC 514.

[135] For more on the feminist critique of the subject see eg James and Palmer (eds), *Visible Women: Essays on Feminist Legal Theory and Political Philosophy* and Lacey, *Unspeakable Subjects: Feminist Essays in Legal and Social Theory*.

[136] See RW Connell, *Masculinities*, (Berkeley, University of California Press, 2005), for an exploration of the complexity surrounding the usage of the term 'masculinity'.

as excluding women.[137] This exclusion was justified on the basis of 'natural' or 'common-sense' understandings about distinctions between the capabilities, characteristics and roles of the genders.[138] I submit that this distinction is a consequence of the liberal understanding of the 'public/private' divide and the duality of gender roles this promotes, with man as the 'breadwinner' and woman as the 'homemaker'. Indeed, I argue that this construction of separate, distinct gender roles continues to manifest itself in the dominant, contemporary legal understanding of the 'family'.[139] The values of the orthodox legal subject are also the values that are associated with the public realm, which was traditionally considered the sole preserve of men.[140] Pateman has argued that 'Only masculine beings are endowed with the attributes and capacities necessary to enter into contracts, the most important of which is ownership of property in the person; only men, that is to say, are "individuals".'[141] The intertwining of the values of the orthodox legal subject and those understood as characteristically 'masculine' is unsurprising because the orthodox subject (based upon the liberal individual) and the public/private divide were both presented as inherent aspects of the 'neutral' and 'natural' social and legal order.[142]

Naffine has argued that the legal person should be understood as 'the man of law':[143]

> The legal model of the person, it will be argued, is a man, not a woman. He is a successful middle-class man, not a working class male. And he is a middle-class man who demonstrates what one writer has termed a form of 'emphasised' middle-class masculinity. In short, he is a man; he is a middle class man; and he evinces the style of masculinity of the middle class.[144]

In a subsequent work, Naffine observes that in addition to embodying these 'masculine' characteristics, the subject is premised upon an explicit rejection of the features traditionally assigned to women, stating that 'he seemed to take his nature from the positive exclusion of those characteristics which have traditionally been associated with women and from the consignment to women of those qualities

[137] See below at subs II(C), '"The Persons Cases": The Rejection of Women as Legal Subjects'. This denial of subjecthood to women was also apparent in the classical societies, as discussed above at subs I(A), '"Family" and the Subject in Historical Societies'.

[138] For example, see the judgment of Lord Neaves in *Jex-Blake v Senatus of University of Edinburgh* (1873) 11 M 784, below at subs II(C), '"The Persons Cases": The Rejection of Women as Legal Subjects'.

[139] As will be shown throughout the remainder of this work, particularly in the course of ch 5, 'The Legal Understanding of the Parental Role'.

[140] See above at subs I(B), 'The Development of the "Public/Private" Divide'.

[141] Pateman, *The Sexual Contract* 5.

[142] Moller Okin, *Women in Western Political Thought* 5, observes more generally, that 'It must be recognised at once that the great tradition of political philosophy consists, generally speaking of writings by men, for men and about men.'

[143] Naffine, *Law and the Sexes: Explorations of Feminist Jurisprudence* 100–123.

[144] ibid, at 100. The description of Lord Denning MR in *Wachtel v Wachtel (No. 2)* [1973] 2 WLR 366, at 376, that, 'The husband will have to go out to work all day and must get some woman to look after the house – either a wife, if he remarries, or a housekeeper, if he does not', illustrates the influence upon judicial reasoning of the construction of the legal subject as a successful middle-class man.

and activities which would represent a diminution of his person'.[145] As previously argued the 'objective' standard of the legal subject permits law to deem certain characteristics and behaviours as inherently appropriate and correct. Therefore, because of the orthodox subject's construction around these 'masculine' values, this will clearly favour the rational, middle-class, 'economic man' of liberalism, described by Naffine as 'the man of law', while consequently being detrimental to the interests of women.[146] This feminist critique argues that despite the eventual inclusion of women within the legal definition of 'person', the legal subject retains elements of this embodiment as a male being of a particular socio-economic class and continues to be constructed on the basis of these idealised 'masculine' characteristics of rationality and self-interest.

C. 'The Persons Cases': The Rejection of Women as Legal Subjects

Cases containing detailed judicial discussion of the nature of the legal subject are limited in number because of the historical dominance of the orthodox construction of the subject, reflecting Naffine's observation that 'Sometimes the nature of the legal person is presumed and implicit rather than expounded or defended.'[147] However, judicial consideration of the subject of law is found in a succession of cases from the late nineteenth and early twentieth centuries. These cases determined whether or not the use of the word 'person'[148] in a variety of statutory provisions[149] relating to the ability and capacity to perform certain public functions included women as well as men. In these cases the judiciary was effectively considering, in a variety of contexts, the extent of the public role which was legally available to women at that point in history.[150] While these cases do not involve disputes regarding the family, nevertheless these cases are valuable in clarifying how the law (at this particular time in history) framed women's role as firmly

[145] Naffine, 'Can Women Be Legal Persons?' in James and Palmer (eds), *Visible Women: Essays on Feminist Legal Theory and Political Philosophy* 81.

[146] ibid, at 82–83, Naffine uses the example of the legal regulation of pregnant women, both through abortion laws and judicial decisions approving caesarean sections against the wishes of those women to illustrate the 'maleness' of the legal subject, she suggests that, at 83 'legal persons do not reproduce and divide in this manner. Certainly they are never pregnant'.

[147] Naffine, *Law's Meaning of Life: Philosophy, Religion, Darwin and the Legal Person* 15.

[148] Or in some statutes (eg Representation of the People Act 1867, s 3) whether the word 'men' included women, due to the Interpretation Act 1850, s 4 (Lord Brougham's Act), stating 'words importing the masculine gender shall be deemed and taken to include females … unless the contrary as to gender … is expressly provided'.

[149] See eg Representation of the People (Scotland) Act 1868, s 27 and Municipal Corporations Act 1882, s 11(1).

[150] See Sachs and Wilson, *Sexism and the Law: A Study of Male Beliefs and Legal Bias in Britain and the United States* 4–66 for a detailed exploration of these cases, which are referred to as 'The Male Monopoly Cases'.

within the private sphere as wives, mothers and 'homemakers' – a role constructed in binary opposition to the public role of men as legal subjects.

The decisions in these cases consistently denied women the right to exercise public functions that were held, at the time, to be the exclusive domain of men. This included women being prohibited from registering to vote,[151] women being prevented from attending university,[152] women being barred from serving as local councillors,[153] women being prevented from serving as either 'law agents'[154] or solicitors[155] and women being held to be unable to sit in the House of Lords.[156] Collectively these decisions amounted to a denial that women were full legal subjects with full access to the public sphere of society.[157] The explicit rejection of the subjecthood of women contained in the judgments demonstrates the rhetorical power that the strict 'public/private' divide and its restriction of women to the private sphere of the home and family held over social and legal understanding at that time in history.[158]

Examining the judgments in these cases reveals certain unifying strands and recurring themes. First, the cases contain repeated and clear rejections of the idea that women should be included within the word 'person' and this exclusion is expressed as self-evident and uncontroversial, reflecting the asserted self-evidence of the legal subject described above. This is exemplified by the judgment of Bovill CJ in *Wilson v Town Clerk of Salford*,[159] where he simply stated that, 'It is clear that only males are "persons" within the meaning of [the relevant provision] … we have therefore no authority to hear this case.'[160] In *Chorlton v Lings*,[161] Willes J described women as having a 'legal incapacity to vote at elections'.[162] The use of this language seems to deny that the legal personhood of women is a legitimate issue, by suggesting that their exclusion is uncontroversial and thus not worthy of any detailed judicial consideration.

Secondly, there are references within the judgments to the previous customary exclusion of women from these activities or functions justifying the continued

[151] *Chorlton v Lings* (1868) LR 4 CP 374 and *Brown v Ingram* (1868) 7 M 281.

[152] *Jex-Blake v Senatus of University of Edinburgh* (1873) 11 M 784, which is referred to as 'Septem contra Edine' – The Edinburgh Seven Case.

[153] *Beresford-Hope v Lady Sandhurst* (1889) 23 QBD 79, however ironically and somewhat absurdly in *De Souza v Cobden* [1891] 1 QB 687, the court was prepared to sanction criminal penalties for those women who 'purported' to act as local councillors.

[154] *Hall v Incorporated Society of Law Agents* (1901) 9 SLT 150.

[155] *Bebb v Law Society* [1914] 1 Ch 286.

[156] *Viscountess Rhondda's Claim* [1922] 2 AC 339.

[157] The 'masculinity' of the legal subject was explored above at subs II(B), 'The Masculinity of the "Legal Subject" Masks Inequality'.

[158] This reflects the historical emphasis within the law on the strict public/private divide discussed above at subs I(A), '"Family" and the Subject in Historical Societies' and subs I(B), 'The Development of the "Public/Private" Divide'.

[159] *Wilson v Town Clerk of Salford* (1868) LR 4CP 398.

[160] ibid, per Bovill CJ, at 399.

[161] *Chorlton v Lings* (1868) LR 4 CP 374.

[162] ibid, per Willes J, at 388.

prohibition of women, unless there is express inclusion of women to the contrary by Parliament.[163] This was exemplified by Lord Robertson in *Nairn v University of St. Andrews and Others*,[164] who stated that 'the central fact in the present appeal is that from time immemorial men only have voted in parliamentary elections'.[165] Recourse to such language allowed the judges to disregard the wider moral implications of their decisions. It is submitted that this judicial statement reflects the orthodox construction of the legal subject as representing an objective standard, which is equally applicable to all, regardless of differences between individuals.

Thirdly, the language and tone of the judgments regarding women is particularly striking; some of the decisions suggest that the exclusion of women from these public functions provided evidence of the *privileged* position women held in society, rather than an indication of their lack of status. Sachs and Wilson observe that throughout the judgments in these cases 'The words that constantly recur in describing their attitudes towards women are decorum, respect and propriety. In their view, this respect for women did not hold women back, but shielded them from the harsh vicissitudes of public life.'[166] This language is typified by Wiles J in *Chorlton v Lings*,[167] who stated that:

> I must protest against its being supposed to arise in this country from any underrating of the sex either in point of intellect or worth. That would be quite inconsistent with one of the glories of our civilization, – the respect and honour in which women are held.[168]

The prohibitions were described, in other cases, as existing to protect women from the stresses of the public sphere, which they were not believed to be suited to for reasons of the supposedly 'natural' distinctions between the capacities of the genders. This is encapsulated by the judgment of Lord Neaves in *Jex-Blake v Senatus of University of Edinburgh*,[169] where he stated:

> The powers and susceptibilities of women are as noble as those of men; but they are thought to be different, and, in particular, it is considered that they have not the same power of intense labour as men are endowed with.[170]

[163] See eg Swinfen Eady LJ in *Bebb v Law Society* [1914] 1 Ch 286, who stated, at 297 'it is sufficient to rest this case upon the inveterate practice of the centuries that, ever since attorneys as a profession have existed, women have never been admitted to the office, and, in my opinion, that shews what the law is and has been'.

[164] *Nairn v University of St Andrews and Others* [1909] AC 147.

[165] ibid, at 164.

[166] Sachs and Wilson, *Sexism and the Law: A Study of Male Beliefs and Legal Bias in Britain and the United States*, at 53.

[167] (1868) LR 4 CP 374.

[168] ibid, at 388.

[169] *Jex-Blake v Senatus of University of Edinburgh* (1873) 11 M 784.

[170] ibid, at 833, he further added to this passage, stating 'I confess that, to some extent, I share in this view, and should regret to see our young females subjected to the severe and incessant work which my own observation and experience have taught me to consider as indispensable to any high attainment in learning'.

I argue that this notion of a 'natural'[171] distinction between the genders continues to be evident within the nuclear family model.[172]

These legal restrictions on women's participation in the public sphere were not removed until the Sex Disqualification Removal Act 1919.[173] Inevitably, after Parliament had legislated to eliminate the majority of these explicit exclusions, the judiciary then reversed its previous position and held, in *Edwards v Attorney General Canada*,[174] that women were after all capable of being 'persons'.[175] The rationale of the earlier court decisions was seemingly questioned by Lord Sankey, who stated 'The exclusion of women from all public offices is a relic from days more barbarous than ours, but it must be remembered that the necessity of the times often forced on man customs which in later years were not necessary.'[176] Regarding the motivation for this complete revision in judicial opinion, Sachs and Wilson have suggested that:

> In the absence of any other satisfactory explanation, the conclusion becomes inescapable that what had changed was not the meaning of the word 'person', nor the modes of reasoning appropriate to lawyers, but the conception of women and women's position in public life held by the judges.[177]

It is submitted that the judgments in these cases illustrate how problematic the self-asserted abstractness, impartiality and dispassion of the legal subject appears once the tangible history of legal decision-making is examined and scrutinised.[178]

Consequently, I contend that the historical exclusion of women from the legal definition of 'person' has influenced the construction of the legal subject and the values which that subject embodies, particularly regarding how these values continue to reflect the historical dominance within western society of the liberal understanding of the public/private divide and its associated gender roles.[179]

[171] The influence of normative and rhetorical appeals to 'nature' will be further considered below at s III, 'The Nuclear Family as the Natural Model of "Family"' in the context of the nuclear family model and in ch 5, s II, 'The Gendered Parenting Roles of the Nuclear Family' in the context of the different constructions of the parenting roles of 'mother' and 'father' within legal understanding.

[172] See the description of the 'nuclear family' given by Bernardes, *Family Studies: An Introduction* 2–3, set out above in ch 1, s II, 'The Law's "Definition(s)" of "Family"'.

[173] Section 1 stated 'A person shall not be disqualified by sex or marriage from the exercise of any public function, or from being appointed to or holding any civil or judicial office or post, or from entering or assuming or carrying on any civil profession or vocation, or for admission to any incorporated society'.

[174] *Edwards v Attorney General Canada* [1930] AC 124.

[175] ibid, at 138, Lord Sankey stated 'The word "person" … may include members of both sexes, and to those who ask why the word should include females the obvious answer is why should it not? In these circumstances the burden is upon those who deny that the word includes women to make out their case.'

[176] ibid, at 128.

[177] Sachs and Wilson, *Sexism and the Law: A Study of Male Beliefs and Legal Bias in Britain and the United States* 41.

[178] Lord Sankey in *Edwards v Attorney General Canada* [1930] AC 124, at 134, observed that 'Customs are apt to develop into traditions which are stronger than law and remain unchallenged long after the reason for them has disappeared.'

[179] As considered above at subs I(B), 'The Development of the "Public/Private" Divide'.

I argue that the remnants of these values and ideals continue to influence the nuclear family model.

III. The Nuclear Family as the Natural Model of 'Family'

In this section, I will show that the recurrence of the nuclear family form throughout history has combined with the influence of the construction of the liberal legal subject and the ideals of the 'public/private' divide to influence the positioning of the nuclear family as the 'natural' and 'common sense' model of the family. I will argue that this construction of the legal subject as rational, autonomous and self-interested, in combination with the historical exclusion of women from the public sphere through the liberal understanding of the 'public/private' divide, have influenced the values of the traditional nuclear family (subsection A). I will further argue that the nuclear family has become the law's idealised image of 'family' as a result of its aforementioned historical dominance, which has allowed it to appear and to be presented as the natural and 'common-sense' understanding of 'family' (subsection B).

A. The Legal Subject and the Nuclear Family

Moller Okin has observed that:

> The traditional, supposedly indispensable, nuclear family is used as the connecting link by which the basic biological differences between the sexes are expanded into the entire set of ascribed characteristics and prescribed functions which make up the conventional female sex role.[180]

Thus, historically the private sphere of home and family was positioned as the appropriate realm for women.[181] As O'Donovan observes 'The insistence on the idea that women belong in the private sphere is part of the cultural superstructure which has been built on biological foundations.'[182] Within the historical, liberal conception of the public/private divide, the private sphere of the home and the family was conceptualised as the place where the liberal individual would be able to escape from the issues, pressures and problems of the public sphere, as Naffine describes:

> Liberal theory describes quite another world operating in the private sphere. To this place the liberal citizen can retreat and feel secure from the interventions of other

[180] Moller Okin, *Women in Western Political Thought* 293.
[181] As considered above in subs I(B), 'The Development of the "Public/Private" Divide'.
[182] O'Donovan, *Sexual Divisions in Law* 16.

> persons and from the state, indeed the vital liberty of the person is thought to depend on the security of the private realm, where the individual can relax, express emotions, love and be loved.[183]

Traditionally the law was largely content to ignore the private sphere, this was exemplified by Bowen LJ in *Re Agar-Ellis*,[184] who stated 'I for one should deeply regret the day, if it ever came, when Courts of Law or Equity thought themselves justified in interfering more than is strictly necessary with the private affairs of the people of this country.'[185] The private sphere was seen as embodying an entirely different set of values from those of the liberal individual or legal subject,[186] Moller Okin has commented that 'Theorists who have assumed a high degree of egoism to determine relations between individuals in the sphere of the market, have assumed almost total altruism to govern interfamilial relationships.'[187] As the critical theorist Unger observes:

> In our public mode of being we speak to common language of reason, and live under laws of the state, the constraints of the market, and the customs of different social bodies to which we belong. In our private incarnation, however, we are at the mercy of our own sense impressions and desires.[188]

There is a clear association of the private sphere with women, which reflects the 'masculinity' of the legal subject; O'Donovan suggests that 'Those areas such as the personal, sexuality, biological reproduction, family home, which are particularly identified socially as the women's domain, are also seen as private.'[189]

Following on from this, I argue that this construction of the rational and autonomous subject encourages the emphasis upon family form and structure within legal definitions of 'family', represented through reliance upon the central nexus of the conjugal and parent/child relationships,[190] rather than an approach to understanding 'family' premised upon 'care' and relationality.[191] Herring suggests that 'The values that are promoted within an ethic of care are not isolated autonomy or the pursuance of individualised rights, but rather those of promoting caring, mutuality and interdependence.'[192] These values of mutuality

[183] Naffine, *Law and the Sexes: Explorations of Feminist Jurisprudence* 69.

[184] (1883) 24 Ch 317.

[185] ibid, at 335. See also the cases discussed above in subs I(B), 'The Development of the "Public/Private" Divide'.

[186] O'Donovan, *Family Law Matters* 23, observes that in the private sphere, 'self-sacrifice and altruism are idealised'.

[187] Moller Okin, *Women in Western Political Thought* 284.

[188] Roberto Unger, *Knowledge and Politics* (New York, Free Press, 1975) 59.

[189] O'Donovan, *Sexual Divisions in Law* 3.

[190] As described above in ch 1, s II, 'The Law's "Definition(s)" of "Family"'.

[191] Subsequently, in ch 6, 'The Possibilities Offered by Alternative Models of the "Family"', I will return to these critiques of the orthodox understanding of the legal subject and explore whether re-constructing the subject on the basis of different normative values would provide an alternative approach (or model) through which to understand the family.

[192] Herring, 'Where are the Carers in Healthcare Law and Ethics?' 66.

and interdependence promoted by the 'ethic of care'[193] are in opposition to those of the orthodox, autonomous, self-interested, liberal legal subject.[194] Therefore, I submit that it is predictable that 'caring' is not privileged within the legal understanding of the 'family'.[195] Indeed, Fineman identifies the fundamental tension that exists due to the continued normative influence of the 'public/'private' divide, commenting, 'In an ultimately disastrous manner for our families, we valorize activities associated with work for wages and the accumulation wealth, while we take for granted dependency work and the production of human beings.'[196] Moreover, the separation of gender roles between breadwinner and homemaker within the traditional nuclear family could be understood as encompassing the distinction between the legal subject (the man) and the other(s)[197] (the woman and any children), who were not considered full legal subjects.[198] Thus, in addition to these non-subjects being unable to gain access to the public sphere, they were also deemed to be subordinate to the subject within the family context.[199] Pateman observes that:

> The antinomy private/public is another expression of natural/civil and women/men. The private, womanly sphere (natural) and the public, masculine sphere (civil) are opposed but gain their meaning from each other, and the meaning of the civil freedom of public life is thrown into relief when counterposed to the natural subjection that characterises the private realm.[200]

Thus, I contend that the orthodox construction of the legal subject has impacted upon the form and values of the nuclear family, particularly influencing the separate and distinct gender roles envisaged within that idealised image of family. These particular constructions of the individual and the family have been consistently

[193] See eg Gilligan, *In a Different Voice: Psychological Theory and Women's Development*, Groenhout, *Connected Lives: Human Nature and an Ethics of Care*, Held, *The Ethics of Care* and Noddings, *Caring: A Feminine Approach to Ethics and Moral Education*.

[194] This opposition illustrates why those theorists have sought to reconceptualise the legal subject around notions of 'relationality' or 'vulnerability', as will be considered further below in ch 6, s I, 'Exploring the Conceptual Influences'.

[195] As observed above in ch 1, s II, 'The Law's "Definition(s)" of "Family"'.

[196] Fineman, *The Autonomy Myth: A Theory of Dependency* 33.

[197] For a detailed theoretical exploration of the role of 'the other' in ethics and morality, see eg Bauman, *Postmodern Ethics* and the work of Emmanuel Levinas, eg *Alterity and Transcendence*, *Totality and Infinity*, and *The Levinas Reader*, Sean Hand (ed).

[198] See eg the repeated judicial denials of the personhood of women, discussed above at subs II(C), '"The Persons Cases": The Rejection of Women as Legal Subjects'.

[199] This subordination in the private sphere replicates the position of women in the Ancient Greece and Ancient Rome (reflecting the concept of *paterfamilias*), discussed above at subs I(A), '"Family" and the Subject in Historical Societies'. This is further shown by the almost complete legal power historically possessed by a father over his children, see eg Brett MR in *Re Agar-Ellis* (1883) 24 Ch 317, at 326, who described the position as follows 'the father has the control over the person, education, and conduct of his children until they are twenty-one years of age. That is the law'. This power has been gradually diminished since the Guardianship of Infants Act 1925, which will be further considered below in ch 5, 'The Legal Understanding of the Parental Role'.

[200] Pateman, *The Sexual Contract* 11.

privileged and promoted within legal understanding, while being presented as abstract, objective and 'natural'.

B. The Historical Significance of the Nuclear Family

Western society, since the classical societies, has been based around a model of family centred on the 'nuclear' core,[201] comprising the nexus of the conjugal relationship and the parent/child relationship.[202] Gittins has commented that:

> [I]deals of family relationships have become enshrined in our legal, social, religious and economic systems which, in turn, reinforce the ideology and penalise those who transgress it. Thus there are very real pressures on people to behave in certain ways, to lead their lives according to acceptable norms and patterns.[203]

The recurrence of the nuclear family as the central family form since the classical period, as described above, has resulted in the nuclear family being positioned not only as the form of family that was traditionally dominant in society, but also as the 'natural' or 'common-sense' model of the family. Torrant has observed that, 'the nuclear family form – that is, its dominance – was underpinned by an interlocking matrix of assumptions that together, constituted an ideology of this family form as "natural"'.[204]

As well as exerting influence upon the legal definitions of 'family' described above,[205] the positioning of the nuclear family as 'natural' and the assumption of a separation between the gender roles in that idealised image of 'family' is apparent in other historical judicial reasoning.[206] One such example, from the early twentieth century, is found in *Short v Poole Corporation*,[207] where Pollock MR referred to 'the incidence of domestic duties which may be presumed to fall with greater weight upon a married woman than upon a single woman'.[208]

[201] See above at subs I(A), '"Family" and the Subject in Historical Societies'.

[202] As described above in ch 1, s II, 'The Law's "Definition(s)" of "Family"'.

[203] Gittins, *The Family in Question: Changing Households and Familiar Ideologies* 72.

[204] Julie P Torrant, *The Material Family* (Rotterdam, Sense, 2011) ix. Torrant goes on to further state that 'These assumptions linked a specific sex/gender/sexuality/procreation relation and understood these as natural and transhistorical.' The influence of the 'natural' construction of the gender roles of the traditional, nuclear family will be considered below in ch 5, s II, 'The Gendered Parenting Roles of the Nuclear Family'.

[205] See the discussion of the role of the 'ordinary man' test with the judicial consideration of the Rent Act definition of 'family member', above in ch 1, subs II(A)(ii), '"Family" as Defined by the "Ordinary Man" Test'.

[206] This is in addition to the cases showing the influence of the orthodox construction of the legal subject considered above at subs II(C), '"The Persons Cases": The Rejection of Women as Legal Subjects'.

[207] *Short v Poole Corporation* (1926) Ch 66, this was a case concerning a local authority policy to terminate the employment of all married women teachers, the validity of the policy was upheld by the judgment, see eg *Price v Rhondda Urban District Council* (1923) 2 Ch 372, for another case concerning a similar factual situation.

[208] ibid, per Pollock MR, at 86. Warrington LJ used similar words in his judgment at 92, referring to 'the privilege and the burden of domestic ties'.

This understanding of a clear division of responsibilities between the genders within (indeed created by) the marital relationship is also evident in cases concerning divorce and judicial separation, from the late nineteenth century[209] into the mid-twentieth century.[210] This distinction of roles was given explicit judicial expression in *Wachtel v Wachtel (No 2)*,[211] where Lord Denning MR stated:

> When a marriage breaks up, there will thenceforward be two households instead of one. The husband will have to go out to work all day and must get some woman to look after the house – either a wife, if he remarries, or a housekeeper, if he does not. He will also have to provide maintenance for the children. The wife will not usually have so much expense. She may go out to work herself, but she will not usually employ a housekeeper. She will do most of the housework herself, perhaps with some help. Or she may remarry, in which case her new husband will provide for her.[212]

This statement clearly associates men with the public sphere and women with the private sphere; it assumes distinct roles for men and women, with husbands as breadwinners and wives as homemakers within the family.[213] Forty-five years ago, then, judicial language reflected the traditional, gendered conception of the nuclear family[214] and this clear division of gender roles within the 'family' was presented matter-of-factly as the 'common sense' or 'natural' understanding of 'family'.

The dominance of the ideology of the nuclear family is noticeable in the work of the early and mid-twentieth century sociologists and anthropologists who studied the family and its organisation.[215] The understanding of the nuclear family as 'natural' is exemplified by Linton, who suggested that 'The ancient trinity of father, mother, and child has survived more vicissitudes than any other human relationship. It is the bedrock underlying all other family structures.'[216]

[209] See eg *Wood v Wood* [1891] P 272, *Dean v Dean* [1923] P 172 and *Gilbey v Gilbey* [1927] P 197, in these cases emphasis is placed upon the husband's duty to provide maintenance for his wife and the marital conduct of the wife is a significant factor in determining the extent of her entitlement.

[210] See eg Pearce J in *Duchense v Duchense* [1951] P 101, who stated, at 114 'The rights of a wife who has always been selfish and unloving ought not to be identical with those of a wife who has always been loving and unselfish.' See further eg *Schlesinger v Schlesinger* [1960] P 191, *Porter v Porter* [1969] 1 WLR 1155 and *Ackerman v Ackerman* [1972] 2 WLR 1253.

[211] *Wachtel v Wachtel (No 2)* [1973] 2 WLR 366.

[212] ibid, at 376, per Lord Denning MR.

[213] The influence of the division of gender roles will be considered in relation to the legal understanding of parenthood and parenting below in ch 5, s II, 'The Gendered Parenting Roles of the Nuclear Family'.

[214] However, it should be noted that the approach set out in *Wachtel* was not followed by the Court of Appeal in *Dart v Dart* [1996] 2 FLR 286 and subsequently the judicial language in divorce cases has departed from explicit endorsement of the traditional division of gendered roles, see eg *White v White* [2001] 1 AC 596.

[215] For a more detailed consideration of the historical development of sociological and anthropological work on the family, see eg Faith Robertson Elliot, *The Family: Change of Continuity?* (Basingstoke, MacMillan, 1986).

[216] Ralph Linton, 'The Natural History of the Family' in Ruth Nanda Anshen (eds), *The Family: Its Function and Destiny*, Revised edition (New York, Harper and Brothers, 1959) 52.

Within this dominant ideology, evidence of the historical incidence of the nuclear family form is combined with an appeal to the rhetorical power of tradition, in an effort to present the nuclear family as something that stands apart from particular social contexts.[217] Murdock observed the existence of the nuclear family across cultures and concluded that:

> The nuclear family is a universal human social grouping. Either as the sole prevailing form of family or as the basic unit from which more complex familial forms are compounded, it exists as a distinct and strongly functional group in every known society.[218]

The nuclear family is therefore presented in this understanding as both unconstructed and ahistorical. Thus, I argue that there is a certain circularity involved in the dominant and orthodox understanding: the nuclear family is constructed as the 'natural' model of family, which is largely premised on its consistent historical importance.[219] On the basis of this 'natural' construction, I suggest that the nuclear family is positioned as the idealised image which underpins the legal understanding of the 'family', which is held to be based upon 'the person in the street's' understanding of 'family', as set out above in chapter one.[220] In this way, I argue that the dominance of the nuclear family model effectively sustains itself, because it is presented as the 'natural' model of family and derives its continued significance from that positioning.

To conclude, in the previous chapter I argued that the traditional nuclear family, comprising the nexus of the conjugal and parent/child relationships, underpins the law's understanding and definition(s) of 'family'. In this chapter, I have considered the reasons for the normative centrality of the nuclear family within legal understanding. I have observed that the nuclear family form recurs as a central family unit throughout history and that this historical prominence of the nuclear family coincides with the historical prevalence of a division of society into public and private spheres. I have argued that the liberal notion of the 'public/private' divide influenced the orthodox construction of the legal subject, and that this orthodox construction embedded the values of the nuclear family, particularly the delineation of gendered roles (the man as 'breadwinner' and the woman as 'homemaker'). I have further argued that the nuclear family model possessed this dominance within the legal understanding of the 'family' because its historical

[217] However, it is worth noting that this approach was not universally accepted within these disciplines at this point in the twentieth century, see eg CC Harris, *The Family: An Introduction* (London, Allen and Unwin, 1969), who argued that the nuclear family resulted from particular social and cultural processes rather than possessing a 'natural' basis.

[218] George P Murdock, 'The Universality of the Nuclear Family' in Norman W Bell and Ezra F Vogel (eds), *A Modern Introduction to The Family*, Revised edition (New York, Free Press, 1968) 38. Notably, these empirical claims of the universality of the nuclear family were questioned within the same volume, by Kathleen E Gough, 'Is the Family Universal? – The Nayar Case', further suggesting that the dominant ideology has always been subjected to criticism.

[219] See above at subs I(A), '"Family" and the Subject in Historical Societies'.

[220] As considered above in ch 1, subs II(A)(ii), '"Family" as Defined by the "Ordinary Man" Test'.

position as a central family form resulted in it becoming viewed as the 'common sense' or 'natural' model of family. Through the judicial adoption of 'common sense' understandings, the nuclear model has also become the idealised image of 'family' within the law, as discussed above in chapter one.

The next three chapters will explore the continuing normative significance of the traditional, nuclear family, given the context (set out above in the introduction) of legislative reforms and changes in familial demographics and practices; by focusing upon the legal regulation of the two relationships (the conjugal relationship and the parent/child relationship) which form the central nexus of the nuclear family.

PART II

The Conjugal Relationship

> marriage is the model for intimate relationships because of its immorality and its status as icon. Whether it is invoked in political rhetoric or religious ideology, marriage and family stand as a totem … Authority, patriarchal society, religion, politics, invoke the totem as a sacred source.

Katherine O'Donovan, *Family Law Matters* (London, Pluto Press, 1993) 56

3

The Legal Regulation of Conjugal Relationships

This chapter will explore the legal regulation of adult relationships and I will argue that the normative dominance of the nuclear family can be shown by the continuing centrality of marriage and 'marriage-like' conjugality to the legal recognition and regulation of adult personal relationships.

Chan comments that, 'marriage is a pre-legal institution, but its modern incarnation is delimited by law'.[1] Historically marriage was central to the understanding of family both in society and in the law.[2] However gradual shifts have taken place in the past century, with fewer people getting married,[3] divorces increasing[4] and much greater numbers of unmarried cohabitating couples.[5] Today, cohabitation is understood in public attitudes as a legitimate alternative to marriage.[6]

[1] Chan, 'Cohabitation, Civil Partnership, Marriage and the Equal Sharing Principle' 48.

[2] As can be seen from the judicial attitude towards unmarried cohabitants in the cases concerning the Rent Act definition of 'family', discussed above in ch 1, subs II(A)(iii), 'Unmarried Cohabitants', see eg *Gammans v Ekins* [1950] 2 KB 328.

[3] ONS, 'Marriages in England and Wales: 2015' (February 2018) 2, shows that there has been a gradual decline from over 400,000 marriages per year to around 250,000 per year in 2015. Statistics showing a similar trend for marriages in Scotland, from 1971–2013, are found in 'Scotland's Population 2013 – The Registrar General's Annual Review of Demographic Trends 159th edition' (August 2014) at 49, available at: www.nrscotland.gov.uk/files//statistics/annual-review-2013/rgar-2013.pdf.

[4] ONS, 'Divorces in England and Wales: 2016' (October 2017) 3, shows the trends in divorce from the 1950s onwards, first showing significant increase from the 1960s onwards, before a gradual decline in the number of divorces from the early 1990s. Indeed, there were under 24,000 divorces in 1960, nearly 120,000 in 1972, a peak of around 165,000 in 1993 and 107,071 (including same-sex couples) in 2015, available at: www.ons.gov.uk/peoplepopulationandcommunity/birthsdeathsandmarriages/divorce/bulletins/divorcesinenglandandwales/2016. Statistics showing a similar trend for divorces in Scotland from 1971–2011 are available in, 'Scotland's Population 2011 – The Registrar General's Annual Review of Demographic Trends 157th edition', (August 2012) 59, available at: www.gro-scotland.gov.uk/files//statistics/annual-review-2011/rgar-2011.pdf. See further ONS, 'Marriages in England and Wales (Provisional), 2012', (June 2014) 9, which shows that in 34% of marriages at least one of the parties had been married previously with 15% being remarriages for both parties, available at: www.ons.gov.uk/peoplepopulationandcommunity/birthsdeathsandmarriages/marriagecohabitationandcivilpartnerships/bulletins/marriagesinenglandandwalesprovisional/2014-06-11.

[5] ONS, 'Families and Households: 2017' (November 2017) 5, shows that there were 3.3 million cohabiting couples in the UK in 2017, which is over double the figure from 1996.

[6] Alison Park and Rebecca Rhead, 'Personal Relationships: Changing Attitudes Towards Sex, Marriage and Parenthood' (2013) 30 *British Social Attitudes Survey* 7–14, illustrates the shift in attitudes towards marriage and cohabitation amongst the UK population.

Additionally, over the past 50 years there has been an ongoing process of recognition and regulation of same-sex relationships, from decriminalisation,[7] through the judicial extension of existing statutory provisions to same-sex relationships,[8] the subsequent explicit inclusion of same-sex couples within legislative provisions,[9] to the specific statutory regulation of same-sex relationships first as civil partnerships[10] and more recently the extension of marriage to same-sex couples.[11] Barlow and James comment that 'British society today comprises a plurality of family structures which our research confirms are considered acceptable personal life-style choices. Marriage, while still highly valued at least in the abstract, has lost its monopoly on sexual intimacy and childbearing in Britain.'[12] In spite of these developments, I will argue that marriage retains a central position within UK law, reflecting the observation of Diduck and Kaganas, that:

> [A]s a social institution marriage represents an idealised rite of passage into adulthood. It marks a heterosexual couple's readiness to assume the "normal" responsibilities of adulthood including home owning, child rearing, legitimate and exclusive sexual activity and financial independence from parents.[13]

Moreover, I will contend that the extension of legal regulation to non-marital adult personal relationships is premised upon the understanding that it is the 'marriage-like' characteristics and features of these relationships, particularly

[7] Through the partial decriminalisation of the Sexual Offences Act 1967, s 1 and the Criminal Justice (Scotland) Act 1980, s 80.

[8] eg Same-sex couples being considered 'family' for the purposes of the Rent Act in *Fitzpatrick v Sterling Housing Association Ltd* [2001] 1 AC 27, as discussed in ch 1, subs II(A)(iv), 'Same-Sex Cohabitants'.

[9] eg Same-sex couples being allowed to adopt children as a couple, Adoption and Children Act 2002, s 50 and Adoption and Children (Scotland) Act 2007, s 29(3), the inclusion of female same-sex couples within the legal parenthood provisions in cases of assisted reproduction, Human Fertilisation and Embryology Act 2008, ss 42–48 and the extension of 'parental orders' in cases of surrogacy to all same-sex couples, Human Fertilisation and Embryology Act 2008, s 54.

[10] Civil Partnership Act 2004, s 1. Given the extension of marriage to same-sex couples, the long-term future of civil partnership remains unclear, see eg Ruth Gaffney-Rhys, 'Same-sex Marriage but not Mixed-sex Partnerships: Should the Civil Partnership Act 2004 be Extended to Opposite-sex Couples?' [2014] 26(2) *Child and Family Law Quarterly* 173. In this regard, both the UK government and the Scottish government have indicated that they will seek to gather further information and additional evidence before consulting on potential law reform; see 'The Future Operation of Civil Partnership: Gathering Further Information', (Department for International Development, May 2018), available at: https://assets.publishing.service.gov.uk/government/uploads/system/uploads/attachment_data/file/705768/Future-Operation-Civil-Partnership.pdf and 'Review of Civil Partnership: Scottish Government Response to the Consultation' (Scottish Government, November 2017), available at: www.gov.scot/Resource/0052/00527978.pdf. Indeed, in *Steinfeld v Secretary of State for Education* [2018] UKSC 32, the Supreme Court issued a 'declaration of incompatibility', under s 4 of the Human Rights Act 1998, regarding the exclusion of opposite-sex couples from civil partnership by s 1 and s 3 of the Civil Partnership Act 2004. The court held those provisions to be incompatible with Art 14 in conjunction with Art 8 of the ECHR. However, at the time of writing, the government have not announced how they intend to respond to the declaration.

[11] Marriage Same-Sex Couples Act 2013 and Marriage and Civil Partnership (Scotland) Act 2014.

[12] Anne Barlow and Grace James, 'Regulating Marriage and Cohabitation in 21st Century Britain' (2004) 67(2) *Modern Law Review* 143, 172.

[13] Diduck and Kaganas, *Family Law, Gender and the State* 37.

their conjugality, that is used to warrant such regulation. Thus, I will argue that marriage and the traditional nuclear family retain significant normative power in the construction of adult (conjugal) relationships within the legal understanding of the 'family'.

In section I, I will consider the question 'What is marriage in UK law?' The legal definition of marriage will be examined and the continuing influence of historical judicial constructions of marriage will be explored. I will consider whether the contemporary understanding of marriage is changing; exploring the impact of the extension of marriage to same-sex couples upon the dominant understanding of marriage. In section II, I will build upon this by examining the centrality of the conjugal relationship to the regulation of adult relationships. I will consider the legal regulation of cohabitation, arguing that relationships between cohabitees are recognised and regulated by the law on the basis that they are sufficiently 'marriage-like' and that this comparison with marriage occurs primarily as a result of their common conjugality.

I. What is Marriage in UK Law?

O'Donovan observes that 'Marriage has contractual and institutional elements, but it is also, sui generis, a law unto itself.'[14] Marriage has been described, both judicially and otherwise,[15] as an 'institution'[16] or as a 'status',[17] and as discussed above in chapters one and two, it occupies a central position within the traditional, nuclear family model.[18] Indeed, in *Corbett v Corbett*,[19] Ormrod J described marriage as, 'the institution on which the family is built'.[20] As Diduck and Kaganas comment, 'Marriage … is accorded a privileged social status which provides a place for the legitimate expression of heterosexual desires, imbuing other types of sexual activity and other relationships with a lesser status.'[21] In the 1970s in *Campbell v Campbell*,[22] marriage was described as being, 'essential to the well-being of

[14] O'Donovan, *Family Law Matters* 44.

[15] Robert Leckey, 'Marriage and the Data on Same-Sex Couples' (2013) 35(2) *Journal of Social Welfare and Family Law* 179, 180, comments that 'The prevailing treatment of marriage takes it as a unitary contract and institution: as forest more than trees.'

[16] See eg Ormrod J in *Corbett v Corbett* [1970] 2 All ER 33, at 48 and Lord Nicholls in *Bellinger v Bellinger* [2003] UKHL 21, [2003] 2 AC 467, at 480, for judicial descriptions of marriage as an 'institution'. Former Prime Minister David Cameron was quoted as describing marriage as 'a great institution', Christopher Hope, 'We Will Legalise Gay Marriage by 2015, says David Cameron' (*Daily Telegraph*, London, 24 July 2012), available at: www.telegraph.co.uk/news/politics/9425174/We-will-legalise-gay-marriage-by-2015-says-David-Cameron.html.

[17] See eg Lord Hoffmann in *Re P (Adoption: Unmarried Couples)* [2008] UKHL 38, [2008] 2 FLR 1084, at 1088, his lordship also described marriage as a 'very important institution' at 1090.

[18] See particularly ch 1, s II, 'The Law's "Definition(s)" of "Family"'.

[19] *Corbett v Corbett* [1970] 2 All ER 33.

[20] ibid, at 48.

[21] Diduck and Kaganas, *Family Law, Gender and the State* 73.

[22] *Campbell v Campbell* [1977] 1 All ER 1.

our society'.[23] This historical emphasis on the societal importance of marriage was re-affirmed, more recently, by Baroness Hale in *Granatino v Radmacher*,[24] where her ladyship stated 'I still believe that it is the public policy of this country to support marriage and to encourage married people to stay married rather than to encourage them to get divorced.'[25] Moreover, similar emphasis on the ongoing social role of marriage was given by the coalition government that took office in 2010, in its response to the consultation on equal marriage,[26] which stated: 'Marriage is a hugely important institution in this country. The principles of long-term commitment and responsibility which underpin it bind generations together, and make our society strong.'[27] Thus, I suggest that marriage is still viewed within legal understanding as representing the pinnacle or 'gold standard'[28] of conjugal relationships and family forms and throughout this chapter I argue that marriage remains the standard against which the law measures all other relationships.[29]

In this section, I will consider the legal definition of marriage, examining the development of the judicial understanding of marriage and exploring how this has evolved over time (subsection A). I will then examine whether the social and legal understanding of marriage is changing (subsection B), considering whether the recent extension of marriage to same-sex couples has affected the fundamental meaning of legal marriage (subsection C).

A. The Legal Definition of Marriage

There is no statutory definition of marriage,[30] and Herring suggests that 'It is impossible to provide a single definition of marriage.'[31] Historically in England and Wales,[32] the Church of England had control over matrimonial law and

[23] ibid, per Sir George Baker, at 6.

[24] *Granatino v Radmacher* [2010] UKSC 42, [2011] 1 AC 534.

[25] ibid, per Baroness Hale, at 584.

[26] 'Equal Marriage: The Government's Response', (HM Government, December 2012), available at: www.gov.uk/government/uploads/system/uploads/attachment_data/file/133262/consultation-response_1_.pdf.

[27] ibid, Ministerial Foreword of the Rt Hon Maria Miller MP, at 4.

[28] See eg Jo Miles, Fran Wasoff and Enid Mordaunt, 'Reforming Family Law – The Case of Cohabitation: "Things May Not Work Out as You Expect"' (2012) 34(2) *Journal of Social Welfare and Family Law* 167, 168 for academic usage of this description.

[29] In some jurisdictions the centrality of marriage is illustrated through explicit constitutional protections, see eg the Constitution of Ireland, Art 41(3), which states 'The State pledges itself to guard with special care the institution of Marriage, on which the Family is founded, and to protect it against attack' and the Basic Law for the Federal Republic of Germany, Art 6(1), which states 'Marriage and the family shall enjoy the special protection of the state.' Furthermore, the European Convention on Human Rights, Art 12, states 'Men and women of marriageable age have the right to marry and to found a family.'

[30] Neither the Marriage Act 1949 nor the Matrimonial Causes Act 1973 provides a definition of the term 'marriage'; this is also the case with the Marriage (Scotland) Act 1977.

[31] Herring, *Family Law* 70.

[32] In Scotland the religious control of marriage operated differently, due to the different role of the Church of Scotland, which was not an organ of the state as the Church of England was.

regulation.[33] As a consequence, even after the creation of civil marriage,[34] the Christian conception of marriage[35] represented the legal understanding of marriage.[36] I argue that the remnants of this dominance are still apparent in the influence of traditional ideals within the legal understanding of marriage.[37]

The starting point for the judicial definition of marriage is the judgment of Lord Penzance[38] in *Hyde v Hyde*,[39] in which he stated: 'I conceive that marriage, as understood in Christendom, may for this purpose be defined as the voluntary union for life of one man and one woman, to the exclusion of all others.'[40] It is also apparent that historically the judicial understanding of marriage was premised upon the construction of separate and distinct gender roles, associated with the public/private divide and the traditional nuclear family.[41] To that end, in *Pretty v Pretty*,[42] Bargrave Deane J stated:

> Some people think that, in such matters, you must treat men and women on the same footing. But this Court has not taken, and, I hope, never will take, that view. I trust that, in dealing with these cases, it will ever be remembered that the woman is the weaker vessel.[43]

Thus, the husband was constructed as the head of the household and breadwinner, while the wife was constructed as the dependent homemaker.[44] This understanding is demonstrated by the judgment of Sir James Hannen, in *Durham v Durham*,[45] who stated that marriage involved 'protection on the part of the man, and submission on the part of the woman.'[46]

[33] The Ecclesiastical Courts retained authority over matrimonial matters until the Matrimonial Causes Act 1857, which set up the Court for Divorce and Matrimonial Causes.

[34] In England and Wales civil marriage was introduced by the Marriage Act 1836 and in Scotland it was not introduced until over 100 years later in the Marriage (Scotland) Act 1939. In 2015, Civil marriages accounted for 74% of marriages, ONS, 'Marriages in England and Wales: 2015' (February 2018) 7.

[35] eg As found in the 'Book of Common Prayer: The Form of Solemnization of Matrimony', available at: www.churchofengland.org/prayer-worship/worship/book-of-common-prayer/the-form-of-solemnization-of-matrimony.aspx.

[36] *Hyde v Hyde* (1866) LR 1 P&D 130.

[37] See eg the judgment of Sir Mark Potter in *Wilkinson v Kitzinger (No. 2)* [2006] EWHC 2022 (Fam), [2007] 1 FLR 295, which refused to recognise a Canadian same-sex marriage as a marriage in the UK, instead converting it to a civil partnership. Indeed, it is notable that the law in the UK still provides for both religious marriage (Marriage Act 1949, Part II and Marriage (Scotland) Act 1977, ss 9–16) and civil marriage (Marriage Act 1949, Part III and Marriage (Scotland) Act 1977, ss 17–20) even though the legal effects of each are the same, with the distinctions relating to the formalities of the marriage and the wedding ceremony.

[38] However, see Rebecca Probert, 'Hyde v Hyde: Defining or Defending Marriage?' [2007] 19(3) *Child and Family Law Quarterly* 322, 325, where she argues that 'Lord Penzance's dictum should not be regarded as a definition of marriage but as a defence, and that it has been used as a defence rather than a definition by subsequent judges.'

[39] *Hyde v Hyde* (1866) LR 1 P&D 130.

[40] ibid, per Lord Penzance, at 130, see further *Re Bethell* (1887) 38 Ch D 220.

[41] As discussed above in ch 2, subs I(B), 'The Development of the "Public/Private" Divide'.

[42] *Pretty v Pretty* [1911] P 83.

[43] ibid, at 88.

[44] See eg the language of Lord Denning MR in *Wachtel v Wachtel (No. 2)* [1973] 2 WLR 366, at 376, quoted above in ch 2, subs III(B), 'The Historical Significance of the Nuclear Family'.

[45] *Durham v Durham* (1885) 10 PD 80.

[46] ibid, per Sir James Hannen, at 82.

The definition of marriage provided by Lord Penzance underpinned the judicial understanding of marriage throughout the twentieth century[47] and the definition has continued to be referenced judicially in recent times.[48] This was illustrated by the judgment of Sir Mark Potter in *Wilkinson v Kitzinger (No 2)*,[49] who commented that 'This definition has been applied and acted upon by the courts ever since.'[50] Later in his judgment, the President went on to observe that:

> It is apparent that the majority of people, or at least of governments, not only in England but Europe-wide, regard marriage as an age-old institution, valued and valuable, respectable and respected, as a means not only of encouraging monogamy but also the procreation of children and their development and nurture in a family unit (or 'nuclear family').[51]

This statement shows the ongoing influence of the traditional conception of marriage and its interrelationship with the nuclear family upon contemporary judicial understanding.[52] This continuing significance was noted by Sir James Munby, who commented extra-judicially that 'Until very recently, family law was concerned largely, if not exclusively, with the family wrought in the image of Lord Penzance's famous definition of marriage'.[53] An example is the description of marriage given by Lord Millett in *Ghaidan v Godin-Mendoza*:[54]

> Marriage is the lawful union of a man and a woman. It is a legal relationship between persons of the opposite sex. A man's spouse must be a woman; a woman's spouse must be a man. This is the very essence of the relationship, which need not be loving, sexual, stable, faithful, long-lasting or contented.[55]

This judicial statement invokes the language of Lord Penzance's definition and illustrates the continuing significance of the historical and traditional definition of marriage within judicial understanding.[56] These various judicial comments

[47] See eg *Corbett v Corbett* [1970] 2 All ER 33, at 48, where Ormrod J observed 'sex is clearly an essential determinant of the relationship called marriage, because it is and always has been recognised as the union of one man and one woman'. However, the continued use of this definition was subject to academic critique, see eg Sebastian Poulter, 'The Definition of Marriage in English Law' (1979) 42(4) *Modern Law Review* 409.

[48] See eg Ward LJ's describing it as 'the hallowed definition of marriage' in *Bibi v Chief Adjudication Officer* [1998] 1 FLR 375, at 379 and Munby J's reference to 'Lord Penzance's famous definition' in *Sheffield City Council v E and S* [2004] EWHC 2808 (Fam), [2005] 1 FLR 965, at 998.

[49] *Wilkinson v Kitzinger (No. 2)* [2006] EWHC 2022 (Fam), [2007] 1 FLR 295.

[50] ibid, per Sir Mark Potter, at 301.

[51] ibid, at 329.

[52] However, it should be noted that the President's reliance on the traditional definition has been the subject of academic criticism, see eg Rosemary Auchmuty, 'What's So Special About Marriage? The Impact of Wilkinson v Kitzinger' [2008] 20(4) *Child and Family Law Quarterly* 475, 480, who observed, in regard to the above quoted passage, that 'This sentence is contentious in almost every aspect.'

[53] Munby, 'Years of Change: Family Law in 1987, 2012 and 2037', 279.

[54] [2004] UKHL 30, [2004] 2 AC 557.

[55] ibid, per Lord Millett, in his dissenting judgment, at 588.

[56] In addition, the final sentence provides significant insight into the judicial understanding of the marital relationship because it makes clear that, in Lord Millet's opinion, the law has little interest in the nature or quality of the relationship between the parties to an on-going marriage. See further eg

show that the definition of marriage encapsulated in *Hyde v Hyde*, and the ideals it embodies, retain significant influence upon the contemporary judicial conception of marriage.

In *Re P (Adoption: Unmarried Couples)*,[57] Baroness Hale stated that 'Marriage brings with it legal rights and obligations between the couple which unmarried couples do not have.'[58] Historically, due to the doctrine known in English law as coverture,[59] marriage resulted in a wife having no legal personality separate from that of her husband.[60] This doctrine was gradually eliminated by the Married Women's Property Acts of the late nineteenth century,[61] which allowed married women to own their own property, effectively eliminating this most substantial of all the legal consequences of marriage.[62] Other previously important consequences of marriage have also now been eliminated, including the husband being the sole legal guardian of children born to the marriage,[63] the 'legitimate' status of children born during a marriage,[64] and the common law rule that a husband could not be found guilty of raping his wife.[65]

With these historical effects abolished,[66] the main legal consequences of marriage are now the financial and economic entitlements and benefits it brings; including access to favourable taxation regimes,[67] consequences for succession[68]

Vervaeke v Smith [1982] 2 All ER 144, where Lord Halisham stated, at 147 'Although valid in point of form that marriage with Smith was not in any sense an ordinary one. There was no intention to cohabit as man and wife.'

[57] *Re P (Adoption: Unmarried Couples)* [2008] UKHL 38, [2008] 2 FLR 1084.

[58] ibid, per Baroness Hale, at 1121.

[59] As considered above in ch 2, subs I(A) '"Family" and the Subject in Historical Societies'. For details on the Ancient Scots law of marriage, see eg the transcription of the 15th century lectures of William Hay, John C Barry, *William Hay's Lectures on Marriage*, (Edinburgh, Stair Society, 1967) and Patrick Fraser, *Treatise on Husband and Wife, According to the Law of Scotland*, 2nd edn (Edinburgh, T & T Clark, 1876–78).

[60] Sir William Blackstone, *Commentaries on the Laws of England*, Vol 1, at 442.

[61] The Married Women's Property Acts 1870, 1882, 1884 and 1893, see also the Married Women's Property (Scotland) Acts 1881 and 1920.

[62] In *Midland Bank Trust Co Ltd v Green* [1982] Ch 529, at 538, Lord Denning MR observed that 'medieval lawyers held that husband and wife were one person in law: and that the husband was that one. It was a fiction then. It is a fiction now'.

[63] Which was effectively abolished by 'welfare test', first established in s 1 of the Guardianship of Infants Act 1925.

[64] The distinction between children born within marriages and those 'illegitimate' children born outside marriage was effectively abolished by the Family Law Reform Act 1987 and the Law Reform (Parent and Child) (Scotland) Act 1986.

[65] Abolished in England and Wales in *R v R (Rape: Marital Exemption)* [1992] 1 FLR 217 and in Scotland in *S v HM Advocate* 1989 SLT 469.

[66] For the abolition of other historical consequences of marriage, see eg the Law Reform (Husband and Wife) (Scotland) Act 1984 and the more recent abolition of the wife's defence to a charge of reset in s 7 of the Marriage and Civil Partnership (Scotland) Act 2014.

[67] eg the spousal exemption for inheritance tax, Inheritance Tax Act 1984, s 18 and the exemption from capital gains tax on transfers between spouses, Taxation of Chargeable Gains Act 1992, s 58.

[68] eg rights for spouses on intestate succession, in England and Wales, Administration of Estates Act 1925, s 46 and prior and legal rights for spouses in Scotland, provided by Pt 2 of the Succession (Scotland) Act 1964.

and access to the regime of financial provision on divorce.[69] Thus, regardless of how marriage is understood in cultural discourse, the legal consequences of marriage are now primarily financial. Despite the diminution in the legal effects of marriage, Hibbs, Barton and Beswick observe that many people who get married have 'misperceptions about the law relating to marriage and cohabitation, and [are] anyway little concerned with the legal consequences of their decision'.[70] In other words, individuals do not generally make decisions about whether or not to get married on the basis of the legal effects of marriage. Moreover, in view of the relatively limited effects of marriage in contemporary society, Herring has observed that 'The law has had much to say about who can marry whom and how the relationship can be ended, but says very little explicitly about the content of the relationship itself'.[71] Against this background, it is perhaps unsurprising that the traditional 'natural' construction of marriage (and the associated gendered roles) has filled the gap. The next section will explore the continued centrality of these traditional ideals and consider whether the social and legal understanding of marriage is changing.

B. Is the Understanding of Marriage Changing?

There is some recent evidence of judicial recognition that the understanding of marriage may be changing,[72] reflecting a movement away from the language of Lord Penzance in *Hyde v Hyde*.[73] In *Sheffield City Council v E and S*[74] Munby J stated that:

> [M]arriage, whether civil or religious is a contract, formally entered into. It confers on the parties the status of husband and wife, the essence of the contract being an

[69] The provisions for 'ancillary relief' in England and Wales, are provided by Pt 2 of the Matrimonial Causes Act 1973; see also ss 8–17 of the Family Law (Scotland) Act 1985 for the Scottish regime of financial provision on divorce.

[70] Mary Hibbs, Chris Barton and Joanne Beswick, 'Why Marry? – Perceptions of the Affianced' [2001] 31(3) *Fam Law* 197, 207, this statement is based on the findings of empirical research, carried out by the authors, with couples preparing to get married.

[71] Herring, *Family Law* 72, the complex provisions governing the formalities of marriage are found in the Marriage Act 1949 and the Marriage (Scotland) Act 1977, in addition the Matrimonial Causes Act 1973, ss 11–16 provide the rules governing nullity of marriage and the distinction between void and voidable marriages, see further Rebecca Probert, 'The Evolving Concept of Non-Marriage' [2013] 25 (3) *Child and Family Law Quarterly* 314.

[72] See eg the dissenting judgment of Thorpe LJ in the Court of Appeal in *Bellinger v Bellinger* [2001] EWCA Civ 1140, [2001] 2 FLR 1048, where he acknowledged, at 1082 'the world that engendered those classic definitions has long since gone … The intervening 130 years have seen huge social and scientific changes … Illegitimacy with its stigma has been legislated away: gone is any social condemnation of cohabitation in advance of or in place of marriage.'

[73] (1866) LR 1 P&D 130. See eg Probert, 'Hyde v Hyde: Defining or Defending Marriage?', who has been critical of the judicial reliance upon *Hyde*, observing, at 336 '*Hyde* should be seen for what it is: a case of considerable historical interest, that tells us a great deal about the attitudes of mid-Victorian England – but nothing about how marriage should be defined today.'

[74] *Sheffield City Council v E and S* [2004] EWHC 2808 (Fam), [2005] 1 FLR 965.

> agreement between a man and a woman to live together, and to love one another as husband and wife, to the exclusion of all others.[75]

While this description still reflects elements of the traditional definition,[76] the emphasis placed on the contractual nature of marriage[77] and the corresponding omission of any reference to the institutional character of marriage, illustrates an apparent shift in understanding away from the dominance of the historical definition. This ostensible shift in the judicial understanding of marriage is also evident from the judgments in *Re P (Adoption: Unmarried Couples)*,[78] where Lord Hoffman stated that 'It is clear that being married is a status'[79] and Baroness Hale observed that 'marriage is not just a contract; it is also a status.'[80]

Given this judicial recognition, combined with the trends in societal demographics[81] and changing social attitudes toward marriage and cohabitation,[82] some academic commentators[83] have suggested that cultural understandings of marriage are evolving.[84] Auchmuty has argued that 'Though the institution retains residual value for some cultural groups … for most of us it is *simply a lifestyle choice*.'[85] On the basis of their empirical research, Eekelaar and MacLean suggest that 'It becomes increasingly difficult to identify being married in itself as *necessarily*, or even *characteristically*, constituting a significant source of personal obligations in the eyes of the participants in such relationships.'[86] Therefore, for many, marriage is now being constructed as a 'partnership of equals' and this has been reflected in some judicial language.[87]

[75] ibid, per Munby J, at 1004.

[76] Particularly through limiting marriage to 'one man and one woman' and retaining 'to the exclusion of all others'.

[77] The contractual nature of marriage was also emphasised by Thorpe LJ in *Bellinger v Bellinger* [2001] EWCA Civ 1140, [2001] 2 FLR 1048, who stated, at 1082 'Marriage has become a state into which and from which people choose to enter and exit. Thus I would now redefine marriage as a contract for which the parties elect but which is regulated by the state'.

[78] [2008] 2 FLR 1084.

[79] ibid, at 1088.

[80] ibid, at 1120. It is not the purpose or intention of this work to explore the academic literature which considers the contractual nature of marriage.

[81] See eg ONS, 'Marriages in England and Wales: 2015' (February 2018) and ONS, 'Families and Households: 2017' (November 2017).

[82] See eg Park and Rhead, 'Personal Relationships: Changing Attitudes Towards Sex, Marriage and Parenthood' *British Social Attitudes Survey* 30.

[83] See eg Carol Smart, 'Law and Family Life: Insights from 25 Years of Empirical Research' [2014] 26(1) *Child and Family Law Quarterly* 14, who observed, at 29 'Marriage remains important but only in as much as it is part of a process of forming kin, alongside other methods of so doing.'

[84] However, other commentators have been more critical, see eg Heather Brook, 'Zombie Law: Conjugality, Annulment and the (Married) Living Dead' (2014) 22(1) *Feminist Legal Studies* 49, who argued, at 50, that marriage, 'is something of a zombie category'.

[85] Rosemary Auchmuty, 'Law and the Power of Feminism: How Marriage Lost its Power to Oppress Women' (2012) 20(2) *Feminist Legal Studies* 71, 74.

[86] John Eekelaar and Mavis MacLean, 'Marriage and the Moral Bases of Personal Responsibility' (2004) 31(4) *Journal of Law and Society* 510, 536.

[87] See eg Lord Emslie's statement in *S v HM Advocate* 1989 SLT 469, at 473, that 'A husband and wife are now for all practical purposes equal partners in marriage' and Munby J's comment in *Sheffield City*

Similarly, Barlow has observed that 'Adult personal relationships are increasingly characterised as equal partnerships where the partners should be at liberty jointly to exercise their autonomy around decision-making on family issues.'[88] Within this construction of marriage, individuals are given the opportunity for personal fulfilment and as a mechanism to express love,[89] show commitment[90] and provide care[91] for each other. Barlow and James observe that:

> [M]arriage has simply lost its power to hold people together and to entice them into lifelong partnerships in the first place. The social structures which gave it this power have been greatly weakened by the lack of religion, women's financial independence, state support for lone parents, separation of sex from marriage and of childbearing from marriage, ease of divorce, ease of cohabitation.[92]

It would seem, therefore, that while the *idea* of marriage retains significant normative power, the understanding of the relationship, for some couples, has shifted away from the traditional construction.[93] However, it is also clear that in spite of this rhetorical shift, the traditional gendered roles of 'breadwinner' and 'homemaker' still exert influence on wider social and familial practices.[94] This continuing significance has been acknowledged judicially; in *Bellinger v Bellinger*[95] Lord Nicholls noted that 'Marriage is an institution, or relationship,

Council v E and S [2004] EWHC 2808 (Fam), [2005] 1 FLR 965, at para 131, that 'Today both spouses are the joint, co-equal heads of the family.'

[88] Anne Barlow, 'Solidarity, Autonomy and Equality: Mixed Messages for the Family?' [2015] 27(3) *Child and Family Law Quarterly* 223, 223. The role of the concept of 'autonomy' in the regulation and understanding of the 'family' will be considered further in ch 6, subs I(C), 'Autonomy and Choice'.

[89] Hibbs, Barton and Beswick, 'Why Marry? – Perceptions of the Affianced', 200, state regarding the individuals they interviewed 'No one claimed, or admitted to, financial reasons for marriage, love was the single highest-ranking reason given for marriage.'

[90] Diduck, *Law's Families* 33, suggests that 'while older married couples spoke of obligations, often stemming from the marriage vows, younger ones spoke of commitments'.

[91] Herring, *Caring and the Law* 199, suggests that 'Marriage should be about the promotion of caring and ensuring justice within the sharing of caring obligations. So understood limitations based on the gender of the parties or their sexual behaviour would be irrelevant.' The normative role of 'care' in defining and understanding the 'family' will be further considered below in ch 6, subs I(A), 'Care and Relationality'.

[92] Barlow and James, 'Regulating Marriage and Cohabitation in 21st Century Britain' 176.

[93] See eg Park and Rhead, 'Personal Relationships: Changing Attitudes Towards Sex, Marriage and Parenthood' *British Social Attitudes Survey* 30, 1–32. Within this, at 4, the authors show there has been a substantial decrease in religious identification in the UK in the past 30 years, finding that 48% of the UK population, in 2012, describe themselves as having no religious affiliation (this figure is down slightly from 51% in 2009), up from 31% in 1983.

[94] See eg ONS, 'Time Use Survey 2005', (July 2006), which suggested that men spend significantly less time per day than women on both childcare and housework, as well as Rosemary Crompton and Clare Lyonette, 'Who Does the Housework? The Division of Labour within the Home', *British Social Attitudes Survey 24*, (SAGE, 2008) and Jacqueline Scott and Elizabeth Clery, 'Gender Roles: An Incomplete Revolution?', *British Social Attitudes Survey 30*, (2013), available at: www.bsa.natcen.ac.uk/media/38723/bsa30_full_report_final.pdf. These issues will be considered further below in ch 5, subs II(B), 'What is the "Father" in the Law?'.

[95] *Bellinger v Bellinger* [2003] UKHL 21, [2003] 2 AC 467.

deeply embedded in the religious and social culture of this country.'[96] Writing extra-judicially, Baroness Hale has commented that 'We do not need to regard marriage as a religious sacrament to believe it is more than a mere individual contract.'[97] As O'Donovan observes:

> The sacred character of marriage as an institution calls on a past, understood and shared tradition, and on an eternal future, a perpetuity. Marriage is an emblem of continuity, of reproduction of the race, of the recruitment of new members, of the creation of new units of generation from one generation to another.[98]

Thus, I contend that these two contrasting conceptions of marriage (the traditional status-based understanding premised upon distinct gendered roles and the modern contract-based understanding of a 'partnership of equals') are both operating simultaneously within contemporary legal and cultural understandings of marriage. However, as noted above,[99] the traditional image of marriage and the gendered roles it reflects still retains substantial normative influence upon the legal understanding of the family.

C. Same-Sex Marriage and the Understanding of Marriage

The clearest example of a change in the legal definition of marriage is the opening of the relationship to same-sex couples[100] through recent legislation.[101] The introduction of this legislation epitomises the remarkable transformation of the legal approach to same-sex relationships in the UK.[102] This is especially notable

[96] ibid, per Lord Nicholls, at 480, for a consideration of the decision in *Bellinger* see eg Stephen Gilmore, '*Bellinger v Bellinger* – Not Quite Between the Ears and Between the Legs – Transsexualism and Marriage in the Lords' [2003] 15(3) *Child and Family Law Quarterly* 295.

[97] Brenda Hale, 'Equality and Autonomy in Family Law' (2011) 33 (1) *Journal of Social Welfare and Family Law* 3, 4.

[98] O'Donovan, *Family Law Matters* 47.

[99] In subs I(A), 'The Legal Definition of Marriage'.

[100] Some differences remain between marriage for same-sex and opposite-sex couples; one of these relates to the availability of certain types of religious marriage. In England and Wales, marriage under the rites of the Church of England will not be available to same-sex couples (Marriage (Same-Sex Couples) Act 2013, s 1(2)), while other religious bodies are required to 'opt-in' if they wish to perform same-sex marriages (Marriage (Same-Sex Couples) Act 2013, s 5). Similarly, in Scotland the legislation requires religious bodies to 'opt-in' (Marriage and Civil Partnership (Scotland) Act 2014, s 12 amends Marriage (Scotland) Act 1977, s 8) to solemnising same-sex marriage. Therefore, in both jurisdictions, those religious bodies who do not wish to allow same-sex marriage are not obligated to solemnise same-sex marriages (Marriage (Same-Sex Couples) Act 2013, s 2 and Marriage and Civil Partnership (Scotland) Act 2014, s 12). The Religious Society of Friends (Quakers), the Unitarian Church, the Movement for Reform Judaism and Liberal Judaism all supported the legislative approach and will perform same-sex marriages.

[101] In England and Wales, through the Marriage Same-Sex Couples Act 2013, which simply states in s 1(1) 'Marriage of same sex couples is lawful', and in Scotland, through the Marriage and Civil Partnership (Scotland) Act 2014.

[102] Given that consensual sexual intercourse between men was only decriminalised within the past 50 years.

given the governmental[103] and judicial[104] language used about homosexuality and same-sex relationships as recently as 25–35 years ago, as well as social attitudes towards same-sex relationships at that time.[105] The legislation opening marriage to same-sex couples follows[106] the ad hoc extension of various statutory provisions to same-sex couples[107] and the legal recognition of same-sex relationships through the Civil Partnership Act 2004.[108]

Some commentators have described the transformative potential[109] of the inclusion of same-sex couples in marriage on the institution itself.[110] Their contention is that the presence of same-sex couples within the institution of marriage could accelerate the aforementioned evolution of the understanding of marriage;[111] because as Harding argues 'Once marriage becomes a formal relationship between two persons (rather than "one man and one woman") the place of gender roles (wife/husband; mother/father) within the family are necessarily disrupted.'[112] However, other scholarship has been more cautious about the consequences and implications of same-sex marriage, suggesting that the inclusion of same-sex couples within marriage could instead act to normalise those

[103] Most infamously in s 28 of the Local Government Act 1988 which prohibited Local Authorities from promoting homosexuality and described it as a 'pretended family relationship'.

[104] See eg *Re D (An Infant) (Adoption: Parent's Consent)* [1977] AC 602, at 623, where Lord Wilberforce spoke of, 'homosexual tendencies, or of any similar abnormal conduct'. See further the child custody cases involving lesbian mothers, which will be discussed below in ch 5, subs III(A), 'The Judicial Approach to Lesbian Mothers'.

[105] In 1987, 64% of those surveyed believed that sexual relations between two adults of the same-sex were 'always wrong', in 2012 the figure was only 22% of those surveyed, Park and Rhead, 'Personal Relationships: Changing Attitudes Towards Sex, Marriage and Parenthood', *British Social Attitudes Survey 30*, 14–17.

[106] The approach in the UK follows the 'standard sequence' of legislative steps, described by Kees Waaldijk, 'Standard Sequences in the Legal Recognition of Homosexuality – Europe's Past, Present and Future' (1994) 4 *Australasian Gay and Lesbian Law Journal* 50, see further eg Lisa Glennon, 'Displacing the "Conjugal Family" in Legal Policy – A Progressive Move' [2005] 17(2) *Child and Family Law Quarterly* 141.

[107] See eg the succession entitlements under the Rent Act, discussed above in ch 1, and the inclusion within those couples who can adopt jointly in the Adoption and Children Act 2002, s 50 and the Adoption and Children (Scotland) Act 2007, s 29(3).

[108] See eg Nicholas Bamforth, '"The Benefits of Marriage in all but Name"? Same-Sex Couples and the Civil Partnership Act 2004' [2007] 19(2) *Child and Family Law Quarterly* 133, for the argument that civil partnership was explicitly designed to replicate the features of opposite-sex marriage.

[109] See eg Thomas B Stoddard, 'Why Gay People Should Seek the Right to Marry' in Mark Blasius and Shane Phelan (eds), *We Are Everywhere: A Historical Sourcebook of Gay and Lesbian Politics* (New York, Routledge, 1997); Cheshire Calhoun, *Feminism, the Family, and the Politics of the Closet: Lesbian and Gay Displacement* (New York, Oxford University Press, 2000) and for a review of some of the literature in this area see Victoria Clarke, 'Lesbian and Gay Marriage: Transformation or Normalisation?' (2003) 13(4) *Feminism and Psychology* 519.

[110] ONS, 'Marriages in England and Wales: 2015', (February 2018) 2, states that in 2015 there were 6493 marriages of same-sex couples in England and Wales, as well as a further 9156 conversions of civil partnerships into marriages; this suggests that so far same-sex marriages have made up a small amount of all marriages. Moreover, National Records of Scotland, 'Marriage and Civil Partnership Time Series Data', (August 2017), provide that in 2016 there were 998 same-sex marriages registered in Scotland.

[111] See above at subs I(B), 'Is the Understanding of Marriage Changing?'

[112] Rosie Harding, 'Sir Mark Potter and the Protection of the Traditional Family: Why Same Sex Marriage is (Still) a Feminist Issue' (2007) 1 (2) *Feminist Legal Studies* 223, 232.

same-sex relationships towards heteronormative standards.[113] On the basis of recent research, Auchmuty has noted that 'Gendered roles, albeit modified as a result of feminist successes, often seem to be the only roles younger gays and lesbians recognise.'[114] Thus, there exists a tension between this potential for transformation and the lived experiences of (particularly younger) same-sex couples which suggests the continuing power and influence of traditional (heterosexual) understandings.[115]

As discussed above, the perception of a division of gender roles continues to exist within a retained and surviving traditional, heterosexual construction of marriage.[116] These distinct gender roles, of male 'breadwinner' and female 'homemaker', were used to define appropriate behaviour for men and women in the private sphere of marriage, the home and the family.[117] In contrast, there was an understanding that same-sex couples were not so constrained by the pressure to replicate these socially constructed roles and thus were able to develop more individualised conceptions of the roles within their own families.[118] Diduck has previously observed that, 'Lesbian women and gay men … create their identities outside the norm, without the constraints it imposes on gender expectations and gender practices, arguably rendering their partnerships and familial identities freely chosen in a way that would be impossible for heterosexual individuals.'[119] However, more recent empirical research suggests that the traditional gendered

[113] Rosie Harding, 'Recognising (and Resisting) Regulation: Attitudes to the Introduction of Civil Partnership' (2008) 11(6) *Sexualities* 740, 748, notes that 'The creation of a legal framework for same-sex relationships becomes a mapping out of how things are supposed to go – two people meet, fall in love, enter into a civil partnership, become more emotionally mature, become financially dependent on each other, and so on – mirroring heteronormative discourse around societal expectations of marriage and life.'

[114] Rosemary Auchmuty, 'Dissolution or Disillusion: The Unravelling of Civil Partnerships' in Nicola Barker and Daniel Monk (eds), *From Civil Partnership to Same-Sex Marriage: Interdisciplinary Reflections* (Abingdon, Routledge, 2015) 216.

[115] Charlotte Bendall, 'A Break Away from the (Hetero)norm?: *Lawrence v Gallagher* [2012] 1 FCR 557; [2012] EWCA Civ 394' (2013) 21(3) *Feminist Legal Studies* 303, considers the influence of such heteronormative ideals on the first Court of Appeal decision regarding the dissolution of a civil partnership, observing, at 306 'what the Court does not say might be considered to be more interesting than what it does. The silences within the judgment may suggest an inability to conceive of a relationship between two men as entailing codependency and shared lives'.

[116] See above at subs I(A), 'The Legal Definition of Marriage'.

[117] See ch 2 above where this issue is explored in some detail. See further eg the Canadian Law Commission Report, 'Beyond Conjugality: Recognising and Supporting Close Adult Personal Relationships' (December 2001) 16, which observes, 'Close personal relationships between women and men have been and still are marked by unequal distributions of income, wealth and power.' Available at: https://dalspace.library.dal.ca/bitstream/handle/10222/10257/Beyond%20Conjugality%20Report%20EN.pdf?sequence=1&isAllowed=y.

[118] See eg Jeffrey Weeks, Brian Heaphy and Catherine Donovan, *Same Sex Intimacies: Families of Choice and Other Life Experiences* (London, Routledge, 2001). Moreover, research on the parenting practice of lesbian families suggests that the traditional gender roles are not replicated by the parenting of lesbian couples, see eg Gabb, 'Lesbian M/Otherhood: Strategies of Familial-linguistic Management in Lesbian Parent Families' and Dunne, 'Opting into Motherhood: Lesbians Blurring the Boundaries and Transforming the Meaning of Parenthood and Kinship'. This research is considered further below in ch 5, s III, 'The Role of Lesbian "Mothers" or "Parents"'.

[119] Diduck, *Law's Families* 30.

roles are exerting influence upon younger same-sex couples in construction of their identities. Heaphy, Smart and Einarsdottir observe that younger same-sex couples 'have a strong sense of the ordinariness of same-sex relationships'[120] and Auchmuty cautions that 'At worst, what we may see (and my findings suggest are already seeing) is same-sex couples behaving "just like" heterosexuals because these are the only spaces they can occupy that will be recognised and protected by law.'[121]

Thus, there seems to be some evidence that the formal equality granted by the legal recognition and regulation of same-sex relationships,[122] as well as the more positive societal attitudes towards same-sex relationships,[123] has shaped the identities of the younger generation of same-sex couples towards the 'ordinary' and an understanding of a closer equivalence with their opposite-sex peers. Indeed, Auchmuty observes that:

> Younger lesbians, like gay men, have no shared memory of the oppressiveness of marriage: marriage for them is simply a lifestyle choice. Similarly, younger gay men have no shared memory of outlaw status. Both sexes act upon the confident, if sometimes misplaced assumption that their relationships will be 'equal' with those of heterosexuals.[124]

The traditional construction of marriage with its separate gendered roles retains significant normative authority within both legal and cultural understandings[125] and these traditional (heteronormative) ideals and values appear to be influencing younger same-sex couples construction of their own relationships. As Heaphy, Smart and Einarsdottir observe 'Compared to previous generations of same-sex relationships as reported by a number of studies, the younger couples we studied appeared to be more actively invested in convention than in radical relational experimentation.'[126] It is submitted that as a consequence of the continuing significance of the traditional 'natural' construction of marriage, a fundamental transformation of the legal and cultural understanding of marriage remains an aspiration. Moreover, given the influence of these traditional roles upon the attitudes and identities of younger same-sex couples, the extent to which the inclusion of same-sex couples within marriage can radically alter

[120] Brian Heaphy, Carol Smart and Anna Einarsdottir, *Same Sex Marriages: New Generations, New Relationships* (Basingstoke, Palgrave MacMillan, 2013) 4.

[121] Rosemary Auchmuty, 'The Experience of Civil Partnership Dissolution: Not "Just Like Divorce"' (2016) 38(2) *Journal of Social Welfare and Family Law* 152, 172.

[122] For an examination of the role of formal and substantive equality in the debates on same-sex marriage, see eg Robert Leckey, 'Must Equal Mean Identical? Same-sex Couples and Marriage' (2014) 10(1) *International Journal of Law in Context* 5.

[123] See eg Park and Rhead, 'Personal Relationships: Changing Attitudes Towards Sex, Marriage and Parenthood' *British Social Attitudes Survey* 30, 14–17.

[124] Auchmuty, 'Dissolution or Disillusion: The Unravelling of Civil Partnerships' in Barker and Monk (eds), *From Civil Partnership to Same-Sex Marriage: Interdisciplinary Reflections* 203.

[125] As discussed above at subs I(B), 'Is the Understanding of Marriage Changing?'.

[126] Heaphy, Smart and Einarsdottir, *Same Sex Marriages: New Generations, New Relationships* 4.

the institution of marriage itself remains unclear. Thus, it appears that tension will continue between the transformative potential of the inclusion of same-sex couples within marriage and the rhetorical power of the traditional understanding of marriage to normalise same-sex relationships towards heteronormative standards and roles.

II. The Centrality of Conjugality

As discussed above, in spite of the decrease in the number of marriages taking place in the UK,[127] marriage remains central to the legal understanding of the 'family'.[128] I will argue that legal regulation is extended to other cohabiting, interdependent, monogamous, sexual relationships on the basis that those relationships are regarded as sufficiently 'marriage-like' because they share enough of the features and characteristics traditionally associated with marriage.[129] In drawing comparisons with marriage, I will suggest that emphasis is placed upon one particular feature of the relationship; the existence of a conjugal or sexual element.[130] The centrality of conjugality to the regulation of other adult relationships is noteworthy, given that conjugality is not a requirement within marriage itself; as Sir James Munby recently observed in *Re X (A Child)*[131] 'In short, the marriage is a marriage. The fact that it is platonic, and without a sexual component, is, as a matter of long-established law, neither here nor there and in truth no concern of the judges or of the State.'[132] Nevertheless, I will contend that the centrality of conjugality (understood as the combination of a sexual relationship, living together and interdependence) within the legal regulation of adult relationships illustrates the continuing influence of the nuclear family upon the legal understanding of the family, because relationships are regulated on the basis that they can be located within the central nexus of that nuclear family.

In this section, I will begin by considering some of the justifications for the legal regulation of cohabitation, before arguing that cohabitation is being

[127] ONS, 'Marriages in England and Wales: 2015', (February 2018) 2.

[128] At subs I(B), 'Is the Understanding of Marriage Changing?'.

[129] Heather Brook, 'Zombie Law: Conjugality, Annulment and the (Married) Living Dead', 61, argues that '"marriage" – as a singular, self-evident entity – can no longer sustain its historical place at the top of a hierarchical order, but must instead be placed alongside a range of conjugal relationships'.

[130] Subsequently in ch 6, subs I(A), 'Care and Relationality', I will explore in more detail the potential of a normative shift from conjugality to care within the legal understanding of the 'family'.

[131] *Re X (A Child)* [2018] EWFC 15.

[132] ibid, at para 7. Indeed, in English Law marriage merely requires to be consummated to be considered valid; marriage is voidable if it has not been consummated due to both 'incapacity' (Matrimonial Causes Act 1973, s 12(a)) and 'wilful refusal' (Matrimonial Causes Act 1973, s 12(b)) see eg *Clarke v Clarke* [1943] 2 All ER 540 and *R v R* [1952] 1 All ER 1194. In Scots Law it is the *potential* for conjugality that is important, as a marriage is voidable on the ground of incurable impotency, see eg *L v L* 1931 SC 477 and *J v J* 1978 SLT 128. Therefore, in neither jurisdiction does marriage need to involve an ongoing sexual relationship. However, I argue that the dominant understanding of marriage is premised upon a conjugal relationship subsisting between the parties.

regulated on the basis that it is a 'marriage-like' relationship (subsection A). I will then explore the justification for the centrality of conjugality to the legal regulation of adult personal relationships, arguing that the conjugal couple form is understood as providing greater social stability particularly in regard to the upbringing of children (subsection B). I will conclude by contending that this emphasis on stability reflects the central nexus of the conjugal relationship and the parent/child relationship within the nuclear family model.

A. The Legal Regulation of Cohabitation

Over the past 50 years there has been a significant demographic shift, away from the dominance of marriage and toward an increase in unmarried cohabitation.[133] Once a small minority, cohabiting couples (and their children) now make up around 17% of families in the UK.[134] Over the same period there has been a corresponding increase in the social acceptance of unmarried cohabitation.[135] Barlow and James suggest that 'the social and cultural norms which made people feel that they had or ought to get married in order to be accepted as a decent member of society, seem to have disappeared. Cohabitation is now a perfectly acceptable family form'.[136] The change in the cultural understanding of cohabitation is apparent from the language of the government, which now endorses a range of family forms. This is exemplified by the previous coalition's 'Programme for Government', which states: 'The Government believes that strong and stable families of all kinds are the bedrock of a strong and stable society'.[137] In spite of this rise in cohabitation, the law in the UK was initially reluctant to acknowledge and regulate these relationships.[138] Indeed, even after such acknowledgment, the subsequent legal responses to cohabitation have been varied, ranging from the inclusion of cohabitants within certain statutory rights[139] on an ad hoc basis,[140] through to essentially

[133] ONS, 'Short Report: Cohabitation in the UK, 2012' (November 2012) 1.

[134] ONS, 'Families and Households: 2017' (November 2017) 5.

[135] Park and Rhead, 'Personal Relationships: Changing Attitudes Towards Sex, Marriage and Parenthood', *British Social Attitudes Survey 30*, 7–14.

[136] Barlow and James, 'Regulating Marriage and Cohabitation in 21st Century Britain', 160, see also Auchmuty, 'Law and the Power of Feminism: How Marriage Lost its Power to Oppress Women', who goes further, suggesting, at 81 'The tipping point has been reached; not only has cohabitation ceased to be a preparation for marriage, and become an alternative to it, but it will soon be the *preferred* alternative.'

[137] 'The Coalition: Our Programme for Government', (May 2010) 19.

[138] See eg the evolution of judicial attitudes concerning the inclusion of cohabitants within the definition of 'family' under the Rent Acts, between the 1950s and the 1970s, discussed above in ch 1, subs II(A)(iii), 'Unmarried Cohabitants'.

[139] See eg Child Support Act 1991, Family Law Act 1996, Pt IV, Fatal Accidents Act 1976, s 1(3)(b) and Matrimonial Homes (Family Protection) (Scotland) Act 1981, s 18.

[140] Rebecca Probert, 'Cohabitation in Twentieth Century England and Wales: Law and Policy' (2004) 26(1) *Law and Policy* 13, 23, observes that in the 1970s 'Parliament was beginning to include cohabitants within the scope of legislation, but in a very ad hoc fashion.'

ignoring the relationship and treating the parties to it as (legal) strangers,[141] to the creation in Scotland of a statutory regime specifically for cohabiting couples.[142]

The inclusion of cohabitants within various statutory provisions suggests recognition that cohabiting couples should be subject to some legal regulation. Scots law differs from English law on whether such regulation should take the form of a statutory regime specifically for cohabitants.[143] A significant reason for the lack of consensus is that, as Baroness Hale observed in *Stack v Dowden*[144] 'Cohabitation comes in many different shapes and sizes.'[145] Such relationships range from those where the parties have actively chosen to reject marriage in order not to subject their relationships to legal regulation,[146] to those relationships where the parties erroneously believe themselves to have formed a 'common law marriage',[147] to those couples that view their cohabitation as a temporary or transitional arrangement, which could be converted to a marriage at an (as yet undetermined) future point.[148] Consequently, Chan observes that 'The understandings that underpin de facto partnerships find no natural, unitary expression to be captured by law.'[149]

Given this diversity of relationships, on what basis does the law seek to regulate cohabitation? I argue that while the law is influenced by both changes in social attitudes and a paternalistic desire to protect vulnerable (female) cohabitants, the central justification for legal regulation of cohabitation is acknowledging that

[141] As occurred in relation to the absence of financial provision upon relationship breakdown in England and Wales, see eg *Burns v Burns* [1984] Ch 317, where May LJ stated, at 334 'the resolution of these disputes must depend upon the ascertainment according to normal principles of the respective property rights between the man and the woman'. Although this position has been altered by the more recent judicial developments regarding constructive trusts, see *Stack v Dowden* [2007] UKHL 17, [2007] 1 FLR 1858 and *Jones v Kernott* [2011] UKSC 53, [2012] 1 FLR 45.

[142] Family Law (Scotland) Act 2006, ss 25–30.

[143] The Law Commission Report, 'Cohabitation: The Financial Consequences of Relationship Breakdown' (Law Com No 307, July 2007), available at: www.gov.uk/government/uploads/system/uploads/attachment_data/file/228881/7182.pdf, proposed a statutory regime for England and Wales similar to the Scottish approach. However, there are currently no plans from the government to act upon the recommendations of the report. In a written Ministerial Statement on 6 September 2011, the Parliamentary Under-Secretary of State, Ministry of Justice, Jonathan Djanogly, stated that 'We do not therefore intend to take forward the Law Commission's recommendations for reform of cohabitation law in this parliamentary term.' (Hansard HC Col 16WS).

[144] *Stack v Dowden* [2007] UKHL 17, [2007] 1 FLR 1858.

[145] ibid, per Baroness Hale, at 1874, see further Lord Hoffman in *Re P (Adoption: Unmarried Couples)* [2008] UKHL 38, [2008] 2 FLR 1084, at 1090, who stated of cohabitation, these 'relationships may vary from quasi-marital to ephemeral'.

[146] Anne Barlow, Carole Burgoyne, Elizabeth Clerly and Janet Smithson, 'Cohabitation and the Law: Myths, Money and the Media' *British Social Attitudes Survey* 24 (SAGE, 2008) 33, observe that 31% of those currently cohabiting had previously been married, compared to 17% of those now married and suggests that 'in some instances, cohabitation might be a refuge for those disillusioned by previous experiences of marriage'.

[147] See Rebecca Probert, 'Common-law Marriage: Myths and Misunderstandings' [2008] 20(1) *Child and Family Law Quarterly* 1, for a consideration of the development of a common law marriage myth within law.

[148] Barlow, Burgoyne, Clerly and Smithson, 'Cohabitation and the Law: Myths, Money and the Media', *British Social Attitudes Survey 24*, 33, observed that, in 2006, 56% of cohabiting relationships ended in marriage.

[149] Chan, 'Cohabitation, Civil Partnership, Marriage and the Equal Sharing Principle', 55.

cohabitation is a 'marriage-like' relationship, based primarily upon the shared conjugality which features in these different types of relationship. The aforementioned changes in social attitudes in the UK have resulted in a far closer equivalence being drawn between marriage and cohabitation than was apparent historically.[150] Eekelaar and MacLean have observed 'Our evidence shows that married and unmarried people who are living together share many values. Indeed, the similarities in the normative determinants of their behaviour may be greater than the dissimilarities.'[151] The dominant cultural understanding now envisages significant similarities between the two relationships and their functions.[152] These shifts have been, and continue to be, a significant factor supporting further legal regulation of cohabitation.[153]

The normative resonance of the unfairly treated, 'deserving' cohabitant (the 'Mrs Burns figure')[154] has resulted in a paternalistic motive for legal regulation; to provide some protection for economically vulnerable cohabitants. This is visible in the Scottish Law Commission Report,[155] upon which the statutory regime for cohabitants was based, which stated that the proposed regime 'should be confined to the easing of certain legal difficulties and the remedying of certain situations which are widely perceived as being harsh and unfair'.[156] The emphasis on vulnerable cohabitants[157] is supported by the existence of a long-standing belief in 'common-law marriage' amongst the general public.[158] The continuing prevalence

[150] Anne Barlow, 'Cohabitation Law Reform – Messages from Research' (2006) 14(2) *Feminist Legal Studies* 167, 173, observes that 'the social norms whereby most people use marriage and cohabitation as a personal lifestyle choice have diverged from the legal norms which continue to privilege marriage over cohabitation in many significant ways, although there is no real understanding of this by the British public, it seems'.

[151] Eekelaar and MacLean, 'Marriage and the Moral Bases of Personal Responsibility' 538.

[152] Park and Rhead, 'Personal Relationships: Changing Attitudes Towards Sex, Marriage and Parenthood', British Social Attitudes Survey 30, 9, observe that only 42% of respondents agree with the statement, 'people who want children ought to get married', this figure is down from 71% in 1989.

[153] See eg The Law Commission Report, 'Cohabitation: The Financial Consequences of Relationship Breakdown', (July 2007), para 1.6, at 2, which states 'Cohabitation outside marriage in England and Wales has become increasingly common over recent decades, and is expected to become more prevalent in the future.'

[154] *Burns v Burns* [1984] Ch. 317, in the course of his judgment, May LJ stated, at 345 'I think that she can justifiably say that fate has not been kind to her.'

[155] Scottish Law Commission, 'Report on Family Law', (No 135, May 1992), available at: www.scotlawcom.gov.uk/files/5912/8015/2668/Report%20on%20family%20law%20Report%20135.pdf.

[156] ibid, para 16.1, at 115, see further the Law Commission Report 'Cohabitation: The Financial Consequences of Relationship Breakdown', (July 2007), para 1.4, at 2, which similarly proposed a regime that 'would provide economically vulnerable members of society with the private means to rebuild their lives and ensure a fairer division of assets on relationship breakdown'.

[157] Such language was also apparent in a written ministerial statement regarding the Bill which subsequently became the Family Law (Scotland) Act 2006, Deputy Minister for Justice, Hugh Henry, 'Response to Justice 1 Committee Stage 1 Report', (August, 2005) 14, stated that 'the law should safeguard the interests of those in cohabiting relationships who may be vulnerable', available at: www.scottish.parliament.uk/S2_Justice1Committee/Reports/SEresponseFamilyLawStage1.pdf.

[158] Fran Wasoff and Claudia Martin, 'Scottish Social Attitudes Survey 2004: Family Module Report' (August 2005) 41, found that 51% of respondents believed that some form of common law marriage existed in Scotland, available at: www.scotland.gov.uk/Resource/Doc/57346/0016386.pdf. See further Barlow, Burgoyne, Clerly and Smithson, 'Cohabitation and the Law: Myths, Money and the

of this belief in common law marriage results in many cohabiting couples incorrectly believing that their relationship will, at some stage, acquire the rights and obligations associated with a marriage.[159] Thus, the existence of these common societal misconceptions regarding common law marriage provides additional paternalistic motivations for the legal regulation of cohabitation.

Wong argues that the legal regulation of cohabitation involves 'a stretching of the marriage model to accommodate the inclusion of other close personal relationship … The basis for inclusion of other types of close personal relationships such as opposite-sex and same-sex cohabitation must thus be based on similarity or sameness'.[160] Therefore, I suggest that the law primarily regulates cohabitation on the basis that cohabiting couples share sufficient features and characteristics with married couples and therefore can be located within the central nexus of the nuclear family. In this regard, legislation often defines cohabitation by comparison with marriage, as is exemplified by the Family Law (Scotland) Act 2006, which defines opposite-sex[161] cohabitants as 'a man and a woman who are (or were) living together as if they were husband and wife'.[162] Thus, cohabitation is regulated because it is constructed and understood as being a 'marriage-like' relationship[163] on the basis of its conjugality.[164] Any legal recognition of cohabitation is premised on the basis that, as Bottomley argues 'by bringing cohabitants into family

Media' *British Social Attitudes Survey* 24, who also found 51% of respondents believed that common law marriage existed in England and Wales.

[159] Prior to its abolition by s 3 of the Family Law (Scotland) Act 2006, in Scotland an 'irregular marriage' could be constituted through marriage by cohabitation with habit and repute, therefore the existence of this doctrine may have contributed to the continued prevalence of the common law marriage myth in Scottish society.

[160] Simone Wong, 'Cohabitation and The Law Commission's Project' (2006) 14(2) *Feminist Legal Studies* 145, 151.

[161] A similar approach is used in relation to same-sex cohabitation, in s 25(1)(b), which is defined as 'two persons of the same sex who are (or were) living together as if they were civil partners', this definition ceases to have effect as a result of s 4(4) of the Marriage and Civil Partnership (Scotland) Act 2014 and is replaced by 'living together as if they were married to each other'.

[162] See Family Law (Scotland) Act 2006, s 25(1)(a) for examples of similar definitions from English Law, see eg Fatal Accidents Act 1976, s 1(3)(iii), Family Law Act 1996, s 62(1) and Inheritance (Provision for Family and Dependants) Act 1975, s 1(1A)(b).

[163] Barlow and James, 'Regulating Marriage and Cohabitation in 21st Century Britain', suggest, at 153 'cohabitation … has taken on the functions of marriage. Conversely, the institution of marriage itself has also changed, perhaps becoming more akin to unmarried cohabitation'.

[164] However, it is worth noting that the law still does not envisage a direct comparison between the two relationships, instead acknowledging that cohabitation shares enough characteristics with marriage to deserve some (lesser) recognition. This distinction is evident from Scottish Law Commission, 'Report on Family Law', (No 135, May 1992), para 16.1, at 115, which states that the proposals should not, 'undermine marriage', as well as the Law Commission Report 'Cohabitation: The Financial Consequences of Relationship Breakdown', (July 2007), para 1.2, which states, at 1 'The scheme would not equate cohabitants with married couples or give them equivalent rights.' As such cohabitation remains understood within the law as an inferior relationship to marriage, which remains the pinnacle or 'gold standard' of legally regulated conjugal relationships. See further Simone Wong, 'Cohabitation and The Law Commission's Project', who comments, at 151 'a distinction is still being drawn between marriage and cohabitation, which emphasises the centrality of commitment. It is, however, not just the notion of commitment but the *type* of commitment that is critical.'

law, a modified marriage law regime, law and social policy might be able to find ways of stabilising domestic units through a reinforcement of family values carried through the application of a marriage (like) model'.[165] The law is able to bring cohabiting couples within the scope of its (nuclear) understanding of family by constructing cohabitation as a 'marriage-like' relationship. Thus, the regulation of cohabiting couples shows that the traditional, nuclear family remains central to the legal understanding of the family.

B. The Justification for the Centrality of Conjugality

Conjugality is central to legal categorisation of relationships as 'marriage-like'.[166] Barker claims that 'By continuing to legally privilege marriage and other conjugal relationships, the state is reinforcing this romantic mystique, drawing a boundary around sexual relationships as the "ideal"'.[167] Through the centrality of the conjugal relationship, the ideals and values of marriage and the traditional nuclear family continue to be promoted. If an adult relationship does not include at least the possibility of conjugality or a sexual partnership,[168] it will be situated outside the boundaries of the law's conception of family.[169] Wong observes that 'cohabitation is being distinguished from other (inter)dependent relationships and a key element of that distinction is that the parties' interdependence stems from being in a relationship involving commitment and intimacy'.[170]

[165] Anne Bottomley, 'From Mrs Burns to Mrs Oxley: Do Co-Habiting Women (Still) Need Marriage Law' (2006) 14(2) *Feminist Legal Studies* 181, 206.

[166] See eg *Crake v Supplementary Benefits Commission* [1982] 1 All ER 498, *Kimber v Kimber* [2000] 1 FLR 383, *Garrad v Inglis* 2014 GWD 1–17 and *M v T* 2011 GWD 40–828, for judicial consideration of the influence of conjugality within the definition of cohabitation, under both English and Scots law.

[167] Nicola Barker, 'Sex and the Civil Partnership Act: The Future of (Non) Conjugality' (2006) 14(2) *Feminist Legal Studies* 241, 248.

[168] Although there is some debate as to the nature and significance of sex within same-sex marriage. This arises because the traditional definition of adultery is retained by the legislation, Sch 4, Pt 3 of the Marriage (Same-Sex Couples) Act 2013 amends s 1 of the Matrimonial Causes Act 1973, providing that 'Only conduct between the respondent and a person of the opposite sex may constitute adultery', see also s 5(2) of the Marriage and Civil Partnership (Scotland) Act 2014, which amends s 1 of the Divorce (Scotland) Act 1976, inserting a similar provision. Furthermore, the other statutory provisions which relate to the importance of sexual activity within marriage are simply not extended to same-sex marriages; in England and Wales Sch 4, Pt 4 of the Marriage (Same-Sex Couples) Act 2013 amends s 12 of the Matrimonial Causes Act 1973 and states that the provisions regarding non-consummation 'do not apply to the marriage of a same sex couple' and in Scotland s 5(1) of the Marriage and Civil Partnership (Scotland) Act 2014, states 'For the avoidance of doubt, the rule of law which provides for a marriage to be voidable by reason of impotence has effect only in relation to a marriage between persons of different sexes.' For a critique of the legislative approach to these issues, which suggests that this approach results in the invisibility of homosexual sex, see eg Lucy Crompton, 'Where's the Sex in Same-Sex Marriage?' [2013] 43(5) *Fam Law* 564.

[169] See eg s 11(a)(i) of the Matrimonial Causes Act 1973 prohibits marriages between people who are related to each other within the 'forbidden degrees' of relationships, for the similar Scots law rule see s 2 and Sch 1 of the Marriage (Scotland) Act 1977.

[170] Simone Wong, 'Shared Commitment, Interdependency and Property Relations: A Socio-Legal Project for Cohabitation' [2012] 24(1) *Child and Family Law Quarterly* 60, 61.

Non-conjugal relationships[171] that have sometimes been suggested as deserving of legal recognition[172] include those between adult siblings who live together,[173] relationships between residential carers and the person cared for[174] and wider recognition and regulation of adult relationships based upon 'care'.[175] Herring has argued 'that what might make a relationship worthy of promotion by the state is care and mutual support, rather than sex'.[176] However, regarding the relationship between adult siblings, in *Burden v UK*[177] the European Court of Human Rights observed that:

> [T]he relationship between siblings is qualitatively of a different nature to that between married couples and homosexual civil partners ... The fact that the applicants have chosen to live together all their adult lives ... does not alter this essential difference between the two types of relationship.[178]

While such relationships share some of the characteristics of those that are regulated and may be deserving of some form of legal recognition,[179] the judgment proceeds on the basis that there is a 'qualitative' or 'essential' difference which limits the scope for comparable legal recognition.[180] Such relationships, because

[171] Under the Rent Acts non-conjugal adult relationships were consistently held to be outside the 'de facto familial nexus' required to be considered a 'family member', see the decisions in *Ross v Collins* [1964] 1 WLR 425, *Joram Developments Ltd v Sharratt* [1979] 1 WLR 928 and *Sefton Holdings v Cairns* [1988] 2 FLR 109, considered above in ch 1, subs II(A)(ii), 'The Role of the "De Facto Familial Nexus"'.

[172] See eg the Canadian Law Commission Report, 'Beyond Conjugality: Recognising and Supporting Close Adult Personal Relationships', (December 2001), which suggested a radical restructuring of the regulation of adult personal relationships in Canada, moving away completely from the centrality of conjugality, however these recommendations were not enacted by the Canadian government.

[173] During debates on the Civil Partnership Act 2004, the image of the 'spinster sisters' was invoked repeatedly by opponents of the Bill.

[174] See further eg Brian Sloan, *Informal Carers and Private Law*, (Oxford, Hart Publishing, 2012) and Beverley Clough, 'What About Us? A Case for Legal Recognition of Interdependence in Informal Care Relationships' (2014) 36(2) *Journal of Social Welfare and Family Law* 129.

[175] The normative role of 'care' within the legal understanding of the 'family' will be considered in more detail below in ch 6, subs I(A), 'Care and Relationality'. See further eg Tronto, *Moral Boundaries: A Political Argument for an Ethic of Care* and Noddings, *Starting at Home: Caring and Social Policy*.

[176] Herring, *Caring and the Law* 192.

[177] *Burden v UK* (2008) 47 EHRR 38, this case involved an unsuccessful challenge, under Art 1 of Protocol 1 in conjunction with Art 14, by two elderly sisters who had lived together for their entire lives, of their exclusion from the spousal/civil partner inheritance tax exemption. See further eg Rosemary Auchmuty, 'Beyond Couples' (2009) 17(2) *Feminist Legal Studies* 205.

[178] ibid, at 876.

[179] Barker, 'Sex and the Civil Partnership Act: The Future of (Non) Conjugality', comments, at 255, that 'It may be that certain parts of the law relating to marriage and divorce would be helpful for many types of relationships not currently recognised, even though other parts of marriage might be deeply problematic.'

[180] Interestingly in *Morgan v Morgan* [1959] P 92, Mr Commissioner Latey QC, at 101, observed that 'Many elderly and aged people intermarry on the basis, implied or agreed upon, that they come together merely for companionship and without any thought of sexual relations.' This statement appears to suggest a judicial acknowledgement that some marriages may be formed without any intention of conjugality. See further the more recent statement of Sir James Munby in *Re X (A Child)* [2018] EWFC 15, at para 8, that 'A sexual relationship is not necessary for there to be a valid marriage.' Although such marriages would remain voidable in terms of s 12 of the Matrimonial Causes Act 1973.

of their inherent and essential lack of conjugality,[181] cannot be located within the central nexus of the nuclear family model[182] and as a consequence these relationships are categorised differently by the law than conjugal relationships.[183]

What then justifies the centrality of the conjugal relationship within the law? I argue that the conjugal couple form is associated with 'stability', which is understood by government as a social value worth promoting,[184] both in terms of the relationship itself and in relation to providing a stable and secure upbringing for children. This association of the conjugal couple and children reflects the central nexus between those two relationships within the nuclear family. This construction is based upon a particular understanding of the purpose of marriage in society, which is premised upon the historical conception that marriage, and the nuclear family, provided significantly more social stability than other, alternative, family forms.[185] As Herring notes 'If a person falls ill, or becomes unemployed, and so no longer has an income, then the financial responsibility is likely to fall on the state if that person is single, whereas spouses or civil partners would depend on each other.'[186] Judicial reliance upon similar ideas about the significance of marriage was evident as recently as the judgment of Lord Hoffmann in *Re P (Adoption: Unmarried Couples)*,[187] where he stated 'Statistics show that married couples, who have accepted a legal commitment to each other, tend to have more stable relationships than unmarried couples'.[188] However, such stability is no longer exclusively associated with marriage; the law now recognises that stability can also be a feature of long-term, cohabiting, conjugal relationships which are non-marital. In her concurring judgment in *Re P*, Baroness Hale acknowledged that 'Some unmarried relationships are much more stable than some marriages, and vice versa.'[189] The law's understanding of family is now organised around the conjugal couple form (rather than marriage specifically), which, I submit, is constructed as performing the same central role that was historically exclusive to marriage. As Stychin observes 'The stable couple form, it is argued, is good for the individual, for the couple and for society (and the economy) as a whole. Long-term, traditional, stable, legally recognised relationships thus become the socially preferred option.'[190]

[181] Baroness Ruth Deech, 'Sisters Sisters – And Other Family Members' [2010] 40(4) *Fam Law* 375, 380, suggests that 'Thus does English law continue to prefer the idle sexual partner over the deserving family member.'

[182] This reflects the approach identified to defining 'family member' in the context of the Rent Acts above in ch 1, subs II(A)(ii), 'The Role of the "De Facto Familial Nexus"'.

[183] See eg Carl Stychin, 'Not (Quite) a Horse and Carriage' (2006) 14(1) *Feminist Legal Studies* 79, who commented, in the context of the debates around civil partnership, at 81, that 'if the state is going to recognise relationship forms outside the institution of marriage, then it should take the opportunity to consider real alternatives to the marriage model, that might be available more widely; a model in which conjugality might be deprivileged'.

[184] See eg 'The Coalition: Our Programme for Government', (May 2010) 19.

[185] See eg *Campbell v Campbell* [1977] 1 All ER 1.

[186] Herring, *Family Law* 122.

[187] [2008] 2 FLR 1084.

[188] ibid, per Lord Hoffmann, at 1090.

[189] ibid, per Baroness Hale, at 1121.

[190] Carl Stychin, 'Family Friendly? Rights, Responsibilities and Relationship Recognition?' in Diduck and O'Donovan (eds), *Feminist Perspectives on Family Law* 24.

Related to this is the emphasis placed on the stable, conjugal couple form and the nuclear family as the environment best suited to achieving the positive development of children, which illustrates the importance of the central nexus between the conjugal relationship and the parental/child relationship. Traditionally, it was marriage that was positioned as providing this stable environment for children.[191] A preference for marriage was evident in the language of government as recently as 1998, when a government consultation stated that 'children need stability and security … marriage is still the surest foundation for raising children and remains the choice of the majority of people in Britain'.[192] This understanding was also reflected in judicial language; writing extra-judicially, Elizabeth Butler-Sloss observed that 'One most important aspect of a child's welfare is the need to grow up in a secure and stable environment and to be loved and cared for … The most secure family is achieved through marriage.'[193] This conception was exemplified by the judgment of Sir Mark Potter in *Wilkinson v Kitzinger (No. 2)*,[194] who describes marriage 'as a means not only of encouraging monogamy but also the procreation of children and their development and nurture in a family unit (or "nuclear family")'.[195] Therefore, I agree with Sheldon's description that 'The importance of providing a "stable" base for children is frequently asserted, with "stability" standing as a shorthand for heterosexual marital monogamy.'[196] Thus, the relationship between marriage and the appropriate development of children was traditionally presented as axiomatic within the law.

However, the law has long recognised that the procreation of children, or even the possibility of such procreation, is not required for a marriage to be valid. The judiciary acknowledged this as early as the 1940s, in *Baxter v Baxter*,[197] where Viscount Jowitt stated that 'It is indisputable that the institution of marriage generally is not necessary for the procreation of children; nor does it appear to be a principal end of marriage as understood in Christendom'.[198] This has also been

[191] In the nineteenth century ecclesiastical courts, in *D-e v A-g* (1845) Rob Ecc 279, Dr Lushington, at 281, described the 'two principal ends of matrimony' as 'a lawful indulgence of the passions to prevent licentiousness, and the procreation of children, according to the evident design of Divine Providence'.

[192] 'Supporting Families: A Consultation Document', (Home Office, December 1998), para 8, available at: http://webarchive.nationalarchives.gov.uk/+/http:/www.nationalarchives.gov.uk/ERORecords/HO/421/2/P2/ACU/SUPPFAM.HTM.

[193] Elizabeth Butler-Sloss, 'Ethical Considerations in Family Law' (2006) *Web Journal of Current Legal Issues* 4.

[194] [2007] 1 FLR 295.

[195] ibid, per Sir Mark Potter, at 329.

[196] Sheldon, 'Fragmenting Fatherhood: The Regulation of Reproductive Technologies', 534, this statement was made in the context of the parliamentary debates on the Human Fertilisation and Embryology Act 1990.

[197] *Baxter v Baxter* [1948] AC 274.

[198] ibid, per Viscount Jowitt, at 286, this contrasted with the decision in *D-e v A-g* (1845) Rob Ecc 279, as to the centrality of procreation to marriage, which had been supported, only three years prior to *Baxter*, by Pilcher J in *Cowen v Cowen* [1945] 2 All ER 197, who stated, at 199, that the procreation of children was 'One of the purposes for which marriage was ordained'.

reflected in contemporary judicial understanding, as illustrated by the judgment of Baroness Hale in *Ghaidan v Godin-Mendoza*,[199] where she stated:

> [T]he capacity to bear or beget children has never been a prerequisite of a valid marriage in English law … A marriage, let alone a relationship analogous to marriage, can exist without either the presence or the possibility of children from that relationship.[200]

Of course, correlation does not prove causation, and as Chan has observed: 'There is little evidence to suggest that stability is caused by rather than correlated with marriage.'[201] More recently this 'stable base' has been extended from only referring to marriage to including other conjugal relationships. This expansion of the law has partly resulted from the social shift toward unmarried cohabitation.[202] The extension to other conjugal relationships has also been supported by evidence from empirical research into children's outcomes, such as that undertaken by Crawford et al, who commented that 'We … regard our results as a strong indication that marriage plays a relatively small role, if any, in promoting children's early cognitive or socio-emotional development.'[203] Thus, I suggest that it is having two parents in an ongoing, stable, monogamous, conjugal, cohabiting relationship which is now understood by the law as being intrinsically favourable to children, regardless of whether that relationship is formalised as marriage. The clear association between the conjugal couple form and the upbringing of children suggests that it is the central nexus of the nuclear family between the conjugal relationship and the parent/child relationship which remains fundamental to the understanding of family within the law.[204]

Herring questions the normative significance granted to conjugality in this context, arguing 'Whether couples are same-sex or opposite sex; married or not; sexual or not, does not, I suggest affect the contribution they make to the social good. They deserve the same support and protection.'[205] However, regardless of this normative argument,[206] it is apparent that the law continues to

[199] [2004] UKHL 30, [2004] 2 AC 557.

[200] ibid, per Baroness Hale, at 606.

[201] Chan, 'Cohabitation, Civil Partnership, Marriage and the Equal Sharing Principle' 52.

[202] See eg ONS, 'Families and Households: 2017' (November 2017).

[203] Claire Crawford, Alissa Goodman, Ellen Greaves and Rob Joyce, 'Cohabitation, Marriage and Child Outcomes: An Empirical Analysis of the Relationship between Marital Status and Child Outcomes in the UK using the Millennium Cohort Study' (2012) 24(2) *Child and Family Law Quarterly* 176, 195.

[204] As discussed above in regards to 'family' under the Rent Act in ch 1, subs II(A)(ii), 'The Role of the "De Facto Familial Nexus"' and in terms of the interpretation of 'family life' in Art 8 of the ECHR in ch 1, subs II(B), 'The Definition of "Family Life" under Article 8 of the European Convention on Human Rights' as well as throughout ch 1 more generally.

[205] Herring, *Caring and the Law* 199.

[206] It is not the intention of this chapter to assess whether the centrality of conjugality is the most appropriate normative approach to regulating adult personal relationships, nor whether an approach based upon mutuality, interdependence and 'care' would better serve the needs of a diversity of relationships. However, these issues will be considered below in ch 6, subs I(A), 'Care and Relationality'.

draw a distinction between relationships on the basis of conjugality and sexual partnership.[207] As Bottomley and Wong comment 'What these emerging patterns make clear is that the extensions to cover others tend to include the drawing of lines around a central nexus of either marriage or sexual partnership.'[208] The legal regulation of non-marital conjugal relationships occurs when these relationships are constructed to some degree as emulating the social functions of marriage and reproducing its characteristics and values. Therefore, as Diduck comments:

> The 'new' families of law thus look remarkably like the old ones. Coupledom and conjugality remain central … it is ironic that at the same time as policy seems increasingly to be moving away from the view that marriage should be the only state sanctioned intimate relationship; the test for others is the degree to which they are 'marriage-like'.[209]

I have argued that the centrality of conjugal relationships is premised upon the perceived value provided by the conjugal couple form regarding social stability and because of the value that relationship possesses in relation to securing the healthy and happy upbringing of children, within the central nexus that comprises the nuclear family. Thus, these relationships are now understood as being as capable as marriage of comprising that central nexus of relationships within the nuclear family.[210] On this basis, I submit that the law continues to base its understanding of 'family' around marriage (and 'marriage-like' conjugal relationships) and the traditional nuclear family.

More generally, in this chapter, I have considered the legal regulation of adult personal relationships and argued that such regulation is centred upon the conjugal relationship and remains influenced by traditional understandings of marriage and the nuclear family. Therefore, I endorse Diduck and Kaganas' observation that 'law's model is still the private heterosexual traditional family. While the range of people who may be allowed into it may have increased, the norms by which they must live remain the same'.[211] To begin, I considered the legal definition and understanding of marriage; I observed that the traditional understanding of marriage and the associated division of gender roles continues to influence the contemporary understanding of marriage. However, I argued that recently there has been some evidence of a shift in the legal and social understanding of marriage, moving away from elements of the historical definition, as indicated by the recent

[207] As illustrated by the decision of the ECHR in *Burden v UK* (2008) 47 EHRR 38 and by the cases concerning the Rent Acts discussed above in ch 1, subs II(A)(ii), 'The Role of the "De Facto Familial Nexus"'.

[208] Anne Bottomley and Simone Wong, 'Shared Households: A New Paradigm for Thinking about the Reform of Domestic Property Relations' in Diduck and O'Donovan (eds), *Feminist Perspectives on Family Law* 48.

[209] Diduck, 'Shifting Familiarity' 248.

[210] As illustrated above in the context of the Rent Acts, in ch 1, subs II(A)(iii), 'Unmarried Cohabitants' and II(A)(iv), 'Same-Sex Cohabitants'.

[211] Diduck and Kaganas, *Family Law, Gender and the State* 23.

legislation extending marriage to same-sex couples. Subsequently, I contended that conjugality is the central factor in the regulation of adult relationships. I observed that cohabiting couples are subject to legal recognition and regulation because they are constructed by the law as sharing some of the features and characteristics of marriage (with particular emphasis on conjugality) and are considered to be 'marriage-like' relationships. I submitted that the conjugal couple form is now understood by the law as providing social stability for the parties to the relationship and constructed as the best environment for securing the upbringing and development of children, within the central nexus of the conjugal relationship and the parent/child relationship.

To conclude, I argued that the nuclear family model has been expanded to include both same-sex couples and unmarried cohabitants, *without* any fundamental revision of the traditional, nuclear family itself. The next two chapters will build upon this conclusion, by examining the influence of the nuclear family (particularly through the traditional gendered parenting roles of 'mother' and 'father') on the other relationship within the central nexus of the nuclear family; the 'parent/child' relationship.

PART III

Parenthood

> Law's simultaneous promotion of social and genetic parenting through the fusion of the two marks a conceptual failure to distinguish between the relative significance of them. It is also indicative of a poverty of legal means with which to recognise the different strands of parenthood.

Julie Wallbank, 'Channelling the Messiness of Diverse Family Lives: Resisting the Calls to Order and De-Centring the Hetero-Normative Family' (2010) 32(4) *Journal of Social Welfare and Family Law* 353, 360

4

The Attribution of Legal Parenthood within UK Law

This chapter will consider the questions: (i) Who does the law deem to be the parents of a child? and (ii) What factors form the basis for this determination? These two questions are intertwined and in the course of answering them I will consider the importance of both genetic parentage and social parenthood to the attribution of legal parenthood.[1] Although in many instances the identity of the legal parent(s) may be simple and unproblematic, in many others the answer may not be as straightforward. In these more complex scenarios, I will observe that different factors appear to be determinative of legal parenthood in different factual circumstances.

Given the discussion in the previous chapters, it is unsurprising that the law is influenced by the idealised image of the nuclear family when making determinations of legal parenthood. Thus, legal parenthood generally vests in two people,[2] traditionally one woman ('the mother') and one man ('the father').[3] Jackson argues that this approach is 'the law's principal stumbling block, namely its assumption that a child can have only two legal parents: one mother and one father'.[4] This binary, two-parent approach often requires the law to choose between competing parental claims and pronounce a 'truth' of parenthood, rather than being able to acknowledge the value and status of multiple, different relationships.[5] Bainham has suggested that, 'Increasingly the question will not be whether to prefer the

[1] Although both of these types of parenthood may lead to legal parenthood being deemed in certain circumstances, eg genetic parenthood is generally now recognised as leading to legal parenthood for fathers in cases of natural reproduction and adoption acts to create legal parenthood for social parents.

[2] While it is possible for a child born of natural reproduction to only have one legal parent, if the father is unknown and not registered on the birth certificate, the provisions of the Human Fertilisation and Embryology Act 2008 allows for the circumstance in which a child only has the *possibility* of one legal parent, ie where donor sperm is used by a single woman.

[3] Although the law has recently allowed for there to be two legal parents of the same sex in certain contexts: with there being the possibility of two parents of the same sex by virtue of adoption, Adoption and Children Act 2002, s 50 and Adoption and Children (Scotland) Act 2007, s 29, two female parents in the context of assisted reproduction, Human Fertilisation and Embryology Act 2008, ss 42–47 (which will be considered in more detail below at subs II(B), 'Non-Gestational Female "Parents"') and two male parents in the context of surrogacy, HFEA 2008, s 54.

[4] Jackson, 'What is a Parent?', in Diduck and O'Donovan (eds), *Feminist Perspectives on Family Law* 59.

[5] Craig Lind and Tom Hewitt have suggested that 'parental status has declined in importance in the last few decades' in 'Law and the Complexities of Parenting: Parental Status and Parental Function' (2009) 31(4) *Journal of Social Welfare and Family Law* 391, 392.

genetic or social parent but how to accommodate *both* on the assumption that they both have distinctive contributions to make to the life of the child.'[6] Herring has proposed a normative underpinning for determining legal parenthood which focuses on social parenting and 'care', arguing that:

> Parental status should be earned by the care and dedication to the child, something not shown simply by a biological link. It is the changing of the nappy; the wiping of the tear; and the working out of maths together that makes a parent, not the provision of an egg or sperm.[7]

While there is evidence of greater significance being accorded to social parenting in some particular contexts,[8] in this chapter I will argue that underpinning the attribution of legal parenthood there remains a binary, two-parent model, in which ideally a child has one 'mother' and one 'father'.

Throughout this chapter, I will examine how the status of legal parenthood is assigned in a variety of circumstances: natural reproduction in section I, assisted reproduction in section II and surrogacy in section III. I will observe that there are clear differences in the attribution of legal parenthood based upon biological sex; with motherhood being determined on the basis of gestation in all contexts and fatherhood being determined by different factors in different factual contexts. I will conclude that legal parenthood is ordinarily premised upon a binary, two-parent model, which is derived from the traditional, heterosexual, nuclear family model.

I. Natural Reproduction

Diduck and Kaganas observe that:

> [W]hile it is usually presented as a question of fact, the determination of which of the features that are normally associated with parenthood should be singled out as identifying the 'real' mother or father of a child is actually a question of judgment.[9]

[6] Bainham, 'Parentage, Parenthood and Parental Responsibility: Subtle, Elusive, Yet Very Important Distinctions' in Andrew Bainham, Shelley Day Sclater and Martin Richards (eds), *What is a Parent?: A Socio-Legal Analysis* (Oxford, Hart Publishing, 1999) 29.

[7] Herring, *Caring and the Law* 200.

[8] Particularly the legislative reforms in the Adoption and Children Act 2002 and Adoption and Children (Scotland) Act 2007, which have sought to introduce greater flexibility to the adoption context through the introduction of 'Special Guardianship' (in England and Wales) and 'Permanence Orders' (in Scotland). These new legal orders provide a long-term option which does not completely replace one set of parents with another and thus recognises the complexity of the interaction between legal, genetic and social parenthood in different individual circumstances. For the policy background to these reforms, see 'Adoption: A New Approach' (Department of Health, December 2000), available at: www.gov.uk/government/uploads/system/uploads/attachment_data/file/263529/5017.pdf and 'Adoption: Better Choices for Our Children', Report of the Adoption Policy Review Group, (June 2005), available at – www.scotland.gov.uk/Resource/Doc/54357/0014208.pdf. See further eg Jane Lewis, 'Adoption: The Nature of Policy Shifts in England and Wales 1972–2002' (2004) 18(2) *International Journal of Law, Policy and the Family* 235 and Deborah Cullen, 'Adoption – a (Fairly) New Approach' [2005] 17(4) *Child and Family Law Quarterly* 475.

[9] Diduck and Kaganas, *Family Law, Gender and the State* 125.

The paradigm context for the determination of legal parenthood is 'natural' reproduction (that is reproduction following heterosexual intercourse). In this section, the basic presumptions that underpin legal parenthood in cases of natural reproduction will be considered and, it will be noted, that the attribution of legal motherhood involves one, simple presumption while that of legal fatherhood involves the use of several related presumptions.

Where natural reproduction is concerned there is only one woman who can be considered the legal mother of a child at birth: the woman who has gestated and given birth to the child *(mater est quam gestatio demonstrat)*. As Lord Simon observed in the *Ampthill Peerage Case*,[10] 'Motherhood, although also a legal relationship, is based on a fact, being proved demonstrably by parturition.'[11] Thus, the attribution of legal motherhood is determined by one factor alone: gestation.

The determination of the legal father of any child is self-evidently not so simple: accordingly, the law operates several presumptions in determining legal paternity. Historically the most important of these presumptions was that legal paternity is determined on the basis of the existence of a marriage to the mother of the child *(pater est quem nuptiae demonstrant)*. Indeed, this remains a common law presumption, as Lord Simon further observed in the *Ampthill Peerage Case* 'Fatherhood, by contrast, is a presumption. A woman can have sexual intercourse with a number of men any of whom may be the father of her child.'[12] This presumption ties men to children through their relationship to the children's mothers; the key factor is the existence of a marriage to the mother.[13] This emphasis on the marital relationship is unsurprising given that historically[14] this presumption existed to protect the 'sanctity' of marriage.[15] Consequently, this presumption supported the traditional, nuclear family model that dominated the legal definition of the family,[16] by assigning legal parenthood on the basis of the existence of marriage,

[10] *Ampthill Peerage Case* [1977] AC 547.

[11] ibid, at 577.

[12] ibid. The presumption is rebuttable on the balance of probabilities, see the Family Law Reform Act 1969, s 26. In Scotland, this presumption is now statutory, s 5(1)(a) of the Law Reform (Parent and Child) (Scotland) Act 1986, which states: 'A man shall be presumed to be the father of a child – if he was married to the mother of the child at any time in the period beginning with the conception and ending with the birth of the child'. This Scottish statutory presumption is also rebuttable on the balance of probabilities, as set out s 5(4).

[13] The presumption could also be understood as being a presumption that the husband of the mother is the genetic father of the child. Indeed, s 5(2) of the Law Reform (Parent and Child) (Scotland) Act 1986 states that the presumption applies 'in the case of a void, voidable or irregular marriage as it applies in the case of a valid and regular marriage'.

[14] Historically the marital status of the parents was used to distinguish between 'legitimate' and illegitimate' children, which had significant legal consequences for the child. This distinction was effectively abolished in the Family Law Reform Act 1987 and the Law Reform (Parent and Child) (Scotland) Act 1986.

[15] The presumption also reflected the historical absence of direct evidence prior to the advent of blood and DNA testing and the common experiences of mankind that the majority of married men were the fathers of their wives' children.

[16] As described above, in ch 1, in subs II(A), 'The Definition of "Family" Under the Rent Acts' and subs II.B, 'The Definition of "Family Life" under Article 8 of the European Convention on Human Rights'.

which historically was the only legally regulated conjugal relationship.[17] I suggest that the continued significance of this presumption should be understood as an indication of the continuing importance of marriage and the nuclear family within UK law.

An alternative presumption, which did not exist at common law, now applies in cases where the mother of the child is unmarried at both birth and at conception.[18] This presumes legal parenthood from the presence of the father's name on the child's birth certificate.[19] The key factors in this context are the willingness of the man to be recognised as the father and the consequent actions of the individual man and woman, through acknowledging the man as the child's father and in registering this on the birth certificate.[20] In these circumstances, it is the willingness to be recognised as the child's father, combined with the public acknowledgment of that willingness that leads to the granting of the legal status of father.

The genetic connection between the man and the child may also determine legal fatherhood in cases of natural reproduction. This would apply in cases of 'disputed paternity', generally either where the mother was unmarried at birth and conception and no man was registered on the birth certificate, or where a man not deemed to be the father as a result of the aforementioned presumptions wishes to assert his paternity.[21] As Beresford comments 'law has a tradition of appealing to "nature" and to "blood"'.[22] Due to advances in DNA testing technology it is now possible[23] to accurately establish genetic paternity through such testing.[24] The identification of the genetic father displaces the aforementioned presumptions of legal fatherhood.[25] Therefore, legal fatherhood can only be attributed to one man and I argue that this exclusivity shows that these presumptions situate the attribution of legal fatherhood, in cases of natural reproduction, within the boundaries of a binary, two-parent model.

[17] See above throughout ch 3, 'The Legal Regulation of Conjugal Relationships'.

[18] The Family Law Reform Act 1987, s 24 inserted s 10 into the Births and Deaths Registration Act 1953.

[19] Provided that the birth registration complies with the terms of s 10(1) of the Births and Deaths Registration Act 1953.

[20] In Scotland, s 5(1)(b) of the Law Reform (Parent and Child) (Scotland) Act 1986 provides that a man is considered the legal father 'if both he and the mother of the child have acknowledged that he is the father and he has been registered as such'. Moreover, his name must have been registered in terms of s 18(1) of the Registration of Births, Deaths and Marriages (Scotland) Act 1965.

[21] The Family Law Act 1986, s 55A sets out the provisions for 'declarations of parentage'. See s 7(1) of the Law Reform (Parent and Child) (Scotland) Act 1986 for the similar Scots law provisions for actions for declarator of either 'parentage' or 'non-parentage'.

[22] Beresford, 'Get Over Your (Legal) "Self": A Brief History of Lesbians, Motherhood and the Law' 95.

[23] See eg *S v S* 2014 SLT (Sh Ct) 165 for an example of a recent Scottish case where DNA testing to establish paternity was refused and the issues that resulted from the refusal.

[24] However, see Helen Draper and Jonathan Ives, 'Paternity Testing: A Poor Test of Fatherhood' (2009) 31(4) *Journal of Social Welfare and Family Law* 407, for a critique of the reliance on paternity testing alone as a method of determining 'fatherhood'.

[25] Law Reform (Parent and Child) (Scotland) Act 1986, s 5(3).

In this way, the law operates a hierarchy of factors in cases of natural reproduction, with proof of genetic relatedness, when established, having precedence over the marital relationship with the child's mother, which in turn has precedence over willingness and public acknowledgment of fatherhood. Judicial opinion has emphasised the significance of determining the genetic 'truth',[26] as seen in *Re H and A (Children) (Paternity: Blood Test)*,[27] where Thorpe LJ stated that 'the interests of justice are best served by the ascertainment of the truth and … the court should be furnished with the best available science and not confined to such unsatisfactory alternatives as presumptions and inferences'.[28] This approach has been applied consistently in other recent cases[29] and in *Re D (A Child) (Paternity)*,[30] Hedley J stated 'the general approach is that it is best for everyone for the truth about a disputed paternity to be known'.[31] This suggests a change from prioritising the relationship with the child's mother toward prioritising the genetic connection[32] with the child in determining legal fatherhood.[33] This is notable as it runs counter to the historical protection of the nuclear family in determinations of legal parenthood. Diduck comments that:

> Now that we *can* know the biological – or at least genetic – 'truth', it seems that in the interests of our well-being, we *must* know. And not only must we know, it has now become our right to know. We seem happy to be in the thrall to biology or nature again in a way that has been unknown for years.[34]

[26] Judicial emphasis on seeking the 'truth' of paternity is apparent in the historical 'blood test' cases. In *S v S* [1972] AC 24, Lord Hodson observed, at 57, that 'The interests of justice in the abstract are best served by the ascertainment of the truth and there must be few cases where the interests of children can be shown to be best served by the suppression of truth.' See further eg *Re L (An Infant)* [1967] 3 WLR 1645 and *B v B* [1968] 3 WLR 566.

[27] *Re H and A (Children) (Paternity: Blood Test)* [2002] EWCA Civ 383, [2002] 1 FLR 1145.

[28] ibid, at 1157, the use of the word 'truth' is particularly notable as it seems to conflate genetic relatedness and 'parenthood'.

[29] See eg *Re R (Parental Responsibility)* [2011] EWHC 1535 (Fam), [2011] 2 FLR 1132, *Re T (Paternity: Ordering Blood Tests)* [2001] 2 FLR 1190 and *Re H (A Minor) (Blood Tests: Parental Rights)* [1996] 2 FLR 65. These cases suggest that the contemporary judicial approach is that carrying out scientific tests to establish paternity is usually in the best interests of the child.

[30] *Re D (A Child) (Paternity)* [2006] EWHC 3545 (Fam), [2007] 2 FLR 26.

[31] ibid, per Hedley J, at 31.

[32] Judicial opinion in this regard has also been influenced by scientific developments which have improved the accuracy of testing, resulting in less need for reliance upon presumptions based on the relationship of the men with the mother of the child, see eg *Re H (A Minor) (Blood Test: Parental Rights)* [1996] 2 FLR 65, where Ward LJ stated, at 77 'Science has now advanced. The whole truth can now be known.'

[33] The historical approach to 'blood test' evidence was that carrying out these tests was often not in the best interests of the child, due to the disruption to the pre-existing nuclear family, see eg *Re F (A Minor) (Blood Tests: Parental Rights)* [1993] Fam 314, where Balcombe LJ stated, at 320 'now and for the first few years of her life E.'s physical and emotional welfare are inextricably bound up with the welfare of the family unit of which she forms part: any harm to the welfare of that unit, as might be caused by an order for the taking of blood tests, would inevitably be damaging to E.'

[34] Diduck, 'If Only we can Find the Appropriate Terms to Use the Issue Will Be Solved: Law, Identity and Parenthood' 468.

This approach is based on the understanding which has developed within the law that genetic connection, in and of itself, has significant importance and value for children.[35] This has led to the genetic relationship being given greater recognition and priority within the law.[36] Sheldon has described this as 'a "geneticisation" of understandings of fatherhood'.[37]

Fortin sees a link between Article 7 of the United Nations Convention on the Rights of the Child (UNCRC), which states that a child has 'the right to know and be cared for by his or her parents'[38] and the developing judicial understanding that an ongoing relationship with the genetic progenitor is in the best interests of the child.[39] On this basis, she has suggested that 'the right to know one's parents is being developed, through faith in the magical properties of biological ties, into the right to be with one's parents'.[40] Bainham has commented that:

> [R]ecent changes in England and elsewhere reflect a heavy emphasis on the importance of biological truth. Ascertaining the truth, if not seen as a right of the child, is certainly viewed as being in the child's best interests most of the time.[41]

Thus, some academic commentators have suggested that the genetic connection has become the crucial factor in judicial determinations of legal fatherhood in cases of natural reproduction. Nevertheless, it is apparent that the determination of legal fatherhood is complex and is based on reliance upon different factors in different factual circumstances. In spite of these differences, however, I argue that the attribution of legal fatherhood, in cases of natural reproduction, is always situated within a binary, two-parent model.

[35] See eg Lord Nicholls' short speech in the House of Lords in *Re G (Children) (Residence: Same-Sex Partner)* [2006] UKHL 43, [2006] 2 FLR 629, particularly his observation, at 631, that 'the court should always have in mind that in the ordinary way the rearing of a child by his or her biological parent can be expected to be in the child's best interests, both in the short term and also, and importantly, in the longer term'.

[36] See eg *Re F (Paternity: Jurisdiction)* [2007] EWCA Civ 873, [2008] 1 FLR 225, where it was held that the courts have jurisdiction to make an order that a child should be told the truth about their genetic origins, regardless of the wishes of the primary caregiver. However, see *L v P (Paternity Test: Child's Objection)* [2011] EWHC 3399, [2013] 1 FLR 578, where an application for a genetic test was rejected on the basis of the 15 year old child's objections to the test being carried out.

[37] Sally Sheldon, 'From "Absent Objects of Blame" to "Fathers who Want to Take Responsibility": Reforming Birth Registration Law' (2009) 31(4) *Journal of Social Welfare and Family Law* 373, 374.

[38] Article 7(1) of the UNCRC states in full: 'The child shall be registered immediately after birth and shall have the right from birth to a name, the right to acquire a nationality and, as far as possible, the right to know and be cared for by his or her parents.' See further eg Katherine O'Donovan, 'A Right to Know One's Parentage' (1988) 2(1) *International Journal of Law and the Family* 27 and Julie Wallbank, 'The Role of Rights and Utility in Instituting a Child's Right to Know Her Genetic History' (2004) 13(2) *Social and Legal Studies* 245.

[39] See eg *Re H (Contact with Biological Father)* [2012] EWCA Civ 281, [2012] 2 FLR 627, *Re L (Contact: Domestic Violence); Re V (Contact: Domestic Violence); Re M (Contact: Domestic Violence; Re H (Contact: Domestic Violence)* [2000] 2 FLR 334 and *White v White* 2001 SLT 485. This issue will also be further considered below in ch 5, subs II(C)(i), 'The Significance of Contact with the Non-Resident Parent'.

[40] Jane Fortin, 'Children's Right to Know Their Origins – Too Far, Too Fast?' [2009] 21(3) *Child and Family Law Quarterly* 336, 338.

[41] Andrew Bainham, 'Arguments About Parentage' (2008) 67(2) *Cambridge Law Journal* 322, 331.

II. Assisted Reproduction

The question of who should be considered the legal parent(s) of a child has been made significantly more complex by advances in medical science that have led to the much more widespread availability and use of 'assisted reproduction technologies',[42] such as IVF, because these medical processes often involve the use of genetic material provided by a donor (or indeed multiple donors).[43] Additional complexities may be introduced through the use of surrogacy,[44] a process which inevitably involves at least one additional person (the surrogate), in addition to the 'intended parent(s)'.[45] Cases of assisted reproduction can give rise to complex factual scenarios which involve competing claims of legal parenthood. The effect of these situations is that the law is required to provide clear statements regarding how legal parenthood is to be assigned, because the 'correct' answer may not be readily apparent. The process of making such determinations requires the law to navigate complex factual circumstances and occasionally difficult choices,[46] and to be more explicit about the meanings of the various terms involved than is necessary in cases of natural reproduction where the attribution of parenthood is viewed as being more straightforward.

[42] Scientific techniques continue to advance rapidly, for example both uterus transplants and artificial wombs are in various stages of development throughout the world. These technologies will raise additional questions for the law in the future, as they will further problematise the paradigm, binary, two-parent model of legal parenthood.

[43] The UK became the first country to allow specialist IVF treatments for mitochondrial disorders in the Human Fertilisation and Embryology (Mitochondrial Donation) Regulations 2015, opening the possibility of children having 3 'genetic parents'. See the Nuffield Council on Bioethics, 'Novel Techniques for the Prevention of Mitochondrial DNA Disorders: An Ethical Review', (June 2012), available at: http://nuffieldbioethics.org/wp-content/uploads/2014/06/Novel_techniques_for_the_prevention_of_mitochondrial_DNA_disorders_compressed.pdf.

[44] The use of surrogacy remains quite limited in the UK due to surrogacy arrangements remaining unenforceable, Surrogacy Arrangements Act 1985, s 1A and commercial surrogacy being prohibited, Surrogacy Arrangements Act 1985, s 2. Marilyn Crawshaw, Eric Blyth and Olga van den Akker, 'The Changing Profile of Surrogacy in the UK – Implications for National and International Policy and Practice' (2012) 34(3) *Journal of Social Welfare and Family Law* 267, 269, on the basis of correspondence with the General Register Office, state that there were 149 parental orders granted in the UK in 2011. See further National Records of Scotland, 'Vital Events Reference Tables 2014, Section 2: Adoption and Re-Registrations' (August 2015), states that there were only nine parental orders granted in Scotland in 2014, available at: www.nrscotland.gov.uk/files//statistics/vital-events-ref-tables/2014/section-2/14-vital-events-ref-tab-2-3.pdf.

[45] The particular issues raised by the factual circumstances of surrogacy will be considered in more detail below at s III, 'Surrogacy'.

[46] These difficult judgments become apparent in some of the high-profile litigation surrounding the HFEA 2008 and its predecessor the HFEA 1990, eg *Evans v Amicus Healthcare Ltd* [2004] EWCA Civ 727, [2004] 3 WLR 681, *Leeds Teaching Hospitals NHS Trust v A* [2003] EWHC 259 (QB), [2003] 1 FLR 1091 and *R v Human Fertilisation and Embryology Authority Ex p Blood* [1997] 2 WLR 806. See further, Sally Sheldon, 'Gender Equality and Reproductive Decision-Making' (2004) 12(3) *Feminist Legal Studies* 303 and Sally Sheldon, 'Evans v Amicus Healthcare; Hadley v Midland Fertility Services – Revealing Cracks in the "Twin Pillars"?' [2004] 16(4) *Child and Family Law Quarterly* 437.

The Human Fertilisation and Embryology Act 2008 ('the 2008 Act')[47] provides the statutory framework for determining legal parenthood in this context.[48] McCandless and Sheldon have commented that 'the model of family underlying these provisions was barely considered by the reformers at all, not forming a core part of the reform project'.[49] This lack of consideration suggests that the values preferenced in the legislation's determination of legal parenthood were not the result of an explicit, conscious choice.[50] Arguably, then, the provisions simply reflect the traditional, nuclear family, which influenced its predecessor legislation; the Human Fertilisation and Embryology Act 1990 ('the 1990 Act').[51] Writing in reference to the 1990 Act,[52] Sheldon has observed that 'in the status provisions, Parliament attempted to foresee every possible reproductive scenario and to provide for the resulting family arrangement to conform as closely as possible to a nuclear family model'.[53] It is notable that the factors established in the legislation do not reflect the approach employed in cases of natural reproduction. This disparity has led some commentators to identify a sense of confusion and incoherence about these concepts within the law in the UK.[54]

In this section, the more complex circumstances created by assisted reproduction will be considered. The distinction between the attribution of motherhood and fatherhood is also apparent in this context,[55] with the use of one, straightforward provision for determining the legal mother (subsection A) compared to several provisions used for the legal father (subsection C). In addition, assisted

[47] This is amending legislation, designed to 'modernise' the original Human Fertilisation and Embryology Act 1990. The reforms of the 2008 Act have been described as 'devoid of any coherent philosophical framework' in Rachel Fenton, Susan Heenan and Jane Rees, 'Finally Fit For Purpose? The Human Fertilization and Embryology Act 2008' (2010) 32(3) *Journal of Social Welfare and Family Law* 275, 285 and as a 'missed opportunity' in Marie Fox, 'The Human Fertilisation and Embryology Act 2008: Tinkering at the Margins' (2009) 17(3) *Feminist Legal Studies* 333, 334.

[48] For assisted reproduction and surrogacy, the determination of legal parenthood is governed through the 'status provisions', found in ss 33–47 of the Human Fertilisation and Embryology Act 2008.

[49] Julie McCandless and Sally Sheldon, 'The Human Fertilisation and Embryology Act (2008) and the Tenacity of the Sexual Family Form' (2010) 73(2) *Modern Law Review* 175, 182.

[50] However, the Joint Committee on the Human Tissue and Embryology (Draft) Bill, 'Human Tissue and Embryos (Draft) Bill, Volume I: Report', (HL Paper 169, HC Paper 630, August 2007) stated, at para 263 'Part 3 of the draft Bill seeks to take a new approach to parenthood, moving towards the concept of parenthood as a legal responsibility rather than a biological relationship.' Available at: http://www.publications.parliament.uk/pa/jt200607/jtselect/jtembryos/169/169.pdf.

[51] Support for the traditional nuclear family is apparent in the report of the Warnock Committee, which led to Human Fertilisation and Embryology Act 1990, 'Report of the Committee of Inquiry into Human Fertilisation and Embryology' (Department of Health and Social Security, July 1984), para 2.11 'we believe that as a general rule it is better for children to be born into a two-parent family, with both father and mother', available at: www.hfea.gov.uk/docs/Warnock_Report_of_the_Committee_of_Inquiry_into_Human_Fertilisation_and_Embryology_1984.pdf.

[52] This issue will be considered in more detail below in subs II(D), 'The Influence of the Nuclear Family Model'.

[53] Sheldon, 'Fragmenting Fatherhood: The Regulation of Reproductive Technologies', 541.

[54] See eg Therese Callus, 'First "Designer Babies", Now a La Carte Parents' [2008] 38(2) *Fam Law* 143 and Bainham, 'Arguments About Parentage'.

[55] Although it could be argued that this distinction simply reflects the factual reality of the very different gendered contributions made to human reproduction (whether 'natural' or medically assisted) by men and women.

reproduction creates the possibility of there being two legal parents of the same gender, which raises issues around choice of terminology (subsection B). I will argue that, in spite of the radical possibilities presented by assisted reproduction, the determination of legal parenthood remains firmly situated within the boundaries of the two-parent model and thus the traditional nuclear family (subsection D).

A. Motherhood

The statutory definition of 'mother' in cases of assisted reproduction reflects the common law approach used in natural reproduction.[56] The 2008 Act provides in section 33(1) that 'The woman who is carrying or has carried a child as a result of the placing in her of an embryo or of sperm and eggs, and no other woman, is to be treated as the mother of the child'.[57] This provision favours gestation over the genetic connection in cases where the two factors do not coincide, therefore privileging gestation in the determination of legal motherhood.[58] In addition to the legislation preferencing gestation in the determination of motherhood, section 47 is titled: 'Woman not to be other parent merely because of egg donation'. Therefore, the legislation is explicit that the genetic connection (through egg donation) does not give rise to any *parental* status;[59] McCandless and Sheldon comment that 'This serves to emphasise the legal irrelevance of whether or not a woman is a genetic parent'.[60] Jones has argued that:

> With this legislation, the birth mother is designated the legal mother, and the significance of genetic links between mothers and children is marginalised. Hence, legal discourse is able to make claims of 'truth' with regard to the ascription of parenthood. Consequently, alternative constructions of 'mother' are disqualified for the purposes of legal status and rights in relation to the donor-conceived child.[61]

[56] As set out above in s I, 'Natural Reproduction'.

[57] HFEA 2008, s 33(1), this provision replicates the provisions for determining motherhood in s 27(1) of the HFEA 1990.

[58] Some empirical research suggests that the legislative position is reflected in the attitudes of many of the women who participate in egg donation or egg-sharing, see eg H. Abdalla, F Shenfield and E Latarche, 'Statutory Information for the Children Born of Oocyte Donation in the UK: What Will They Be Told in 2008?' [1998] 13(4) *Human Reproduction* 1106 and K Ahuja, E Simons, B Mostyn and P Bowen-Simpkins, 'An Assessment of the Motives and Morals of Egg Share Donors: Policy of "Payments" to Egg Donors Requires a Fair Review' [1998] 13(10) *Human Reproduction* 2671.

[59] See eg *Re G (Children) (Shared Residence Order: Biological Non-Birth Mother)* [2014] EWCA Civ 336, [2014] 2 FLR 897 for judicial consideration of the role of the 'genetic mother' (who was not a legal parent) in the context of a dispute with the gestational (and legal) mother. In her judgment, at 910, Black LJ stated 'I accept the appellant's submission that the judge failed to give weight to the fact that she is the biological mother of the children. The judge was absolutely correct to observe that the appellant is not the parent of the children in law. That was undoubtedly a significant factor, but it was not the end of the story as one might think the judge thought it was.'

[60] McCandless and Sheldon, 'The Human Fertilisation and Embryology Act (2008) and the Tenacity of the Sexual Family Form' 187.

[61] Caroline Jones, 'Parents in Law: Subjective Impacts and Status Implications around the Use of Licensed Donor Insemination' in Diduck and O'Donovan (eds), *Feminist Perspectives on Family Law* 80.

This definition partly represents a pragmatic response; the woman who initiates the assisted reproduction process will be the gestational mother and she is also (usually) the intended social mother.[62] More importantly, however, this choice to privilege gestation over the genetic connection reflects UK law's construction of motherhood as a 'natural', indivisible, process.[63] The use of this construction reflects the fact that, as O'Donovan suggests 'The distinction between maternity and motherhood … is the distinction between giving birth and being a mother. In common parlance in Britain, this distinction is not made, nor even seen. Nor is it made in law.'[64] The law does not separate the status of legal motherhood from the process of carrying a baby and giving birth. Cases of assisted reproduction and surrogacy, which do not follow this natural process, challenge the dominant construction, but these cases nevertheless follow the gestational paradigm of motherhood through the provisions of the 2008 Act. In this way, the apparently straightforward, 'common-sense' approach to the legal attribution of motherhood in cases of natural reproduction, involves a choice when utilised in cases of assisted reproduction.

B. Non-Gestational Female 'Parents'

The law's reliance upon this natural, indivisible construction of motherhood is reinforced by its response to lesbian couples who have children together using assisted reproduction.[65] As a result of reforms in the 2008 Act, the non-gestational female 'parent'[66] is to be treated as 'a parent of the child'[67] provided certain consent requirements are met.[68] While both members of the couple are legal parents, it is notable that gender-neutral terminology is used to describe the parenthood of one.[69] This is in clear contrast to the gendered language used in the legislation to describe the parental roles of 'mother'[70] and 'father';[71] gender-neutral terminology

[62] Except in cases of surrogacy, which are considered below at s III, 'Surrogacy'.

[63] The construction of 'motherhood' within UK law will considered further below in ch 5, subs II(A), 'What is the "Mother" in the Law?'.

[64] O'Donovan, 'Constructions of Maternity and Motherhood in Stories of Lost Children' in Bridgeman and Monk (eds), *Feminist Perspectives on Child Law* 73.

[65] Under the provisions of HFEA 1990 it was not possible for both members of a lesbian couple to be considered a child's legal parents at birth. The fundamental basis of these reforms have been questioned by some commentators, see eg Callus, 'First "Designer Babies", Now à La Carte Parents', 146, 'By recognising the status of two female parents, the child's identity is thrown into disarray because the recognition of two female parents conceals the necessary heterosexual element of human existence'.

[66] A variety of terms are employed to describe this role, eg 'Co-Mother', 'Co-Parent', 'Other Mother', 'Second Female Parent', amongst others. As this section will suggest, these issues of terminology are fundamental to any consideration of this role. Throughout this work the terms non-gestational female 'parent' and 'second female parent' will be used to describe the role, reflecting the statutory terminology.

[67] Following provisions similar to those determining 'father' detailed below: HFEA 2008, s 42(1) for those in a civil partnership and s 43 for those not.

[68] These are found in 'the agreed female parenthood conditions', HFEA 2008, s 44.

[69] This approach shows the 'enduring grip' of the two-parent model, according to Leckey in 'Law Reform, Lesbian Parenting, and the Reflective Claim' 338.

[70] HFEA 2008, s 33.

[71] HFEA 2008, ss 35–37 these provisions are considered below at subs II(C), 'Fatherhood'.

is only used to describe the parenthood of the non-gestational female 'parent'.[72] This use of the terminology of 'parent' to describe the legal parenthood of one member of the lesbian couple means that, as Probert says, 'there is not even a name to make her visible'.[73] As a result of this approach, Diduck has commented:

> Motherhood remains exclusive; no alternative terms were attempted. Secondly, where a woman is treated as a parent, no man may be treated as the father of the child so that legal parenthood remains limited in number to two. In fact, by making it difficult for partnered lesbian women to parent alone, the proposals reinforce the traditional hetero-familial ideal of two parents; the equality imposed upon lesbian parents by the proposals in effect imposes heterosexual norms upon them.[74]

While the reforms of the 2008 Act[75] amount to an attempt to acknowledge the diversity of family forms that exist in contemporary society,[76] in the process these provisions reinforce the assumption that a child can only have one mother. Thus, the traditional construction of motherhood, and the binary, two-parent model of parenthood are supported and remain unquestioned. Notably, this exclusivity of motherhood and the absence of an obvious term to describe the non-gestational female 'parent' role is reflected in the views of lesbian parents themselves: Gabb found that 'the vast majority of "other mothers" in my study not only felt uneasy about calling themselves mothers, they also contested the use of non-reductive "special terms" such as "co-parent"'.[77] Fenton, Heenan and Rees suggest that:

> [T]he parentage provisions for same-sex couples are set out as a mirror image to that of heterosexual couples. It is arguable that this is, by effect if not design, a heterocentric statement based on the primacy of the biogenetic two-parent model of the sexual family.[78]

[72] The implications of this terminological distinction upon the legal understanding of the parental roles of both members of lesbian couples will be considered below in ch 5, s III, 'The Role of Lesbian "Mothers" or "Parents"'.

[73] Rebecca Probert, 'Families, Assisted Reproduction and the Law' [2004] 16(3) *Child and Family Law Quarterly* 271, 278.

[74] Diduck, 'If Only we can Find the Appropriate Terms to Use the Issue Will Be Solved: Law, Identity and Parenthood' 466.

[75] The approach of the HFEA 2008 differs substantially from the HFEA 1990, which stated in s 13(5) 'A woman shall not be provided with treatment services … unless account has been taken of the welfare of any child who may be born as a result of the treatment (including the need of that child for a father)'. For consideration of this controversial legislative provision, see eg Gillian Douglas, 'Assisted Conception and the Welfare of the Child' (1993) 46 *Current Legal Problems* 53 and Emily Jackson, 'Conception and the Irrelevance of the Welfare Principle' (2002) 65(2) *Modern Law Review* 176.

[76] The reforms were premised upon addressing the inequality between same-sex and opposite-sex couples as regards access to assisted reproduction, see, 'Review of the Human Fertilisation and Embryology Act', (Department of Health, December 2006), para 2.67, 'In undertaking its review of the HFE Act, the Government aimed to consider the extent to which changes may be needed to better recognise the wider range of people who seek and receive assisted reproduction treatment in the early 21st Century.' Available at: https://assets.publishing.service.gov.uk/government/uploads/system/uploads/attachment_data/file/272391/6989.pdf.

[77] Gabb, 'Lesbian M/Otherhood: Strategies of Familial-linguistic Management in Lesbian Parent Families', 595. See further Dunne, 'Opting into Motherhood: Lesbians Blurring the Boundaries and Transforming the Meaning of Parenthood and Kinship'.

[78] Fenton, Heenan and Rees, 'Finally Fit For Purpose? The Human Fertilization and Embryology Act 2008' 279.

It is submitted that the reforms of the 2008 Act, which extend legal parenthood to both members of a lesbian couple, do not alter the reliance upon a binary, two-parent model, based upon the traditional, heterosexual, nuclear family.[79]

C. Fatherhood

In contrast with the clarity of a single criterion – gestation – for determining motherhood, the 2008 Act provides for different factors to be decisive of legal fatherhood in different factual circumstances; in this sense, UK law's approach to fatherhood in the context of assisted reproduction reflects that in natural reproduction. As Sheldon and Collier observe 'While motherhood is legally firmly rooted in gestation, fatherhood is an altogether more complex and fragmented status.'[80] In determining legal fatherhood in cases of assisted reproduction, the legislation makes a distinction between married and unmarried couples, and different statutory provisions apply depending on relationship status. However, the factors used to determine legal fatherhood in cases of assisted reproduction do not reflect the hierarchy of presumptions that operates in cases of natural reproduction.

In cases where the mother is married and donor sperm is used,[81] the legislation provides that 'the other party to the marriage is to be treated as the father of the child unless it is shown that he did not consent to [the treatment]'.[82] The key factor here is that of consent, and it is notable that, taking account of the law's privileging of marriage and the nuclear family, what is required is evidence of lack of consent: in other words, consent is assumed due to the status of the relationship, as a marriage.[83]

[79] Writing in the context of the HFEA 1990, Julie Wallbank, 'Reconstructing the HFEA 1990: Is Blood Really Thicker Than Water?' [2004] 16(4) *Child and Family Law Quarterly* 387, stated 'the current law is both over-simplistic and biased towards the traditional heterosexual model of family life, which is no longer wholly appropriate or realistic in terms of contemporary family formations'. While the HFEA 2008 went some way to addressing some concerns by providing recognition for lesbian-led families, it is suggested that the provisions still illustrate the dominance of the traditional, nuclear family model in the framework for determining legal parenthood.

[80] Sheldon and Collier, *Fragmenting Fatherhood: A Socio-Legal Study* 87. It is also arguable that the distinction between the statutory approaches to determining legal motherhood and legal fatherhood to some extent reflects the reality of the different mechanism of proof of legal parenthood for 'mothers' and 'fathers'.

[81] If the sperm of the husband is used, legal fatherhood would be determined on the basis of the presumptions described above for cases of natural reproduction, eg the *pater est* presumption and additionally the genetic connection between father and child. Further, those situations involving known donors and home-based insemination outside of licensed clinics will be considered below within this section.

[82] HFEA 2008, s 35(1).

[83] Interestingly, HFEA 2008, s 38(2) states 'In England and Wales and Northern Ireland, sections 35 and 36 do not affect any presumption, applying by virtue of the rules of common law, that a child is the legitimate child of the parties to a marriage.' Similarly, s 38(3) provides 'In Scotland, sections 35 and 36 do not apply in relation to any child who, by virtue of any enactment or other rule of law, is treated as the child of the parties to a marriage.' These provisions effectively restate the pre-eminence of the aforementioned *pater est* presumption, meaning that even in situations where s 35(1) does not apply (due to lack of consent), the common law rebuttable presumption still applies. This illustrates the continuing significance of marriage within the 2008 Act's regime for determining legal parenthood in cases of assisted reproduction.

In cases where the mother is not married and donor sperm is used,[84] the 'agreed fatherhood conditions'[85] need to be satisfied for fatherhood to be conferred. These conditions provide that a man will be deemed the father if he 'has given the person responsible a notice stating that he consents to being treated as the father of any child resulting from treatment provided to W under the licence'.[86] While consent is again the determinative factor,[87] here it is not assumed and must take the specific form prescribed by the legislation.[88] Dame Elizabeth Butler-Sloss P stated, in *Leeds Teaching Hospitals NHS Trust v A*,[89] that:

> The husband is to be treated as the father, unless it is shown that he did not consent, that he "opted out". In subsection (3) the boot is on the other foot. The acceptance of fatherhood has to be shown. The man has to show commitment and that commitment has to be demonstrated by his active involvement. In other words, he must "opt in".[90]

This judicial language of 'opt out' and 'opt in' captures the conceptual distinction in the 2008 Act's approach to consent for married and unmarried men. This distinction in the consent requirements for married and unmarried men illustrates the importance of the existence of marriage in the attribution of legal fatherhood, because consent is effectively assumed for married men, purely on the basis of their relationships status, whereas for unmarried men there is no such assumption of consent.[91]

[84] If the sperm of the unmarried partner is used, legal fatherhood would be determined on the basis of the presumptions described above for cases of natural reproduction, e.g. through registration on the birth certificate and through the genetic connection between father and child.

[85] Section 36(b) and detailed in HFEA 2008, s 37.

[86] HFEA 2008, s 37(1)(a).

[87] In addition, the agreed fatherhood conditions include a requirement of the consent of the mother, s 37(1)(b), to treat an unmarried man as the legal father.

[88] However, in a series of cases involving significant errors regarding appropriate paperwork made by numerous fertility clinics, consent was held to be valid in spite of not taking the precise form set out in the legislation, see eg *Re P (Human Fertilisation and Embryology Act 2008: Assisted Reproduction: Parent)* [2017] EWHC 49 (Fam) and *B v B (Fertility Treatment: Paperwork Error)* [2017] EWHC 599 (Fam). Moreover, these issues regarding systematic paperwork errors originally arose regarding the consent of non-gestational female 'parents', see eg *Re E (Assisted Reproduction: Parent)* [2013] EWHC 1418 (Fam) [2013] 2 FLR 1357 and *Re A (Human Fertilisation and Embryology Act 2008: Assisted Reproduction: Parent)* [2015] EWHC 2602 (Fam), [2016] 1 WLR 1325.

[89] *Leeds Teaching Hospitals NHS Trust v A* [2003] EWHC 259 (QB), [2003] 1 FLR 1091, this case was considering the HFEA 1990 which employed different language in relation to unmarried couples, but it is suggested that the general principles are still relevant. The interpretation of the previous legislation, particularly the reference in s 28(3) to 'treatment together' was subject to judicial consideration, see eg *Re R (A Child) (IVF: Paternity of Child)* [2005] UKHL 33, [2005] 2 AC 621 and *Re R (A Child)* [2003] EWCA Civ 182, [2003] 1 FLR 1183.

[90] ibid, per Dame Elizabeth Butler-Sloss P, at 1103, the President was referring to the language of HFEA 1990, s 28(3).

[91] These provisions in relation to unmarried fathers only apply to 'treatment services' carried out by licensed UK clinics, HFEA 2008, s 36(a) states 'in the course of treatment services provided in the United Kingdom by a person to whom a licence applies'. Therefore, in either private 'known donor' cases or in cases where treatment (using donor sperm) is carried out at foreign clinics these provisions do not apply and the sperm donor would have a claim to legal fatherhood on the basis of the genetic connection. There is no similar requirement in relation to married men; indeed, s 35(2) explicitly applies to artificial insemination outside the UK.

Regardless of whether the mother and father are married, sperm donors are not treated as legal fathers provided the conditions in the Act are satisfied.[92] This is also based upon consent; the donor has consented to the use of his genetic material on the condition that he is *not* treated as the father.[93] Indeed, the report of the Warnock Committee,[94] upon which the provisions of the 1990 Act were based, was clear in its recommendation that 'the donor should have no responsibilities towards the child'.[95] This principle of removal of responsibilities, both parental and financial, from the donor has continued to underpin the regulation of legal parenthood in cases of assisted reproduction. However, those donating sperm are no longer granted anonymity;[96] legislation now allows for children conceived using donated material, after 1 April 2005,[97] to request certain identifying information about their donors.[98] This change in UK law reflects the understanding, discussed above, that the genetic connection itself is now granted significant importance within the law.[99] By removing donor anonymity the law is seeking to give some recognition to the continued importance (at least in the perception of those whose origins are different from the norm) of the genetic link.[100] This partial recognition exists notwithstanding that legal parenthood is not being determined by the genetic connection in this context.[101] Indeed, I argue that this approach illustrates that the attribution of legal fatherhood, in cases of assisted reproduction, continues to be determined within the confines of a binary, two-parent model.

The emphasis on consent in preference to the genetic connection in cases of assisted reproduction runs in direct contradiction to the hierarchy of presumptions established in cases of natural reproduction.[102] McAvoy notes that 'The common law's traditional emphasis on genetic parenthood has been made to appear inappropriate by scientific advancements in the field of assisted reproduction.'[103]

[92] HFEA 2008, s 41(1).

[93] HFEA 2008, s 41(1) states 'Where the sperm of a man who had given such consent … was used for a purpose for which such consent was required, he is not to be treated as the father of the child.'

[94] 'Report of the Committee of Inquiry into Human Fertilisation and Embryology' (July 1984).

[95] ibid, at para 4.22.

[96] This change was as a result of the Human Fertilisation and Embryology Authority (Disclosure of Donor Information) Regulations 2004.

[97] HFEA 1990, s 31ZA as amended by HFEA 2008, s 24.

[98] Human Fertilisation and Embryology Authority (Disclosure of Donor Information) Regulations 2004, reg 2(3) details the identifying information that is required to be retained about the sperm donor: full name, date of birth, appearance and last known address.

[99] As discussed above at s I, 'Natural Reproduction'.

[100] Prior to the change in the law, in *R (On the Application of Rose) v Secretary of State for Health* [2002] EWHC 1593 (Admin), [2002] 2 FLR 962, a claim for judicial review as to the lack of availability of non-identifying information about donors, by children born as a result of anonymous sperm donation, Scott Baker J stated, at 967 'The claimants' requests were for information about their biological fathers which went to the very heart of their identity, and to their make-up as people.'

[101] See further eg Catherine Donovan, 'Genetics, Fathers and Families: Exploring the Implications of Changing the Law in Favour of Identifying Sperm Donors' (2006) 15(4) *Social and Legal Studies* 494.

[102] As set out above in s I, 'Natural Reproduction'.

[103] Sharon McAvoy, 'Modern Family: Parenthood' [2013] *Fam Law* 1421, 1422.

The genetic connection is privileged over social parenting when determining legal parenthood in natural reproduction, whereas in assisted reproduction the significance of the donor's genetic connection is diminished in favour of recognising the consent of the intended (social) parents. This has prompted Callus to observe that:

> [T]here are competing tendencies in the law on the one hand with reliance on biological truth where no recourse to assisted conception is required, and, on the other, a complete isolation of the biological component of parenthood to take into account social parenting.[104]

This disparity of approaches reinforces the concern expressed by some commentators (referenced above) that the law lacks a coherent, principled approach to determining legal parenthood.[105]

The complexity of assigning legal parenthood is further increased in circumstances involving home-based insemination and the use of a known sperm donor.[106] The 2008 Act applies to those in marriages and civil partnerships in all cases of 'artificial insemination',[107] whereby the other party to the relationship will be the child's legal parent when a known donor was used.[108] However, for unmarried couples the legislation applies only to treatment carried out by licensed clinics,[109] therefore in cases where unmarried couples use home-based insemination the known donor will be considered the legal father, traced to his genetic connection with the child. Thus, in spite of the presence of this additional potential parental figure the binary, two-parent model is still applied in these situations.[110] Evidence suggests that in practice the vast majority of

[104] Callus, 'First "Designer Babies", Now à La Carte Parents' 147.

[105] Furthermore, some commentators have been critical of the perceived lack of transparency, within law, regarding the genetic origins of children conceived using donor sperm; see eg Bainham, 'Arguments About Parentage' 332. For the opposing argument, see eg Carol Smart, 'Family Secrets: Law and Understandings of Openness in Everyday Relationships' (2009) 38(4) *Journal of Social Policy* 551.

[106] This is another area where terminology has proved somewhat controversial, the judiciary has often used the term 'biological father' to describe the donors in circumstances involving lesbian couples, eg *Re P & L (Contact)* [2011] EWHC 3431 (Fam), [2012] 1 FLR 1068, *Re B (Role of the Biological Father)* [2007] EWHC 1952 (Fam), [2008] 1 FLR 1015 and *Re D (Contact and Parental Responsibility: Lesbian Mothers and Known Father)* [2006] EWHC 2 (Fam), [2006] 1 FCR 556. See further Julie Wallbank and Chris Dietz, 'Lesbian Mothers, Fathers and Other Animals: Is the Political Personal in Multiple Parent Families?' [2013] 25(4) *Child and Family Law Quarterly* 451. The issues that arise in disputes between lesbian couples and 'known donors' are discussed more below in ch 5, subs III(A)(ii), '"Known Donor" Disputes'.

[107] HFEA 2008, s 35 for married couples and s 42 for civil partners.

[108] However, for children conceived by women in civil partnerships using 'known donors', prior to the 2008 Act coming into force, the known donor would be the legal father, see eg *A v B and C (Role of Father)* [2012] EWCA Civ 285, [2012] 2 FLR 607.

[109] HFEA 2008, s 36 for opposite-sex couples and s 43 for same-sex couples.

[110] Julie Wallbank, 'Channelling the Messiness of Diverse Family Lives: Resisting the Calls to Order and De-Centring the Hetero-Normative Family' (2010) 32(4) *Journal of Social Welfare and Family Law* 353, 359 argues that 'When the heterosexual or now hetero-normative family is reproduced, the genetic link diminishes in significance and when sanctioned by the law or legal framework the donor is expunged.'

known donor cases involve lesbian couples rather than opposite-sex couples.[111] On this basis, Smith observes that 'Excluding known donors from legal recognition through a system which recognises only two parents validates and protects lesbian families but also reinforces the dyadic parenting norm based on heterosexual reproduction.'[112] It is clear that the reliance on the binary, two-parent model becomes particularly problematic in cases involving same-sex couples and 'known donors' and therefore I agree with Wallbank's observation that 'The current framework of allocating parental status to only two people is simply inadequate for responding to the innovative parenting practices adopted by some lesbian parents and their co-parents.'[113]

D. The Influence of the Nuclear Family Model

From all of the foregoing, it is apparent that the law's approach to determining fatherhood in cases of assisted reproduction is complex and applies different rules in different circumstances. However, there are certain universal truths that seem to be unchallenged: as Sheldon notes, for example, central to the attribution of fatherhood under the legislation has been the notion that:

> [T]he symbolism of fatherhood and replication of the nuclear family is crucial: each child should ideally have a father who is married to her mother or, failing that, a father who is committed to the mother and intending to create a child with her.[114]

Thus, I argue that the attribution of legal fatherhood in cases of assisted reproduction is determined within the boundaries of a binary, two-parent model.

Moreover, I submit that the diminishing of the significance of the genetic connection between donors and children is premised upon the continued promotion of the nuclear family, because as Diduck and Kaganas observe:

> [F]atherhood by consent is contrary to law's privileging of biology and things "natural" but [the law] contradicts this position when there is a marriage or marriage-like partnership to privilege above nature … Reliance upon this relationship, now in extended form, continues to privilege the "sexual family".[115]

[111] Research evidence suggests that lesbian couples were more likely to enter into 'known donor' arrangements than use anonymous donors, prior to the reforms of the 2008 Act, see eg Smith, 'Is Three a Crowd? Lesbian Mothers Perspectives on Parental Status in Law' 234 and Dunne, 'Opting into Motherhood: Lesbians Blurring the Boundaries and Transforming the Meaning of Parenthood and Kinship' 16. It is possible that the existence of legal parenthood for both members of a lesbian couple, through the reforms of the 2008 Act, will encourage greater usage of anonymous donors than under the previous regime.

[112] Smith, 'Tangling the Web of Legal Parenthood: Legal Responses to the Use of Known Donors in Lesbian Parenting Arrangements' 378.

[113] Wallbank, 'Channelling the Messiness of Diverse Family Lives: Resisting the Calls to Order and De-Centring the Hetero-Normative Family' 360.

[114] Sheldon, 'Fragmenting Fatherhood: The Regulation of Reproductive Technologies' 541, this comment was made in the context of the provisions of the 1990 Act.

[115] Diduck and Kaganas, *Family Law, Gender and the State* 170.

Thus, ignoring the genetic link confers parenthood on men who are married to mothers or in marriage-like relationships[116] with mothers, rather than on sperm donors, who are unknown to the mother and this approach illustrates the significance of the nuclear family model. Research evidence suggests that relatively few (heterosexual) parents inform their children that they have been conceived using donor sperm[117] and as Fortin states 'any child born by donor conception looks as if he or she has been born into a "normal" nuclear family with one mother and one father. The legislation in this context ignores the biological connectedness between sperm donor and child'.[118]

The report of the Warnock Committee upon which the provisions of the Human Fertilisation and Embryology Act 1990 were based made its preference for the two-parent model and the 'nuclear family' very obvious when it stated, 'we believe that as a general rule it is better for children to be born into a two-parent family, with both father and mother'.[119] It can be seen clearly from this that the promotion and protection of the nuclear family was influential in shaping the legislative approach to determining legal parenthood across the variety of different circumstances in cases of assisted reproduction.[120] While the reforms of the 2008 Act have widened the scope of legal parenthood to allow for the possibility of two female parents, this has been done without altering or challenging the model on which the provisions are based,[121] namely the two-parent model, based upon the traditional, heterosexual, nuclear family. As such, I agree with Smith's observation that, 'legal parenthood remains an exclusive concept – albeit an exclusive concept that is now capable of embracing two parents of the same sex – designed to shore up nuclear families against the disruptive potential of the fragmentation of parenthood'.[122]

[116] The significance given to 'marriage-like' relationships in this context reflects the discussion of the legal regulation of cohabitation on the basis that such relationships are 'marriage-like', set out above in ch 3, subs (II)(A), 'The Legal Regulation of Cohabitation'.

[117] See eg S Golombok, A Braeways, MT Giavazzi, D Guerra, F MacCallum and J Rust, 'The European Study of Assisted Reproduction Families: The Transition to Adolescence' [2002] 17(3) *Human Reproduction* 830, 836, found only 8.6% of the families in their study had told their children (aged 11–12 at the time). See also, S Golombok, C Murray, V Jadva, E Lycett, F MacCallum and J Rust, 'Non-Genetic and Non-Gestational Parenthood: Consequences for Parent-Child Relationships and the Psychological Well-Being of Mothers, Fathers and Children at Age 3' [2006] 21(7) *Human Reproduction* 1918, 1921, where it was observed that 46% of parents of donor conceived children (aged 3) had already decided not to inform their children at any point.

[118] Fortin, 'Children's Right to Know Their Origins – Too Far, Too Fast?' 344.

[119] 'Report of the Committee of Inquiry into Human Fertilisation and Embryology', (July 1984), para 2.11.

[120] Dewar, 'The Normal Chaos of Family Law' 482, observed in the context of the 1990 Act 'The definition of paternity … reflects, more than anything, the type of parents whom the state is prepared to reproduce through the provision of fertility services: namely, the two parent, heterosexual, preferably married, parents.'

[121] Although it should be noted that in contrast, Sheldon and Collier, *Fragmenting Fatherhood: A Socio-Legal Study*, 80, suggest that 'The fierce protection of the heterosexual nuclear family form entrenched in the 1990 legislation gives way to a more fluid and complex sense of familial relationships.'

[122] Smith, 'Clashing Symbols? Reconciling Support for Fathers and Fatherless Families After the Human Fertilisation and Embryology Act 2008' 70.

III. Surrogacy

Horsey and Sheldon have observed that 'The law relating to the attribution of legal parenthood is poorly designed to respond to surrogacy arrangements.'[123] This occurs because of the greater complexity that is introduced into the determination of legal parenthood in cases of surrogacy, where it is possible that, as Horsey identifies:

> [A] child can have up to six potential "parents": two gamete providers, the gestational/birth mother and her husband or partner (if she has one) and the two intending parents, where these are different people. Notably this number is only limited to six because the law is only prepared to recognise two parents, the number could be greater were this not the case.[124]

The complex factual circumstances that may be present in cases of surrogacy sit uneasily within the general approach to legal parenthood in cases of assisted reproduction. This is due to the law's reliance upon a binary, two-parent model.[125] The distinct issues raised by the determination of legal parenthood in cases of surrogacy are not dealt with explicitly by the 2008 Act's framework for determining legal parenthood.[126] Simply put, as Fenton-Glynn observes, 'The status provisions … were not designed with surrogacy in mind'.[127]

Moreover, the issues regarding surrogacy are magnified because UK law currently treats surrogacy arrangements as unenforceable between the parties[128] and organising commercial surrogacy remains prohibited;[129] consequently, surrogacy arrangements remain unregulated by the Human Fertilisation and Embryology Authority. This relatively restrictive legal regime is based upon the report of the Warnock Committee, which was opposed to surrogacy and commented that 'Even in compelling medical circumstances the danger of exploitation of

[123] Kirsty Horsey and Sally Sheldon, 'Still Hazy After All These Years: The Law Regulating Surrogacy' (2012) 20(1) *Medical Law Review* 67, 87. See further eg Emily Jackson, *Regulating Reproduction: Law, Technology and Autonomy* (Oxford, Hart Publishing, 2001), who similarly observes, at 283, 'The Human Fertilisation and Embryology Act's status provisions apply awkwardly and inappropriately to surrogacy arrangements.'

[124] Kirsty Horsey 'Challenging Presumptions: Legal Parenthood and Surrogacy Arrangements' [2010] 22(4) *Child and Family Law Quarterly* 449, 453.

[125] Although the provisions of HFEA 2008, s 54 that set out the procedures for 'parental orders' allow for the possibility that the intended social reality of the parties to the surrogacy arrangement will be given effect to within six months of the child being born; s 54(6) states that 'the court must be satisfied that both … [the surrogate mother and her husband, if he is deemed the legal father] … have freely, and with full understanding of what is involved, agreed unconditionally to the making of the order'.

[126] Horsey, 'Challenging Presumptions: Legal Parenthood and Surrogacy Arrangements', suggests that consideration of surrogacy did not form a major part of the reform proposals that led to HFEA 2008, stating, at 451 'where a child is born using surrogacy (with or without donated gametes) the law regarding parenthood was left almost entirely untouched'.

[127] Claire Fenton-Glynn, 'The Regulation and Recognition of Surrogacy Under English Law: An Overview of the Case-Law' [2015] 27(1) *Child and Family Law Quarterly* 83, 84.

[128] Surrogacy Arrangements Act 1985, s 1A states 'No surrogacy arrangement is enforceable by or against any of the persons making it.'

[129] Surrogacy Arrangements Act 1985, s 2. This section prohibits the operation of a commercial surrogacy agency, making it 'an offence' in terms of s 2(2).

one human being by another appears ... far to outweigh the potential benefits, in almost every case.'[130] Thus, the legal regulation of surrogacy arrangements has always been premised upon this exploitative conception of surrogacy and Alghrani and Griffiths observe that 'since 1985, the law governing surrogacy has developed in a haphazard fashion and piecemeal changes made over the years have resulted in a regulatory framework that is contradictory and confusing for all involved'.[131]

Historically, as a consequence of the regulatory regime surrogacy was not widely used within the UK.[132] More recently, however, there has been evidence of increasing use of surrogacy,[133] with particular growth observed in international surrogacy arrangements.[134] As well as this, there is evidence of evolving attitudes towards the practice of surrogacy.[135] Therefore, it is unsurprising that in December 2017, the Law Commission announced the inclusion of surrogacy within its 13th Programme of Law Reform,[136] commenting that 'We take the view that the law relating to surrogacy is outdated and unclear, and requires comprehensive reform.'[137] Consequently, proposals for law reform concerning the legal regulation of surrogacy arrangements will be forthcoming.[138] However, the manner in which

[130] 'Report of the Committee of Inquiry into Human Fertilisation and Embryology', (July 1984), para 8.17.

[131] Amel Alghrani and Danielle Griffiths, 'The Regulation of Surrogacy in the United Kingdom: The Case for Reform' [2017] 29(2) *Child and Family Law Quarterly* 165, 166.

[132] Official figures as to the number of surrogacies are difficult to obtain due to the unregulated nature of surrogacy. However, the non-profit organisation 'Childlessness Overcome Through Surrogacy' (COTS), state they have been involved in over 1,000 surrogate births since 1988, available at: www.surrogacy.org.uk/.

[133] Crawshaw, Blyth and van den Akker, 'The Changing Profile of Surrogacy in the UK – Implications for National and International Policy and Practice', 269, the authors present data based on correspondence with the General Register Office, which shows that there has been a sharp increase in the number of parental orders granted in the UK, with 149 in 2011 compared to 51 in 2007. See also National Records of Scotland, 'Vital Events Reference Tables 2014, Section 2: Adoption and Re-Registrations', (August 2015), where, curiously, parental orders after surrogacy are listed as a 'Type of Adoption', show that in the six years between 2003 (when the first parental order was made in Scotland) and 2008 there were 15 such orders made by the Scottish courts, while in the six years between 2009 (when the rules for eligibility to apply were expanded) and 2014 there were 52 such orders.

[134] ibid, at 271, the authors note that in 2011 26% of parental orders in England and Wales involved a child that had been born abroad, compared to only 2% in 2008.

[135] See eg Kirsty Horsey, 'Surrogacy in the UK: Myth Busting and Reform', Report of the Surrogacy UK Working Group on Surrogacy Law Reform, (November 2015), paras 3.1–3.2, at 19–25, which provides data regarding the attitudes of those involved in surrogacy arrangements, available at: https://www.surrogacyuk.org/Downloads/Surrogacy%20in%20the%20UK%20Report%20FINAL.pdf.

[136] Law Commission, 'Thirteenth Programme of Law Reform', (Law Com No 377, December 2017). This will be a joint project with the Scottish Law Commission, 'Tenth Programme of Law Reform', (Scot Law Com No 250, February 2018).

[137] ibid, para 2.44, at 21.

[138] ibid, para 2.43, at 21, the Law Commission sets out a range of issues that may be considered in the upcoming law reform project, stating 'There are, therefore, significant questions relating to the procedure for the grant of Parental Orders to the intended parents. But these are only some of the issues that arise. Surrogacy arrangements also raise issues of children's rights to access information about their parentage, both genetic and gestational, while there are wider questions around the basis on which surrogacy arrangements should be permitted. International surrogacy arrangements bring into focus problems surrounding the nationality of children born to surrogates (including the risk of statelessness), bringing surrogate-born children into the UK, and the risk of exploitation of all the parties involved.'

the specific issues regarding surrogacy and the determination of legal parenthood will be approached in these proposed reforms remains to be seen.

Nevertheless, regardless of this potential law reform, it is clear that the use of surrogacy as a method of reproduction challenges some of the fundamental underpinning assumptions of parenthood, as Cook et al state:

> Surrogacy is problematic for traditional notions of "mother", "father" and "family" when it introduces a third (or even fourth) party into reproduction, when it introduces contractual or "public" arrangements into "private" affairs and when it fragments motherhood. Surrogacy makes motherhood negotiable and confounds both social and biological bases of claims to parenthood.[139]

In this section, the additional complexity that results from the process of surrogacy will be explored, and in particular, I will argue that the reliance upon a binary, two-parent model of legal parenthood fits uneasily with the factual circumstances of surrogacy; considering the attribution of both motherhood (subsection A) and fatherhood (subsection B). As well as this, I will argue that, the 'parental order' (the order through which legal parenthood can be transferred from the surrogate to the intended parents) continues to reinforce the two-parent model (subsection C).

A. Motherhood

Douglas has commented that 'English law views the gestational mother as the legal mother because this will produce the right result in terms of parentage for all cases except for surrogacy.'[140] The seemingly straightforward approach to maternity, which applies across contexts, creates complexity in cases of surrogacy, because there are two women with competing claims to 'motherhood'. As Cook observes 'A major moral concern in relation to these types of family formation is the fragmentation of parenthood. This fragmentation is more explicit in surrogacy than any other reproductive option: it separates social motherhood from gestation and genetics.'[141] However, the law relies upon the binary two-parent model and thus determines motherhood on the basis of gestation, which results in the surrogate being recognised as the child's legal mother at birth.[142] Thus, I argue that surrogacy presents a factual context where the reliance upon the traditional, indivisible, 'natural' construction of 'mother' creates issues in the attribution of legal

[139] Rachel Cook and Shelley Day Sclater with Felicity Kaganas (eds), *Surrogate Motherhood: International Perspectives* (Oxford, Hart Publishing, 2003) 4.

[140] Douglas, 'The Intention to Be a Parent and the Making of Mothers' 640.

[141] Rachel Cook, 'Donating Parenthood: Perspectives on Parenthood from Surrogacy and Gamete Donation' in Bainham, Day Sclater and Richards (eds), *What is a Parent?: A Socio-Legal Analysis* 122.

[142] See eg *Re Z (A Child) (Surrogacy Arrangement: Child Arrangements Orders)* [2017] EWCA Civ 228, for a rare example of the breakdown of a surrogacy arrangement, and the resultant dispute between the surrogate and the intended parents regarding the child's residence.

parenthood.[143] This approach to determining legal motherhood gives limited significance or recognition to the intended social reality in surrogacy cases, where the process of gestation and giving birth is separated from the social practice of 'mothering', as they will be undertaken by different women. As a consequence of the law's reliance upon a binary, two-parent model, it is necessary for an explicit choice to be made between these competing claims to motherhood and Wallbank suggests that 'by adopting the either/or approach it reinforces the ideology inherent in much of family law and social policy that children's best interests are served by being raised in the traditional two-parent family'.[144] Thus, the approach to determining motherhood in cases of surrogacy diminishes the importance of the intention of the parties and social parenting,[145] instead preferencing a unified construction of motherhood based upon gestation.[146] I suggest that this reflects the rhetorical power of the law's construction of mother as 'natural',[147] since legal motherhood is exclusively determined on the basis of gestation and no other factors are considered.[148] Moreover, I argue that this approach illustrates the significance of the binary, two-parent model of the nuclear family in the attribution of legal parenthood, in spite of the more complex factual circumstances which exist in cases of surrogacy.

B. Fatherhood

Surrogacy can also complicate the attribution of legal fatherhood, because the provisions of the 2008 Act apply to all forms of assisted reproduction, meaning

[143] The situation of non-gestational female 'parents' provides another example of the problematic consequences of the 'natural' indivisible construction of the 'mother' upon the determination of legal parenthood, see above at, subs II(B), 'Non-Gestational Female "Parents"'. Although it should be noted that in the context of surrogacy the privileging of gestation could also be seen as a protective measure, which ensures that the woman who carried the child ('the gestational mother') always retains the option to change her mind.

[144] Julie Wallbank, 'Too Many Mothers? Surrogacy, Kinship and the Welfare of the Child' (2002) 10(3) *Medical Law Review* 271, 286.

[145] However, it is notable that the significance of social parenting and 'care' are recognised in this context by 'parental orders', under HFEA 2008, s 54 which transfer parenthood to the commissioning couple after birth, these essentially operate as a form of fast-track adoptions. These orders will be considered in more detail below at subs III(C), 'Parental Orders'.

[146] The approach also does not reflect the research into the perspectives of surrogates themselves, see eg Vasanti Jadva, Clare Murray, Emma Lycett, Fiona MacCallum and Susan Golombok, 'Surrogacy: The Experiences of Surrogate Mothers' [2003] 18(10) *Human Reproduction* 2196, who find that 59% of surrogates felt they had no 'special bond' with the child and go on to find, at 2203, that 'none of the women in the present study had any doubts about their decision to hand over the child to the commissioning couple'. See also, Fiona MacCallum, Emma Lycett, Clare Murray, Vasanti Jadva and Susan Golombok, 'Surrogacy: The Experience of Commissioning Couples' [2003] 18(6) *Human Reproduction* 1334.

[147] This construction will be explored in more detail below in ch 5, subs II(A), 'What is the "Mother" in the Law?'.

[148] However, the provisions of HFEA 2008, s 54(2) governing applications for 'parental orders', include civil partners and both opposite-sex and same-sex cohabitants, therefore the act is expressly allowing for situations in which a child would be legally motherless, through the granting of a parental order to two men.

that in most cases where the surrogate is married, it will be her husband who is likely to be presumed to be the child's father at birth.[149] This applies regardless of whether the sperm of the commissioning father is used; in such circumstances the commissioning father is effectively in a position equivalent to that of a 'known donor' and therefore has no legally recognised parental relationship with the child at birth.[150] This result illustrates, even more clearly than the determination of legal motherhood that a binary two-parent model is an inappropriate fit with the factual circumstances of surrogacy arrangements. This is because legal parenthood is attributed to a man with no genetic relationship to the child, who also has no intention of having any social relationship with that child in the future,[151] purely on the basis of the existence of a marital relationship. Consequently, relationship status is being privileged over other factors; genetic connection, the intention of the parties and social parenting. In Horsey's view 'this is a wholly unnecessary legal fiction and, while reinforcing the notion that motherhood is determined by gestation, does not mirror the way that father following other forms of assisted reproduction is regulated'.[152] I submit that this result acutely illustrates the law's promotion of marriage, a binary, two-parent model and the idealised image of the nuclear family, regardless of the existence of complex factual circumstances which may justify alternative, more nuanced approaches.[153]

Thus, the application of a unified approach to legal parenthood in cases of assisted reproduction has the consequence in some surrogacy cases of assigning legal fatherhood in a manner that ignores both the genetic connections and the intentions of the parties as to future social parenting. This stands in contrast to both the law's emphasis on consent and reflecting social parenting when determining legal fatherhood in other types of assisted reproduction[154] and the emphasis on the significance of the genetic connection in cases of natural reproduction.[155]

[149] Except in cases where he didn't consent to his wife's treatment, HFEA 2008, s 35(1).

[150] Although as this is merely a presumption of fatherhood, the intended father in such circumstances would be able to assert his genetic paternity through testing, as described above in cases of natural reproduction, at s I, 'Natural Reproduction'. However, the determination of legal parenthood at birth remains premised upon the centrality of marriage and the nuclear family.

[151] In comparison to the surrogate, whose legal parenthood is premised upon her having a gestational connection.

[152] Horsey 'Challenging Presumptions: Legal Parenthood and Surrogacy' 450.

[153] ibid, at 455–474, Horsey argues for the development of an approach to determining legal parenthood in cases of assisted reproduction that is premised upon intention. Indeed, it is submitted that the approach to the attribution of legal parenthood in cases of surrogacy should be reconsidered. I suggest that this should be premised upon legal parenthood in cases of surrogacy being attributed under different legislative provisions than other types of assisted reproduction. Such an alternative approach would allow the particular issues regarding legal parenthood in the context of surrogacy to be addressed by the law. As mentioned above, the Law Commission are currently reviewing the regulation concerning surrogacy arrangements, it is hoped that this will result in the proposal of an alternative regime for the determination of legal parenthood in cases of surrogacy.

[154] As set out above in subs II(C), 'Fatherhood'.

[155] As discussed above in s I, 'Natural Reproduction'.

C. Parental Orders

The law's attempt to provide a partial solution to the specific problems of the attribution of legal parenthood in cases of surrogacy was to create the 'parental order'.[156] This is the post-birth order through which legal parenthood is transferred from the surrogate mother (and in some cases her husband)[157] to the intended parents, without the need to go through the full adoption process.[158] However, as with the determination at birth, these orders continue to reflect the binary two-parent model, allowing for legal parenthood to be granted to the intended parents[159] at the same time as it is removed from the surrogate, rather than acknowledging the potential for three (or more) 'parental' roles to exist simultaneously from birth. Indeed, when parental orders were created by section 30 of the 1990 Act, they were consciously designed to protect the traditional nuclear family, as the orders were originally only available to married couples,[160] who represent the archetypical couple within the idealised image of the nuclear family model. Furthermore, parental orders did not originally form part of the planned regime for the attribution of legal parenthood in cases of assisted reproduction. Instead, the provision

[156] The judicial interpretation of the conditions for granting a 'parental order' in HFEA 2008, s 54 in a range of cases, including s 54(8) in *Re X and Y (Children) (Parental Order: Foreign Surrogacy)* [2008] EWHC 3030 (Fam), [2009] 1 FLR 733, s 54(4) and (5) in *A v P (Surrogacy: Parental Order: Death of Applicant)* [2011] EWHC 1738 (Fam), [2012] 2 FLR 145, s 54(3) *Re X (A Child) (Parental Order: Time Limit)* [2014] EWHC 3135 (Fam), [2015] 1 FLR 349 and s 54(1) *Re Z (A Child) (Surrogate Father: Parental Order)* [2015] EWFC 73, [2017] 1 FLR 472, has prompted significant academic criticism. Mary Welstead, 'Surrogacy: One More Nail in the Coffin' [2014] *Fam Law* 1637, 1637, described the decision in *Re X* as 'hammering the nails into the coffin of s 54 of the Human Fertilisation and Embryology Act 2008'. See further eg Kirsty Horsey, 'Fraying at the Edges: UK Surrogacy Law in 2015' (2016) 24(4) *Medical Law Review* 608, Philip Bremner, 'Surrogacy and Single Parents Following *Re Z*' (2017) 21(2) *Edinburgh Law Review* 281 and Kenneth Norrie, 'English and Scottish Adoption Orders and British Parental Orders After Surrogacy: Welfare, Competence and Judicial Legislation' [2017] 29(2) *Child and Family Law Quarterly* 93. Moreover, these interpretative issues were a significant impetus for the inclusion of surrogacy within the Law Commission's '13th Programme of Law Reform'.

[157] HFEA 2008, s 35(1) as discussed above at subs III(B), 'Fatherhood'. Moreover, HFEA 2008, s 54(6) provides that the surrogate (and her husband) must 'have freely, and with full understanding of what is involved, agreed unconditionally to the making of the order'. See *Re AB (Surrogacy: Consent)* [2016] EWHC 2643 (Fam), [2017] 2 FLR 217, for an example of such consent being withheld.

[158] HFEA 2008, s 54(1) states 'On an application made by two people ("the applicants"), the court may make an order providing for a child to be treated in law as the child of the applicants'. There are various beneficial consequences for the intended parents of not having to utilise the adoption procedure. For example, a parental order can be granted in a shorter timeframe than an adoption order and there is no requirement for an independent assessment to be made of the suitability of the intended parents in order for a parental order to be granted (as there would be for an adoption order).

[159] Section 54(1) explicitly excludes the possibility of single applicants for parental orders. However, a 'declaration of incompatibility' was made under s 4 of the Human Rights Act 1998 in *Re Z (A Child) (Surrogate Father: Parental Order) (No 2)* [2016] EWHC 1191 (Fam), [2016] 2 FLR 327, on the basis that this provision was incompatible with Art 14 in conjunction with Art 8. The government introduced a remedial order in November 2017 to address this issue and allow single applicants, see Ministerial Statement of Philip Dunne, 'Human Fertilisation and Embryology Act 2008: Remedial Order: Written Statement', 29 November 2017, HCWS282. At the time of writing (June 2018) the remedial order has not been passed by Parliament, but it is expected later in Summer 2018.

[160] Section 30(1) of the 1990 Act stated: 'The court may make an order providing for a child to be treated in law as the child of the parties to a marriage.'

creating the orders was inserted at a late stage of the legislative process, in response to a complaint received by a backbench MP from constituents who had undertaken a surrogacy arrangement[161] and who objected to 'having to adopt "their children"'.[162] Consequently, the resulting provisions, which attempted to ameliorate some of the problematic consequences of the attribution of legal parenthood in cases of surrogacy, were 'rapidly drafted'.[163] Therefore, under the 1990 Act, the 'solution' of the parental order was only made available to those people (married couples) who fit within the traditional, binary, two-parent model. While the reforms of the 2008 Act expanded the scope of those couples who can apply for a parental order, to include same-sex couples and unmarried couples,[164] this expansion did not include single applicants,[165] and as set out above, the underlying model of family was not challenged or altered during the reform process.[166] Therefore, I argue that the parental order provides further illustration of the continuing significance of the binary, two-parent model to the attribution of legal parenthood in cases of surrogacy.[167]

Consequently, I contend that the attribution of legal parenthood in cases of surrogacy sits uneasily within a legislative framework that is premised upon the exclusive, binary, two-parent model, because the factual circumstances of surrogacy arrangements introduce additional potential 'parents' into the 'natural' factual scenario, but this cannot be taken into account by that model.

To conclude, in this chapter, I have argued that UK law's approach to the attribution of legal parenthood is based upon a binary, two-parent model. I have observed that the legal determination of motherhood employs a simple test in all circumstances; motherhood is based upon gestation. Although the chapter has also noted that this simple test is complicated by the contexts of egg donation and surrogacy arrangements. By contrast, the legal attribution of fatherhood involves different factors being prioritised in different circumstances; the existence of a marriage between the mother and father, the consent and actions of the parties and the genetic connection between the father and

[161] Their dispute with the local authority became *Re W (Minors) (Surrogacy)* [1991] 1 FLR 385, prior to the coming into force of s 30 of the 1990 Act in November 1994.

[162] The Brazier Report, 'Surrogacy: Review for Health Ministers Current Arrangements for Payments and Regulation', (Department of Health, October 1998), para 3.12, at 20, available at: http://webarchive.nationalarchives.gov.uk/20130107105354/http://www.dh.gov.uk/prod_consum_dh/groups/dh_digitalassets/@dh/@en/documents/digitalasset/dh_4014373.pdf.

[163] Claire Fenton-Glynn, 'Outsourcing Ethical Dilemmas: Regulating International Surrogacy Arrangements' (2016) 24(1) *Medical Review Law* 59, 61.

[164] HFEA 2008, s 54(2).

[165] Ibid, s 54(1). Although, as set out above, reforms to this provision are currently before Parliament.

[166] See eg McCandless and Sheldon, 'The Human Fertilisation and Embryology Act (2008) and the Tenacity of the Sexual Family Form'.

[167] I have previously advanced this argument in greater detail in Alan Brown, 'Two Means Two, but Must Does Not Mean Must: An Analysis of Recent Decisions on the Conditions for Parental Orders in Surrogacy' [2018] 30(1) *Child and Family Law Quarterly* 23.

the child are all used to determine fatherhood in different contexts. Jackson has commented that the approach taken to the determination of legal parenthood has occurred:

> Because the law has been stymied by the principle of parental exclusivity, its response to the splitting of the normal incidents of parenthood has been to try to identify a hierarchy of criteria which will result in one putative parents claim trumping the others. In so doing, it has become spectacularly confused and confusing, not least because different hierarchies operate in different circumstances.[168]

In addition, I have argued that historically, the law sought to promote the traditional nuclear family (comprising one mother and one father, who are married) when making determinations of legal parenthood.[169] This approach has recently been supplanted, in cases of natural reproduction, by a focus on the genetic connection between father and child. However, I have argued that these developments occurred within an overarching framework premised upon a binary, two-parent model. Moreover, I have observed that the emphasis on genetic connection has not been evident in the contexts of assisted reproduction and surrogacy. Instead, in these contexts, the existence of marital relationships and the consent of individual men are privileged. Thus, I argued that a binary two-parent model and the traditional nuclear family continue to underpin the framework for determining legal parenthood in cases of assisted reproduction, even though these provisions have been reformed to include legal parenthood for both members of same-sex couples.

The next chapter will build upon this identification of a binary, two-parent model within the attribution of legal parenthood by considering the legal understanding of the parental role and arguing that this understanding is premised upon the traditional, gendered roles of 'mother' and 'father' of the nuclear family model.

[168] Jackson, 'What is a Parent?' in Diduck and O'Donovan (eds), *Feminist Perspectives on Family Law* 60.

[169] Through the usage of the *pater est* presumption, which was influenced by the consequences of the statuses of legitimacy and illegitimacy.

5

The Legal Understanding of the Parental Role

This chapter will contend that the legal understanding of the parental role is dependent upon the 'natural' constructions of the gendered parenting roles of 'mother' and 'father', derived from the traditional nuclear family model. Collier argues that within the law there has developed, 'a notion of the responsible parent as formally gender-neutral … Yet the concept of gender neutrality is itself, as a growing number of scholars have argued, extremely questionable in several respects.'[1] Indeed, the chapter will argue that the law's starting point is an overarching conception of the parental role, which encompasses all parents.[2] However, I will argue that this overarching 'parental role' remains opaque within legal discourse and judicial interpretation; in sharp contrast to the traditional gendered parenting roles, the role of 'parent' lacks any 'natural' or 'common-sense' construction.[3] As Diduck comments, 'Both law and parents tend to reward fathers for caring about their children, while mothers' caring for them is unremarkable, taken for granted and thus unrewarded.'[4] These different gendered constructions of parental role permeate legal discourse; Kaganas and Day Sclater have commented that:

> Good mothers not only refrain from obstructing contact but actively facilitate it. Good fathers, at least for the purposes of contact, take some interest in their children and do not harm them or, generally speaking, behave violently to mothers. Good parents co-operate and do not litigate.[5]

[1] Richard Collier, 'A Hard Time to Be a Father?: Reassessing the Relationship Between Law, Policy, and Family (Practices)' (2001) 28(4) *Journal of Law and Society* 520, 535.

[2] See eg Children Act 1989, s 3(1) which provides the meaning of 'parental responsibility' in an entirely gender-neutral form. See further Children (Scotland) Act 1995, which details 'parental responsibilities', s 1, and 'parental rights', s 2, in Scots law in similarly gender-neutral language.

[3] The association of these gendered roles with the nuclear family and the public/private divide was discussed above throughout ch 2, particularly at subs I(B) 'The Development of the "Public/Private" Divide' and subs III(A), 'The Legal Subject and the Nuclear Family'.

[4] Diduck, *Law's Families* 86.

[5] Kaganas and Day Sclater, 'Contact Disputes: Narrative Constructions of "Good" Parents' 13.

I will argue that, consequently, it is the gendered roles which shape the legal understanding of the role of the 'parent' and through this I will show the continuing significance of the idealised image of the nuclear family.[6]

This chapter will illustrate the influence of the gendered parenting roles of 'mother' and 'father' by examining how the law constructs the parental role. In section I, I will explore the understanding of the 'parent' within the law; considering the statutory concepts of 'parental responsibilities'[7] and 'parental rights'[8] and suggesting that these provide limited specific guidance as to the role of the 'parent'. In section II, I will argue that when the parental role is considered and interpreted by the judiciary, the gap created by this lack of guidance is filled by relying upon the readily identifiable and easily understandable archetypes of the traditional, gendered parenting roles of 'mother' and 'father'. Finally, in section III, I will consider the legal understanding of lesbian parenthood, which provides a situation where one parental role (that of the non-gestational female 'parent') is explicitly described in legislation as the 'parent'.[9] I will argue that the lack of exposition or detailed consideration of the role of the non-gestational female 'parent', in this context where neither gendered role is available, further illustrates the privileging of the traditional gendered parenting roles of the nuclear family.

I. What is the 'Parent' in the Law?

Diduck observes that 'Law "speaks" of parents and spouses rather than of mothers, fathers, husbands, wives'.[10] It is evident that the government consistently emphasises the importance of parenting using gender-neutral language; for example 'Good parenting therefore reduces the risks that children experience poor behavioural outcomes, criminality and anti-social behaviour'[11] and 'Parenting has a greater impact on children's wellbeing, learning and development than anything else'.[12]

[6] Recent research suggests that in 2011 the proportion of families in the UK with two full-time earners had risen to 29%, from 26% in 2001, while the proportion where the father works full-time and the mother works part-time had fallen to 31%, from 37% in 2001. The proportion of sole male breadwinners remained stable at 22% throughout the period, whereas the total proportion of families where women were the main earner was only 12%. This suggests that the traditional gendered roles are still influencing the practices of a significant proportion of families in contemporary society, 'Modern Fatherhood: Fathers, Work and Families in the 21st Century', available at: www.modernfatherhood.org/themes/fathers-and-work/?view=key-facts-and-figures.

[7] Children Act 1989, s 3 see also Children (Scotland) Act 1995, s 1.

[8] Children Act 1989, s 3(1), see also Children (Scotland) Act 1995, s 2.

[9] Human Fertilisation and Embryology Act 2008, ss 42–47.

[10] Diduck, *Law's Families* 41.

[11] 'Supporting Families in the Foundation Years', (Department for Education, October 2011), 36, para 73, available at: www.gov.uk/government/uploads/system/uploads/attachment_data/file/184868/DFE-01001-2011_supporting_families_in_the_foundation_years.pdf.

[12] 'Positive for Youth: A New Approach to Cross-Government Policy for Young People Aged 13 to 19', (Department for Education, February 2010), 13, para 3.7, available at: https://assets.publishing.service.gov.uk/government/uploads/system/uploads/attachment_data/file/175496/DFE-00133-2011.pdf.

However, such statements are generally expressed in vague terms[13] and consequently do not provide any substantive insight into the understanding of the role of the 'parent', nor any guidance as to the specific details and characteristics of that role.[14] Similarly, legislation often utilises the gender-neutral terminology of 'parent',[15] most obviously through the concepts of 'parental responsibilities'[16] and 'parental rights'.[17] Notably, those people who can be granted parental responsibilities and rights by the law are a wider group than merely the legal parents of a child.[18] Although legal parents[19] automatically possess parental responsibilities and rights, it is also possible for 'natural fathers'[20] who do not have automatic responsibilities and rights to acquire them.[21] The statutory definitions and judicial interpretation of these terms should provide some indication of the legal understanding of the role and functions of the 'parent'; however, I will argue that there is an absence of clarity about the meaning of these terms and consequently about the characteristics of the parental role. I will argue, therefore, that when the law uses the gender-neutral language of the 'parent', this role is judicially interpreted by defaulting back to the 'natural' and 'common sense' constructions of the archetypical gendered parenting roles of 'mother' and 'father', derived from the traditional nuclear family.

[13] See 'Support for All: The Families and Relationships Green Paper', (Department for Children, Schools and Families, January 2010), for a further example of the vague, gender-neutral language used to describe parenting, at 56, para 3.2, which stated 'Parents are the most profoundly important people in the world for babies and younger children and remain hugely significant to children as they grow up. Good parenting is crucial for children's outcomes and can protect them against other disadvantages.' Available at: https://assets.publishing.service.gov.uk/government/uploads/system/uploads/attachment_data/file/329448/Support_for_All.pdf.

[14] Felicity Kaganas and Alison Diduck, 'Incomplete Citizens: Changing Images of Post-Separation Children' (2004) 67(6) *Modern Law Review* 959, 959, observe that 'The images of "good" parents that populate law's discourse, therefore, are very close to those apparent in the dominant discourse espoused by policy-makers and within popular culture.'

[15] See eg the amendment of Children Act 1989, s 1 by Children and Families Act 2014, s 11, which states 'as respects each parent … to presume, unless the contrary is shown, that involvement of that parent in the life of the child concerned will further the child's welfare'.

[16] Children Act 1989, s 3, see also Children (Scotland) Act 1995, s 1.

[17] Children Act 1989, s 3(1) defines 'parental responsibility' as including 'rights'. In contrast, in Scots law there is a separate statutory definition for 'parental rights' in the Children (Scotland) Act 1995, s 2.

[18] Under English law there is a specific procedure (Children Act 1989, s 4A) for step-parents to acquire parental responsibilities and other individuals require 'the leave of the court' (Children Act 1989, s 10) to make such applications. In Scots law, under the Children (Scotland) Act 1995, s 11(3)(a)(i) the court is able to grant orders for 'parental responsibilities and rights' to any person, 'who – not having, and never having had, parental responsibilities or parental rights in relation to the child, claims an interest'.

[19] 'Legal parents' have such responsibilities and rights in terms of the following provisions, Children Act 1989 s 2(1) for mothers and married fathers, s 2(1A) for non-gestational female parents with legal parenthood and s 2(2)(b) for unmarried fathers who satisfy the terms of s 4(1). In Scotland, the relevant provision are as follows, Children (Scotland) Act 1995, s 3(1)(a) for mothers, s 3(1)(b) for married fathers and Family Law (Scotland) Act 2006, s 23(2) for unmarried fathers whose name is on the birth certificate.

[20] This is the term used by the legislation; it is taken to mean unmarried 'genetic' fathers without parental responsibilities and rights.

[21] Either by agreement with the child's mother, Children Act 1989, s 4(1)(b), or through the granting of a court order to that effect, Children Act 1989, s 4(1)(c). See s 4(1) and Children (Scotland) Act 1995, s 11 for the relevant Scots law provisions for acquisition of parental responsibilities by unmarried fathers.

In this section, I will consider the role of the 'parent', suggesting that there is not a clear understanding of this overarching parental role, independent from the traditional gendered roles. The statutory concepts of parental responsibilities and parental rights will be considered and I will suggest that these concepts are defined in vague terms and consequently offer limited guidance as to the role of the 'parent' (subsection A). I will argue that the law relies instead upon the 'natural' gendered roles of 'mother' and 'father' when constructing the role of the 'parent' (subsection B).

A. The Content of Parental Responsibilities and Parental Rights

The approach taken to defining the content of parental responsibilities differs under the relevant English and Scottish legislation. However, I will observe that the approaches in both jurisdictions provide a general, overarching definition of the concept, which does not provide significant specific guidance as to the role of the 'parent'.

In England and Wales, the statutory provision is imprecise, defining 'parental responsibility' as 'all the rights, duties, powers, responsibilities and authority which by law a parent of a child has in relation to the child and his property'.[22] In this definition 'parental rights' are explicitly included as part of 'parental responsibilities', illustrating that these rights are understood as forming one part of the responsibilities. This vague statutory definition has left the content of parental responsibilities to be established and considered by the courts; Bainham suggests that this approach presupposes, 'some knowledge of the effects of being a parent which the courts have formulated over a long period of time at common law'.[23] However, this approach has resulted in contradiction and apparent divergence between competing authorities.[24] Black LJ has observed that 'Parental responsibility can be a difficult concept to grasp, particularly when it comes to the details of how it works in practice'[25] and Bridgeman has commented that 'the concept of parental responsibility has been developed into a confused, contradictory concept with little meaning in relation to the responsibility of caring for children'.[26] This confusion about the meaning of parental responsibilities is illustrated by the contrast between judicial descriptions of parental responsibility

[22] Children Act 1989, s 3(1).

[23] Bainham, 'Parentage, Parenthood and Parental Responsibility: Subtle, Elusive, Yet Very Important Distinctions' in Bainham, Day Sclater and Richards (eds), *What is a Parent?: A Socio-Legal Analysis* 35.

[24] Stephen Gilmore, Jonathan Herring and Rebecca Probert, 'Introduction: Parental Responsibility – Law, Issues and Themes' in Rebecca Probert, Stephen Gilmore and Jonathan Herring (eds), *Responsible Parents and Parental Responsibility* (Oxford, Hart Publishing, 2009) 12, observe that in English law 'the concept of parental responsibility is far from straightforward'.

[25] *T v T (Shared Residence)* [2010] EWCA Civ 1366, [2011] 1 FCR 267, at para 23.

[26] Jo Bridgeman, 'Parental Responsibility, Responsible Parenting and Legal Regulation' in Jo Bridgeman, Craig Lind and Helen M. Keating (eds), *Responsibility, Law and the Family* (Aldershot, Ashgate, 2008) 237.

as a 'stamp of approval'[27] or 'essentially an acknowledgment of status'[28] and other decisions which suggest parental responsibility should not be granted unless it could be exercised effectively.[29] This judicial approach to parental responsibilities has led Herring to observe that 'there is a real tension in the case law as to whether parental responsibility is about real decision-making power, or whether it is of more symbolic value',[30] and Harris and George to comment that 'it has become increasingly uncertain what the purpose and effect of parental responsibility is'.[31] I contend that, as a result of the lack of clarity within the authorities as to the meaning of 'parental responsibility' and the extent of the practical decision-making power that derives from this responsibility, this statutory concept does not provide clarification of the legal understanding of the role of the 'parent'.

In Scotland, the relevant legislation defines both 'parental responsibilities' and 'parental rights'. The former are defined as including two general 'responsibilities', which are 'to safeguard and promote the child's health, development and welfare'[32] and 'to provide, in a manner appropriate to the stage of development of the child – (i) direction; (ii) guidance, to the child'.[33] These two responsibilities overlap and are expressed in a relatively vague and universal way, providing for general rather than specific guidance to parents, and are designed to cover virtually every aspect of a child's upbringing.[34] The legislation then defines the more specific responsibility 'if the child is not living with the parent, to maintain personal relations and direct contact with the child on a regular basis'.[35] I suggest that this emphasis on

[27] Ward LJ in *Re S (A Minor) (Parental Responsibility)* [1995] 2 FLR 648, at 657, see further John Eekelaar, 'Rethinking Parental Responsibility' [2001] 31(6) *Fam Law* 426.

[28] Thorpe LJ in *Re H (A Child) (Parental Responsibility)* [2002] EWCA Civ 542, at para 15.

[29] See eg *M v M (Parental Responsibility)* [1999] 2 FLR 737, where parental responsibility was denied on the basis that the father lacked the mental capacities to make decisions on behalf of the child, *Re G (A Child) (Parental Responsibility Order)* [2006] EWCA Civ 745, [2006] 2 FLR 1092, where the first instance judge had purported to grant 'suspended parental responsibility', which was rejected by the Court of Appeal, with Hedley J stating, at 1096 'to make a parental responsibility order and then effectively draw all its teeth is something that would be a most unusual thing to do' and *Re B (Role of the Biological Father)* [2007] EWHC 1952 (Fam), [2008] 1 FLR 1015, where parental responsibility was denied to a 'known donor' on the basis that his use of parental responsibility would diminish the parental status of the lesbian nuclear family.

[30] Herring, *Family Law* 436, see also Helen Reece, 'The Degradation of Parental Responsibility' in Probert, Gilmore and Herring (eds), *Responsible Parents and Parental Responsibility*, who suggests, at 102 'there is a trend away from parental responsibility as parental authority towards parental responsibility as nothing more than official approval'.

[31] Peter G Harris and Robert H George, 'Parental Responsibility and Shared Residence Orders: Parliamentary Intentions and Judicial Interpretation' [2010] 22(2) *Child and Family Law Quarterly* 151, 170. The authors suggest that the judicial interpretation of parental responsibility has not reflected the concept as it was originally envisaged in the Children Act 1989.

[32] Children (Scotland) Act 1995, s 1(1)(a).

[33] Children (Scotland) Act 1995, s 1(1)(b).

[34] Children (Scotland) Act 1995, s 1(4) states 'The parental responsibilities supersede any analogous duties imposed on a parent at common law'. Thus, the statutory definition was required to provide for the entirety of the child's upbringing.

[35] Children (Scotland) Act 1995, s 1(1)(c), the section defines one additional specific responsibility, Children (Scotland) Act 1995, s 1(1)(d) 'to act as the child's legal representative'. However, it is suggested that this provides a very specific responsibility which addresses the issue of the lack of legal capacity of the child.

maintaining contact should be viewed in the context of the law's understanding that, in the event of the breakdown of the relationship between the parents, the continuation of both parent/child relationships is prima facie beneficial for the child.[36] 'Parental rights' are defined as existing to 'enable [the parent] to fulfil his [or her] parental responsibilities'.[37] Therefore these rights seem to be conceptualised as subordinate to, and as flowing from, the associated responsibilities.[38] The statute provides for the rights: '(a) to have the child living with him or otherwise to regulate the child's residence; [and] (b) to control, direct or guide, in a manner appropriate to the stage of development of the child, the child's upbringing'.[39] As with the definition of parental responsibility, I suggest that there seems to be a generality to the definition of these rights. The second right essentially mirrors one of the parental responsibilities, which further emphasises that the rights are conceptualised as being subsidiary to the responsibilities.[40] Therefore, I suggest that the generality of these definitions does not provide significant insight into the legal understanding of the role of the 'parent'.

Regardless of the specific differences between English and Scots law, the approaches taken in both jurisdictions provide only vague definitions of 'parental responsibilities', and neither approach offers significant substantive guidance regarding the legal understanding of the role of the 'parent'.

B. The Role of the 'Parent'

Bainham, Day Sclater and Richards ask 'can parenting ever be a truly gender-neutral activity?'[41] Parental responsibilities are defined using gender-neutral language and therefore do not differ between mothers and fathers, suggesting that the law's starting point is an overarching understanding of the role of the 'parent',

[36] See eg the judgment of Lord Rodger in *White v White* 2001 SLT 485, who stated at 489 'The point of reference to which they have regard – and which they take because it represents the consensus of society – is that "it may normally be assumed that the child will benefit from continued contact with the natural parent"'. The issue of contact will be explored in more detail below at subs II(C)(i), 'The Significance of Contact with the Non-Resident Parent'.

[37] Children (Scotland) Act 1995, s 2(1). See further, Scottish Law Commission, 'Report on Family Law', (No 135, May 1992), para 2.1, at 3, which states 'it would enable the law to make it clear that parental rights were not absolute or unqualified, but were conferred in order to enable parents to meet their responsibilities'.

[38] And as such the more specific 'responsibilities' of subss (c) and (d), detailed above, are repeated as 'rights'.

[39] Children (Scotland) Act 1995, s 2(1), J Thomson, *Family Law in Scotland*, 7th edn (London, Bloomsbury Professional, 2014) 251, states that 'the nature of a parental right alters as the child matures: beginning with the right to take decisions on the child's behalf, it becomes, in time, a right merely to give guidance to the child'.

[40] In the English case of *Gillick v West Norfolk and Wisbech Area Health Authority* [1986] AC 112, at 170, Lord Fraser observed, 'parental rights to control a child do not exist for the benefit of the parent. They exist for the benefit of the child and they are justified only in so far as they enable the parent to perform his duties towards the child'.

[41] Andrew Bainham, Shelley Day Sclater and Martin Richards, 'Introduction' in Bainham, Day Sclater and Richards (eds), *What is a Parent?: A Socio-Legal Analysis* 2.

which provides the framework for both of the gendered parental roles.[42] However, the lack of a clear definition of 'parental responsibilities' in either Scotland or England and Wales results in limited guidance being provided as to the nature of that overarching parental role. Reece comments that, 'parental responsibility is no longer predominantly about parental authority or decision-making'.[43] I argue that due to the lack of detail and specification provided by the statutory definition and judicial interpretation of 'parental responsibilities', this concept does not assist us significantly in our understanding of the law's construction of the role of the 'parent'.

Interestingly, the 'parent' is primarily defined by its abstract, statutory 'responsibilities' and 'rights', this parent is constructed as a rational and autonomous figure, arguably embodying the influence of the orthodox legal subject and its values.[44] I suggest that the influence of these values within the construction of the 'parent' illustrates why any alternative, relational understanding of the subject, associated with the ethical concept of 'care',[45] does not have a substantial normative influence in the legal construction of this parental role. As mentioned above in chapter two,[46] the law is premised upon a particular understanding of the individual (the legal subject) and I suggest that it is unsurprising that the legal understanding of the role of the 'parent' reflects the values of that legal subject. However, I argue that recognition of the influence of the orthodox construction of the legal subject upon the understanding of the overarching parental role does not provide greater clarity as to the nature, features or characteristics of that role within the law, because the legal subject itself represents an abstract standard.

Moreover, it is apparent from judicial language that these definitions are not designed to prescribe to parents how they should perform their parenting or to interfere with the day to day detail of that parenting.[47] Baroness Hale has stated that 'it is important in a free society that parents should be allowed a large measure of autonomy in the way in which they discharge their parental responsibilities'[48]

[42] The impact of the use of gender-neutral language will be considered below, in the context of contact with the non-resident parent, in subs II(C)(ii), 'Contact and Gender Neutrality'.

[43] Reece, 'The Degradation of Parental Responsibility' in Probert, Gilmore and Herring (eds), *Responsible Parents and Parental Responsibility* 94.

[44] Which were set out above and described as 'liberal values', at ch 2, subs I(C), 'The Orthodox Understanding of the "Legal Subject"'.

[45] See eg Herring, 'Where are the Carers in Healthcare Law and Ethics?', Herring, 'The Disability Critique of Care' and Herring and Foster, 'Welfare Means Relationality, Virtue and Altruism'. The literature on 'care' and its potential to ground an alternative construction of the 'family' will be considered below in ch 6, subs I(A), 'Care and Relationality'.

[46] See ch 2 above, particularly subs II(A), 'The Legal Subject Favours Specific Individuals'.

[47] This lack of interference with day-to-day parenting practices illustrates the continuing significance of the public/private divide within UK law, considered above in ch 2, subs I(B), 'The Development of the "Public/Private" Divide'.

[48] Baroness Hale in *R (On the Application of Williamson) v Secretary of State for Education and Employment* [2005] UKHL 15, [2005] 2 AC 246, at 271, an application for judicial review, which considered whether the ban on corporal punishment in all schools violated the ECHR, Art 9 right to religious freedom of the head teachers, teachers and parents at four independent 'Christian' schools.

and in *Christian Institute v Lord Advocate*,[49] the judgment of the Supreme Court observed 'Different upbringings produce different people … Within limits, families must be left to bring up their children in their own way.'[50] Thus, parental responsibilities and rights are understood as merely providing an overall *framework* for parenting. In *Re L (A Child) (Care: Threshold Criteria)*,[51] Hedley J stated 'Society must be willing to tolerate very diverse standards of parenting, including the eccentric, the barely adequate and the inconsistent.'[52] I suggest that the judicial acknowledgment of parental autonomy,[53] as well as the recognition of the diversity of acceptable parenting standards and practices further contributes to the lack of clarity as to the legal understanding of the role of the 'parent'. This statement of Hedley J reflects the oft-quoted language of Lord Templeman in *Re KD (A Minor) (Ward: Termination of Access)*[54] that 'It matters not whether the parent is wise or foolish, rich or poor, educated or illiterate, provided the child's moral and physical health are not endangered. Public authorities cannot improve on nature.'[55] Thus, while the law's starting point is the overarching concept of the 'parent', I argue that the legal understanding of the role tends to default to the easily understandable, 'natural' and 'common sense' constructions of the archetypical gendered parenting roles. Diduck has observed that 'The importance of father(ing) and mother(ing) to a child's welfare if not always clear for the law, is at least meaningful. The role, on the other hand, of a de-gendered "parent" is opaque and, as yet, imaginary.'[56] Over the course of the rest of the chapter, I will argue that the legal understanding of role of the 'parent' is dependent and reliant on the 'natural' constructions of the traditional gendered roles of 'mother' and 'father'.

II. The Gendered Parenting Roles of the Nuclear Family

As discussed above in chapters one and two, within the traditional nuclear family model the gendered parenting roles of mother and father are constructed with emphasis on their differing functions and they are understood as inherently

[49] *Christian Institute v Lord Advocate* [2016] UKSC 51, 2017 SC (UKSC) 29. This decision held that the provisions of Pt 4 of the Children and Young People (Scotland) Act 2014, concerning the Scottish Government's plan to introduce a 'named person' for every child in Scotland, were not within the legislative competence of the Scottish Parliament.

[50] ibid, at 55.

[51] *Re L (A Child) (Care: Threshold Criteria)* [2007] 1 FLR 2050.

[52] ibid, at 2063.

[53] The literature on the concept of 'autonomy' and the significance of autonomy within the legal regulation of the family will be considered in more detail in ch 6, subs I(C), 'Autonomy and Choice'.

[54] *Re KD (A Minor) (Ward: Termination of Access)* [1988] AC 806.

[55] ibid, at 812.

[56] Diduck, 'If Only we can Find the Appropriate Terms to Use the Issue Will Be Solved: Law, Identity and Parenthood' 464.

possessing different characteristics.[57] These distinct roles were premised upon the historical separation of gender roles envisaged within the public/private divide.[58] O'Donovan has argued:

> The heterosexual dyad is a union of opposites, a bi-polar model of attributes, bodies, gestures, conduct, aptitudes and expectations of what a gendered person is and what a gendered person does. The notion of parenthood is not gender neutral. In culture, in popular morality, in juridical and 'psy' discourses, parents are mothers and fathers with all that these distinct terms imply.[59]

Under these traditional gendered constructions, the mother is conceptualised as 'the homemaker' and viewed as the primary care figure for children. Furthermore, as previously mentioned, motherhood is constructed and presented as a 'natural' and indivisible status within the law.[60] Thus, I suggest that the significance of 'care' is understood through the prism of the gendered parenting roles and the imagery of the mother as primary carer retains normative resonance,[61] regardless of any changes in familial caring practices.[62] In contrast, the law has a more 'fragmented'[63] construction of the father, as a result of a complicated understanding of the development of that role.[64] Historically, the role of the father was constructed primarily in economic terms, as 'the breadwinner'. Changing demographics and practices[65] have led to a more contradictory construction of the role,[66] with ongoing attempts to define a specific and distinct male role ('the father as carer')

[57] See above in ch 1, s II, 'The Law's "Definition(s)" of "Family"'.

[58] As discussed above throughout ch 2, but particularly subs I(B), 'The Development of the "Public/Private" Divide' and subs III(A), 'The Legal Subject and the Nuclear Family'.

[59] O'Donovan, *Family Law Matters* 61.

[60] See above at ch 4, subs II(A), 'Motherhood'.

[61] The gendered nature of 'care' will be further considered in ch 6, subs I(A), 'Care and Relationality'.

[62] The empirical research set out below in subs II(B), 'What is the "Father" in the Law?', suggests that men continue to spend significantly less time per day than women on both childcare and housework, see eg ONS, 'Time Use Survey 2005', (July 2006) and therefore the traditional gendered parenting roles continue to exert significant influence on familial practices.

[63] Sheldon and Collier, *Fragmenting Fatherhood: A Socio-Legal Study*.

[64] See eg Coltrane, *Family Man: Fatherhood, Housework and Gender Equality*, Collier, *Masculinity, Law and the Family*, Graeme B Wilson, 'The Non-Resident Parental Role for Separated Fathers: A Review' (2006) 20(3) *International Journal of Law, Policy and the Family* 286 and Brid Featherstone, 'Taking Fathers Seriously' (2003) 33(2) *British Journal of Social Work* 239.

[65] ONS, 'Women in the Labour Market', (September 2013), available at: www.ons.gov.uk/ons/dcp171776_328352.pdf, shows that the percentage of women aged 16–64 in employment has risen from 53% in 1971 to 67% in 2013. This corresponds to a decline in the numbers of men in work from 92% to 76% over the same time frame. Interestingly, however, 42% of those women are in part-time employment compared to only 12% for men.

[66] This shift in construction has also, quite pointedly, led to a media backlash against the implied suggestion that traditional 'fathers' are no longer a necessary component for families and the development of a popular narrative suggesting that society is undergoing a 'Crisis of Masculinity'; see eg Glen Poole, 'How Tackling the "Crisis of Masculinity" Creates a Crisis for Feminism', (*The Guardian*, London, 15 May 2013), available at: www.theguardian.com/commentisfree/2013/may/15/why-crisis-masculinity-feminism and Kunal Dutta, 'Masculinity in Crisis: "There is a Battle Going on Inside Us That is Never Discussed"', (*The Independent*, London, 19 May 2013), available at: www.independent.co.uk/life-style/love-sex/masculinity-in-crisis-there-is-a-battle-going-on-inside-us-that-is-never-discussed-8622992.htm.

in the caring, nurture and development of children.[67] However, I submit that the traditional construction continues to exert significant influence and consequently any alternative understanding of the role of the 'father' has yet to be fully developed within legal understanding, nor has it substantially influenced social attitudes and familial practices. Indeed, the 2013 British Social Attitudes survey observes 'The overall story is that there has been very little change over the past two decades in the percentage of couple households dividing household responsibilities along traditional gender lines.'[68]

The following section will consider the influence of these traditional gendered parenting roles of the mother (subsection A) and the father (subsection B) within the legal understanding of the role of the parent. Thereafter, this section will examine the significance of these gendered roles within the welfare test, focusing upon the support for contact with the non-resident parent after parental separation (subsection C). I will argue that the traditional constructions of these roles retain normative significance, because they remain understood by the judiciary as the 'common-sense' and 'natural' constructions of the parenting roles.

A. What is the 'Mother' in the Law?

Historically the mother was not viewed as possessing any legal role, which reflected the influence of the public/private divide[69] and women's resultant exclusion from the public sphere of society as legal subjects.[70] Blackstone observed that 'for a mother, as such, is entitled to no power, but only to reverence and respect'.[71] This remained the legal understanding of the role,[72] until the Guardianship of Infants Act 1925 stated that courts 'shall not take into consideration whether … the claim of the father … is superior to that of the mother, or the claim of the mother is superior to that of the father'.[73] This legislation first statutorily established that 'the welfare of the child'[74] was to be the paramount consideration in decisions concerning children.

[67] See eg Hodson (ed), *Making Men into Fathers: Men, Masculinities and the Social Politics of Fatherhood* and Dienhart, *Reshaping Fatherhood: The Social Construction of Shared Parenting*. It is arguable that the development of a construction of the role as 'father as carer' shows the normative influence of the literature on 'care'.

[68] Scott and Clery, 'Gender Roles: An Incomplete Revolution?', *British Social Attitudes Survey* 30, 127.

[69] As set out above in ch 2, subs I(B), 'The Development of the "Public/Private" Divide'.

[70] Which was illustrated in the 'persons cases', discussed above in ch 2, subs II(C), '"The Persons Cases": The Rejection of Women as Legal Subjects'.

[71] Sir William Blackstone, *Commentaries on the Laws of England*, Vol 1, at 453.

[72] The Guardianship of Infants Act 1886 established that mothers could become sole guardians of children in the event of the death of the father.

[73] Guardianship of Infants Act 1925, s 1.

[74] ibid, the section further states that when making decisions about the 'custody and upbringing of children', courts, 'shall regard the welfare of the infant as the first and paramount consideration'. The so-called 'welfare principle' continues to govern disputes concerning children, see eg Children Act 1989, s 1(1) and Children (Scotland) Act, s 11(7).

There has been a consistently expressed judicial understanding that in a dispute between the parents over the residence of the children, the mother was the best person to raise the children,[75] and this was considered to be particularly true in the case of younger children.[76] This preference was judicially presented as being based upon 'common sense' or reflecting 'nature'.[77] Over 50 years ago in *Re B (An Infant)*,[78] Lord Evershed MR stated that 'as a matter of human sense a young child is better with its mother and needs a mother's care'.[79] The subsequent passage of 30 years did not lead to any significant alteration in judicial language, as illustrated in *Re H (A Minor: Custody)*,[80] where O'Connor LJ stated 'it is well recognised that the natural person to have the care and control of a little child is the mother of the child'.[81] In the Scottish House of Lords case of *Brixey v Lynas*,[82] Lord Jauncey observed that this understanding amounted to 'recognition of a widely held belief based on practical experience and the workings of nature'.[83] I suggest that invoking 'practical experience' and 'nature' to justify the preference for mothers as the primary carers of children is a reflection of the 'natural' gender roles of the traditional, nuclear family.[84] In the more recent decision of *Re T (A Child)*,[85] Wall LJ stated that 'as a matter of practice, very small babies are usually cared for by their mothers'.[86] The reference to 'a matter of practice' illustrates the continuing judicial recognition of the social reality[87] that the vast majority

[75] Although in *W v W and C* [1968] 1 WLR 1310, Lord Denning MR, at 1312, referred to 'the general principle that a boy of this age, some eight years of age, is, on the whole, other things being equal, better to be with his father'. However, the existence of such a principle was rejected by the Court of Appeal in *Re C (A) (An Infant)* [1970] 1 WLR 288. See further *Re N* [2009] EWHC 1807 (Fam), [2010] 1 FLR 272, for a more recent decision which dismisses the existence of such a presumption.

[76] In *Re W (A Minor) (Residence Order)* [1992] 2 FLR 332, Lord Donaldson MR in relation to very young children, stated, at 336 'I think there is a rebuttable presumption of fact that the best interests of a baby are served by being with its mother, and I stress the word "baby"'.

[77] See eg Donovan LJ in *Re B (An Infant)* [1962] 1 All ER 872, at 875.

[78] ibid.

[79] ibid, per Lord Evershed MR, at 873, see further *Re L (Infants)* [1962] 3 All ER 1.

[80] *Re H (A Minor: Custody)* [1990] 1 FLR 51.

[81] ibid, per O'Connor LJ, at 53. For further examples of such judicial language, see *Re A (A Minor: Custody)* [1991] 2 FLR 394, *Re W (A Minor) (Residence Order)* [1992] 2 FLR 332, *Re S (A Minor) (Custody: Children's Welfare)* [1991] 2 FLR 388.

[82] *Brixey v Lynas* 1997 SC (HL) 1.

[83] ibid, per Lord Jauncey, at 6, see further eg *Re W (Residence)* [1999] 2 FLR 390 and *Re A (Children: 1959 UN Declaration)* [1998] 1 FLR 354. His lordship also stressed, at 6, that there was, 'neither a presumption nor a principle' in favour of mothers being awarded residence. See Jonathan Herring and Oliver Powell, 'The Rise and Fall of Presumptions Surrounding the Welfare Principle' [2013] 43(5) *Fam Law* 553, 556, who observe that, 'any presumption that children are best cared for by mothers has been whittled away to vanishing point'.

[84] This reflects the construction of the nuclear family as 'natural', considered above in ch 2, s III, 'The Nuclear Family as the Natural Model of "Family"'.

[85] *Re T (A Child)* [2005] EWCA Civ 1397.

[86] ibid, per Wall LJ, at para 5.

[87] It could also be argued that this approach reflects the importance placed upon not disturbing the 'status quo', see Children Act 1989, s 1(3)(c).

of young children simply are cared for by their mothers.[88] It seems, therefore to remain a judicial understanding that mothers are usually best suited to the role of the primary carer of children (particularly young children)[89] because they are understood as inherently possessing characteristics and traits that men do not. This preference for mothers as the primary carer of children illustrates the continuing normative influence of the archetypical gendered parenting role of the 'mother' derived from the traditional nuclear family.

In view of this, I observe that the law places normative significance upon the role of the mother as the 'natural' primary carer of children. The rhetorical positioning of motherhood as a 'natural' status,[90] which is primarily associated with the care of children, is evident from *Re S (A Minor) (Custody: Children's Welfare)*,[91] where Butler-Sloss LJ stated that 'it is natural for young children to be with mothers'.[92] This emphasis on the 'natural' construction of motherhood is supported by Lord Jauncey's observation in *Brixey v Lynas*,[93] that 'Nature has endowed men and women with very different attributes and it so happens that mothers are generally better fitted than fathers to provide for the needs of very young children.'[94]

The significance given to the role of the mother was made apparent in the House of Lords decision in *Re G (Children) (Residence: Same-Sex Partner)*,[95] particularly in Lord Scott's comment that 'Mothers are special'[96] and Baroness Hale's statement that 'Her contribution to the welfare of the child is unique'.[97] Indeed, her ladyship

[88] See eg Joan Hunt and Alison MacLeod, 'Outcomes of Applications to Court for Contact Orders After Parental Separation or Divorce', (Ministry of Justice, September 2008), 239, which shows that fathers accounted for 91.6% (265 out of 289) of the non-resident parents making applications for contact in the research sample, illustrating the continued preference for mothers in the vast majority of cases, available at: http://dera.ioe.ac.uk/9145/1/outcomes-applications-contact-orders.pdf. See further Maebh Harding and Annika Newnham, 'How Do County Courts Share the Care of Children Between Parents?', (Nuffield Foundation, July 2015) 11, whose research into the approach of County courts to disputes between parents shows that fathers accounted for 96% (68 out of 71) of the applicants for contact in their research sample, available at: www.nuffieldfoundation.org/sites/default/files/files/Full%20report.pdf.

[89] See eg *Re K (Residence Order: Securing Contact)* [1999] 1 FLR 583, where Hirst LJ, at 529, stated that 'I fully recognise that to award a residence order of a 2-year-child in the father's favour is somewhat unusual'.

[90] O'Donovan and Marshall, 'After Birth: Decisions about Becoming a Mother' in Diduck and O'Donovan (eds), *Feminist Perspectives on Family Law*, provide a useful exploration of the feminist literature on the construction of motherhood. See above in ch 4, subs II(A), 'Motherhood'.

[91] *Re S (A Minor) (Custody: Children's Welfare)* [1991] 2 FLR 388.

[92] ibid, at 390.

[93] 1997 SC (HL) 1.

[94] ibid, per Lord Jauncey, at 6.

[95] *Re G (Children) (Residence: Same-Sex Partner)* [2006] UKHL 43, [2006] 2 FLR 629.

[96] ibid, per Lord Scott, at 631.

[97] ibid, per Baroness Hale, at 641. Indeed, given the particular factual circumstances of this case (a dispute between a separated lesbian couple) it would not be terminologically inaccurate to state that two women were 'mothering' the children. Therefore, I suggest that a deliberately narrow construction of 'mother' was being employed within the judgments.

reflected the 'natural', gestational construction of motherhood earlier in her judgment in *Re G*, where she stated that:

> [I]t also recognises a deeper truth: that the process of carrying a child and giving him birth (which may well be followed by breast-feeding for some months) brings with it, in the vast majority of cases, a very special relationship between mother and child, a relationship which is different from any other.[98]

This construction of motherhood reflects back to the public/private divide and the traditional nuclear family, with mothers understood primarily in terms of their care for their (young) children.[99] Diduck has powerfully observed that 'The romantic "good" mother is self-sacrificing in her care for her child. She is most fundamentally a nurturer, because nature (or God) made her that way'.[100] Within legal understanding, mothers remain constructed as part of the private sphere, viewed as the 'natural'[101] carers of children, as wives, as the gate-keepers of the nuclear family and therefore as mothers, 'in every sense of that term'.[102] Consequently, women are generally constructed as 'mothers', rather than as 'parents', by the law. Indeed, it is for this reason I observe that the 'mother' does not share the characteristics of the rational, autonomous legal subject.[103] This reflects Diduck's suggestion that the 'mother-child dyad resides firmly in the romantic private domain of instinct or love and lies in contrast with the rational legal world'.[104] Thus, the law is content to affirm 'motherhood' as a 'natural', quasi-mystical relationship and view this solely as a result of gender. When constructing the role of the mother, the judiciary has tended to view the gendered role as offering a more valuable caring role, particularly in relation to the care of young children,[105] than is entailed by the gender-neutral language of 'parent'.[106] It is submitted that this repeated and consistent judicial emphasis on 'mothers' as the 'natural' carers of children illustrates the continuing significance of the gendered parenting roles, instead of an overarching understanding of the parental role.

[98] *Re G (Children) (Residence: Same-Sex Partner)* [2006] UKHL 43, [2006] 2 FLR 629, per Baroness Hale, at 641.

[99] The wider significance of the gendered construction of 'care' within the legal understanding of the 'family' will be considered in ch 6, subs I(A), 'Care and Relationality'.

[100] Diduck, *Law's Families* 84.

[101] This reflects the positioning of the nuclear family as the 'natural' model of family, discussed above in ch 2, s III, 'The Nuclear Family as the Natural Model of "Family"', see further eg Collier, 'A Hard Time to Be a Father?: Reassessing the Relationship Between Law, Policy, and Family (Practices)' 526, who has suggested that 'Motherhood has appeared at once both "natural" and yet also deeply problematic and dangerous in the way it has been constituted as in need of surveillance, regulation and discipline.'

[102] In the words of Baroness Hale in *Re G (Children) (Residence: Same-Sex Partner)* [2006] UKHL 43, [2006] 2 FLR 629, at 643.

[103] As discussed above in ch 2, subs I(C), 'The Orthodox Understanding of the "Legal Subject"'.

[104] Diduck, *Law's Families* 84.

[105] See eg *Re W (A Minor) (Residence Order)* [1992] 2 FLR 332.

[106] See below at s III, 'The Role of Lesbian "Mothers" or "Parents"', for how the 'natural' construction of the 'mother' impacts upon the understanding of the parenting of lesbian couples, where one member is the 'mother' and the other is explicitly labelled as the 'parent' by legislation.

B. What is the 'Father' in the Law?

Historically the role of the father was understood in terms of his power and authority over his wife and children and the 'rights of the father' were emphasised.[107] In the late nineteenth century in *Re Agar-Ellis*[108] Brett MR observed that 'the father has control over the person, education, and conduct of his children until they are twenty-one years of age. That is the law'.[109] This view of the complete authority of the father was combined with an understanding of the role as embracing what Blackstone referred to as the 'natural obligation of the father to provide for his children'.[110] The role of the 'father' was the traditional gendered role of head of the household[111] and the 'breadwinner'. Thus, I observe that the gendered division of the roles of mother and father, derived from the public/private divide and the traditional nuclear family historically underpinned the legal understanding of the role of the father. While this common law authority of the father was effectively eliminated by the reforms of the Guardianship of Infants Act 1925, subsequent to the passage of this legislation the law continued to construct the role of the father on the basis of the traditional, gendered role of the 'breadwinner'.[112]

More recently there has been an apparent shift in the construction of the role of the father,[113] which has been evident in government policy,[114] reflecting the understanding that, 'Fathers want – and increasingly are – becoming more involved in caring for their children'.[115] Under this construction greater emphasis is being placed on the caring features of the role of father,[116] in addition to the

[107] Historically this power of the father was over his legitimate children, it should be noted that a distinction between the role of married and unmarried fathers has been made by law consistently throughout history.

[108] (1883) 24 Ch. 317.

[109] ibid, per Brett MR, at 326.

[110] Sir William Blackstone, *Commentaries on the Laws of England*, Vol 1, at 447.

[111] Reflecting to a lesser extent the Roman law concept of *pater families*, discussed above at ch 2, subs I(A), '"Family" and the Subject in Historical Societies'.

[112] See eg *Wachtel v Wachtel (No 2)* [1973] 2 WLR 366 and other cases noted above in ch 2, subs III(B), 'The Historical Significance of the Nuclear Family'.

[113] See Lupton and Barclay, *Constructing Fatherhood: Discourses and Experiences*, for a consideration of the development of the role of fatherhood, both through an examination of the sociological and psychological literature, but also through analysis of popular representations of fatherhood in the media. See further eg Coltrane, *Family Man: Fatherhood, Housework and Gender Equality* and Collier, *Masculinity, Law and the Family*.

[114] This shift was initially associated with the reforms and ideals of the New Labour government. It is suggested that this construction of 'involved fatherhood' has been largely reflected by the policies of subsequent governments.

[115] 'Support for All: The Families and Relationships Green Paper', (January 2010) 94, para 5.12.

[116] See eg Equal Opportunities Commission, 'Fathers: Balancing Work and Family', (March 2003), where it was stated, at 2 'fatherhood is in a state of change. The everyday, traditional role of providing economic support for the family now takes place alongside activities previously regarded as maternal', available at: www.fatherhoodinstitute.org/uploads/publications/285.pdf. See further eg Margaret O'Brien, 'Shared Caring: Bringing Fathers into the Frame', (Equal Opportunities Commission, 2005), available at: http://dera.ioe.ac.uk/5299/1/1.73363!shared_caring_wp18.pdf.

traditional breadwinner role. The perception of this shift in the understanding of fatherhood is evident in judicial language,[117] as illustrated by the observation of Lord Nicholls in *White v White*[118] that:

> Traditionally, the husband earned the money, and the wife looked after the home and the children. This traditional division of labour is no longer the order of the day. Frequently both parents work. Sometimes it is the wife who is the money-earner, and the husband runs the home and cares for the children during the day.[119]

Subsequently, Baroness Hale employed similar language in *Ghaidan v Godin-Mendoza*[120] stating:

> The law now differentiates between husband and wife in only a very few and unimportant respects. Husbands and wives decide for themselves who will go out to work and who will do the homework and child care. Mostly each does some of each. The roles are interchangeable.[121]

However, in spite of this rhetoric suggesting that there has been fundamental change in family practice, relatively recent research evidence indicates that even though the traditional breadwinner/homemaker division is no longer the dominant form of family,[122] in the vast majority of families men are still the main earner[123] and women remain the primary carers of children.[124] As Scott and Clery comment 'the public retains a view that there should be a gender divide in terms of caring responsibilities: the shift has been in accepting the idea that a mother works part-time, rather than not at all'.[125] This is supported by

[117] See eg the observation of Lord Donaldson MR in *Re S (A Minor) (Custody: Children's Welfare* [1991] 2 FLR 388, at 392, that 'What is clear is that there is a change in the social order, in the organisation of society, whereby it is much more common for fathers to look after young children than in bygone days.'

[118] *White v White* [2001] 1 AC 596.

[119] ibid, per Lord Nicholls, at 605.

[120] [2004] UKHL 30, [2004] 2 AC 557.

[121] ibid, at 607.

[122] 'Modern Fatherhood: Fathers, Work and Families in the 21st Century', referenced above, suggests that the sole male breadwinner model only exists in 22% of families, see further eg Man Yee Kan, Oriel Sullivan and Jonathan Gershuny, 'Gender Convergence in Domestic Work: Discerning the Effects of Interactional and Institutional Barriers from Large-Scale Data' (2011) 45(2) *Sociology* 234.

[123] 'Trends in Fathers Work-Family Arrangements and Fathers Working Hours (2001–2011)', in the sample of families in this study, the mother was the 'main earner' in only 12% of families, available at: www.modernfatherhood.org/wp-content/uploads/2014/01/Nuffield-PRESENTATION-FATHERS-FINAL-2.pdf.

[124] ONS, 'Time Use Survey 2005', (July 2006), suggests that men spend significantly less time per day than women on both childcare and housework, see further Crompton and Lyonette, 'Who Does the Housework? The Division of Labour within the Home', *British Social Attitudes Survey* 24. This research contains a survey on the extent to which social attitudes in the UK about the roles of men and women in the family have shifted in recent years.

[125] Scott and Clery, 'Gender Roles: An Incomplete Revolution?', *British Social Attitudes Survey* 30, 124. Indeed, at 125, the authors further note that 31% of people think that a male full-time breadwinner, women full-time homemaker is the best way to organise the family when children are under school age and 38% believe that father working full-time while the mother works part-time is the best method, in contrast only 4% of people favour both parents working full-time.

research into the parenting patterns of families involved in court applications;[126] with Harding and Newnham commenting that 'It is likely that social expectations of parenting had shaped gendered parenting roles long before the parties came to court.'[127] Therefore, I agree with Sheldon and Collier when they say that 'The "father as breadwinner" model, and the masculinities with which it has been associated have not been supplanted in law. Rather, they exist alongside, and in tension with, the new ideology of "father as carer".'[128] Smart has drawn upon Tronto's distinction between 'caring for' and 'caring about'[129] to note that this shift in normative construction is not necessarily based upon a shift in the caring practices of fathers, observing that 'when fathers articulated their care about their children, even if they had never really cared for them, their utterances seemed to reverberate around the courts with a deafening significance'.[130] Thus, this emphasis on the caring role of the father appears to largely represent a rhetorical shift, rather than a structural change in social behaviour.[131] I contend that the increased emphasis on the idealised 'father as carer' role remains significantly influenced by replicating particular normative roles, rather than reflecting the reality of societal parenting practices.

As a result of increased divorce,[132] relationship breakdown among cohabiting couples and the rise in lone-parent families,[133] the vast majority of which are headed by single mothers,[134] more fathering is now being performed

[126] Harding and Newnham, 'How Do County Courts Share the Care of Children Between Parents?', July 2015, 20–21, find that mothers were the primary carer in 60% (104 out of 174) and fathers in only 10% (17 out of 174) of County Court applications in their research sample. Moreover, 17% (30 out of 174) of the applications were classed as 'initial family breakdown', where the status quo had been the intact family living together, and as such no primary carer was identified.

[127] ibid, at 80.

[128] Sheldon and Collier, *Fragmenting Fatherhood: A Socio-Legal Study* 136. See also Collier, 'A Hard Time to Be a Father?: Reassessing the Relationship Between Law, Policy, and Family (Practices)', Hodson (ed), *Making Men into Fathers: Men, Masculinities and the Social Politics of Fatherhood* and Dienhart, *Reshaping Fatherhood: The Social Construction of Shared Parenting.*

[129] See eg Joan Tronto, 'Women and Caring: What Can Feminists Learn about Morality from Caring?' in Alison Jaggar and Susan Bordo (eds), *Gender/Body/Knowledge: Feminist Reconstructions of Being and Knowing*, (New Brunswick, Rutgers University Press, 1989) and Tronto, *Moral Boundaries: A Political Argument for an Ethic of Care.* Tronto's work, and the other theoretical literature on the ethical concept of 'care', will be considered in more detail in ch 6, subs I(A), 'Care and Relationality'.

[130] Carol Smart, 'Losing the Struggle for Another Voice: The Case for Family Law' (1995) 18(2) *Dalhousie Law Journal* 173, 177. This will be further explored below at subs II(C)(ii), 'Contact and Gender Neutrality'.

[131] Harding and Newnham, 'How Do County Courts Share the Care of Children Between Parents?', July 2015, 130, in relation to their sample of County Court applications relating to children, observe that 'Near equal shared care arrangements were rarely sought, logistically difficult to manage and often precluded by most families work patterns and accommodation limitations.'

[132] See eg ONS, 'Divorces in England and Wales: 2016', showing the fluctuation of divorces from the 1950s onwards.

[133] See eg ONS, 'Families and Households: 2017', (November 2017) 5, showing that single-parent families represent 14.8% of all families in 2017.

[134] ibid, the statistics show that lone-mother families amount to 14.1% of all families, therefore around 87% of single-parent families were headed by women.

outside the traditional two-parent, nuclear family[135] and consequently without day-to-day contact with children.[136] On this point, Simpson, Jessop and McCarthy have observed that:

> Whereas in conventional family settings fathers may be physically close to their children their role is apt to leave them emotionally distant from them. Conversely, and somewhat paradoxically, divorce usually results in fathers being physically separated but does create the possibility that kinds of emotional closeness can develop which might not have been possible in marriage.[137]

This change has resulted because non-resident fathers have no option but to take on the role of the primary carer in their more limited time with their children,[138] rather than defaulting to the traditional gendered roles that still exert influence within parenting by heterosexual couples.[139] However, the late twentieth and early twenty-first century increase in the number of non-resident fathers also led to a renewed focus on the financial obligations of those fathers,[140] which resulted in the controversial provisions of the (frequently restructured) Child Support Act 1991.[141] Collier comments that 'The experience of "being a father" continues to involve, for most men, a temporal and spatial trade-off between the domains of work and family.'[142]

Thus, I observe that the traditional construction of the role of the father as the 'breadwinner' still possesses significant normative influence, even on those fathers who are now living and 'fathering' outside the boundaries of the nuclear family. Moreover, I argue that this focus upon understanding and constructing a specific role for the 'father', in the day-to-day upbringing of children, shows that it is the gendered role which is shaping legal understanding, not an overarching conception of the role of the 'parent'.

[135] In 2004 it was suggested that there were around 2 million non-resident fathers in the UK, Joan Hunt with Ceridwen Roberts, 'Family Policy Briefing 3: Child Contact with Non-Resident Parents', University of Oxford, available at: www.spig.clara.net/reports/hunt.pdf.

[136] 'Judicial and Court Statistics 2011', (Ministry of Justice, June 2012), for England and Wales, state that there were 109,656 children involved in private law applications in 2011, of which around one-third were applications relating to the residence and contact of those children, available at: https://www.gov.uk/government/uploads/system/uploads/attachment_data/file/217494/judicial-court-stats-2011.pdf.

[137] Bob Simpson, Julie A Jessop and Peter McCarthy, 'Fathers After Divorce' in Andrew Bainham, Bridget Lindley, Martin Richards and Liz Trinder (eds), *Children and Their Families: Contact, Rights and Welfare* (Oxford, Hart Publishing, 2003) 215.

[138] ibid, see further eg Carol Smart, 'The New Parenthood: Fathers and Mothers after Divorce' in Silva and Smart (eds), *The New Family?*, S Kielty, 'Similarities and Differences in the Experiences of Non-Resident Mothers and Non-Resident Fathers' (2006) 20(1) *International Journal of Law Policy* and the Family 74 and Wilson, 'The Non-Resident Parental Role for Separated Fathers: A Review'.

[139] See eg Clare Lyonette and Rosemary Crompton, 'Sharing the Load? Partners Relative Earnings and the Division of Domestic Labour' (2015) 29(1) *Work, Employment and Society* 23 and Jacqueline Scott, 'Family and Gender Roles: How Attitudes are Changing?', (GeNet Working Paper, No 21, 2006), available at: https://pdfs.semanticscholar.org/50c3/a2740ddafdb438df4b920304262533128253.pdf.

[140] Which reflects the historical 'obligations' of the 'father', considered above at subs II(B), 'What is the "Father" in the Law?'

[141] For a detailed consideration of the legal regulation of child support and maintenance obligations, see Nicholas Wikeley, *Child Support: Law and Policy* (Oxford, Hart Publishing, 2006).

[142] Collier, 'A Hard Time to Be a Father?: Reassessing the Relationship Between Law, Policy, and Family (Practices)', 533.

C. The Gendered Parenting Roles within the Welfare Principle

The statutory language of the welfare principle provides that 'the child's welfare shall be the court's paramount consideration',[143] in any decision concerning the 'child's upbringing'.[144] The welfare principle appears to be 'child-centred',[145] placing the focus of decision making on the 'best interests' of children, with those interests being preferenced to all other considerations, including the rights of parents.[146] However, as O'Donovan has observed 'Behind the word "welfare" lies a claim to knowledge of what is in the child's interests.'[147] Thus, an examination of the judicial interpretation of 'welfare' should provide further insight into the law's construction of the role of the parent.[148] I will argue that the law's understanding of the welfare of the child is influenced by the gendered parenting roles of 'mother' and 'father' derived from the traditional nuclear family.

The welfare principle has been subjected to significant and sustained critique.[149] Freeman notes that 'Critics have emphasised its indeterminacy, its vagueness, its values and its absence of normative content.'[150] I will focus upon

[143] Children Act 1989, s 1(1), the equivalent Scottish provision, found in Children (Scotland) Act 1995, s 11(7)(a), is worded slightly differently, stating that the court, 'shall regard the welfare of the child concerned as its paramount consideration'.

[144] Children Act 1989 s 1(1)(a) and similar language is employed in different statutes, see eg in the context of adoption, Adoption and Children Act 2002, s 1(2) and Adoption and Children (Scotland) Act 2007, s 14(3).

[145] White Paper, 'Scotland's Children: Proposals for Child Care Policy and Law', (The Scottish Office, August 1993), para 2.2, at 5, states that children 'should be viewed as individuals in their own right, whose wants and needs must be taken seriously.' Available at: https://www.gov.uk/government/uploads/system/uploads/attachment_data/file/271973/2286.pdf.

[146] See the judgment of Lord MacDermott in *J v C* [1970] AC 668, where he stated, at 715 'the rights and wishes of parents, whether unimpeachable or otherwise, must be assessed and weighed in their bearing on the welfare of the child'.

[147] O'Donovan, *Family Law Matters* 92.

[148] Herring, *Caring and the Law*, proposes an alternative normative construction of the 'welfare principle' underpinned by care, mutuality and interdependence, which he describes as 'relationship-based welfare', he states, at 203 'A care-centred approach would require us to consider the child in the network of relationships within which they live. Relationship-based welfare argues that children should be brought up in relationships which overall promote their welfare.' In ch 6, 'The Possibilities Offered by Alternative "Models" of the "Family"', I will consider whether the legal understanding of 'family' could be reconstructed based upon alternative conceptions of the individual, including those based upon care and relationality.

[149] See eg Robert Mnookin, 'Child-Custody Adjudication: Judicial Functions in the Face of Indeterminancy' (1975) 39(3) *Law and Contemporary Problems* 226, Helen Reece, 'The Paramountcy Principle: Consensus or Construct?' (1996) 49(1) *Current Legal Problems* 267 and Adrienne Barnett, 'The Welfare of the Child Re-Visited: In Whose Best Interests? Part 1' [2009] 39(1) *Fam Law* 50 and 'Part 2' [2009] 39(2) *Fam Law* 135.

[150] Michael Freeman, 'Feminism and Child Law', in Bridgeman and Monk (eds), *Feminist Perspectives on Child Law* 30, see also Stephen Parker, 'The Best Interests of the Child – Principles and Problems' (1994) 8(1) *International Journal of Law and the Family* 26 and John Eekelaar, 'Beyond the Welfare Principle' [2002] 14(3) *Child and Family Law Quarterly* 237.

only one aspect of this critique, the lack of normative content; I will argue that this has resulted in the influence of the gendered parenting roles of 'mother' and 'father' upon the understanding of the role of the parent within the welfare principle. While the welfare principle appears to allow some scope for judicial discretion, the principle lacks specified normative content, at least as set out by statute.[151] As a result of this, the judiciary has developed several shared understandings,[152] which provide the normative content used in determining the best interests of the child.[153] Montgomery has described the welfare principle as an 'ideological construction'[154] and observed that 'the extent to which proposals for the care of children are seen by the courts to promote the welfare of those children is determined by the degree to which they diverge from establishment expectations of "normal" family life'.[155] I argue that some of these shared judicial understandings of the welfare of the child are underpinned by the idealised image of the nuclear family,[156] and its construction of separate gendered parenting roles, because that archetype of family has been positioned as the 'natural'[157] model of family.[158]

[151] Nevertheless, judgments often claim that the welfare of the child is the *only* principle driving the outcome, see eg the Supreme Court decision in *Re B (A Child)* [2009] UKSC 5, [2010] 1 FLR 551 and the statement of Baroness Hale in *Re J (A Child) (Custody Rights: Jurisdiction)* [2005] UKHL 40, [2006] 1 AC 80, at 94, that 'we do not have any fixed concept of what will be in the best interests of the individual child.'

[152] These 'shared understandings' include: (i) the understanding that children are best cared for by their natural parents, see eg *J v C* [1970] AC 668 and *Re KD (A Minor) (Ward: Termination of Access)* [1988] AC 806, (ii) the preference for mothers as the primary carers of children after relationship breakdown, see eg *Re B (An Infant)* [1962] 1 All ER 872 and *Brixey v Lynas* 1997 SC (HL) 1, (iii) the proposition that siblings should continue to reside together after parental separation, see eg *C v C (Minors: Custody)* [1988] 2 FLR 291, (iv) the support for ongoing contact with the non-resident parent, see eg *White v White* 2001 SLT 485 and *Re O (Contact: Imposition of Conditions)* [1995] 2 FLR 124, and (v) the contrary proposition in favour of allowing the reasonable proposals of resident parents in relocation applications, see eg *Payne v Payne* [2001] EWCA Civ 166, [2001] 1 FLR 1052.

[153] There is significant academic debate surrounding whether judicial 'presumptions' exist within the welfare test, see eg Herring and Powell, 'The Rise and Fall of Presumptions Surrounding the Welfare Principle', Jonathan Herring, 'The Welfare Principle and the Children Act: Presumably it's About Welfare?' (2014) 36(1) *Journal of Social Welfare and Family Law* 14 and Christine Piper, 'Assumptions about Children's Best Interests' (2000) 22(3) *Journal of Social Welfare and Family Law* 261. It is not my intention to determine, one way or the other, whether or not these shared judicial understandings amount to 'presumptions', nor is such a determination necessary to advance the central argument of this chapter.

[154] Jonathan Montgomery, 'Rhetoric and "Welfare"' (1989) 9(3) *Oxford Journal of Legal Studies* 395, 396.

[155] ibid.

[156] The preference for mothers, discussed above at subs II(A), 'What is the "Mother" in the Law?' and the support for contact with the non-resident parent, which will be discussed below at subs II(C)(i), 'The Significance of Contact with the Non-Resident Parent'.

[157] See eg *Re B (An Infant)* [1962] 1 All ER 872, per Donovan LJ, at 875.

[158] Discussed above in ch 2, s III, 'The Nuclear Family as the Natural Model of "Family"'.

The reliance upon these central factors is apparent both from judicial language[159] and from recent legislative provisions.[160] In *White v White*,[161] Lord Rodger observed that:

> [W]hen Parliament says that judges are to have regard to the welfare of the child, it must consider that judges will, by and large, have a common conception of what that involves – of what will advance the welfare of children in regard to these matters.[162]

Therefore the interpretation of the welfare principle is premised upon judicial understandings about what serves the best interests of the child.[163] Diduck and Kaganas comment that the interpretation of the welfare principle 'owes less to scientific "truths" than to understandings of the welfare of children that accord with prevailing beliefs about how families should be structured and what the roles of family members should be'.[164] I will argue that the judicial interpretation of the best interests of the child is premised upon the distinct gendered parenting roles, mother as 'homemaker' and father as 'breadwinner', derived from the traditional, nuclear family, but that these values are hidden behind references to 'nature'[165] and simple 'common sense'[166] rationality within the welfare principle.

i. The Significance of Contact with the Non-Resident Parent

Following the breakdown of a relationship between parents (or where the parents were never in a cohabiting relationship), in the absence of agreement between the parents,[167] it is often necessary for a court to make an order[168] regarding which

[159] Various terms have been employed by the judiciary, including: 'presumption', *Re W (A Minor) (Residence Order)* [1992] 2 FLR 332, 'assumption', *Re L (Contact: Domestic Violence); Re V (Contact: Domestic Violence); Re M (Contact: Domestic Violence; Re H (Contact: Domestic Violence)* [2000] 2 FLR 334, 'strong supposition', *Re H (A Minor) (Custody: Interim Care and Control)* [1991] 2 FLR 109, 'policy', *Re B (Contact: Stepfathers Opposition)* [1997] 2 FLR 579 and 'consideration', *Re S (A Minor) (Custody: Children's Welfare)* [1991] 2 FLR 388.

[160] Children and Families Act 2014, s 11(2) amends Children Act 1989, s 1, inserting a presumption in favour of contact with both parents. Kaganas, 'A Presumption that "Involvement" of Both Parents is Best: Deciphering Law's Messages' 288, describes this as 'symbolic legislation'.

[161] *White v White* 2001 SLT 485.

[162] ibid, per Lord Rodger, at 489.

[163] ibid, per Lord McCluskey, at 494, 'The judge who approaches the issues raised in an application for a s.11 order does not do so value free.'

[164] Diduck and Kaganas, *Family Law, Gender and the State* 373.

[165] See eg *Brixey v Lynas* 1997 SC (HL) 1, per Lord Jauncey, at 6.

[166] See eg Latey J in *M v M (Child: Access)* [1973] 2 All ER 81, at 88.

[167] The vast majority of separated parents reach agreement as to residence and contact without any involvement from the courts. In England and Wales there were 111,302 contact orders made in 2011, 'Judicial and Court Statistics 2011', (June 2012) 26. Estimates for the number of non-resident fathers vary, eg in 'What Do We Know about Nonresident Fathers?' (Modern Fatherhood) 2, it was estimated that there are around 980,000 non-resident fathers in the UK, available at: www.modernfatherhood.org/wp-content/uploads/2013/11/Briefing-paper-Non-resident-fathers.pdf, whereas Hunt with Roberts, 'Family Policy Briefing 3: Child Contact with Non-Resident Parents', University of Oxford, suggested, in 2004, that there may be up to 2 million non-resident fathers.

[168] Known in England and Wales as a 'Child Arrangements Order' subsequent to Children and Families Act 2014, s 12, which amended Children Act 1989, s 8(1) replacing both the 'residence order' and the 'contact order'.

parent the child will live with[169] and detailing the contact[170] between the other parent and the child(ren). In determining such disputes, judicial reasoning has generally observed that it is in the best interests of a child to continue to have a relationship with both parents; which is reflected in judicial support for ongoing contact with the 'non-resident parent'.[171]

In an early decision 'access' (as it was then known), was described as 'the basic right of any parent'.[172] This language was quickly altered to reflect 'a basic right in the child rather than a basic right in the parent'.[173] Subsequent judicial formulations[174] have generally reflected the observation of Sir Thomas Bingham MR in *Re O (Contact: Imposition of Conditions)*,[175] that 'where parents of a child are separated and the child is in the day-to-day care of one of them, it is almost always in the interests of the child that he or she should have contact with the other parent'.[176] In the more recent decision in *Re W (Children) (Direct Contact)*,[177] this understanding was reiterated by McFarlane LJ, who referred to 'the well known case law which stresses the benefit children will normally gain from maintaining a meaningful relationship with both of their parents following a split in the family'.[178] Research into outcomes of court applications, conducted in 2008, identified that, 'while there is no statutory presumption, the courts operate on a *de facto*

[169] Children Act 1989, s 8(1) defines a 'child arrangements order' as 'an order regulating arrangements relating to any of the following – (a) with whom a child is to live, spend time or otherwise have contact, and (b) when a child is to live, spend time or otherwise have contact with any person', see Children (Scotland) Act 1995, s 11(2)(c) for the Scottish provision relating to 'residence orders'.

[170] Children (Scotland) Act 1995, s 11(2)(d) provides the Scottish provision for 'contact orders'.

[171] In spite of the removal of 'residence orders' in the 2014 Act, this book will continue to use the term 'non-resident parent' to describe the parent who is not the children's primary carer.

[172] *S v S & P* [1962] 2 All ER 1, per Wilmer LJ, at 3. In Scotland, Lord Dunpark stated in *Porchetta v Porchetta* 1986 SLT 105, at 105 'A father does not have an absolute right to access to his child. He is only entitled to access if the court is satisfied that this is in the best interests of the child.' See further eg Joseph Thomson, 'Whither the "Right" of Access?' 1989 *Scots Law Times (News)* 109.

[173] *M v M (Child: Access)* [1973] 2 All ER 81, per Wrangham J, at 85. Judicial descriptions of contact as a right of the child continued into the early 1990s, see eg *Re S (Minors) (Access)* [1990] 2 FLR 166, *Re W (A Minor) (Contact)* [1994] 2 FLR 441 and *Re J (A Minor) (Contact)* [1994] 1 FLR 729.

[174] In *Re M (Contact: Welfare Test)* [1995] 1 FLR 274, at 279, Wilson J referred to 'the strong presumption in favour of contact', see further *Re A (Contact: Domestic Violence)* [1998] 2 FLR 171 and *Re P (Contact: Discretion)* [1998] 2 FLR 696. However, Thorpe LJ rejected the use of the term presumption in *Re L (Contact: Domestic Violence); Re V (Contact: Domestic Violence); Re M (Contact: Domestic Violence; Re H (Contact: Domestic Violence)* [2000] 2 FLR 334. There continues to be academic argument about whether there is a presumption in favour of contact, see eg Stephen Gilmore, 'Disputing Contact: Challenging Some Assumptions' [2008] 20(3) *Child and Family Law Quarterly* 285, who argues against the existence of such a presumption and Andrew Bainham, 'Contact as a Right and Obligation' in Bainham, Lindley, Richards and Trinder (eds), *Children and Their Families: Contact, Rights and Welfare*, who observes, at 61, 'those who assert that there is no right or presumption of contact are not merely misguided, but are plainly wrong'.

[175] *Re O (Contact: Imposition of Conditions)* [1995] 2 FLR 124.

[176] ibid, per Sir Thomas Bingham MR, at 128, see further eg the Scottish House of Lords' decision *Sanderson v McManus* 1997 SC (HL) 55, where Lord Hope stated, at 64, 'It may normally be assumed that the child will benefit from continued contact with the natural parent'.

[177] *Re W (Children) (Direct Contact)* [2012] EWCA Civ 999, [2013] 1 FLR 494.

[178] ibid, per McFarlane LJ, at 504, see further eg *Re K (A Child)* [2010] EWCA Civ 478 and *Re H (Contact with Biological Father)* [2012] EWCA Civ 281, [2012] 2 FLR 627.

presumption that unless there were good reasons to the contrary there should be contact'.[179] Indeed, the judicial preference for contact is illustrated by the fact that contact orders[180] are issued in the majority of cases.[181]

Various justifications have been employed by the judiciary in support of contact;[182] I will focus upon judicial language which suggests that the support for contact is based upon reflecting 'common sense' or 'nature'.[183] In *White v White*,[184] Lord Rodger referred to 'a working hypothesis born of human experience'.[185] Kaganas suggests that the courts are 'simply stating the proposition as axiomatic; in this way it becomes indisputable',[186] and indeed in *Re O (Contact: Imposition of Conditions)*,[187] Sir Thomas Bingham MR observed that 'The reason for this scarcely needs spelling out.'[188] By presenting the benefits as self-evident, this approach illustrates the reliance upon 'nature' and 'common sense' as founding the judicial support for contact.[189]

[179] Hunt and MacLeod, 'Outcomes of Applications to Court for Contact Orders After Parental Separation or Divorce', (September 2008) 189, similarly Herring and Powell, 'The Rise and Fall of Presumptions Surrounding the Welfare Principle' refer to the 'wide academic consensus' of a 'de facto presumption in favour of contact', at 556.

[180] Jonathan Herring, *Family Law*, 6th edn (Harlow, Pearson Longman, 2013) 550, notes that, in England and Wales, 'In 2011 there were 111,302 applications for a contact order heard and in 108,557 cases were contact orders made, and in only 333 were contact orders refused.'

[181] Hunt and MacLeod, 'Outcomes of Applications to Court for Contact Orders After Parental Separation or Divorce', (September 2008) 11, found that 70% of cases in their sample resulted in a contact order, while 16% of applications were withdrawn, 7% resulted in no order and only 7% were dismissed. Moreover, Harding and Newnham, 'How Do County Courts Share the Care of Children Between Parents?', July 2015, 62, found that within their sample, 85% of applications for contact were successful, with that figure rising to 88% for contact applications made by fathers. See further the 'Judicial and Court Statistics 2011', (June 2012) 26, which states that there were 183,718 children involved in disposals of private law applications in which 178,517 orders were made.

[182] Notably, there have been judicial references to the benefit of contact being demonstrated by 'scientific' evidence, external to law. See eg *Re L (Contact: Domestic Violence); Re V (Contact: Domestic Violence); Re M (Contact: Domestic Violence; Re H (Contact: Domestic Violence)* [2000] 2 FLR 334 and *Re G (Contact)* [2006] EWCA Civ 1507, [2007] 1 FLR 1663, where Ward LJ stated, at 1672 'every psychiatrist that has ever given evidence to me on this question will have told me the serious consequences if that contact is denied'. These judicial references to evidence from experts are especially notable because there is far from a consensus in the research that contact itself is beneficial for children, see eg Stephen Gilmore, 'Contact/Shared Residence and Child Well-Being: Research Evidence and its Implications for Legal Decision-Making' (2006) 20(3) *International Journal of Law, Policy and the Family* 344, Paul Amato and Joan Gilbreth, 'Nonresident Fathers and Children's Well-Being: A Meta-Analysis' (1999) 61(3) *Journal of Marriage and the Family* 557 and Judy Dunn, Helen Cheng, Thomas G O'Connor, and Laura Bridges, 'Children's Perspectives on their Relationships with their Nonresident Fathers: Influences, Outcomes and Implications' (2004) 45(3) *Journal of Child Psychology and Psychiatry* 55.

[183] This reflects the judicial reliance upon the 'natural' construction of motherhood, discussed above in subs II(A), 'What is the "Mother" in the Law?'

[184] 2001 SLT 485.

[185] ibid, per Lord Rodger, at 490.

[186] Felicity Kaganas, 'Regulating Emotion: Judging Contact Disputes' [2011] 23(1) *Child and Family Law Quarterly* 63, 69.

[187] [1995] 2 FLR 124.

[188] ibid, per Sir Thomas Bingham MR, at 128.

[189] This reflects the positioning of the nuclear family as the 'natural' model of 'family' discussed above in ch 2, s III, 'The Nuclear Family as the Natural Model of "Family"'.

Moreover, the understanding that contact is beneficial is now adduced in the language of government reports; for example 'Children generally do better if both their parents are involved in their lives, irrespective of whether the parents live together'[190] and 'We believe that children normally benefit from the continued involvement of both parents in their lives'.[191] In England and Wales, section 11 of the Children and Families Act 2014 amends section 1 of the Children Act 1989 by inserting the provision[192] that the court is 'to presume, unless the contrary is shown, that involvement of [the] parent in the life of the child concerned will further the child's welfare'.[193] This presumption of 'parental involvement' was to some extent premised upon the government seeking 'to dispel the perception that there is an in-built legal bias towards fathers or mothers'.[194] Harding and Newnham comment that 'the new presumption … will make little practical difference to the way in which the courts approach the issue of contact'.[195] Indeed, given the social reality of mothers as primary carers in the vast majority of cases,[196] Kaganas has observed that 'The new presumption makes a statement about the importance of fathers and so symbolically restores their status'.[197] I submit that this legislative approach is underpinned by support for 'fathering', which is constructed as providing a different form of parenting than that provided by the mother.[198] Thus, I contend it is not the capacity of the father to provide 'care' or social parenting that is being granted normative significance within legal understanding, but rather it is the symbolic importance of the 'father' as completing the gendered archetype

[190] 'Positive for Youth: A New Approach to Cross-Government Policy for Young People Aged 13 to 19', (February 2010) 14, para 3.7.

[191] 'The Government Response to the Family Justice Review: A System with Families and Children at its Heart', (Ministry of Justice and Department for Education, February 2012) 18, para 57, available at: www.gov.uk/government/uploads/system/uploads/attachment_data/file/177097/CM-8273.pdf.

[192] Children Act 1989, s 1(2A).

[193] Section 11(2), this provision also inserts s 1(2B) into the Children Act 1989, which provides that '"involvement" means involvement of some kind, either direct or indirect, but not any particular division of a child's time'. This legislative support for parental 'involvement' proved controversial, because the insertion of this provision went directly against the recommendations of the independent, 'Family Justice Review: Final Report', (November 2011) 139–141, paras 4.29–4.40, available at: www.gov.uk/government/uploads/system/uploads/attachment_data/file/217343/family-justice-review-final-report.pdf.

[194] Department for Education and Ministry of Justice Consultation, 'Co-operative Parenting Following Family Separation: Proposed Legislation on the Involvement of Both Parents in a Child's Life', (July 2012) para 4.3, available at: http://dera.ioe.ac.uk/14682/.

[195] Harding and Newnham, 'How Do County Courts Share the Care of Children Between Parents?', July 2015, 131.

[196] As discussed above in subs II(A), 'What is the "Mother" in the Law?', see eg Hunt and MacLeod, 'Outcomes of Applications to Court for Contact Orders After Parental Separation or Divorce', (September 2008) 239, which shows that fathers accounted for 91.6% (265 out of 289) of the non-resident parents making applications for contact.

[197] Kaganas, 'A Presumption that "Involvement" of Both Parents is Best: Deciphering Law's Messages' 293.

[198] As discussed above in subs II(B), 'What is the "Father" in the Law?' Indeed, the significance granted to the role of the 'father' creates additional complexity in cases involving disputes between lesbian couples and known sperm donors, which are considered below at subs III(A)(ii), '"Known Donor" Disputes'.

of the nuclear family. Kaganas and Diduck comment that 'The nuclear family has long been accorded an idealised status and the "good" post-separation family has been moulded in its image.'[199] Thus, I suggest that the support for contact is premised upon the need for continued male parental involvement, which reflects the distinct gendered parenting roles of the nuclear family.

ii. Contact and Gender Neutrality

Kaganas and Day Sclater observe that 'contact, despite law's propensity to cast parenting as a gender-neutral activity, remains very much a gender issue and the meaning of a contact dispute to parents varies with gender'.[200] The gendered dimension of contact, with mothers being the resident parent and fathers the non-resident parent in the vast majority of cases,[201] is often obscured by the gender-neutral language employed by the law,[202] particularly through the language of the statutory provisions,[203] which refer to 'parents'[204] rather than to mothers and fathers.[205] Interestingly, in spite of the apparent gender neutrality of the law[206] some judges have felt it necessary to acknowledge the gendered context in which contact disputes occur; for example in *Re O (Contact: Withdrawal of Application)*[207] Wall J commented that 'The courts are not anti-father and pro-mother or vice-versa'.[208] Similarly, based upon their analysis of County Court applications, Harding and Newnham observe that 'the County courts showed no indication of gender bias in contested cases about where the child should live'.[209]

Various academic commentators have contended that judicial considerations of contact are influenced by the different constructions of the gendered

[199] Kaganas and Diduck, 'Incomplete Citizens: Changing Images of Post-Separation Children' 981.

[200] Kaganas and Day Sclater, 'Contact Disputes: Narrative Constructions of "Good" Parents' 6.

[201] Hunt and MacLeod, 'Outcomes of Applications to Court for Contact Orders After Parental Separation or Divorce', (September 2008) 239.

[202] As discussed above in s I, 'What is the "Parent" in Law?'

[203] See eg the definitions of 'parental responsibilities' and 'parental rights' in Children (Scotland) Act 1995, ss 1–2 and Children Act 1989, s 3.

[204] See eg *Re M (Contact: Welfare Test)* [1995] 1 FLR 274 and *Re P (Contact: Discretion)* [1998] 2 FLR 696 for judicial examples of the use of such gender-neutral language.

[205] Although for examples of the judicial use of gendered terminology in the context of contact, see eg Wall J's reference in *Re O (Contact: Withdrawal of Application)* [2003] EWHC 3031 (Fam), [2004] 1 FLR 1258, at 1260, that 'the courts recognise the vital importance of the role of non-resident fathers in the lives of their children' and *Re G (Contact)* [2006] EWCA Civ 1507, [2007] 1 FLR 1663.

[206] This reflects the political and cultural power that the 'father's rights' organisations (eg Fathers4Justice) have achieved. On the influence of father's rights campaigners within legal debates, see eg Richard Collier and Sally Sheldon (eds), *Fathers Rights Activism and Law Reform in Comparative Perspective* (Oxford, Hart Publishing, 2006) and Carol Smart, 'The Ethic of Justice Strikes Back: Changing Narratives of Fatherhood' in Diduck and O'Donovan (eds), *Feminist Perspectives on Family Law*.

[207] *Re O (Contact: Withdrawal of Application)* [2003] EWHC 3031 (Fam), [2004] 1 FLR 1258.

[208] ibid, at 1260, see further eg Wall J's similar comments in *Re M (Intractable Contact Dispute: Interim Care Order* [2003] EWHC 1024 (Fam), [2003] 2 FLR 636, at 641.

[209] Harding and Newnham, 'How Do County Courts Share the Care of Children Between Parents?', July 2015, 56.

parenting roles of mothers and fathers within the traditional, nuclear family.[210] In this regard, Trinder suggests 'underpinning the discussion of the respective rights of resident and non-resident parents are, of course, sets of ideas about the respective rights of mothers and fathers, despite the gender neutral use of "parent"'.[211] Collier claims that 'The good father and the good mother continue to be seen as having different albeit overlapping roles'[212] while Diduck observes that 'fathers' expressions of care about the children are valued more highly than mothers' actions of caring for them'.[213] Moreover, Smart observes, on the basis of empirical research into the language of parents themselves, that:

> [M]others, when they spoke about the work they did in caring for their children and the sacrifices they made, were hardly acknowledged. These actions were seen as being as normal as breathing and thus as worthy of as much acknowledgement as such taken for granted activities usually generate.[214]

Thus, the actual caring activities undertaken by the mother as primary carer are diminished and understood as part of her 'natural' role, yet when a father performs 'caring' activities, this is in addition to his 'natural' role, thus demonstrating that he is a 'good' father.[215] Indeed, this distinction between the expectations placed upon men and women in their parenting clearly illustrates the influence of the gendered parenting roles.[216]

In addition, mothers who do not embrace the dominant understanding that contact with the non-resident father is beneficial to their children can be the subject of judicial criticism; Wallbank observes that, 'women who are constructed as wilfully depriving their children of the right to contact with their father are subjected to the court's often vehement disapproval'.[217] Historically this led to repeated judicial references to the 'implacably hostile' mother.[218] While such

[210] The different conceptions of these gendered parenting roles were discussed above in chs 1 and 2, as well as earlier in this chapter at subss II(A), 'What is the "Mother" in the Law?' and II(B), 'What is the "Father" in the Law?'

[211] Liz Trinder, 'Introduction' in Bainham, Lindley, Richards and Trinder (eds), *Children and Their Families: Contact, Rights and Welfare* 10.

[212] Richard Collier, 'Anxious Parenthood, the Vulnerable Child and the "Good Father": Reflections on the Legal Regulation of the Relationship between Men and Children', in Bridgeman and Monk (eds), *Feminist Perspectives on Child Law* 112.

[213] Diduck, *Law's Families* 86.

[214] Smart, 'Losing the Struggle for Another Voice: The Case for Family Law' 177.

[215] This reflects Tronto's distinction between 'caring for' and 'caring about', See eg Tronto, 'Women and Caring: What Can Feminists Learn about Morality from Caring?' in Jaggar and Bordo (eds), *Gender/Body/Knowledge: Feminist Reconstructions of Being and Knowing* and Tronto, *Moral Boundaries: A Political Argument for an Ethic of Care*, which is mentioned above in subs II(B), 'What is the "Father" in the Law?'

[216] The gendered dimensions of 'care' and care work will be further explored in ch 6, subs I(A), 'Care and Relationality', which explores the potential of 'care' to provide an alternative understanding of the 'family'.

[217] Julie Wallbank, 'Castigating mothers: The Judicial Response to "Wilful" Women in Disputes over Paternal Contact in English Law' (1998) 20(4) *Journal of Social Welfare and Family Law* 357, 358.

[218] See eg *Re D (A Minor) (Contact: Mother's Hostility)* [1993] 2 FLR 1, *Re P (A Minor) (Contact)* [1994] 2 FLR 374, *Re P (Minors) (Contact: Parental Hostility)* [1996] 2 FLR 314 and *Re J (A Minor) (Contact)* [1994] 1 FLR 729.

language has subsequently been the subject of judicial criticism[219] and is no longer readily employed, milder judicial criticism of mothers resisting giving effect to judicial decisions is still evident, as illustrated by the comment of Ward LJ, in *Re G (Contact)*,[220] that 'This mother has got to appreciate that contact with father is in the best interests of her son. It may not be pleasant for either of them at this particular point in time.'[221] The judicial language in contact cases has prompted Kaganas and Day Sclater to observe:

> For the most part, it remains the case that fathers have to do very little to qualify as "good" fathers. And, for the most part, it remains the case that mothers who oppose contact for reasons other than "genuine" and "reasonable" fears of physical violence are considered selfish and as harming their children.[222]

I would adopt the analysis of these authors and thus make the point that the law expects more from resident parents than non-resident parents within the contact discourse and, given that resident parents are overwhelmingly mothers, it is submitted that the law generally expects more from mothers than fathers in relation to contact. Wallbank suggests 'that where disputes arise between mothers and fathers, because of the strength of the presumption in favour of contact, mothers will inevitably have higher hurdles to jump in order to have their fears about it taken seriously'.[223] I submit that this distinction is based upon reference to the differing constructions of the archetypical gendered parenting roles, with mothers presented as the 'natural' carers of children,[224] derived from the traditional, nuclear family. Thus, I argue that the judicial support for contact provides further illustration of the influence of the gendered roles of 'mother' and 'father' and the nuclear family model upon the legal understanding of parenthood.

III. The Role of Lesbian 'Mothers' or 'Parents'

This section considers the legal understanding of lesbian parents, focusing on the role of non-gestational female 'parent', which provides an example of individuals whose parental role has been created and explicitly defined by legislation as the 'parent'.[225] This section will argue that the lack of legal engagement with the

[219] See eg Hale J in *Re D (Contact: Reasons for Refusal)* [1997] 2 FLR 48, who stated, at 53 'It is important to bear in mind that the label "implacable hostility" is sometimes imposed by the law reporters and can be misleading.'

[220] *Re G (Contact)* [2006] EWCA Civ 1507, [2007] 1 FLR 1663.

[221] ibid, Ward LJ, at 1672.

[222] Felicity Kaganas and Shelley Day Sclater, 'Contact and Domestic Violence – The Winds of Change?' [2000] 30(9) *Fam Law* 630, 635.

[223] Julie Wallbank, 'Getting Tough on Mothers: Regulating Contact and Residence' (2007) 15(2) *Feminist Legal Studies* 189, 216.

[224] As discussed above in subs II(A), 'What is the "Mother" in the Law?'

[225] Human Fertilisation and Embryology Act 2008, ss 42–47. See above in ch 4, subs II(B), 'Non-Gestational Female "Parents"'.

role of the non-gestational female 'parent' reflects the dominance of the 'natural' gendered parental roles of the nuclear family within the legal understanding of the role of the 'parent'. In this section, I will consider the legal understanding of the role of lesbian parents, focusing upon the constructions of the role of the non-gestational female 'parent' in two contexts: disputes between the members of a lesbian couple (subsection A(i)) and disputes between lesbian couples and (male) 'known donors' (subsection A(ii)). I will conclude that the lack of a clear legal understanding of the role of the non-gestational female 'parent' reflects the rhetorical power of the traditional gendered constructions of 'mother' and 'father' (subsection B).

A. The Judicial Approach to Lesbian Mothers

The UK legal system first systematically encountered lesbian mothers in the early 1980s in the context of child 'custody'[226] disputes involving mothers who had entered lesbian relationships after the breakdown of relationships with male partners. The initial judicial response was characterised by hostility towards these mothers,[227] and references to their 'sexual deviance'.[228] As recently as 1991, Glidewell LJ expressed the view that 'a lesbian relationship between two adult women is an unusual background in which to bring up a child'.[229] Beresford observes that 'legal discourse largely presents motherhood as having essentialist, and naturalistic qualities, [and] a lesbian mother appears in the court room without those qualities'.[230] The approach of the judiciary to lesbian motherhood in these early cases is exemplified by the statement of Watkins LJ in *Re P (A Minor) (Custody)*[231] that:

> I accept that it is not right to say that a child should in no circumstances live with a mother who is carrying on a lesbian relationship with a woman who is also living with her, but I venture to suggest that it can only be countenanced by the court when it is driven to the conclusion that there is in the interests of the child no other acceptable alternative form of custody.[232]

While lesbian mothers were not prevented in these cases from being the primary carer for their children, their role was distinguished from the heterosexual, 'natural'

[226] As it was then known.

[227] Judicial hostility was also evident regarding the fatherhood of gay men, see eg Lord Kilbrandon's reference in *Re D (An Infant) (Adoption: Parent's Consent)* [1977] AC 602, at 641, to 'those whose sexual abnormalities have denied them the possibility of a normal family life'.

[228] This term is used by both Orr LJ in *S v S (Custody of Children)* [1980] 1 FLR 143 and Watkins LJ in *Re P (A Minor) (Custody)* [1983] 4 FLR 401.

[229] *C v C (A Minor) (Custody Appeal)* [1991] 1 FLR 223, per Glidewell LJ, at 228.

[230] Beresford, 'Get Over Your (Legal) "Self": A Brief History of Lesbians, Motherhood and the Law' 104.

[231] *Re P (A Minor) (Custody)* [1983] 4 FLR 401.

[232] ibid, per Watkins LJ, at 405.

ideal of motherhood.[233] Consequently, their parenting was considered unable to offer the same qualities as the traditional, gendered nuclear family.[234] At this time, the 'lesbian mother' could not be positioned within the idealised image of the (heterosexual) nuclear family. Therefore, it was not the actual care she provided that was granted normative significance, but rather her differences from the traditional, gendered construction of the 'mother' as the primary carer. The gendered, binary, two-parent model of the nuclear family remained the model of parenting preferred by the judiciary, as made clear by Glidewell LJ's observation in *C v C*[235] that 'I regard it as axiomatic that the ideal environment for the upbringing of a child is the home of loving, caring and sensible parents, her father and her mother.'[236]

Subsequent legislative developments, including the legal regulation of lesbian relationships through the Civil Partnership Act 2004, followed by the more recent same-sex marriage legislation,[237] and the recognition of lesbian parenting in relation to assisted reproduction[238] and adoption[239] show that there has been an increasing acceptance of lesbian mothers within the law and a corresponding movement away from these early negative judicial attitudes.[240] However, this initial hostility towards lesbian parenting provides further evidence of the normative and rhetorical significance of the 'natural', gendered parenting roles of the traditional nuclear family model.

i. Disputes Between Lesbian Couples

Legal recognition of the existence of a parental relationship between a non-gestational female 'parent' and her children has only been achieved relatively recently, both through the status of legal parenthood in assisted reproduction[241]

[233] Calman J in *B v B (Minors) (Custody, Care and Control)* [1991] 1 FLR 402, distinguished between 'militant lesbians' and 'lesbians in private', noting, at 410, that the lesbian couple in this case were 'private persons who both do not believe in advertising their lesbianism and acting in the public field in favour of promoting lesbianism'.

[234] ibid, at 408, however it is interesting to note that Calman J emphasised that 'The mother has been a blameless, faultless mother so far as care of her children is concerned'.

[235] *C v C (A Minor) (Custody Appeal)* [1991] 1 FLR 223.

[236] ibid, at 228.

[237] Marriage (Same Sex Couples) Act 2013 and the Marriage and Civil Partnership (Scotland) Act 2014.

[238] Described above in ch 4, at subs II(B), 'Non-Gestational Female "Parents"'.

[239] Adoption and Children Act 2002, s 144(4)(b) and Adoption and Children (Scotland) Act 2007, s 29(3) allowed same-sex couples to adopt jointly, see also the decisions in *Re E (Adoption: Freeing Order)* [1995] 1 FLR 382, *T, Petitioner* 1997 SLT 724 and *Re W (A Minor) (Adoptions: Homosexual Adopter)* [1997] 3 WLR 768, which allowed adoption by individual homosexual applicants.

[240] More recent judicial language has been much more supportive of same-sex families, see eg Girvan LJ's statement in *Northern Ireland Human Rights Commission's Application* [2013] NICA 37, [2014] NI 263, at 276, that 'the status of civil partners is closely analogous to that of married partners' and Baroness Hale's statement in *Hall v Bull* [2013] UKSC 73, [2013] 1 WLR 3741, at 3752, that 'same sex couples can enter into a mutual commitment which is the equivalent of marriage'.

[241] As set out above in ch 4, subs II(B), 'Non-Gestational Female "Parents"'. In addition, s 4ZA was inserted into the Children Act 1989 to provide for the acquisition of parental responsibilities by the 'second female parent'.

and in terms of judicial acknowledgement that hers is a parental role.[242] However, as discussed above in chapter four, in the attribution of legal parenthood the term 'mother' remains exclusive to the *gestational* mother, based on the dominant construction of motherhood as 'natural' and indivisible.[243] Both in legislation[244] and in the courts[245] non-gestational female 'parents' are usually referred to using the gender-neutral terminology of 'parents' rather than as 'mothers'.[246] I argue that the use of this terminology is significant, because as Everett and Yeatman comment 'The words we choose to use to describe relationships have power and we must choose them with care'.[247] In spite of these non-gestational female 'parents' now being granted recognition *as* legal parents, the terminological distinction made between the two roles seems to suggest that the law takes there to be essential differences between this parenting role and that of the 'mother'. As Diduck points out, this approach leads to a situation where '"Doing" parenting may make lesbian parents "parents", but it is not enough to make them mothers and the difficulties presented by the limitation of language for that form of parenthood are clear'.[248] This could result in a hierarchy of parenting roles being created within lesbian couples, because of the widely different idealised constructions of these two roles. As described above, the law has an understanding of the 'natural' role of the mother which underpins its construction of motherhood.[249] In contrast, the gender-neutral terminology of 'parent' possesses less cultural resonance because it lacks a similar readily identifiable and easily understandable archetypical role.[250]

This distinction between the two roles is evidenced in the House of Lords judgment in *Re G (Children) (Residence: Same-Sex Partner)*,[251] where in the context of a residence dispute between two lesbians who were formerly a couple, Baroness Hale states that 'the issues arising are just the same as those which may arise between heterosexual couples. The legal principles are also the same'.[252] I suggest

[242] See eg the judgment of Hedley J in *Re P & L (Contact)* [2011] EWHC 3431 (Fam), [2012] 1 FLR 1068.

[243] Described above at subs II(A), 'What is the "Mother" in the Law?'

[244] Human Fertilisation and Embryology Act 2008, ss 42–47.

[245] Although the courts will still not always even use terminology which gives recognition to the role as being parental, eg Lord Nicholls referred to the 'former partner' of the mother in *Re G (Children) (Residence: Same-Sex Partner)* [2006] UKHL 43, [2006] 2 FLR 629, at 631, see also Thorpe LJ referring to the 'long-term lesbian partner', in *A v B and C (Role of Father)* [2012] EWCA Civ 285, [2012] 2 FLR 607, at 608.

[246] For an exception to the judicial use of this terminological distinction, see *Re G (Children) (Shared Residence Order: Biological Non-Birth Mother)* [2014] EWCA Civ 336, [2014] 2 FLR 897, where Black LJ, at 910, uses the term 'biological mother' to describe a non-gestational female 'parent' whose gametes had been used in the creation of the child. Although, it is notable that even in this judgment the gender-neutral terminology of 'genetic parent' was her Ladyship's preferred descriptor.

[247] Everett and Yeatman, 'Are Some Parents More Natural Than Others?' 306.

[248] Diduck, 'If Only we can Find the Appropriate Terms to Use the Issue Will Be Solved: Law, Identity and Parenthood' 465.

[249] As discussed above in ch 4, subs II(A), 'Motherhood'.

[250] See above at subs I(B), 'The Role of the "Parent"'.

[251] [2006] UKHL 43, [2006] 2 FLR 629, see further Elizabeth Woodcraft, '*Re G*: A Missed Opportunity' [2007] 37(1) *Fam Law* 53.

[252] ibid, per Baroness Hale, at 632.

that this is a problematic approach because it explicitly applies the standards of the traditional, heterosexual, nuclear family to the circumstances of a lesbian-led family, which had been purposely designed outside that framework.[253] The judgment also includes the observation of Baroness Hale that:

> The fact [CG] is the natural mother of these children in every sense of that term, while raising no presumption in her favour, is undoubtedly an important and significant factor in determining what will be best for them now and in the future.[254]

This emphasis on the importance of the 'natural mother'[255] to the child's welfare seems to contradict her description of the case as identical to one that arises with opposite-sex couples, and also seems to create a de facto presumption in favour of genetic relationships.[256] Such a presumption would be problematic for lesbian couples where, unlike in most heterosexual relationships,[257] the mother will usually have a genetic connection with the children which the non-gestational female 'parent' will not possess.[258] Beresford suggests that 'the case firmly restated so-called traditional values. It stated that the biological connection is of fundamental importance and it did this by appealing to the rhetorical importance of that which is "natural"'.[259] It is submitted that through the attempt to analogise a lesbian couple with a heterosexual couple, the law reflects the aforementioned hierarchy of parenting roles within lesbian relationships; with the 'parent' constructed as a

[253] See eg Fiona Kelly, 'Nuclear Norms or Fluid Families? Incorporating Lesbian and Gay Parents and Their Children into Canadian Family Law' (2004) 21(1) *Canadian Journal of Family Law* 133.

[254] *Re G (Children) (Residence: Same-Sex Partner)* [2006] UKHL 43, [2006] 2 FLR 629, per Baroness Hale, at 643.

[255] Baroness Hale defines a 'natural parent' as encompassing 'genetic', 'gestational' and 'social and psychological' parenthood, therefore she distinguishes the 'natural mother' from other 'natural parents', including the non-gestational female 'parent', who generally only possesses 'psychological parenthood'. Interestingly in *Re G, Re Z (Children: Sperm Donors: Leave to Apply for Children Act Orders)* [2013] EWHC 134 (Fam), [2013] 1 FLR 1334, a case involving a lesbian couple and a known sperm donor, at 1365, Baker J, comments that 'the potential importance of genetic and psychological parenthood is not automatically extinguished by the removal of the status of legal parenthood, and that social and psychological relationships amounting to parenthood can and often do co-exist with legal parenthood'.

[256] Subsequently the Supreme Court in *Re B (A Child)* [2009] UKSC 5, [2010] 1 FLR 551 made clear that there exists no 'presumption' and that all decisions must be made on the basis of the 'welfare test'. However, the factual circumstances were very different, involving a dispute between a genetic father and maternal grandmother as opposed to dispute between lesbian couple. Therefore, the differing gendered parenting roles this case involved may have influenced this different approach. See further eg Andrew Bainham, 'Rowing Back from *Re G*? Natural Parents in the Supreme Court' [2010] 40(4) *Fam Law* 394 and Everett and Yeatman, 'Are Some Parents More Natural Than Others'.

[257] However, the implications of the judgment in *Re G* may also be problematic for fathers in disputes with mothers, because they can only possess 'genetic' and 'psychological' parenthood, whereas only the mother can have 'gestational' parenthood and therefore possess all three characteristics.

[258] In cases of assisted reproduction where the eggs of the non-gestational female 'parent' are used, both parties would possess two of the three incidences of 'natural parenthood' described above by Baroness Hale. However, it is suggested that the influence of the traditional construction of motherhood, premised around gestation, would result in the gestational mother retaining the exclusive term 'mother', over the claim of the 'genetic mother'. See further *Re G (Children) (Shared Residence Order: Biological Non-Birth Mother)* [2014] EWCA Civ 336, [2014] 2 FLR 897.

[259] Beresford, 'Get Over Your (Legal) "Self": A Brief History of Lesbians, Motherhood and the Law' 102.

second-class parental role in comparison with the 'mother'; thus illustrating the normative significance of the gendered parenting roles. I argue that this is needlessly problematic and the courts' choice to view lesbian family disputes through a heterosexual prism once again illustrates the influence of the traditional, nuclear family model.

ii. 'Known Donor' Disputes

This hierarchy of roles becomes even more problematic for the non-gestational female 'parent' in the context of disputes between lesbian couples and male 'known donors'.[260] It is notable that the terms 'father' and 'biological father' are used to describe the men in these cases.[261] In *A v B and C (Role of Father)*,[262] Black LJ observed that:

> The practice has grown up of referring to the father in circumstances such as this as a 'donor' … it seems to me that the label might merit reconsideration … as it is capable of conveying the impression that the father is giving his child away and that is misleading.[263]

In a commentary on this case Zanghellini describes the decision as being based upon a series of 'heteronormative assumptions'.[264] I want to suggest that such assumptions feature throughout the known donor decisions and consequently position the donor in the readily identifiable gendered role of the 'father', to the significant diminishment of the role of the non-gestational female 'parent', a role which lacks the rhetorical power possessed by the gendered parenting roles.[265]

[260] Prior to the reforms of the Human Fertilisation and Embryology Act 2008 the non-gestational female 'parent' could not possess the status of legal parenthood; instead the 'known donor' would have been the legal parent on the basis of the genetic connection, making her position even weaker. All but one of the decisions discussed in this section concerned children born prior to the legislative reforms.

[261] See eg *Re P and L (Contact)* [2011] EWHC 3431 (Fam), [2012] 1 FLR 1068, *T v T (Shared Residence)* [2010] EWCA Civ 1366, [2011] 1 FCR 267, *R v E and F (Female Parents: Known Father)* [2010] EWHC 417 (Fam), [2010] 2 FLR 383, *Re B (Role of the Biological Father)* [2007] EWHC 1952 (Fam), [2008] 1 FLR 1015 and *Re D (Contact and Parental Responsibility: Lesbian Mothers and Known Father)* [2006] EWHC 2 (Fam), [2006] 1 FCR 556. See further eg Therese Callus, 'A New Parenthood Paradigm for Twenty-First Century Family Law in England and Wales?' (2012) 32(3) *Legal Studies* 347.

[262] *A v B and C (Role of Father)* [2012] EWCA Civ 285, [2012] 2 FLR 607.

[263] ibid, per Black LJ, at 617. Similarly, in *JB v KS (Contact: Parental Responsibility)* [2015] EWHC 180 (Fam), [2015] 2 FLR 1180 in different factual circumstances, Hayden J stated, at 1192 'I cannot easily contemplate any factual circumstance where its use is anything other than belittling and disrespectful to all concerned, most importantly the child.'

[264] Aleardo Zanghellini, '*A v B and C* [2012] EWCA Civ 285 – Heteronormativity, Poly-Parenting, and the Homo-Nuclear Family' [2012] 24(4) *Child and Family Law Quarterly* 475. However, see Philip Bremner, 'Collaborative Co-Parenting and Heteronormativity: Recognising the Interests of Gay Fathers' [2017] 27(4) *Child and Family Law Quarterly* 293, who observes, at 307 'while some may perceive a legal framework that facilitates the involvement of the biological father alongside a lesbian couple as heteronormative because it promotes gendered parenting, others may perceive a legal framework that did not facilitate the involvement of the biological father alongside a lesbian couple as heteronormative because it promoted dyadic parenting based on conjugality'.

[265] Fox, 'The Human Fertilisation and Embryology Act 2008: Tinkering at the Margins', suggests at 338, that 'adopting the terminology of "fathers" and "female parents" tends to suggest that the two roles are not equally valorised by law'.

Boyd has observed that 'The problem is that the legal system still seems tempted to impose a father figure on families that are headed, and sometimes carefully designed, by women'.[266] The role of the father, and therefore the specifically male perspective, seems to be understood by the courts to be a necessary and valuable part of a child's life, on the basis of the traditional gendered construction of the role derived from the nuclear family.[267] This understanding of the importance of the role of the 'father' is evident from the statement of Black J in *Re D (Contact and Parental Responsibility: Lesbian Mothers and Known Father)*[268] that 'Perhaps most importantly of all, I am considerably influenced by the reality that [Mr B] is [D's] father. Whatever new designs human beings have for the structure of their families, that aspect of nature cannot be overcome'.[269] As Smith observes, this creates a problematic dichotomy because 'whereas lesbian parents tend to emphasise that genetic fathers have less authority and significance than co-parents, law takes the opposite approach'.[270]

The use of the terminology of 'biological fathers' is also notable because research has found that a variety of different terms are used within lesbian-led families who involve known donors in their parenting, Donovan has observed that '[for] the biological father the terms can range from "donor" through to "daddy", "uncle" or "adult friend"'.[271] I argue that the judicial use of the term 'biological father' results in greater normative significance being placed on these relationships than would be likely if the term 'known donor' was used in these cases, because of the resonance of the 'natural' role of the 'father'.[272] Smith states that the approach of

[266] Boyd, 'Gendering Legal Parenthood: Bio-Genetic Ties, Intentionality and Responsibility' 92.

[267] *JB v KS (Contact: Parental Responsibility)* [2015] EWHC 180 (Fam), [2015] 2 FLR 1180, a case involving a single lesbian woman and a single straight man who had acted as her 'known donor'. This judgment was considered in Mary Welstead, 'The Parenthood War: Biological Fathers, Lesbian Mothers and the Best Interests of Their Children' [2015] *Fam Law* 431. Indeed, in this context where there is not a second female parent, the normative influence of the traditional nuclear family model is apparent, in spite of the explicit choices of the individuals involved. See further Fiona Kelly, 'Autonomous from the Start: Single Mothers by Choice in the Canadian Legal System' [2012] 24(3) *Child and Family Law Quarterly* 257, for a consideration of similar issues in the Canadian context; Kelly notes that, at 258 'single mothers and their children are vulnerable to having families reconstituted by judges who typically treat the lack of a second (male) parent as a gap that needs to be filled'.

[268] *Re D (Contact and Parental Responsibility: Lesbian Mothers and Known Father)* [2006] EWHC 2 (Fam), [2006] 1 FCR 556.

[269] ibid, at para 89.

[270] Smith, 'Is Three a Crowd? Lesbian Mothers Perspectives on Parental Status in Law' 244.

[271] Catherine Donovan, 'Who Needs a Father? Negotiating Biological Fatherhood in British Lesbian Families Using Self-Insemination' (2000) 3(2) *Sexualities* 149, 156, see also the accounts of similar families in Kathryn Almack, 'Seeking Sperm: Accounts of Lesbian Couples' Reproductive Decision-Making and Understandings of the Needs of the Child' (2006) 20(1) *International Journal of Law, Policy and the Family* 1.

[272] Kelly, '(Re)Forming Parenthood: The Assignment of Legal Parentage Within Planned Lesbian Families', 205, refers to the accounts of lesbian mothers and notes their acknowledgment of the, '"utter failure" of language to capture the identities created', in 'known donor' situations.

the courts[273] could be 'just as easily interpreted as a regressive effort to insert identifiable fathers into lesbian families. Such capitulation to the prevailing ideology of essential fathers demeans the parenting capacities of lesbian couples and devalues the integrity of their families'.[274] I submit that the approach of the courts in these 'known donor' cases, particularly the consistent use within the judgments of the language of 'biological fathers' further illustrates the influence of the gendered parenting roles upon the legal understanding of the parental role, to the disadvantage of the non-gestational female 'parent'. Indeed, Yeatman comments that 'some of the judiciary in this country remain firmly attached to the importance of the genetic family and are still struggling to recognise the completeness of the lesbian headed family despite the legislative changes'.[275]

B. The Construction of the Role of the Non-Gestational Female 'Parent'

It is submitted that there is a lack of judicial consideration throughout all of these different types of cases as to the role performed by the non-gestational female 'parent',[276] which reflects the lack of clarity of the legal understanding of the overarching parental role.[277] Everett and Yeatman observe that 'Lesbian families are in essence different from heterosexual families, not only because they defy the primacy of the biological link as the defining factor in parenthood, but also because they have two mothers'.[278] However, given that the legislation explicitly makes the terminological distinction between 'parent'[279] and 'mother',[280] it is clear that the non-gestational female 'parent' is not treated as an 'additional mother'.[281]

[273] Smith was writing of the judicial approach prior to the reforms of the Human Fertilisation and Embryology Act 2008, although it is notable that the language of 'biological fathers' was still employed by Baker J in *Re G, Re Z (Children: Sperm Donors: Leave to Apply for Children Act Orders)* [2013] EWHC 134 (Fam), [2013] 1 FLR 1334, the only reported decision subsequent to the HFEA 2008 where the lesbian couple were both legal parents. The donors in this case were granted leave to apply for contact orders, but no substantive judgment was made as to the merits of their application. I have previously considered the approach and language of Baker J in *Re G, Re Z* in Alan Brown, 'Re G; Re Z (Children: Sperm Donors: Leave to Apply for Children Act Orders): Essential "Biological Fathers" and Invisible "Legal Parents"' [2014] 26(2) *Child and Family Law Quarterly* 237.

[274] Smith, 'Tangling the Web of Legal Parenthood: Legal Responses to the Use of Known Donors in Lesbian Parenting Arrangements' 377.

[275] Lucy Yeatman, 'Lesbian Co-Parents: Still Not Real Mothers' [2013] *Fam Law* 1581, 1587.

[276] It is arguable that this lack of consideration reflects the limited normative significance accorded to social parenting and 'care' within the legal understanding of parenthood in contrast to reproducing the gendered roles of the nuclear family.

[277] As set out above in s I, 'What is the "Parent" in Law?'

[278] Everett and Yeatman, 'Are Some Parents More Natural Than Others?' 304.

[279] HFEA 2008, s 33.

[280] ibid, ss 42–47.

[281] Millbank, 'The Limits of Functional Family: Lesbian Mother Litigation in the Era of the Eternal Biological Family', 158, comments that 'The co-mother in a lesbian family by contrast is viewed as just an *extra* mother and *only* through her care giving, she is viewed as a not-really-real or not-complete mother'.

Although there is no distinction between the legal (parental) status of the 'mother' and the 'parent', I contend that the explicit difference in terminology influences judicial understandings of the two roles and this, as illustrated by the cases considered above, appears to be influencing judicial outcomes.[282] This is underscored by the exclusivity inherent in the traditional, 'natural' construction of mother,[283] with its fundamental link to the process of gestation, which the 'parent' self-evidently does not and cannot possess.

Alternatively, it is possible that the role of the non-gestational female 'parent' could be understood as essentially replicating the role of father within the traditional nuclear family.[284] Hedley J in *Re P & L (Contact)*[285] did describe the role as 'second parent which in a traditional family would have been fulfilled by the father'.[286] This understanding of parent could be read as having the radical implication that fatherhood does not actually have distinctly 'male' features and therefore that it is not necessary for children to have (male) fathers.[287] However, the approach adopted by the courts in the known donor decisions does not support this construction of the role of 'parent'. These decisions[288] suggest that the father fulfils a specific, significant and gendered role which is understood as being additional to the day-to-day parenting performed by the lesbian couple; as Millbank has commented 'Lesbian mothers may be a functional family but they are not a complete family'.[289] I argue that the presence of a (male) father, completing the gendered binary of parenting roles within the nuclear family, possesses greater normative resonance in judicial reasoning than the practical contributions of the non-gestational female 'parent' in caring for the children. Thus, in its legal construction, the second female 'parent' is, as Golombok observes 'more likely to be viewed as an additional parent than as a replacement parent'.[290] It is my contention

[282] Both in the context of disputes between lesbian couples, eg *Re G (Children) (Residence: Same-Sex Partner)* [2006] UKHL 43, [2006] 2 FLR 629 and *Re G (Children) (Shared Residence Order: Biological Non-Birth Mother)* [2014] EWCA Civ 336, [2014] 2 FLR 897 and in the 'known donor' cases, eg *A v B and C (Role of Father)* [2012] EWCA Civ 285, [2012] 2 FLR 607 and *Re G, Re Z (Children: Sperm Donors: Leave to Apply for Children Act Orders)* [2013] EWHC 134 (Fam), [2013] 1 FLR 1334.

[283] As set out above in ch 4, subs II(A), 'Motherhood'.

[284] It is suggested that the possibility of the role being viewed as replacing that of the father could be implied by the exclusion of the possibility of their being a legal 'father' when there is a 'parent' in HFEA 2008, s 45(1), which states 'Where a woman is treated by virtue of section 42 or 43 as a parent of the child, no man is to be treated as the father of the child'.

[285] *Re P and L (Contact)* [2011] EWHC 3431 (Fam), [2012] 1 FLR 1068.

[286] ibid, per Hedley J, at 1069.

[287] Such an approach, which explicitly treats fatherhood as secondary to motherhood would be in contradiction with the wider policy agenda emphasising the importance of fatherhood, discussed above at subs II(B), 'What is the "Father" in the Law?'

[288] See eg *Re P and L (Contact)* [2011] EWHC 3431 (Fam), [2012] 1 FLR 1068, *T v T (Shared Residence)* [2010] EWCA Civ 1366, [2011] 1 FCR 267, *R v E and F (Female Parents: Known Father)* [2010] EWHC 417 (Fam), [2010] 2 FLR 383 and *Re B (Role of the Biological Father)* [2007] EWHC 1952 (Fam), [2008] 1 FLR 1015.

[289] Millbank, 'The Limits of Functional Family: Lesbian Mother Litigation in the Era of the Eternal Biological Family' 162.

[290] Susan Golombok, 'Lesbian Mother Families' in Bainham, Day Sclater and Richards (eds), *What is a Parent?: A Socio-Legal Analysis* 172.

that, within the law, the role of the non-gestational female 'parent' is not being constructed as an equivalent to either mother *or* father.

While there has been scant specific consideration of the latter role within the judicial decisions, sociological research suggests that lesbian couples do not necessarily reflect the traditional gendered parenting roles of the nuclear family. Instead, lesbian couples have been observed to adopt a more egalitarian form of parenting, with Gabb observing that 'Femininity and masculinity are practised without regard to their cultural referents of female and male bodies, as lesbians raise children as both mothers and fathers – beyond gender'[291] and Dunne commenting that 'Without exception, respondents believed that they approached and experienced parenting in ways that were very different from the heterosexual norm'.[292] In spite of this, as illustrated above, within judicial decisions there has been little or no engagement with the radical possibilities created by lesbian-led families, who may aim to parent outside of the boundaries of the heterosexual nuclear family.

The importance of language in this context should also be emphasised; the absence of an obvious ordinary language term for the role of the non-gestational female 'parent' results in law employing the gender-neutral term 'parent'.[293] This term lacks the easily understood, traditional, 'common-sense' construction possessed by the gendered roles of mother and father. Thus, the social parental role undertaken and the caring activities performed by the 'parent' cannot grant the status of 'mother', which remains exclusively premised upon gestation. This illustrates the tremendous power possessed by language, represented through the traditional nuclear family, to exclude those who do not fit within its boundaries.[294] I argue that the lesbian-led family is constantly being judged against heteronormative standards of parenting and the nuclear family ideal with which it is not and cannot be truly analogous, because as Diduck points out:

> [L]esbian co-parenthood is like nothing else. It is unlike step-parenthood, heterosexual parenthood by assisted reproduction or even single parenthood, all of which bear some similarity to it but are practised within a heterosexual norm that gives meaning to the concepts and practices of motherhood and fatherhood.[295]

I submit that it is because of this lack of understanding of the reality of lesbian parenting that the role of the non-gestational female 'parent' has not been fully explored or articulated within the law. The positioning of this role illustrates the

[291] Gabb, 'Lesbian M/Otherhood: Strategies of Familial-linguistic Management in Lesbian Parent Families' 592.

[292] Dunne, 'Opting into Motherhood: Lesbians Blurring the Boundaries and Transforming the Meaning of Parenthood and Kinship' 25.

[293] As considered above in ch 4, at subs II(B), 'Non-Gestational Female "Parents"', see eg Diduck, 'If Only we can Find the Appropriate Terms to Use the Issue Will Be Solved: Law, Identity and Parenthood' and Probert, 'Families, Assisted Reproduction and the Law'.

[294] See eg Jones, 'Parents in Law: Subjective Impacts and Status Implications around the Use of Licensed Donor Insemination' in Diduck and O'Donovan (eds), *Feminist Perspectives on Family Law*.

[295] Diduck, 'If Only we can Find the Appropriate Terms to Use the Issue Will Be Solved: Law, Identity and Parenthood' 473.

continuing normative power of the gendered parenting roles of 'mother' and 'father' upon the legal understanding of the role of the 'parent'.

To conclude, this chapter has argued that the gendered parenting roles of 'mother' and 'father', derived from the traditional nuclear family model, underpin the legal understanding of the role of the 'parent'. It has been argued that law's starting point is an overarching conception of parenting which applies equally to all parents, and this is illustrated by legislative usage of the gender-neutral language of 'parent'.[296] I have suggested, however, that the legal understanding of the role of this 'parent' is unclear. In judicial interpretation of the parental role, significant reliance is placed upon the archetypical gendered parenting roles of 'mother' and 'father', which are understood as the 'natural' and 'common sense' parenting roles. I have argued that these roles are understood by the law on the basis of their distinct functions within the traditional, nuclear family: the 'mother' is constructed as the 'natural' primary carer for children, whereas the 'father' is understood as the breadwinner. I have argued that the understanding of the role of the 'parent' which is evident within the judicial interpretation of the welfare principle illustrated the influence of these gendered parental roles. Considering the law's approach to the role of the non-gestational female 'parent' in lesbian couples, it has been observed that this parental role is not fully explored or developed within the case law. Moreover, the gender-neutral term 'parent' lacks the kind of 'natural' or 'common-sense' construction possessed by the gendered roles of mother and father, which reinforces the significance of those traditional, gendered parenting roles.

My overarching claim in this chapter has been that the legal understanding of the role of the 'parent', regardless of the usage of gender-neutral terminology, is substantially underpinned by the distinct, gendered parenting roles of 'mother' and 'father' derived from the nuclear family.

[296] Through the definitions of 'parental responsibilities' and 'parental rights' in Children Act 1989, s 3 and Children (Scotland) Act 1995, ss 1–2.

PART IV

The Future

> From family unit and village community through region and religion to class, corporation and gender role, what used to provide a framework and rules for people's daily lives has become increasingly brittle. New space and new options have thereby opened up for individuals. Now men and women can and should, may and must, decide for themselves how to shape their lives – within certain limits, at least.

Elisabeth Beck-Gernsheim, *Reinventing the Family: In Search of New Lifestyles*, (Cambridge, Polity Press, 2002) Preface to the English Edition, ix

6

The Possibilities Offered by Alternative 'Models' of the 'Family'

The central argument that runs throughout, and connects, the preceding chapters of this book has been that the traditional nuclear family model continues to possess substantial normative influence within the contemporary legal understanding of the 'family' in the UK. This influence has been identified and discussed across a variety of contexts; statutory definitions of 'family',[1] the legal regulation of adult personal relationships,[2] the attribution of legal parenthood[3] and the legal understanding and construction of the parental role.[4] One consequence of this continuing normative hold of the nuclear family model is that, as Wallbank has previously observed 'Relying on established norms and traditions about the family saves the legislators, users and wider society from having to rethink, revise, let alone challenge the assumptions which are held about what constitutes a family'.[5] Thus, the idealised image of the nuclear family and its underlying values and assumptions have dominated within the legal understanding of 'family' without any significant assessment or consideration of their continued relevance to twenty-first century family life.

Building upon that premise, which has been established throughout the book, this chapter considers the consequences of deprivileging the traditional nuclear family within legal understanding. To that end, two related questions are considered: (1) What alternative 'models' could replace the nuclear family model?, and (2) Should the legal regulation of families and family life be centred around a conceptual model of 'family' at all? In attempting to answer these questions this chapter will explore a range of potential conceptual influences[6] on the understanding

[1] Ch 1, 'What is the Law's "Family"?'

[2] Ch 3, 'The Legal Regulation of Conjugal Relationships'.

[3] Ch 4, 'The Attribution of Legal Parenthood within UK Law'.

[4] Ch 5, 'The Legal Understanding of the Parental Role'.

[5] Wallbank, 'Channelling the Messiness of Diverse Family Lives: Resisting the Calls to Order and De-Centring the Hetero-Normative Family', 365.

[6] It should be noted, at the outset, that some potential influences are not considered in any detail in this chapter; for example, 'emotion', 'love' and 'intimacy'. On 'emotion', as Herring, 'The Disability Critique of Care', 3, argues 'the law tends to be suspicious of emotion. Much of the law emphasises the importance of rationality and intellect and downplays the importance of emotion'. On the law's relationship with the concept of 'love', see eg Renata Grossi, *Looking for Love in the Legal Discourse of Marriage* (Canberra, ANU Press, 2014) and Renata Grossi, 'The Meaning of Love in the Debate

of 'family',[7] including 'care',[8] 'relationality',[9] 'vulnerability',[10] 'autonomy',[11] 'choice'[12] and 'individualism'.[13] Therefore, this chapter will involve a critical exploration of how these concepts can be utilised to create potential alternative 'models of family' to the traditionally dominant nuclear family ideal.[14] Throughout this chapter, I will also consider the potential impact of these alternative conceptual 'models' of 'family' upon the legal regulation of family life and future family law reform. Within this, it is possible to identify a spectrum of approaches that could be taken to the regulation of families and family life; and Westwood notes the tension between 'whether the solution involves more legal recognition of newer relationship forms, or de-regulation of those relationships which are currently privileged'.[15] As previous chapters have set out, the trend within the UK has been towards extending legal regulation outwards to include new forms and types of relationship, on the basis of analogy with those relationships that form the central nexus of the nuclear family model.[16] However, as Herring has previously observed 'While public support and recognition of a relationship is important, whether that needs to be in the form of a legal status, or even in the form of state-approved status may be questioned'.[17] As I have suggested in earlier chapters of this book, legal status and regulation is

for Legal Recognition of Same-Sex Marriage in Australia' (2012) 8(4) *International Journal of Law in Context* 487. Moreover, within the relevant literature, the notion of 'intimacy' is not restricted to conjugal or consanguineous relationships; see eg Sue Westwood, '"My Friends are my Family": An Argument about the Limitations of Contemporary Law's Recognition of Relationships in Later Life' (2013) 35(3) *Journal of Social Welfare and Family Law* 347, who observes, at 349 'the word friendship is also insufficient to describe the range of depth of intimate non-biological and non-conjugal relationships'. See further eg Weeks, Heaphy and Donovan, *Same Sex Intimacies: Families of Choice and Other Life Experiences*.

[7] Many of these concepts are inter-related and overlapping, consequently, this means that it is often difficult to draw conceptual boundaries between them. Moreover, there is an apparent contestability regarding the meaning and definition of many of these terms. The impact of these two 'issues' will be explored subsequently throughout this chapter.

[8] See eg Herring, *Caring and the Law* and Tronto, *Moral Boundaries: A Political Argument for an Ethic of Care*.

[9] See eg Rosie Harding, *Duties to Care: Dementia, Relationality and Law* (Cambridge, Cambridge University Press, 2017) and Herring, *Relational Autonomy and Family Law*.

[10] See eg Wallbank and Herring (eds), *Vulnerabilities, Care and Family Law* and Fineman and Grear (eds), *Vulnerability: Reflections on a New Ethical Foundation for Law and Politics*.

[11] See eg Fineman, *The Autonomy Myth: A Theory of Dependency* and John Christman and Joel Anderson (eds), *Autonomy and the Challenges to Liberalism* (Cambridge, Cambridge University Press, 2005).

[12] See eg Susan Boyd, Dorothy Chunn, Fiona Kelly and Wanda Wiegers, *Autonomous Motherhood? A Socio-Legal Study of Choice and Constraint* (Toronto, University of Toronto Press, 2015).

[13] See eg Ulrich Beck and Elisabeth Beck-Gernsheim, *Individualization: Institutionalized Individualism and its Social and Political Consequences* (London, SAGE, 2002) and Lukes, *Individualism*.

[14] It should be noted that a detailed exploration of the literature on each of these concepts, and the definitional, conceptual and linguistic internal debates within such literature is outside the scope of this chapter; which instead is focused on considering the role (if any) that these conceptual influences have on our social and legal understanding(s) of the 'family'.

[15] Westwood, '"My Friends are my Family": An Argument about the Limitations of Contemporary Law's Recognition of Relationships in Later Life' 360.

[16] This argument is particularly evident in ch 3, 'The Legal Regulation of Conjugal Relationships' and ch 4, 'The Attribution of Legal Parenthood within UK Law'.

[17] Herring, *Relational Autonomy and Family Law* 28.

not a panacea; nor does recognition of particular relationship types and family forms necessarily indicate a fundamental shift in the dominant legal understanding of 'family', because traditional norms and ideals continue to exert significant influence in spite of seemingly 'progressive' legal reforms.

The previous chapters of this book have been critical of the continued gravitational force of the traditional, nuclear family model upon contemporary legal understanding of the 'family'. Therefore, in this chapter I argue that no single concept, image or 'model' can encompass the multitude of relationships, meanings and forms that are captured by the term 'family'. Thus, while this chapter will suggest that a radical re-imagining of the 'family' is essential to reflect the diversity of families and family life in twenty-first century society; I will argue that conceiving of the 'family' in terms of 'models' obscures the complexity, individual nature and 'messy' reality of contemporary family life. As Diduck has previously commented 'Our lived relationships are thus complex and contradictory: they are moral, emotional, rational, sacred, reflexive and static. They often reinforce traditional gender and class stereotypes even while they attempt to democratise relationships'.[18] I agree with this need to acknowledge these competing normative tendencies which exist within contemporary families, and it is the attempt to recognise the complex and contradictory reality of the nature of families and family life that underpins the various concepts that are considered in this chapter.

This chapter will begin in section I by considering the literature on these various conceptual factors, identified above, as well as how they influence our understanding of the 'family'. Building upon this, in section II, the chapter will explore the wider question of the relationship between abstract conceptual and philosophical models of 'family' and the diversity of contemporary family life; concluding that while radical rethinking of family law and policy is necessary, it is far from clear that the approaches discussed would address the underlying issues raised in earlier chapters. Simply put, the chapter argues that the traditional, nuclear family should not be replaced within legal understanding by an alternative model of 'family'. Instead, the entire normative approach which relies upon constructing a model of 'family' and regulating relationships based on their similarity to that model should be rejected. Consequently, the law should be underpinned by an attempt to fully and properly recognise, appreciate and regulate the diversity of individual families in contemporary society.

I. Exploring the Conceptual Influences

Families are diverse, they are multi-faceted, they are made up of complex bonds constructed by the individuals within them and, as has been discussed earlier in this book, it is difficult to provide a simple definition that encompasses the variety

[18] Diduck, *Law's Families* 2.

of relationships and forms of contemporary family life.[19] As I have argued in the preceding chapters, this search for clarity and simplicity within the law has led to the continuing normative significance within legal understanding of the idealised image of the nuclear family.[20] However, I would also suggest that once the normative centrality of that model of family is questioned and if it is ultimately rejected, Cheal's observation, quoted above in chapter one, still remains 'There is no single concept of the family which is true for all historical periods and in all places'.[21] With that in mind, this section will explore some of the theoretical, philosophical and ethical concepts that may contribute to moving the legal understanding of the 'family' beyond the idealised image of the traditional nuclear family.[22]

Consequently, this section will briefly consider the developing literature on the following concepts: 'care' and 'relationality' (subsection A), 'vulnerability' (subsection B) and 'autonomy' and 'choice' (subsection C), examining the relationship between this literature and the construction and understanding of the 'family', family life and family law. It is important to note at the outset that there is a significant degree of overlap between these conceptual and terminological categories (which will be explored below) and that these categories have been chosen as much for linguistic simplicity and structural clarity than for any normative claim about the bounds of these concepts.[23] With that said, this section will consider the nature of this conceptual literature, focusing upon its potential impact upon the legal understanding of the 'family'.

A. Care and Relationality

As set out in earlier chapters,[24] traditionally within the law 'care', caring and 'care work' were given limited significance, instead these features were largely ignored or invisible.[25] With that said, it is trite to note that everybody 'cares' in the widest

[19] The issues with the lack of overarching definition of 'family' within the sociological literature were considered above in ch 1, s I, '"Family" as a Social Concept'.

[20] See above throughout, but particularly in ch 1, 'What is the Law's "Family"?'

[21] Cheal, *Sociology of Family Life* 4.

[22] Douzinas and Warrington, *Justice Miscarried: Ethics, Aesthetics and the Law* 1, argue that 'the task [is] to find grounds for arguing that there can be an ethical substance for law, without reproducing the discredited essentialism of Enlightenment thinking'.

[23] Moreover, I recognise that there is some debate within the literature on these concepts as to their definitions, which will be acknowledged where appropriate throughout this chapter.

[24] See particularly ch 1, s II, 'The Law's "Definition(s)" of "Family"' and ch 3, s II, 'The Centrality of Conjugality'.

[25] See eg Ann Stewart, 'From Family to Personal Responsibility: the Challenges for Care of the Elderly in England' (2012) 34(2) *Journal of Social Welfare and Family Law* 179, 181, who argues that 'Because caring relationships do not form the basis for societal wellbeing more generally, the costs to those involved in them are not adequately addressed either within private family law or public social welfare and employment laws'.

abstract sense, it is also true that everybody provides and receives 'care' in one form or another, but this section is interested in 'care' as a moral or ethical ideal. The starting point for understanding this concept, as Herring has argued, is that, 'caring is the very essence of life. It is part of being human.'[26] In recognition of this, as set out in previous chapters,[27] there is now substantial literature on the moral and ethical significance of 'care';[28] as Held describes 'the central focus of the ethics of care is on the compelling moral salience of attending to and meeting the needs of particular others for whom we take responsibility.'[29] As a result of this literature, there has been increasing focus upon the role of 'care' within the law and legal discourse.[30] This has combined with consideration of how this literature on 'care' could be used to redefine our understanding of the 'family'.[31] These attempts to define and conceptualise the 'family' on the basis of 'care' are unsurprising, because the family remains the foremost site of such 'caring' work and activity within contemporary society.[32] The burden of this work is performed asymmetrically within families, as Wallbank and Herring have observed 'Central to understanding the treatment of care is its gendered nature.'[33] The gendered nature of the societal division of 'care' reflects the continuing social power of the gendered roles (of 'breadwinner' and 'homemaker') within the traditional nuclear family model, which are premised upon the historical centrality of the 'public/private' divide.[34] Thus, even in this context, the continuing influence of these traditional norms is clear. The consequence of this historical association of the 'family' with the 'private' (unregulated) sphere of society was that, as Stewart observes 'Although the breadwinner/homemaker model has never existed in reality, the traditional family with its gendered division of labour moulded by the emerging discipline

[26] Herring, 'Where are the Carers in Healthcare Law and Ethics?' 67.

[27] See particularly 'Introduction' and ch 1, 'What is the Law's "Family"?'

[28] See eg Gilligan, *In a Different Voice: Psychological Theory and Women's Development*, Friedman, *Liberating Care*, Groenhout, *Connected Lives: Human Nature and an Ethics of Care* and Noddings, *Caring: A Feminine Approach to Ethics and Moral Education.*

[29] Held, *The Ethics of Care* 10.

[30] This has been both general, see eg Herring, *Caring and the Law*, and more specifically directed towards the legal recognition for 'caring' relationships, see eg Sloan, *Informal Carers and Private Law* and Clough, 'What About us? A Case for Legal Recognition of Interdependence in Informal Care Relationships'. Interestingly, Joanne Conaghan and Emily Grabham, 'Sexuality and the Citizen Carer' (2007) 58(3) *Northern Ireland Legal Quarterly* 325, 341, argue that 'Rights for carers require an intelligible model of the family that has no space for non-standard intimacies: polyamory, non-standard parental relationships, independent financial arrangements between partners, and close ties between friends'. On the interaction of 'care' and the law, see further eg Lydia Hayes, *Stories of Care: A Labour of Law* (Basingstoke, Palgrave MacMillan, 2017).

[31] See eg Young, *Intersecting Voices* 106.

[32] See the empirical data on the gendered division of labour within households cited above in ch 5, for example Crompton and Lyonette, 'Who Does the Housework? The Division of Labour within the Home', *British Social Attitudes Survey* 24 and Scott and Clery, 'Gender Roles: An Incomplete Revolution?', *British Social Attitudes* Survey 30.

[33] Julie Wallbank and Jonathan Herring, 'Introduction' in 'Autonomy and Vulnerability in Family Law' in Wallbank and Herring (eds), *Vulnerabilities, Care and Family Law* 12.

[34] Which was considered in some detail above in ch 2, subs I(B), 'The Development of the "Public/Private" Divide'.

of family law was assumed to take responsibility for caring relationships'.[35] The relationship between the 'family', 'care' and female responsibility for ('private') care work is implicit and assumed within the dominant and orthodox understanding of the gendered familial roles.[36] Thus, by explicitly focusing on the ethical and moral significance of 'care', this literature seeks to challenge the normative power of the traditional gendered roles of the nuclear family model.

As well as this, the growing conceptual focus upon 'care' explicitly challenges the centrality of the orthodox construction of the rational, self-interested and autonomous legal subject.[37] There is an inherent tension between this rational and autonomous subject and a philosophical emphasis on 'care', because as Bridgeman argues 'The work of caring for dependents and emotional interdependency with our children, spouses, partners and families must remain concealed lest we appear not to be independent souls suited for the public world'.[38] Historically, 'care' has been solely associated with the 'private' sphere of the home and the family, while the 'legal subject' is constructed as a purely 'public' being.[39] It is axiomatic that the work of 'care' involves tasks that cannot generally be performed individually, as Whitney comments 'Consider those kinds of care that are by their very character things we can't do for ourselves: love, affection, support, a hug, companionship, friendship'.[40] Therefore, when care is deployed conceptually there is an intrinsic recognition of the relationships of (and between) individuals and crucially within the literature on 'care' there is focus on the moral and ethical significance of those relationships and the interdependence of those within them. As Noddings notes 'Caring is not controlled entirely by the carer – it is a mode of shared control'.[41] 'Care' is mutual, it is not individual, it is centred on the relationship, not upon the subject; thus, the literature on 'care' inevitably questions the orthodox and dominant understanding of the individual 'subject' as the central social and legal unit. In the orthodox understanding, as Naffine has observed:

> [L]aw is for rational human subjects, for sane rational adults, intelligent agents who because of their capacity to reason can assume moral as well as legal responsibility for their actions and so enter into moral and legal community with others of a similarly rational nature.[42]

[35] Stewart, 'From Family to Personal Responsibility: the Challenges for Care of the Elderly in England' 192.

[36] Which were explored above in ch 5, s II, 'The Gendered Parenting Roles of the Nuclear Family'.

[37] This orthodox construction of the 'legal subject' and the influence of this 'subject' upon the traditional, nuclear family model was explored above in ch 2, subs I(C), 'The Orthodox Understanding of the "Legal Subject"'.

[38] Jo Bridgeman, 'Accountability, Support or Relationship? Conceptions of Parental Responsibility' (2007) 58(3) *Northern Ireland Legal Quarterly* 307, 308.

[39] See above in ch 2, subs II(B), 'The Masculinity of the "Legal Subject" Masks Inequality'.

[40] Shiloh Whitney, 'Dependency Relations: Corporeal Vulnerability and Norms of Personhood in Hobbes and Kittay' (2011) 26 *Hypatia* 554, 562.

[41] Noddings, *Starting at Home: Caring and Social Policy* 14.

[42] Naffine, *Law's Meaning of Life: Philosophy, Religion, Darwin and the Legal Person* 23.

Indeed, given the centrality of the autonomous, individualised 'subject' to Western political, philosophical and legal systems, this centring of 'care' and thus relationships represents a profound breach with the philosophical valorisation of the 'individual' and the rational, autonomous 'legal subject'.[43] As Sevenhuijsen comments 'An ethics of care implies a radically different argument on the relationship between morality and politics, and thus responsibility and obligation'.[44] Therefore, I argue that this literature should be understood as proposing a radical, alternative conceptual model of the self, and consequently, this different understanding of the self will inevitably result in a different understanding of the 'family'. Given the influence that the orthodox understanding of the 'legal subject' has exerted upon the traditional nuclear family model,[45] such a radical shift in conceptual understanding of the individual will inevitably have significant consequences for the resulting conceptualisation of the 'family'.

Consequently, a key aspect of this writing on 'care' has been to challenge the centrality of the individual 'subject' (and associated philosophical values such as 'autonomy' and 'choice') and instead emphasise the 'relational subject'; as Herring describes 'Ethics of care is based on the belief that people are relational. People understand themselves in terms of their relationships'.[46] This repositioning of the social gaze, from the individual to the relationship as the focal point,[47] results in the developing conceptual emphasis on mutuality, interdependence and 'care' that has been explored throughout this book. Herring and Foster explicitly link this approach to an attempt to reflect the diverse reality of the lived experiences of families, observing 'Anyone with experience of family life will recognise as absurd the notion that one can identify the interests of a single family member without taking account of the interest of other family members'.[48] At its core the 'relational subject' reconceives the conceptual starting point of our understanding of the individual and consequently of the 'family', because as Herring puts it: 'A relational approach starts with responsibilities and connections as a norm.'[49] On this basis, an understanding (or perhaps a 'model') of 'family' premised on 'care' and 'relationality' would be functional rather than formal.[50] As quoted above in chapter one, Herring provides the following definition of 'family' premised upon 'care',

[43] The continuing significance attached to individual autonomy within conceptual understandings of the 'family' will be considered below at subs I(C), 'Autonomy and Choice'.

[44] Selma Sevenhuijsen, 'Caring and the Third Way: the Relation Between Obligation, Responsibility and Care in Third Way Discourse' (2000) 20(1) *Critical Social Policy* 5, 6.

[45] See above in ch 2, subs III(A), 'The Legal Subject and the Nuclear Family' for an exploration of how the dominant and orthodox understanding of the rational and autonomous legal subject exerted substantial influence upon the values of the traditional, nuclear family.

[46] Herring, 'The Disability Critique of Care' 3.

[47] Foster and Herring, *Identity, Personhood and the Law* 35, argue that this emphasis on relationships reflects moral values, stating 'It is people's relationships, rather than any inherent characteristics of a person, which have moral value and are deserving of special moral status'.

[48] Herring and Foster, 'Welfare means Relationality, Virtue and Altruism' 489.

[49] Herring, *Relational Autonomy and Family Law* 16.

[50] To utilise the terminology of Herring, *Family Law*, set out above in ch 1, s II, 'The Law's "Definition(s)" of "Family"'.

as 'People providing each other with a substantial amount of care in a relationship marked by commitment'.[51] I argue that such an understanding of 'family' based upon 'care', would not solely focus on the central 'nexus' of the 'parent/child' relationship and the conjugal relationship of the traditional nuclear family model, which this book has identified, instead encompassing a wider and more diverse range of relationship types and forms.[52] Within this, there would necessarily be a deprivileging of the conjugal or sexual relationship[53] in terms of the legal recognition and regulation of adult personal relationships,[54] a shift from the genetic connection to social parenting in the attribution of legal parenthood[55] and the development of an understanding of the role of the parent that is not constrained by the 'natural' constructions of the gendered parenting roles of 'mother' and 'father'.

However, there are two strands of critique of this conceptual focus on 'care' and 'relationality' and the resulting 'model' of family that I believe are important and necessary to acknowledge.[56] The first is that the focus on interdependence and relationality appears to assume (either explicitly or implicitly) that these are universally positive values, thus obscuring the potential for relationships themselves to be the sources of unequal power, harm and individual suffering. Bauman cautions us that 'the impulse to care for the other, when taken to the extreme, leads to the annihilation of the autonomy of the other, to domination and oppression'.[57] In this regard, even those who advocate for greater emphasis on 'care' and 'relationality' are themselves aware of this potential for problematic power dynamics within relationships; Wallbank and Herring have simply observed that 'the concepts of care and vulnerability are troublesome'.[58] Building upon this, Clough has acknowledged that:

> [I]t is salient to note that if we focus purely on relational interdependence, not only do we run the risk of essentialising those within the relationship in terms of pre-defined

[51] Herring, *Caring and the Law* 194.

[52] The boundaries of a 'care' based understanding of the 'family', and the significance of whether such an approach has any boundaries will be considered in more detail below at s II, 'Abstract Models and Real Families'.

[53] See above at ch 3, s II, 'The Centrality of Conjugality', where the importance of the conjugal relationship within the orthodox, contemporary legal understanding of the 'family' is considered.

[54] Herring, *Caring and the Law* 192, expressively justifies this shift by stating: 'To be blunt, society does not really gain much from a couple having sex, however pleasurable it may be for the participants! However, the state does benefit from care, particularly where that is of a person whose needs would otherwise fall on the state.'

[55] ibid, at 200, 'Parental status should be earned by the care and dedication to the child, something not shown simply by a biological link.'

[56] As with the consideration of the literature itself, these critiques are only briefly explored in this chapter, as a more detailed examination is outside the scope of their impact upon social and legal understandings of the 'family'.

[57] Bauman, *Postmodern Ethics* 11.

[58] Wallbank and Herring, 'Introduction' in 'Autonomy and Vulnerability in Family Law' in Wallbank and Herring (eds), *Vulnerabilities, Care and Family Law* 1.

> roles and obligations, we also run the risk of subjugating individual interests to the interests of the family as a whole. Relationships are not always benign.[59]

Consequently, it is necessary to be aware of the possibility of approaches based upon 'care' or 'relationality' replacing a problematic and exclusionary focus upon the individual, with an antithetical approach where the interests of the individual become entirely obscured, or even subsumed, within a focus upon the interests of the relationship or the 'family'.[60]

The second strand of critique relates to the resulting understanding of 'family' and is based on the premise that 'care' and 'relationality' lack the precision and clarity required by the law (which favours and desires certainty above all)[61] to produce a workable definition. It is consistently accepted within the literature itself that providing a definition of 'care' is complex;[62] this is encapsulated by Clough, who notes that 'Challenging legal individualism will be an important starting point for progress here. Yet relational approaches may be difficult to translate into legal doctrine'.[63] This relates back to arguments I have made in earlier chapters suggesting that the traditional, nuclear family provides a simple, readily understandable image of the 'family', which has resulted in its being granted normative significance as the idealised image of 'family' within legal understanding.[64] I suggest that the lack of a precise definition is an inherent (and fundamental) part of an approach based upon 'care', 'relationality', 'mutuality' and 'interdependence'. Nevertheless, there exists a conceptual gap between the precision of what the law appears to require from an understanding of 'family' and what appears to be offered by the relational or care-centred approach.[65] This highlights the problematic nature of

[59] Clough, 'What About Us? A Case for Legal Recognition of Interdependence in Informal Care Relationships' 139.

[60] However, see eg Foster and Herring, *Identity, Personhood and the Law*, who state, at 40 'We are not claiming that all relationships are of value: that would be foolish. Clearly many relationships are abusive. It is only relationships of care (in the sense described above), which are of the highest moral value.'

[61] Jonathan Herring, *Vulnerable Adults and the Law* (Oxford, Oxford University Press, 2016) 264, observes 'The law loves its categorisations and the drawing of boundaries. We are boxed in as the competent, the vulnerable and the self. Yes these boxes, like the concepts they represent, are porous'.

[62] This criticism was considered above in ch 1, s I, '"Family" as a Social Concept', see eg Herring, *Caring and the Law* 13, who notes that 'Producing a definition of care is far from straightforward'. To that end, Herring does not attempt to provide a definition of care, instead his approach to care is based around the 'four markers of care', set out at 14–26: 'meeting needs', 'respect', 'responsibility' and 'relationality'. However, by explicitly rejecting the opportunity to provide a definition, Herring does not directly address the criticism that the concept of 'care' is insufficiently precise to underpin legal understanding.

[63] Clough, 'What About Us? A Case for Legal Recognition of Interdependence in Informal Care Relationships', 143.

[64] This argument is made throughout the book, but see particularly ch 1, 'What is the Law's "Family"?'

[65] Although, it is worth drawing a distinction here between identifying when a 'caring relationship' begins and retrospectively identifying that the markers of such a relationship were present after the relationship has broken down. The latter of these may be more readily reconciled with the certainty required by law. This distinction is relevant because much of legal intervention in adult relationships only occurs after relationship breakdown, as discussed above in ch 3, subs I(A), 'The Legal Definition of Marriage'. I would like to thank Jonathan Herring for bringing this point to my attention.

attempting to provide any singular 'model' of 'family', or to utilise specific concepts to provide a unifying conceptual framework.[66]

Furthermore, I argue that elements and aspects of these two critiques resonate and recur in the exploration of the roles of 'vulnerability'[67] and 'autonomy'[68] in providing alternative models of the 'family', which this chapter will subsequently consider, illustrating that the concepts considered in this chapter have fluid boundaries and cannot be easily and neatly placed in isolation.

B. Vulnerability

The similarities, connections and overlap between the concepts of 'vulnerability' and 'care' are clear from their underlying conceptualisations. As with 'care', the literature on 'vulnerability' begins from the premise that vulnerability is a central and intrinsic part of human existence, expressed in the idea that, 'Human life is conditioned by vulnerability'.[69] Or as the postmodernist ethical philosopher Levinas more lyrically expressed it 'The I, from head to foot to the bone-marrow, is vulnerability'.[70] In addition to this, there is an emphasis within the literature on (re)affirming the positive nature of 'vulnerability', which is encapsulated by Herring's statement that 'Vulnerability and dependence are not only inevitable parts of humanity … they are to be greatly welcomed. They are virtues, not vices'.[71] This virtuous construction of 'vulnerability' is central to its deployment as an ethical value. Building upon this, Fineman observes that 'properly understood in the context of the human condition, vulnerability is also generative. Importantly, our vulnerability presents opportunities for innovation and growth, creativity and fulfilment. It makes us reach out to others, form relationships, and build institutions'.[72] From these statements, it is immediately apparent that within this literature 'vulnerability' is being understood and constructed in opposition to the traditionally dominant understanding of the term, which connotes with weakness, limitation and is fundamentally negative.

Moreover, another notable similarity with 'care' is the haziness and ambiguity of the concept itself; as Bridgeman notes 'The concept of vulnerability may be

[66] Section II, 'Abstract Models and Real Families' below will consider whether this lack of specification is normatively significant, and relatedly, whether the law actually requires an overarching model of the 'family'.

[67] Which will be considered below at subs I(B), 'Vulnerability'.

[68] See Harding, 'Legal Constructions of Dementia: Discourses of Autonomy at the Margins of Capacity' 439, who notes that 'relational approaches to autonomy are imperfect. Such an approach can prioritise the values of discussion, communication and interpersonal relationships over individual values'.

[69] Catriona Mackenzie, Wendy Rogers and Susan Dodds, 'Introduction' in Mackenzie, Rogers and Dodds (eds), *Vulnerability: New Essays in Ethics and Feminist Philosophy* 3.

[70] Emmanuel Levinas, *Humanismo Del Otro Hombre*, (Madrid, Siglo, 1993) 123.

[71] Herring, 'The Disability Critique of Care' 13.

[72] Fineman, '"Elderly" as Vulnerable: Rethinking the Nature of Individual and Societal Responsibility' 96.

used inconsistently in different disciplines'[73] and Herring acknowledges that 'Vulnerability is a notoriously vague term'.[74] I suggest that this uncertainty creates two related definitional problems, one at each end of the boundary of the concept; it is not necessarily apparent what should be included within or excluded from this understanding of 'vulnerability', nor how such distinctions would be made. However, Wallbank and Herring address that point by stating:

> Unfortunately, it is simply impossible to come up with a comprehensive account of the very different ways in which humans experience vulnerability. This is of course easily explainable by the very fact that vulnerability is ubiquitous. We therefore make no apologies for the gaps.[75]

In this way, the lack of delineated boundary is understood as a feature, rather than a weakness, of the concept of 'vulnerability'. Bridgeman comments that 'however it is defined it is grounded in our susceptibility to damage, injury or harm'.[76] This illustrates that this construction of 'vulnerability' is understood by reference to general, rather than specific characteristics. As Collins puts it: '"Vulnerability" has emerged as a very important idea for those interested in family law. But it is an abstruse concept without further explanation.'[77] Therefore, it appears that the concept of 'vulnerability' is taking on theoretical and ethical significance without unity as to its definition within the literature. As discussed above in the context of the literature on 'care', there is an ambiguity and a tension inherent to the term and this clearly affects how it is utilised. I recognise that there are different understandings of 'vulnerability' set out within the literature and this is reflected in legal understanding and deployment of the term 'vulnerable' within the law.[78] The nature of this conceptual and definitional disjuncture is summarised by Herring as follows:

> At the heart of the disputes is a disagreement between those who claim that vulnerability is universal and is an inevitable part of the human experience; and those who argue that it is more profitable to recognize that there are particular individuals or groups of individuals who suffer particular vulnerabilities.[79]

Consequently, it is crucial to be clear that, in this section, I am focusing on work within the literature which involves an attempt to construct a universal

[73] Jo Bridgeman, 'Relational Vulnerability, Care and Dependency' in Wallbank and Herring (eds), *Vulnerabilities, Care and Family Law* 201.

[74] Herring, *Vulnerable Adults and the Law* 6.

[75] Wallbank and Herring, 'Introduction' in 'Autonomy and Vulnerability in Family Law' in Wallbank and Herring (eds), *Vulnerabilities, Care and Family Law* 21.

[76] Bridgeman, 'Relational Vulnerability, Care and Dependency' in Wallbank and Herring (eds), *Vulnerabilities, Care and Family Law* 201.

[77] Jennifer Collins, 'The Contours of "Vulnerability"' in Wallbank and Herring (eds), *Vulnerabilities, Care and Family Law* 22.

[78] See eg s 60(1) and Sch 4, para 7 of the Safeguarding Vulnerable Groups Act 2006 which provide a statutory definition of 'vulnerable adults' which utilises a widely drawn list of 'regulated activities' which relate to the provision of care and assistance to determine vulnerability.

[79] Herring, *Vulnerable Adults and the Law* 2.

'vulnerability';[80] shifting the term away from the conception which has previously been utilised as a means of excluding certain groups from full legal subjecthood (including children, elderly people and adults lacking legal capacity).[81] This understanding of vulnerability was traditionally how the terminology was employed within the law,[82] reflecting the orthodox understanding of the rational and autonomous subject; this is illustrated by Fineman's statement that:

> The designation of vulnerable (inferior) populations reinforces and valorizes the ideal liberal subject, who is positioned as the polar opposite of the vulnerable population. This liberal subject is thus constructed as invulnerable, or at least differently vulnerable, and represents the desirable and achievable ideals of autonomy, independence and self-sufficiency.[83]

However, instead of adopting this approach to 'vulnerability' which divides individuals into the categories of the (invulnerable) 'liberal subject' and the 'vulnerable' non-subject,[84] the developing literature attempts to set out a universal understanding of 'vulnerability'[85] and therefore of the 'vulnerable subject'. This 'vulnerability' is constructed on the basis that, as Rogers, MacKenzie and Dodds comment 'all human life is conditioned by vulnerability, as a result of our embodied, finite, and socially contingent existence. Vulnerability is the ontological condition of our humanity'.[86] Thus, 'vulnerability' is not solely understood as representing the features of particular individuals or groups of people, but rather, it is constructed as a moral characteristic shared by all legal subjects. To that end, Fineman comments that 'Every actual adult human being, no matter how strong and independent he or she may seem, is both presently and has been in the past reliant on others and social institutions'.[87] Therefore, I argue that the universal

[80] However, this should not be understood as a rejection of the notion that different individuals are differently vulnerable, but rather of the conceptual barriers between the vulnerable subject and the autonomous subject.

[81] See eg Laura Pritchard-Jones, 'The Good, the Bad and the "Vulnerable Older Adult"' (2016) 38(1) *Journal of Social Welfare and Family Law* 51, 55, who comments, 'This idea of "vulnerability" (or "adult at risk") promulgated both by the courts and safe-guarding law and policy more generally, then, is two-dimensional – the meeting of an inherent characteristic, such as disability or age, with a risk of being subjected to some form of harm.'

[82] ibid, at 58, the author further suggests that 'the association of vulnerability with old age, and certain corporeal or cognitive impairments associated with old age such as frailty or incapacity … indicates that the courts are deploying the terms as a concept that attaches to those who demonstrate such characteristics'.

[83] Fineman, '"Elderly" as Vulnerable: Rethinking the Nature of Individual and Societal Responsibility' 86.

[84] ibid, at 85, Fineman critiques the alternative conception of 'vulnerability', stating 'This targeted group approach to the idea of vulnerability ignores its universality and inappropriately constructs relationships of difference and distance between individuals and groups within society.'

[85] Martha Fineman, 'Responsibility, Family and the Limits of Equality: An American Perspective' in Craig Lind, Heather Keating and Jo Bridgeman (eds), *Taking Responsibility, Law and the Changing Family* (Aldershot, Ashgate, 2011), observes, at 46: 'Vulnerability is inherent in the human condition. It comes partly from our materiality – our embodiment – and, as such, it is both universal and constant.'

[86] Wendy Rogers, Catriona Mackenzie and Susan Dodds, 'Why Bioethics Needs a Concept of Vulnerability' (2012) 5 *International Journal of Feminist Approaches to Bioethics* 11, 12.

[87] Fineman, '"Elderly" as Vulnerable: Rethinking the Nature of Individual and Societal Responsibility' 88.

understanding of 'vulnerability', which is present within the literature, appears to be potentially all-encompassing; it represents nothing less than a conceptual means of describing the inherent humanity of all individuals.

Stychin observes that 'the concept of vulnerability has had significant impact in legal and political theory as a response to the primacy of the discourse of rights'.[88] Therefore, challenging the centrality of the orthodox construction of the rational and autonomous legal subject and instead developing a construction of the 'vulnerable subject' is a core purpose, which is shared across the emerging literature which places a moral and philosophical emphasis on universal 'vulnerability'. This opposition to the orthodox construction of the autonomous 'legal subject' is inherent to the concept of vulnerability, because as Tronto notes:

> Vulnerability belies the myth that we are always autonomous, and potentially equal citizens … A political order that presumes only independence and autonomy as the nature of human life thereby misses a great deal of human experience, and must somehow hide this point elsewhere.[89]

This critique of the orthodox, rational and autonomous legal subject connects to, and overlaps with, the focus, discussed above, on the potential of 'relationality' and the 'relational subject' to similarly challenge the legal subject.[90] This shows that these alternative conceptual approaches are united in their focus on shifting the underlying paradigms by which individuals are constructed and understood within the law. There is also an inherent conceptual connection between 'vulnerability' and 'autonomy'; in the traditional understanding the 'vulnerable individual' was constructed in opposition to the dominant, autonomous (and rational) subject. This orthodox construction has prompted Diduck to observe that 'autonomy cannot exist without its "other", which in current rhetoric has become vulnerability. In the same way that autonomy may be the "friendly face" of individual responsibility, vulnerability may be the friendly face of dependence'.[91] As will be discussed in more detail below,[92] the dichotomy between 'vulnerability' and 'autonomy' reflects the other binary oppositions of 'self/other',[93] 'public/private',[94] 'breadwinner/homemaker'[95] and 'father/mother',[96] discussed throughout the

[88] Carl Stychin, 'The Vulnerable Subject of Negligence Law' (2012) 8(3) *International Journal of Law in Context* 337, 337.

[89] Tronto, *Moral Boundaries: A Political Argument for an Ethic of Care* 135.

[90] See above at ch 2, s II, 'Critiquing the Orthodox Construction of the Legal Subject' for more on the critique of the dominant, orthodox understanding of the 'legal subject'.

[91] Alison Diduck, 'Autonomy and Vulnerability in Family Law' in Wallbank and Herring (eds), *Vulnerabilities, Care and Family Law* 97.

[92] This connection between 'vulnerability' and 'autonomy' will be considered further at subs I(C), 'Autonomy and Choice'.

[93] Considered above in ch 2, s II, 'Critiquing the Orthodox Construction of the Legal Subject'.

[94] As explored above in ch 2, subs I(B), 'The Development of the "Public/Private" Divide'.

[95] See the normative influence of these traditional gendered roles identified above in ch 5, s II, 'The Gendered Parenting Roles of the Nuclear Family'.

[96] See ch 4, 'The Attribution of Legal Parenthood within UK Law'; which sets out the centrality of the binary, two-parent model of legal parenthood.

earlier chapters, which underpin the traditional, nuclear family model that dominates the legal understanding of the 'family'.

As mentioned at the outset of this consideration of 'vulnerability', within the literature there are clear links between this developing conceptual understanding of 'vulnerability' and the literature on 'care'. This is because, as Herring describes 'Relationships, intimacy, care; all of these things in their nature render us vulnerable',[97] and as he also puts it 'If care is an essential part of what it is to be a person and care produces vulnerability then vulnerability is an essential part of being a person'.[98] I argue that the recognition of vulnerability within the construction of the 'legal subject' (the 'vulnerable subject') would provide an understanding (or 'model') of the 'family' which is substantially similar to that described above in the context of 'care' and 'relationality'.[99] The underlying point of such a 'model' of family would be that form and structure would cede importance to function in the determination of which relationships were subject to regulation and correspondingly, which relationships were not. Relatedly, the conceptual emphasis on 'vulnerability' would shift the focus of legal regulation from specific categories of relationship, particularly those of the central nexus of the conjugal relationship and the 'parent/child' relationship within the traditional, nuclear family model, to a wider understanding of 'family' that was potentially directed towards all relationships.[100] However, due to the inherent connection with 'care' and 'relationality', this understanding of 'family', premised on recognising universal vulnerability, would be subject to the same criticisms relating to lack of certainty and precision that were set out above in the context of 'care'. It is uncontroversial to suggest that the law seeks clarity, but 'vulnerability' (as with 'care') is deliberately constructed to be ambiguous, this renders clarity of definition difficult (if not impossible) to achieve.[101]

Moreover, the uncritical promotion of the moral value of 'vulnerability' has been critiqued because of the cultural associations of the terminology; as Brown argues 'far from being innocuous, the concept of "vulnerability" is so loaded with political, moral and practical implications that it is potentially damaging to the pursuit of social justice'.[102] This relates to the critique, set out above in relation to 'relationality', that there is clear potential for oppression, harm and suffering within relationships, where vulnerability is likely to operate differentially between the members. This problematic issue is also acknowledged within the literature on 'vulnerability', where writers are not entirely blind to the potential inequalities

[97] Herring, *Vulnerable Adults and the Law* 38.

[98] ibid, at 14.

[99] At subs I(A), 'Care and Relationality'.

[100] See the consideration of the potential regulation of non-conjugal adult relationships above in ch 3, subs II(B), 'The Justification for the Centrality of Conjugality'.

[101] As with an understanding of 'family' premised upon recognising 'care' and 'relationality', whether this definitional ambiguity is normatively problematic to these conceptual ideas providing the foundation for the legal understanding of 'family' will be considered below at s II, 'Abstract Models and Real Families'.

[102] Kate Brown, '"Vulnerability": Handle with Care' (2011) 5(3) *Ethics and Social Welfare* 313, 314.

within relationships; as Whitney comments 'Dependencies may be enabling, nourishing, and caring. But surely dependency is not wholly without danger: dominating, exploitative responses to vulnerability are still possible'.[103] Similarly, Bridgeman expresses the tension between the previously asserted positive aspects of relationality and universal vulnerability and seeking to recognise these risks inherent to relationships; commenting that 'we also need to acknowledge the extent to which our connectedness to others makes us vulnerable, exposing us to the risk of damage, injury or harm. Humans are vulnerable also because we care, love, are intimately connected to others'.[104] As with 'care', it is necessary to acknowledge that the emphasis on 'vulnerability' has these potentially damaging consequences, because asserting the universal 'vulnerability' of all legal subjects raises the possibility of ignoring the multitude of ways in which the vulnerability of real individuals will operate differently.[105] Thus, the critique of 'care' and 'relationality', set out above, is reflected in the critique of 'vulnerability', providing further evidence of the difficulty of separating these values into neat and clear conceptual categories.

C. Autonomy and Choice

The concept of 'autonomy' is intrinsically associated with the ability of the individual to exercise rational choice(s);[106] Sellers observes that, 'Autonomy signifies the right to decide for oneself.'[107] Building upon this,[108] Christman and Anderson offer the more expansive definition that:

> [T]he notion of autonomy still finds its core meaning in the idea of being one's own person, directed by considerations, desires, conditions, and characteristics that are not simply imposed externally on one, but are part of what can somehow be considered one's authentic self.[109]

[103] Whitney, 'Dependency Relations: Corporeal Vulnerability and Norms of Personhood in Hobbes and Kittay' 565.

[104] Bridgeman, 'Relational Vulnerability, Care and Dependency' in Wallbank and Herring (eds), *Vulnerabilities, Care and Family Law* 201.

[105] However, see eg Wallbank and Herring, 'Introduction' in 'Autonomy and Vulnerability in Family Law' in Wallbank and Herring (eds), *Vulnerabilities, Care and Family Law* 8, who argue that 'Vulnerabilities are not equally distributed between human beings. Although we share the commonality of being born, living lives and dying, the ways we live a vulnerable life are likely to be highly differentiated and affected by factors such as ethnicity, sexuality, gender, age, health, social class, employment status and care responsibilities'.

[106] Helen Reece, 'Divorcing Responsibly' (2002) 8(1) *Feminist Legal Studies* 65, 66, observes that 'The responsible post-liberal individual is judged, not by what he does but by how profoundly he has thought about what he does'.

[107] Mortimer Sellers, 'An Introduction to the Value of Autonomy in Law' in Mortimer Sellers (ed), *Autonomy in the Law* 2.

[108] ibid, at 1, Sellers offers the slightly more detailed explanation that: 'Autonomy, in its simplest and most natural sense, signifies self-rule: the right of states, or of families, or of associations or individuals to make their own laws for themselves.'

[109] Christman and Anderson (eds), *Autonomy and the Challenges to Liberalism* 3.

Autonomy, therefore, is fundamentally linked to the dominant, orthodox notions of subjecthood.[110] There are philosophical, ideological and political aspects to the normative significance granted to 'autonomy' in contemporary legal and social discourse, and this is illustrated by Diduck's observation that:

> Autonomy is in many ways the friendly face of individual responsibility. Autonomy in the liberal policy and in liberal law is like motherhood – it is hard to argue against it, even while interrogating its content, consequences and import means those arguments are sometimes necessary.[111]

Social policy is increasingly premised around the growing centrality of this autonomous individual.[112] Thus, in contrast with the values of 'care', 'relationality' and 'vulnerability', discussed above, which are utilised to suggest a radical re-imagining of the subject, the concept of 'autonomy' is fundamentally bound up with the orthodox, liberal understanding of the self – the 'legal subject'; as O'Donovan succinctly put it 'The ideal legal subject in liberal theory is a rational, choosing person, capable of decision, an autonomous individual.'[113] This legal subject is also the 'economic man' of Western capitalism[114] and Fineman describes this connection between the privileging of individual 'autonomy' and the ideals of the capitalist market: 'The autonomous individual is anchored in a world of paid labor either directly, as a worker, or indirectly, through marriage to a wage earner. Autonomy is the absence of economic dependence on outsiders, particularly the government.'[115] As I argued above in chapter two, the dominant, orthodox construction of the rational and autonomous 'legal subject' exerted significant normative influence upon the traditional nuclear family model, shaping both its form and its values.[116]

From this, it is clear that 'autonomy' is a fundamental aspect of the dominant, orthodox understanding of the individual and the 'legal subject', and therefore the promotion of 'autonomy', in and of itself, within the law cannot represent a radical proposition.[117] One consequence of this centrality is that, as Silva and Smart

[110] As set out above in ch 2, subs I(C), 'The Orthodox Understanding of the "Legal Subject"'. See further eg O'Donovan, 'With Sense, Consent, or Just a Con?: Legal Subjects in the Discourse of Autonomy', in Naffine and Owens (eds), *Sexing the Subject of Law* and Lukes, *Individualism.*

[111] Diduck, 'Autonomy and Vulnerability in Family Law' in Wallbank and Herring (eds), *Vulnerabilities, Care and Family Law* 97.

[112] This is apparent from the consistent emphasis on the language of 'choice' by the UK government in a variety of different context; for example healthcare: www.gov.uk/government/publications/the-nhs-choice-framework, childcare: www.childcarechoices.gov.uk/ and education.

[113] O'Donovan, 'With Sense, Consent, or Just a Con?: Legal Subjects in the Discourse of Autonomy', in Naffine and Owens (eds), *Sexing the Subject of Law* 47.

[114] As Zygmunt Bauman, *Liquid Love: On the Frailty of Human Bonds*, (Cambridge, Polity Press, 2003), simply observes, at 75, 'Human solidarity is the first casualty of the triumph of the consumer market.'

[115] Fineman, *The Autonomy Myth: A Theory of Dependency* 9.

[116] As set out above in ch 2, subs III(A), 'The Legal Subject and the Nuclear Family'.

[117] Which contrasts with the radicalism inherent in the promotion of the 'care', 'relationality' or 'vulnerability' suggested by the literature set out above.

observe 'In a world where the individual becomes a central reference point, families help in the constitution of personal autonomy … Families endure or are transformed, according to whether they continue to serve these needs'.[118] However, in spite of the fundamentally orthodox nature of the concept of 'autonomy', I argue that this idea of utilising 'autonomy' to underpin the legal understanding of the 'family' or family law more widely, does represent a potentially radical shift in understanding. I argue that this developing emphasis on individual 'autonomy' in governing the regulation of families and family life represents an uneasy fit within the dominant conceptual understandings of the 'family', because these understandings are inherently based upon recognising and regulating relationships, not individuals;[119] as Diduck observes:

> [I]t is a curious principle to privilege in family justice because autonomy is not something that fits easily into ideas of 'family', the relations of which are normally thought to remain in the realm of altruism, connection, love, (inter) dependency and the greater good.[120]

In spite of the wider centrality of 'autonomy' within the legal understanding of the individual, to privilege autonomy in the context of the 'family' appears antithetical to our social understanding of 'family';[121] as Herring comments 'Independence and freedom have become the icons of our age. Yet, it will be argued, in the context of family law these are false gods'.[122] Thus, there exists a tension between the societal promotion of individualised autonomy and the traditionally dominant social understanding of the 'family' and its role and function within society.

Nevertheless, it is clear that the explicit utilisation of the language of 'autonomy' in judicial discourse concerning the 'family' and familial relationships is a recent normative and rhetorical development, and this has been noticeable in a variety of contexts. The majority judgment of the Supreme Court in *Granatino v Radmacher*,[123] which recognised the validity of 'pre-nuptial' agreements in English law,[124] makes clear the centrality of respecting the 'autonomy' of individuals to the decision, with the court stating 'The reason why the court should give weight to a nuptial agreement is that there should be respect for

[118] Silva and Smart, 'The "New" Practices and Politics of Family Life' in Silva and Smart (eds), *The New Family?* 6.

[119] As discussed above throughout the previous chapters, the legal understanding of the 'family' has been premised upon the central nexus of relationships (the conjugal relationship and the 'parent/child' relationship) within the traditional nuclear family.

[120] Diduck, 'Autonomy and Vulnerability in Family Law' in Wallbank and Herring (eds), *Vulnerabilities, Care and Family Law* 96.

[121] Which was explored above in ch 1, s I, '"Family" as a Social Concept'. See further eg McKie and Callan, *Understanding Families: A Global Introduction*, Morgan, *Family Connections: An Introduction to Family Studies* and Williams, *Rethinking Families*.

[122] Herring, *Relational Autonomy and Family Law* 2.

[123] [2010] UKSC 42, [2011] 1 AC 534.

[124] For a detailed academic analysis of the issue of pre-nuptial agreements, see Sharon Thompson, *Prenuptial Agreements and the Presumption of Free Choice: Issues of Power in Theory and Practice* (Oxford, Hart Publishing, 2015).

individual autonomy'.[125] I argue that this statement illustrates the influence of ideas of 'autonomy' upon contemporary judicial understandings of the marital relationship more generally.[126] The language of 'autonomy' has also been used by the courts in the context of the 'parent/child' relationship; in *R (On the Application of Williamson) v Secretary of State for Education and Employment*,[127] Baroness Hale stated 'it is important in a free society that parents should be allowed a large measure of autonomy in the way in which they discharge their parental responsibilities'.[128] This illustrates that the language of 'autonomy' has been judicially employed in relation to both relationships which form the central nexus of the traditional nuclear family model. Furthermore, evidence of this language of 'autonomy' has also been apparent in the recent jurisprudence of the European Court of Human Rights concerning the right to respect for private and family life;[129] in *Ternovszky v Hungary*[130] the court stated that 'The notion of personal autonomy is a fundamental principle underlying the interpretation of the guarantees of Article 8'.[131] From these examples, which encompass both different familial relationships and different legal regimes, I suggest that it is clear that the language of 'autonomy' is being invoked as an important normative principle in the context of the legal regulation and understanding of the 'family'.

The dichotomy between 'autonomy' and 'vulnerability', referred to above, is crucial within the theoretical understanding of these concepts. The relationship and dualism between 'autonomy' and 'vulnerability' reflects the distinction between the 'self' and the 'other', and as Diduck observes 'like other dichotomies in liberalism, the autonomy-vulnerability dichotomy is gendered. While the actual autonomous or vulnerable person is not always sexed male or female, the vulnerable side of the dichotomy is feminised and the autonomous side is masculinised'.[132] Consequently, it is apparent that there are gendered implications to any utilisation of the language and rhetoric of 'autonomy' in the context of the 'family', due to both this gendered dichotomy between 'autonomy' and 'vulnerability' and, to the historical relationship between the autonomous liberal subject and the 'public/private' divide.[133] This liberal construct continues to have gendered consequences

[125] ibid, at 564.

[126] This can also be seen from the developing judicial understanding of marriage as a 'partnership of equals', see eg Munby J's comment in *Sheffield City Council v E and S* [2004] EWHC 2808 (Fam), [2005] 1 FLR 965, at para 131, that, 'Today both spouses are the joint, co-equal heads of the family'.

[127] *R (On the Application of Williamson) v Secretary of State for Education and Employment* [2005] UKHL 15, [2005] 2 AC 246.

[128] ibid, at 271.

[129] Art 8(1) states: 'Everyone has the right to respect for his private and family life, his home and his correspondence.'

[130] *Ternovszky v Hungary* (2015) 61 EHRR 35.

[131] ibid, at 938. See eg *AM v Hungary* (2017) 65 EHRR SE2 for an additional example of the language of 'autonomy' being used in the context of Art 8.

[132] Diduck, 'Autonomy and Vulnerability in Family Law' in Wallbank and Herring (eds), *Vulnerabilities, Care and Family Law* 113.

[133] As discussed above in ch 2, subs I(C), 'The Orthodox Understanding of the "Legal Subject"'.

for men and women performing their roles within the contemporary 'family',[134] as Boyd comments:

> [A] responsible mother is still expected to nurture a child's relationship with the father, unless he is proven to be harmful … The ability of women to be at all autonomous from the fathers of their children in the face of this normative expectation is dubious, even when the adults live separately.[135]

Therefore, the promotion of the value of 'autonomy' within the understanding of the 'family' may result in the continued valorisation of the traditional conceptual division between the public sphere of the autonomous masculine 'legal subject'[136] and the private sphere of the family, which is associated with the 'vulnerable' feminised 'non-subject'.[137] Thus, as Fineman argues:

> [F]amilies also have the expectation of autonomy placed on them in today's political culture. An autonomous family is a family perceived to be self-sufficient, providing for the needs of its members. The autonomy of the family in relation to society is expressed in the idea that it occupies a 'separate sphere,' and is a 'private' institution governed by distinct rules.[138]

This illustrates how the discourse of 'autonomy' exerts influence on different levels, through notions of the 'autonomous individual' (which affects the understanding of the family) and through the image of the 'autonomous family'.

At the outset of this consideration of 'autonomy', the relationship between autonomy and the concept of 'choice' was noted;[139] promoting 'choice' is increasingly seen as intrinsically valuable within contemporary political discourse. This ideological emphasis on 'choice' connects to the legal understanding of 'family' through Diduck and O'Donovan's observation that 'Rooted in the rhetoric of choice and located in the ethic of self-responsibility and equality with others, normalisation aims to make a good society by making good families'.[140] Therefore,

[134] The nature of this influence was considered above in ch 5, s II, 'The Gendered Parenting Roles of the Nuclear Family'.

[135] Susan Boyd, 'Autonomy for Mothers' (2010) 18(2) *Feminist Legal Studies* 137, 144.

[136] See eg Naffine, *Law and the Sexes: Explorations of Feminist Jurisprudence* 100, who stated 'The legal model of the person, it will be argued, is a man, not a woman. He is a successful middle-class man, not a working class male'. See further eg Naffine, 'Can Women Be Legal Persons?' in James and Palmer (eds), *Visible Women: Essays on Feminist Legal Theory and Political Philosophy*, Lacey, *Unspeakable Subjects: Feminist Essays in Legal and Social Theory* and Pateman, *The Sexual Contract*.

[137] See eg Moller Okin, *Women in Western Political Thought*, O'Donovan, *Sexual Divisions in Law* and Boyd (ed), *Challenging the Public/Private Divide: Feminism, Law and Public Policy*.

[138] Fineman, *The Autonomy Myth: A Theory of Dependency* 21.

[139] Jeffrey Weeks, Catherine Donovan and Brian Heaphy, 'Everyday Experiments: Narratives of Non-Heterosexual Relationships' in Silva and Smart (eds), *The New Family?*, link the concept of 'choice' to the contemporary understanding of 'intimacy', arguing, at 85, 'Intimacy, in its modern form, implies a radical democratization of the interpersonal domain because it assumes not only that the individual is the ultimate maker of his or her own life, but also equality between partners, and their freedom to choose lifestyles and forms of partnership'.

[140] Alison Diduck and Katherine O'Donovan, 'Feminism & Family Law: Plus Ca Change?' in Diduck and O'Donovan (eds), *Feminist Perspectives on Family Law* 17. This notion of 'normalisation' is heavily associated with the seminal work of twentieth-century French philosopher Michel Foucault,

this wider emphasis on choice is reflected in the promotion of 'autonomy' within familial relationships that, as identified above, is becoming more apparent within legal discourse. Indeed, Torrant has suggested that 'the dominant understanding of the new family in contemporary social and cultural theory and cultural studies posits family relations as no longer relations of need, but *affective* relations of "desire", "affinity" or "choice"'.[141] However, the promotion of 'autonomy' and 'choice' in the normative understanding of such relationships is far from universally or uncritically accepted by academic commentators; because, as Herring argues 'Intimate relationships inevitably lead to a loss of freedom of choice as how to live your life on a daily basis'.[142] As well as that, 'choice' is self-evidently not a useful concept in understanding many other forms of familial relationships, where the connection between individuals cannot be said to have been chosen in any meaningful sense.[143] The problematic relationship between dominant understandings of the 'family' and the growing political and rhetorical centrality of 'choice' is encapsulated by Bauman's comment that:

> The founding act of choice, its original sin, is bound to cast a long shadow and darken even the brightest togetherness called "affinity": choice, unlike the fate of kinship, is a two-way street. One can always turn back, and the knowledge of such a possibility makes the task of keeping direction all the more daunting.[144]

Certainly, within the dominant understanding of the traditional nuclear family, set out in earlier chapters,[145] 'choice' does not form a core part of how the central nexus of the 'parent/child' relationship and the conjugal relationship are constructed; as the sociologist Chambers notes:

> Individualism seems, then, to conflict with the needs of the family, with the former emphasizing individual choice and the latter relying on commitment, stability and permanence. The new emphasis on individual choice and self-fulfilment has created new *risks* as well as *opportunities*.[146]

Therefore, there appears to be the presence of competing normative values within contemporary understandings of the individual and the family; in this regard, Diduck observes that 'At the same time … narratives of stability, tradition,

eg *Madness and Civilization: A History of Insanity in the Age of Reason* (London, Routledge, 2001) and *Discipline and Punish: The Birth of the Prison* (London, Penguin, 1991). See further Douzinas and Geary, *Critical Jurisprudence: The Political Philosophy of Justice* 55, who observe that 'The birth of the modern man is accompanied by a new type of normalising judgment … The norm, keeping to the norm and being normal become the form of law and morality.'

141 Torrant, *The Material Family* xiv.

142 Herring, *Relational Autonomy and Family Law* 17.

143 Most obviously, this includes the relationship between children and their parents, the relationships between siblings, and indeed many relationships between parents and children were not formed by any conscious choice (to become a parent) on the part of the parents.

144 Bauman, *Liquid Love: On the Frailty of Human Bonds* 29.

145 See eg Bernardes, *Family Studies: An Introduction* and Gittins, *The Family in Question: Changing Households and Familiar Ideologies*.

146 Chambers, *A Sociology of Family Life: Change and Diversity in Intimate Relationships* 36.

loyalty and bounded gender-identity are called upon by individuals and by law to constitute normative familial identities and relationships expressed in an idealised discourse'.[147] I argue that the promotion of these individualistic values of 'autonomy' and 'choice' ignores the significance of these contradictory normative tendencies that exists within social (and legal) understandings of the 'family'.

The criticisms of the orthodox construction of the rational and autonomous legal subject, discussed above,[148] have led to theoretical and conceptual attempts to redefine 'autonomy'; because, as Fineman comments:

> The very terms of autonomy – as exemplified by economic independence and a detached notion of self-sufficiency – might well be redefined or reimagined in the public mind. Independence is not the same as being unattached. Independence from subsidy and support is not attainable, nor is it desirable; we want and need the webs of economic and social relationships that sustain us.[149]

This redefinition is premised upon situating the 'autonomy' of individuals more explicitly within the social context of lived reality.[150] Fineman has further observed that the basis for this potential redefinition is that 'We delude ourselves when we think that many (perhaps any) endeavours in our complex modern society can be undertaken in an autonomous and independent manner'.[151] Given the nature of the conceptual ideals considered earlier in this chapter, such reimagining has often been premised upon a radically different underlying construction of the individual; the 'relational subject'. In this way, as Harding comments 'Rather than considering adults with capacity as atomistic individuals, we should consider autonomy as created by, dependent on, and exercised through relationships with other people'.[152] Therefore, this alternative approach to understanding and defining 'autonomy' has been described as 'relational autonomy'.[153] This concept is explained by MacKenzie and Stoljer as follows:

> '[R]elational autonomy' is an umbrella term, designating a range of related perspectives … premised upon a shared conviction that persons are socially embedded, that agents' identities are formed in the context of social relationships and shaped by a complex of intersecting social determinants, such as race, class, gender and ethnicity.[154]

[147] Diduck, *Law's Families* 42.

[148] Both in ch 2, s II, 'Critiquing the Orthodox Construction of the Legal Subject' and, in earlier in this chapter in subss I(A), 'Care and Relationality' and I(B), 'Vulnerability'.

[149] Fineman, *The Autonomy Myth: A Theory of Dependency* 28.

[150] Mary Midgley and Judith Hughes, 'Are Families Out of Date?' in Hilde Lindemann Nelson (ed), *Feminism and Families* (New York, Routledge, 1997) 65, comment that 'In an age when loneliness is so pressing, we need to talk less about freedom in the abstract and more about the balance between particular freedoms, the relation between the various evils from which people need to be free'.

[151] Fineman, *The Autonomy Myth: A Theory of Dependency* 33.

[152] Harding, 'Legal Constructions of Dementia: Discourses of Autonomy at the Margins of Capacity' 430.

[153] See eg Herring, *Relational Autonomy and Family Law*.

[154] Catriona Mackenzie and Natalie Stoljar, 'Introduction' in Catriona Mackenzie and Natalie Stoljar (eds), *Relational Autonomy: Feminist Essays on Autonomy, Agency and Social Self*, (New York, Oxford University Press, 2000) 4.

Thus, it appears that this concept of 'relational autonomy' involves a theoretical attempt to move beyond the binary between 'individualism' and 'relationality', and bridge the conceptual gap, by simultaneously recognising both the centrality of social relationships and of individual autonomy. As Herring suggests 'Once put in the context of other values that society and law values autonomy can be said to play its part in promoting individualism. Individualism ignores the complex web of relations and connections which make up most people's lives'.[155]

However, the concept of 'relational autonomy' has been critiqued for its vagueness and ambiguity, as Harding notes 'A key limitation therefore, of the "relational" view of autonomy is the lack of definitional interrogation of what relationality means in the everyday, situated, lives of individuals'.[156] Notably, this reflects the critique made of both 'care' and 'vulnerability', as to the ambiguity of their definitions.[157] This is unsurprising because the concept of 'relational autonomy' clearly derives from the normative values of 'care' and 'relationality' discussed above, and therefore the same critiques can be levelled against this concept. Moreover, the critique of 'relational autonomy' fundamentally questions the coherency of the attempt to recognise these two competing normative values within one overarching concept. As Harding further observes:

> If relationality means something else, perhaps rather than having the ability to come to any decision that we want on any given issue, our decision is pre-determined by the social relationships or relations of power in which we as individuals are immersed, then it seems to be too far removed from any possible common sense understanding of 'autonomy'.[158]

Thus, the critique suggests that both terms are effectively stripped of their meaning through this conceptual combination. In essence, the problem caused by seeking to redefine 'autonomy' in a manner that is compatible with a relational perspective is that the resulting concept ('relational autonomy') is rendered so ambiguous as to be almost incoherent.

II. Abstract Models and Real Families

The different conceptual factors considered in the previous section each provide a normative basis on which the legal understanding of the 'family' could rest,

155 Herring, *Relational Autonomy and Family Law* 20. Indeed, as he goes on to state, at 21 'we do not start from the atomised self and ask what choices they have made and whether this includes entering relationships. Rather the relationships are not means of perusing an individual's autonomy, but define the individual'.

156 Harding, 'Legal Constructions of Dementia: Discourses of Autonomy at the Margins of Capacity' 431.

157 As described above at subss I(A), 'Care and Relationality' and I(B), 'Vulnerability'.

158 Harding, 'Legal Constructions of Dementia: Discourses of Autonomy at the Margins of Capacity' 431.

instead of relying upon the idealised image of the traditional, nuclear family model.[159] However, each of these concepts can be critiqued for their ambiguity and for lacking the necessary specification to provide a comprehensible 'model' that would underpin the legal understanding of the family. Given the overarching and overlapping nature of the critique of these different concepts, in this section, I will unpick the idea that a conceptual model of the 'family' is necessary as a framework for the legal regulation of family life. My argument here is founded on the same scepticism of overarching models that has been evident throughout the exploration of the continuing normative influence of the traditional, nuclear family model in the preceding chapters of this book.[160] Thus, I argue that to seek to construct an alternative model of 'family', or a different philosophical understanding of the individual 'legal subject', represents a misguided approach to re-imagining the legal regulation of the 'family' in a manner which truly recognises and respects the diversity of contemporary UK families and family life. Therefore, my conclusion is ultimately more modest than that offered by the literature considered in this chapter; that the legal understanding of the 'family' should not be based upon attempts to construct an abstract model of family, but instead should be much more explicitly grounded in the lived reality of families themselves.

This section will return to the complexity of attempting to define the 'family', which was considered in chapter one, before considering the wider question, which has arisen throughout the book, of whether the law requires the definitional certainty it appears to desire in this context (subsection A). The section will then conclude by examining what embracing complexity and uncertainty, in this context, might mean for the legal regulation of families and family life (subsection B).

A. The Inherent Complexity of 'Family' and the Potential of Uncertainty

The preceding chapters of this book argue that the legal understanding of the 'family' continues to be premised upon the traditional, nuclear family model, comprising the central nexus of the conjugal relationships and the 'parent/child' relationship. Those chapters also suggested that this idealised image is an increasingly inappropriate model, given the diversity of family forms, practices and structures that are present within twenty-first century UK society. Given this conclusion, the previous section of this chapter explored the possibilities offered by various alternative, conceptual 'models' of the family. However, in that section,

[159] As, I have argued in previous chapters, the legal understanding of the 'family' currently continues to rely upon.

[160] This scepticism is particularly apparent in the substantive and detailed consideration of the legal regulation of the conjugal relationship and the 'parent/child' relationship that takes place within chs 3, 4 and 5.

I argued that these potential, 'alternative' conceptual understandings of the 'family' struggle, due to their inherent ambiguity, to provide the clear and logical 'model' which the law appears to desire. Thus, there is a recurring tension, both within the literature and within legal discourse, between recognition of the complexity of the meaning of 'family' and the strictures that the law places upon itself; as Herring states, 'The law loves its categorisations and the drawing of boundaries.'[161] As I have argued throughout, it is because of this need within the law for simple and readily understandable categories and definitions that the traditional, nuclear family has come to exert such normative significance upon the legal understanding of the 'family'.[162]

At this point, I believe that it is useful to return to the observation of Coltrane that 'we can never be quite sure what family means unless we can understand the context in which it is used'.[163] Previously, I argued that this lack of a readily identifiable definition of family as a social concept[164] created the conceptual space that allowed the traditional nuclear family model to provide the certainty sought by the law.[165] However, in this section, I want instead to suggest that this conceptual uncertainty is not necessarily problematic; I argue that it is recognition of the situational context of the social understanding of the 'family' that should be embraced within legal understanding. This involves the acknowledgment that it is difficult (if not impossible) to provide a universally applicable model of the 'family', whether that is the traditional, nuclear family model,[166] or an 'alternative' model based on the various conceptual factors discussed earlier in the chapter.[167] Therefore, I argue that the law should not base its recognition and regulation of families and family life upon any 'model' of the family; because as Leeder observes the 'family' is 'a highly elastic and changeable form'.[168] I recognise the radicalism inherent to this proposition, given the previously noted valorisation of certainty within the law.[169] However, throughout this book, I have argued

[161] Herring, *Vulnerable Adults and the* Law 264.

[162] See in particular the argument advanced by chs 1 and 2.

[163] Coltrane, *Gender and Families* 5. This was quoted above in ch 1, s I, '"Family" as a Social Concept'. This recognition of context reflects the language Lord Nicholls in *Fitzpatrick v Sterling Housing Association Ltd* [2001] 1 AC 27, at 41, where he stated: 'Family is a word with several different meanings. In some contexts family means children ("when shall we start a family?") In other contexts it means parents and child ("accommodation suitable for families"). It may mean all persons connected however remotely by birth, marriage or adoption ("family tree").'

[164] See the literature cited above in ch 1; for example, Bernardes, *Family Studies: An Introduction*, Gittins, *The Family in Question: Changing Households and Familiar Ideologies*, Leeder, *The Family in Global Perspective: A Gendered Journey*, Morgan, *Family Connections: An Introduction to Family Studies* and McKie and Callan, *Understanding Families: A Global Introduction*.

[165] See particularly ch 1, s II, 'The Law's "Definition(s)" of "Family"'.

[166] I have argued throughout the previous chapters of this book as to the various ways in which the traditional, nuclear family model represents an uneasy fit with contemporary family life.

[167] Or indeed on other proposed conceptual factors that are not discussed in this chapter.

[168] Leeder, *The Family in Global Perspective: A Gendered Journey* 2.

[169] See eg Diduck and Kaganas, *Family Law, Gender and the State*, as quoted above in ch 1, at 21: 'How can law, which depends on certainty, cope with this lacuna?'.

that this need for certainty has resulted in the awkwardness of the continuing normative significance of the traditional, nuclear family model. Moreover, the earlier sections of this chapter have set out the inherently problematic nature of attempts to 'model' the family around various conceptual factors; including 'care', 'relationality'[170] or 'vulnerability'.[171] Therefore, given this context, my argument is that the legal understanding of the 'family' should seek to embrace the elasticity and uncertainty inherent to the concept of 'family'. The result of this would be a legal understanding that sought to recognise the situated context of individual families and relationships, rather than attempting to apply an overarching conceptual understanding (or 'model') of the 'family' to the regulation of family life.

B. Future Legal Regulation of the 'Family'

As Foster and Herring have previously argued in a different context: 'We will have better laws if they do not make ludicrous assumptions.'[172] This statement is difficult to argue with in the context of the regulation of the 'family',[173] and this entire book has sought to unpack the assumptions (whether ludicrous or otherwise) that the law is making about the 'family'.[174] Therefore, the intention behind the suggestion that the reliance upon an overarching model or idealised image of family should be rejected, is to avoid the normative dominance of such implicit assumptions about what is and is not a 'family' within the legal understanding of the 'family'. At this stage, it is important to acknowledge that I am aware that this suggestion represents a completely different conceptual basis on which the law would approach the understanding and definition of the 'family'. This section does not seek to deny that there are significant potential difficulties associated with this idea,[175] but I argue that such a radical re-imagining of the underlying approach to the legal understanding of the 'family' is necessary to allow the law to respond more appropriately to the dynamic changes in contemporary family forms, structures and practices.

Relatedly, I argue that this approach is supported by the inherent conceptual complexity of the 'family', which cannot be simply or easily captured. The 'family'

[170] See above at subs I(A), 'Care and Relationality'.

[171] See above at subs I(B), 'Vulnerability'.

[172] Foster and Herring, *Identity, Personhood and the Law* 3.

[173] Or for that matter the legal understanding of the individual, through the construction of the 'legal subject'.

[174] Whether those are assumptions about the centrality of the nuclear family, assumptions about the differences between the 'appropriate' gender roles within that idealised image (ch 2), the assumption of the centrality of conjugality to the regulation of adult relationships (ch 3), the assumption that a child can only have two legal parents (ch 4) and the related assumption about the different roles of those parents (ch 5).

[175] However, I would note that in this book there is not the space or scope for a complete exploration of this proposed conceptual understanding and its difficulties (which would be both practical and doctrinal). Therefore, the suggestion of this section is made despite knowledge of these limitations and is therefore necessarily provisional in nature.

is an institution through which traditional social norms have been reproduced across the generations, while it also represents the location of the vast majority of society's 'care' and 'care work'. In addition, it can provide 'stability' and happiness for many,[176] but at the same time it is the source of 'vulnerability' and violence for many others. In contemporary discourse it is also increasingly understood as the vehicle through which 'autonomous' individuals choose to come together and structure their lives. Crucially, the concept of the 'family' can represent these contradictory ideas simultaneously and indeed it already does so in contemporary social understanding. This complexity of the 'family' is encapsulated by Diduck's comment that:

> Law may reflect what appear to be antagonistic values in families in order to sustain a particular vision of society that embraces both traditional and modern values. In this vision, 'the family' can retain its iconic status, while a moral imperative is created for individuals to *choose* it and to assume personal responsibility for that nurturing it.[177]

Thus, because the family is a complex concept it cannot be reduced to a simple conceptual definition[178] and I argue that it is necessary to embrace this uncertainty and complexity, rather than recoiling from it.

However, I also want to stress that this proposed approach does not represent the rejection of the normative value of 'care' and 'interdependence' in relationships, nor does it seek to diminish the significance of recognising 'vulnerability' within relationships, which have been explored earlier in this chapter. Rather, I argue that seeking to utilise any of these moral and ethical concepts to underpin the definition of the 'family' represents an imperfect and inappropriate solution to recognising and regulating the diversity of familial relationships, because the central idea of a conceptual 'model' itself should be rejected. In terms of the recognition of relationships, Herring has previously commented 'I would argue that what might make a relationship worthy of promotion by the state is care and mutual support, rather than sex'.[179] In this section, my purpose is not to deny Herring's premise that these are normative concepts that the state and family law should deem worthy of recognition, but instead to argue that these concepts should no more be used to construct an idealised image of the 'family', than the traditional, nuclear family model should come to represent that image. I would agree with the various bodies of literature considered earlier in the chapter that the

[176] Hans S. Reinders, 'The Power of Inclusion and Friendship' (2011) 15(4) *Journal of Religion, Disability and Health* 431, 432, states that 'Being loved by someone is what matters most in our lives'.

[177] Diduck, *Law's Families* 36.

[178] Diduck, 'Autonomy and Vulnerability in Family Law' in Wallbank and Herring (eds), *Vulnerabilities, Care and Family Law*, has previously recognised the existence of such conceptual complexity within family law itself, in the context of the dichotomy between 'autonomy' and 'vulnerability' discussed in the previous section, commenting, at 103, 'And so we have autonomy and vulnerability as the twin focuses in family law. The law acknowledges both statuses and that a person may inhibit each at different moments in their lives, but not that they can coexist'.

[179] Herring, *Caring and the Law* 192.

law should recognise a wider variety of relationships as familial and attach legal consequences to those relationships. Such a widening of the types of relationship that would be subject to legal regulation inevitably leads back to the spectrum of approaches, identified at the start of this chapter,[180] as to whether the consequences that currently attach to relationships deemed 'family' should be extended to other relationship forms, or whether there should be a reduction in the legal consequences which are granted to all relationships. However, I argue that there does not have to be a binary choice between these constructed opposites. Instead, I suggest that such a shift in the understanding of 'family' will inevitably lead to more fundamental questions regarding the purpose the law is seeking to achieve through relationship recognition and therefore, to a reconsideration of some of the rights and obligations that currently attach to various relationships.[181]

To conclude, this chapter has strongly cautioned against the potential of any alternative 'model' of the family, based upon a 'one-size-fits-all' conceptual solution (regardless of whether that model is based upon 'care', 'relationality', 'vulnerability' or 'autonomy') to replace the traditional nuclear family model as the idealised image within the legal understanding of the 'family'. This chapter has argued that this legal understanding should not be premised upon any model or image of the 'family'. Instead this chapter has suggested that a new approach should be taken to the legal understanding of the 'family', this re-imagined approach would more clearly situate the legal understanding of the 'family' within the context of individual, contemporary familial relationships. Consequently, I argue that this proposed approach to the legal understanding of the 'family' would be more capable of properly recognising the diversity of family structures and the proliferation of non-traditional family forms within twenty-first century UK society. As well as this, I argue that this understanding would be better able to reflect and acknowledge the inherent complexity of contemporary family life and the concept of the 'family' itself.

[180] Westwood, '"My Friends are my Family": An Argument about the Limitations of Contemporary Law's Recognition of Relationships in Later Life' 360.

[181] Moreover, I accept that this argument also raises the question of whether the concept of 'family' itself continues to represent the most appropriate organising concept for the legal regulation of personal relationships, or whether there should be an entirely different conceptual basis for the determination of legal recognition and regulation. I would suggest that this represents a further question that deserves sustained and wide-ranging consideration, which is outside the scope of this work.

Conclusion

This book began by observing that no single, universal definition of 'the family' exists within English law, Scots law, academic literature, or lay discourse within the United Kingdom. Instead, I have argued throughout that a particular, idealised image of family dominates our cultural and legal understandings: the nuclear family, comprising the nexus of the conjugal relationship and the 'parent/child' relationship. The impetus for the consideration of the legal understanding of the 'family', undertaken throughout the preceding chapters, was provided by the major reforms that have taken place within family law over the past several decades and the significant evolution in familial demographics within UK society during the same period. My concern has been to examine the extent to which the traditional archetype of family continues to exert rhetorical and normative influence upon the legal understanding of the 'family' despite the apparent radicalism of the recent changes. As Diduck and O'Donovan comment:

> [T]he notion of "family" may appear to have become complex and contested and infinitely extendable, and one way to describe our family living may be as "chaos". But when one looks closer at the partnerships and the relationships that attract "family" recognition, there is less scope for diversity than first appears, and law's response can be characterised perhaps less as chaotic than as normalising.[1]

To that end, I noted the absence of an agreed social or legal definition of the 'family'. A number of alternative definitions of 'family' were identified within the law. An examination of these definitions and their judicial interpretation revealed the centrality of the idealised image of the traditional, nuclear family. I argued for an understanding of the nuclear family as encompassing the nexus of the conjugal relationship and the 'parent/child' relationship (chapter one). I observed that this idealised image of family had recurred consistently throughout history and had come to be positioned as the 'natural' and 'common sense' model of the 'family'. I contended that the nuclear family is underpinned *both* by the orthodox, liberal construction of the 'legal subject' as rational, autonomous and self-interested *and* by the particular liberal understanding of the 'public/private' divide which, historically, envisaged separate and distinct roles for men (as 'father' and 'breadwinner') and women (as 'mother' and 'homemaker') (chapter two).

[1] Diduck and O'Donovan, 'Feminism & Family Law: Plus Ca Change?' in Diduck and O'Donovan (eds), *Feminist Perspectives on Family Law* 6.

Throughout, I have argued that this idealised image of family exerts significant influence upon the *legal* understanding of what 'family' means. This argument has been advanced both by examining various legal definitions of 'family', in chapter one, and by exploring how law constructs the two relationships identified as forming the nexus which comprises the nuclear family; the conjugal relationship, in chapter three, and the 'parent/child' relationship, in chapters four and five. I observed the influence of the idealised image of the family upon the legal regulation of conjugal relationships, arguing that legal recognition and regulation of adult relationships is extended only to those relationships which can be situated within the boundaries of the nuclear family model. I noted that the traditional understanding of marriage retains normative significance within the legal understanding of marriage, despite recent legislation opening marriage to same-sex couples. I argued that legal recognition and regulation has been extended to other, non-marital adult conjugal relationships on the basis that they are constructed as being sufficiently 'marriage-like' to fulfil the same functions as marriage within the nuclear family (chapter three).

I noted the influence of the nuclear family model and its construction of the distinct, gendered parenting roles of 'mother' and 'father' upon the attribution of legal parenthood (chapter four) and in the legal construction of the role of the 'parent' (chapter five). In chapter four, I argued that legal parenthood is premised around a binary, two-parent model, which ideally comprises one mother and one father. I contended that this approach was particularly problematic for determining legal parenthood in the contexts of medically assisted reproduction and surrogacy, because of the additional factual complexity introduced by those circumstances. In chapter five, I argued that the impact of these gendered roles upon the legal construction and understanding of the role of the 'parent' was evident. I observed that despite the use of the gender-neutral terminology of 'parent', the judicial understanding of parenthood and parenting continues to be underpinned by the traditional, *gendered* parenting roles of 'mother' and 'father', as derived from the idealised image of the nuclear family.

Finally, I considered the possibilities offered by alternative models of the 'family', based upon various conceptual values, including 'care', 'vulnerability' and 'autonomy' (chapter six). I argued that rather than attempting to reconceive the legal understanding of the 'family' on the basis of such an alternative model, this reliance upon such models should itself be rejected. Instead, I suggested a radical re-imagining of the way in which the concept of 'family' was constructed and understood; based around situating this legal understanding much more explicitly within the diversity, complexity and uncertainty of the lived reality of contemporary family relationships and family life.

Previously, Diduck has commented that:

> [T]he moral attributes we ascribe to the families we live by are also those we ascribe to the traditional family – romantic love, stability, loyalty and unity. They are important to us as individuals because they reflect the expectations or hopes we have for our

> relationships, and they are also important socially as they embody what we would like family life to mean in a seemingly amoral society. That they may exist on only an ideal or mythical level is not important.[2]

Therefore, the central conclusion of this book is that the understanding of 'the family' within the law remains premised upon the traditional, nuclear family, comprised of the nexus of the conjugal relationship and the 'parent/child' relationship, and that the continuing centrality of the nuclear model sits uneasily against the complex and diverse family forms, practices and structures within twenty-first century UK society. I concluded that the extension of legal regulation to adult relationships which possess 'marriage-like' conjugality illustrates the significance of this idealised image of the nuclear family within the legal understanding of the family. I further concluded that the influence of this archetype of family was evident from the continued normative significance of the gendered parenting roles of 'mother' and 'father' in the legal understanding of the role of the 'parent'. Ultimately, I have sought to establish, by detailed and systemic analysis, that, in spite of the aforementioned law reforms and changes in social and familial demographics, the traditional nuclear family retains its centrality within the legal understanding and construction of the 'family', while its core ideals and values have remained virtually unchanged and unchallenged. As Nicolson observes 'the belief in the "traditional" family has been sustained, even in the context of widespread changes, because of the surface invisibility of many of the changes. This surface invisibility allows people to impose "traditionality" even where it does not exist'.[3] Thereafter, I considered whether this reliance upon the traditional, nuclear family could be replaced by an alternative conceptual model of 'family', based upon recognition of moral and ethical values. After this examination, I concluded that a radical re-imagining of the approach to defining and regulating the 'family' was required; in which the normative construction of a model of the 'family' should be rejected and replaced by an attempt to embrace the uncertainty inherent to the concept of 'family' itself.

My overall conclusion then is that the law reforms are less radical than they might appear at first sight and that their reflection of changes in demographics and changes in social acceptability of family forms must not blind us to the continuing gravitational pull of the traditional nuclear family model. Family law has not shifted its focus to a care-based, or a multi-layered, model. The parameters of the legal understanding of the 'family' were set long ago and while family law now regulates more family forms than it did 50 years ago, the parameters themselves remain steadfast.

In 1997, Mrs Justice Hale (as she then was), writing extra-judicially, asked of family law 'Can it evolve further to meet its new role: of encouraging families to go

[2] Diduck, *Law's Families* 22.

[3] Linda Nicholson, 'The Myth of the Traditional Family', in Lindemann Nelson (ed), *Feminism and Families* 37.

on meeting the responsibilities which we all need them to meet, despite a rapidly changing pattern of family relationships?'[4] I regard this question as being as relevant now as it was then, given the demographic, social, and legislative changes that have occurred since then. Diduck has commented that 'Family law determines the responsibilities of individuals to each other and by extension, the responsibilities of families and the state and the community to each other'.[5] I agree that family law will continue to serve these same functions in response to additional legislative reform,[6] as well as to further evolutions in social practices and attitudes. As has been described here, social demographics and familial structures continue to change;[7] parenting practices and the roles of mothers and fathers are still evolving,[8] and medical and scientific progress continues to open up additional possibilities in the context of assisted reproduction.[9] Smart has commented that:

> As family life has become more fluid and diverse, with mixtures of cohabitation, marriage, remarriage, children from different relationships, a foreseeable rise in donor conceived children and surrogacy, and more transnational relationships, family's law purpose is increasingly to give recognition and legitimacy to different forms of relationship and kinship.[10]

How will the legal understanding of 'the family' respond and develop as a result of these changes? Eekelaar observes that:

> The very fluidity and complexity of 'real-life' family problems means that neat solutions cannot always be found, and it may take time to move to work towards the most satisfactory (or sometimes the 'least worst') solutions. Sometimes there will be no solutions.[11]

[4] Hale, 'Private Lives and Public Duties: What is Family Law For?' 126.

[5] Diduck, 'What is Family Law For?' 292.

[6] It is necessarily difficult to predict the future of legislative reform, but in the short to medium term there will be the Government's response to the 'declaration of incompatibility' in *Steinfeld v Secretary of State for Education* [2018] UKSC 32, which should lead to reform of the current exclusion of opposite-sex couples from civil partnership and the Law Commission's inclusion of surrogacy within its 13th Programme of Law Reform, which will lead to some proposals regarding reform of the legal regulation of surrogacy arrangements. Beyond that, there are a range of potential areas of reform (most obviously the legal regime for cohabitants in England and Wales) which are likely to be considered in the future.

[7] Chambers, *A Sociology of Family Life: Change and Diversity in Intimate Relationships* 53, argues that 'As the modern family changes during the early twenty-first century, emotional relations and friendships evolve as new and enduring forms of intimacy that can act as a surrogate family.'

[8] See eg Liz Trinder, 'Climate Change? The Multiple Trajectories of Shared Care Law, Policy and Social Practices' [2014] 26(1) *Child and Family Law Quarterly* 30, 49, who observes that 'Shared care in its widest sense has achieved the status of a social norm but shared time is not that much more common as a social practice'.

[9] A child being born with 3 'genetic parents' is now a scientific possibility, see eg Nuffield Council on Bioethics, 'Novel Techniques for the Prevention of Mitochondrial DNA Disorders: An Ethical Review' (June 2012). Indeed, the UK became the first country to allow such research as a result of the Human Fertilisation and Embryology (Mitochondrial Donation) Regulations 2015. Moreover, there continues to be scientific developments relating to other potential assisted reproductive technologies (for example uterus transplants and artificial wombs). It is likely that various technologies which are not currently generally available will become more readily available as scientific technology advances.

[10] Smart, 'Law and Family Life: Insights from 25 Years of Empirical Research' 29.

[11] Eekelaar, 'Then and Now – Family Law's Direction of Travel' 422.

I anticipate that the law, due to its abstract and objective nature, will continue to encounter such difficulties in responding to family problems and resolving familial disputes. It is possible that these are insoluble problems that relate to the essential incompatibility of the law as an instrument for the regulation of family life.[12] However, as well as this, there are conceptual and theoretical difficulties that will continue to arise in the context of the legal engagement with familial problems due to the way that the law itself is presently constructed; as Diduck has commented:

> [T]o the extent that family law reinforces the dichotomy between the vulnerable and the autonomous at the same time as it seeks to protect both, it remains blind to the reality of family living and to the gendered justice it endorses for family subjects.[13]

Unless and until there is an overarching and fundamental shift in the legal understanding of the 'family', the law will remain underpinned by the traditional, nuclear family and the gendered constructions of the roles of men and women, both as partners and as parents, which that model is premised upon.

Finally, as Sir James Munby has noted extra-judicially 'past judicial utterances that we now find almost absurd should serve as a terrible warning of how history will no doubt come, in due course, to judge the present generation'.[14] With this in mind, I am conscious that it is impossible to predict how the law might react to unknown future social developments. Nevertheless, as I have argued throughout this book, despite the recent major legislative reforms and substantial changes in social demographics, the traditional, nuclear family model, comprising the nexus of the conjugal relationship and the 'parent/child' relationship, has retained its normative significance as the 'common sense' and 'natural' idealised image of 'the family'. I have found no evidence to suggest that the substantial normative and rhetorical endurance of the nuclear family, this nexus of two relationships, is diminishing. It may well continue to underpin the legal understanding of 'family' for a long time to come.

[12] Bauman, *Liquid Love* 2, argues that 'People seek partners and "enter relationships" in order to escape the vexation of frailty, only to find that yet more vexing and painful than before. What was meant/hoped/expected to be a shelter (perhaps the shelter) against fragility proves time and again to be its hothouse.'

[13] Diduck, 'Autonomy and Vulnerability in Family Law' in Wallbank and Herring (eds), *Vulnerabilities, Care and Family Law* 114.

[14] Munby, 'Years of Change: Family Law in 1987, 2012 and 2037' 279.

REFERENCES

Books

Austin, John, *Lectures on Jurisprudence or the Philosophy of Positive Law*, revised and edited by Robert Campbell, 3rd edn (London, John Murray, 1869)

Barry, John C, *William Hay's Lectures on Marriage* (Edinburgh, Stair Society, 1967)

Bauman, Zygmunt, *Postmodern Ethics* (Oxford, Blackwell, 1993)

Bauman, Zygmunt, *Liquid Love: On the Frailty of Human Bonds* (Cambridge, Polity Press, 2003)

Beck, Ulrich and Beck-Gernsheim, Elisabeth, *Individualization: Institutionalized Individualism and its Social and Political Consequences* (London, SAGE, 2002)

Beck-Gernsheim, Elisabeth, *Reinventing the Family: In Search of New Lifestyles* (Cambridge, Polity Press, 2002)

Bernardes, Jon, *Family Studies: An Introduction* (London, Routledge, 1997)

Blackstone, Sir William, *Commentaries on the Laws of England*, Vol 1, 4th edn (Oxford, J Exshaw, 1771)

Bottomley, Stephen and Bronitt, Simon, *Law in Context*, 4th edn (Annandale, Federation Press, 2012)

Boyd, Susan, Chunn, Dorothy, Kelly, Fiona and Wiegers, Wanda, *Autonomous Motherhood? A Socio-Legal Study of Choice and Constraint* (Toronto, University of Toronto Press, 2015)

Calhoun, Cheshire, *Feminism, the Family, and the Politics of the Closet: Lesbian and Gay Displacement* (New York, Oxford University Press, 2000)

Cane, Peter, *Responsibility in Law and Morality* (Oxford, Hart Publishing, 2002)

Carty, Anthony (ed), *Post-Modern Law: Enlightenment, Revolution and the Death of Man* (Edinburgh, Edinburgh University Press, 1990)

Cassirer, Ernst, *The Philosophy of the Enlightenment* (Boston, Beacon Press, 1955, translated from the original German edition, 1932)

Chambers, Deborah, *A Sociology of Family Life: Change and Diversity in Intimate Relationships* (Cambridge, Polity Press, 2012)

Cheal, David, *Sociology of Family Life* (Basingstoke, Palgrave, 2002)

Christman, John and Anderson, Joel (eds), *Autonomy and the Challenges to Liberalism* (Cambridge, Cambridge University Press, 2005)

Collier, Richard, *Masculinity, Law and the Family* (London, Routledge, 1995)

Collier, Richard and Sheldon, Sally (eds), *Fathers Rights Activism and Law Reform in Comparative Perspective* (Oxford, Hart Publishing, 2006)

Collins, Hugh, *Marxism and Law* (Oxford, Oxford University Press, 1982)

Coltrane, Scott, *Family Man: Fatherhood, Housework and Gender Equality* (New York, Oxford University Press, 1996)

Coltrane, Scott, *Gender and Families* (Lanham, Rowman and Littlefield, 1998)

Connell, RW, *Masculinities* (Berkeley, University of California Press, 2005)

Cook, Rachel and Day Sclater, Shelley with Kaganas, Felicity (eds), *Surrogate Motherhood: International Perspectives* (Oxford, Hart Publishing, 2003)

Cotterrell, Roger, *The Sociology of Law: An Introduction* (London, Butterworths, 1992)

Davies, Margaret, *Asking the Law Question*, 3rd edn (Sydney, Lawbook Co, 2008)

Dickenson, Donna, *Property, Women and Politics: Subjects or Objects?* (Cambridge, Polity Press, 1997)

Diduck, Alison, *Law's Families* (London, Markham, 2003)

Diduck, Alison and Kaganas, Felicity, *Family Law, Gender and the State*, 3rd edn (Oxford, Hart Publishing, 2012)

Diduck, Alison and O'Donovan, Katherine (eds), *Feminist Perspectives on Family Law* (Abingdon, Routledge-Cavendish, 2006)
Dienhart, Anna, *Reshaping Fatherhood: The Social Construction of Shared Parenting* (London, SAGE, 1998)
Douzinas, Costas and Geary, Adam, *Critical Jurisprudence: The Political Philosophy of Justice* (Oxford, Hart Publishing, 2005)
Douzinas, Costas and Warrington, Ronnie, *Justice Miscarried: Ethics, Aesthetics and the Law* (New York, Harvester Wheatsheaf, 1994)
du Plessis, Paul, *Borkowski's Textbook on Roman Law*, 4th edn (Oxford, Oxford University Press, 2010)
Elliot, Faith Robertson, *The Family: Change of Continuity?* (Basingstoke, Macmillan, 1986)
Fineman, Martha, *The Autonomy Myth: A Theory of Dependency* (New York, The New Press, 2004)
Fineman, Martha and Grear, Anna (eds), *Vulnerability: Reflections on a New Ethical Foundation for Law and Politics* (New York, Routledge, 2014)
Foster, Charles and Herring, Jonathan, *Identity, Personhood and the Law* (Springer, 2017)
Foucault, Michel, *Discipline and Punish: The Birth of the Prison* (London, Penguin, 1991)
Foucault, Michel, *Madness and Civilization: A History of Insanity in the Age of Reason* (London, Routledge, 2001)
France, Anatole, *Le Lys Rouge* (Paris, Calmann-Levy, 1894)
Fraser, Patrick, *Treatise on Husband and Wife, According to the Law of Scotland*, 2nd edn (Edinburgh, T & T Clark, 1876–78)
Friedman, Marilyn, *Liberating Care* (Ithaca, Cornell University Press, 1993)
Frier, Bruce W and McGinn, Thomas AJ, *A Casebook on Roman Family Law* (Oxford University Press, 2004)
Gaius, *Institutes of Gaius*, Francis de Zulueta (ed) (Oxford, Clarendon Press, 1946–53)
Gay, Peter, *The Enlightenment: An Interpretation – The Rise of Modern Paganism*, 4th edn (New York, WW Norton, 1995)
Gilligan, Carol, *In a Different Voice: Psychological Theory and Women's Development* (Cambridge, Harvard University Press, 1982)
Gittins, Diana, *The Family in Question: Changing Households and Familiar Ideologies*, 2nd edn (Basingstoke, Macmillan, 1993)
Goodsell, Willystine, *A History of Marriage and the Family*, 2nd edn (New York, The Macmillan Company, 1934)
Govier, Trudy, *Dilemmas of Trust* (Montreal, McGill's-Queen's University Press, 1998)
Grassby, Richard, *Kinship and Capitalism: Marriage, Family and Business in the English-Speaking World, 1580–1740* (New York, Cambridge University Press, 2001)
Groenhout, Ruth, *Connected Lives: Human Nature and an Ethics of Care* (Lanham, Rowman and Littlefield, 2004)
Grossi, Renata, *Looking for Love in the Legal Discourse of Marriage* (Canberra, ANU Press, 2014)
Hand, Sean (ed), *The Levinas Reader* (Oxford, Blackwell, 1989)
Harding, Rosie, *Duties to Care: Dementia, Relationality and Law* (Cambridge, Cambridge University Press, 2017)
Harris, CC, *The Family: An Introduction* (London, Allen and Unwin, 1969)
Harris, DJ, O'Boyle M, Bates EP and Buckley, M, *Law of the European Convention on Human Rights* (Oxford, Oxford University Press, 2009)
Harrison, AW, *The Law of Athens: The Family and Property* (New York, Oxford University Press, 1968)
Hayes, Lydia, *Stories of Care: A Labour of Law* (Basingstoke, Palgrave MacMillan, 2017)
Heaphy, Brian, Smart, Carol and Einarsdottir, Anna, *Same Sex Marriages: New Generations, New Relationships* (Basingstoke, Palgrave MacMillan, 2013)
Held, Virginia, *The Ethics of Care* (New York, Oxford University Press, 2006)
Hennon, Charles B and Wilson, Stephan M, *Families in a Global Context* (New York, Routledge, 2008)
Herring, Jonathan, *Caring and the Law* (Oxford, Hart Publishing, 2013)
Herring, Jonathan, *Family Law*, 6th edn (Harlow, Pearson Longman, 2013)

Herring, Jonathan, *Family Law*, 7th edn (Harlow, Pearson Longman, 2015)
Herring, Jonathan, *Relational Autonomy and Family Law* (Springer, 2014)
Herring, Jonathan, *Vulnerable Adults and the Law* (Oxford, Oxford University Press, 2016)
Hobbes, Thomas, *Leviathan* (First published 1651, reprinted by Cambridge University Press, 1991)
Hodson, Barbara (ed), *Making Men into Fathers: Men, Masculinities and the Social Politics of Fatherhood* (Cambridge, Cambridge University Press, 2002)
Houlbrooke, Ralph A, *The English Family: 1450–1700* (London, Longman, 1984)
Hume, David, *A Treatise of Human Nature* (First published 1739, reprinted by Clarendon Press, 1896)
Hunt, Alan and Wickham, Gary, *Foucault and Law: Towards a Sociology of Law as Governance* (Boulder, Pluto Press, 1994)
Jackson, Emily, *Regulating Reproduction: Law, Technology and Autonomy* (Oxford, Hart Publishing, 2001)
Jaggar, Alison, *Feminist Politics and Human Nature* (Lanham, Rowman and Littlefield, 1988)
James, Susan and Palmer, Stephanie (eds), *Visible Women: Essays on Feminist Legal Theory and Political Philosophy* (Oxford, Hart Publishing, 2002)
Kelsen, Hans, *General Theory of Law and State* (New York, Russell and Russell, 1945)
Kelsen, Hans, *Pure Theory of Law* (Berkeley, University of California Press, 1967)
Lacey, Nicola, *Unspeakable Subjects: Feminist Essays in Legal and Social Theory* (Oxford, Hart Publishing, 1998)
Lacey, WK, *The Family in Classical Greece* (Ithaca, Cornell University Press, 1984)
Leeder, Elaine, *The Family in Global Perspective: A Gendered Journey* (Thousand Oaks, SAGE, 2003)
Levinas, Emmanuel, *Alterity and Transcendence* (Athlone, Linton, 1999)
Levinas, Emmanuel, *Humanismo Del Otro Hombre* (Madrid, Siglo, 1993)
Levinas, Emmanuel, *Totality and Infinity* (Pittsburgh, Duquesne University Press, 1999)
Lind, Craig, Keating, Heather and Bridgeman, Jo (eds), *Taking Responsibility, Law and the Changing Family* (Aldershot, Ashgate, 2011)
Lukes, Steven, *Individualism* (Oxford, Blackwell, 1973)
Lupton, Deborah and Barclay, Lesley, *Constructing Fatherhood: Discourses and Experiences* (Thousand Oaks, SAGE, 1997)
Mac Chombaich De Colquhoun, Patrick, *A Summary of the Roman Civil Law*, Vol 1 (London, V and R Stevens and Sons, 1849)
MacFarlane, Alan, *The Origins of English Individualism: The Family, Property and Social Transition* (Oxford, Blackwell, 1978)
MacFarlane, Alan, *Marriage and Love in England: Modes of Reproduction, 1300–1840* (Oxford, Blackwell, 1986)
Mackenzie, Catriona, Rogers, Wendy and Dodds, Susan (eds), *Vulnerability: New Essays in Ethics and Feminist Philosophy* (Oxford, Oxford University Press, 2014)
Mackenzie, Catriona and Stoljar, Natalie (eds), *Relational Autonomy: Feminist Essays on Autonomy, Agency and Social Self* (New York, Oxford University Press, 2000)
McKie, Linda and Callan, Samantha, *Understanding Families: A Global Introduction* (London, SAGE, 2012)
McPherson, CB, *The Political Theory of Possessive Individualism: Hobbes to Locke* (Oxford, Clarendon Press, 1962)
Mill, John Stuart, *On Liberty and Other Writings*, Stefan Collins (ed) (Cambridge, Cambridge University Press, 1989)
Moller Okin, Susan, *Women in Western Political Thought* (London, Virago, 1980)
Morgan, David, *Family Connections: An Introduction to Family Studies* (Cambridge, Polity Press, 1996)
Naffine, Ngaire, *Law and the Sexes: Explorations of Feminist Jurisprudence* (Sydney, Allen and Unwin, 1990)

Naffine, Ngaire, *Law's Meaning of Life: Philosophy, Religion, Darwin and the Legal Person* (Oxford, Hart Publishing, 2009)

Naffine, Ngaire and Owens, Rosemary J (eds), *Sexing the Subject of Law* (North Ryde, LBC Information Services, 1997)

Nekam, Alexander, *The Personality Conception of the Legal Entity* (Cambridge, Harvard University Press, 1938)

Noddings, Nel, *Caring: A Feminine Approach to Ethics and Moral Education* (Berkeley, University of California Press, 1984)

Noddings, Nel, *Starting at Home: Caring and Social Policy* (Berkeley, University of California Press, 2002)

O'Donovan, Katherine, *Sexual Divisions in Law* (London, Weidenfeld and Nicholson, 1985)

O'Donovan, Katherine, *Family Law Matters* (London, Pluto Press, 1993)

Pashukanis, Evgenii, *Law and Marxism: A General Theory*, Chris Arthur (ed) (London, Pluto Press, 1989)

Pateman, Carole, *The Sexual Contract* (Cambridge, Polity Press, 1988)

Perkin, Joan, *Women and Marriage in Nineteenth-Century England* (London, Routledge, 1988)

Rousseau, Jean-Jacques, *Of the Social Contract, Or Principles of Political Right* (First published 1762, reprinted by Dent, 1973)

Sachs, Albie and Hoff Wilson, Joan, *Sexism and the Law: A Study of Male Beliefs and Legal Bias in Britain and the United States* (Oxford, Martin Robertson, 1978)

Sealey, Raphael, *The Justice of the Greeks* (Ann Arbor, University of Michigan Press, 1994)

Sellers, Mortimer (ed), *Autonomy in the Law* (Aa Dordrecht, Springer, 2007)

Sheldon, Sally, and Collier, Richard, *Fragmenting Fatherhood: A Socio-Legal Study* (Oxford, Hart Publishing, 2008)

Sloan, Brian, *Informal Carers and Private Law* (Oxford, Hart Publishing, 2012)

Smart, Carol, *Personal Life: New Directions in Sociological Thinking* (Cambridge, Polity Press, 2007)

Smart, Carol, Neale, Bren and Wade, Amanda *The Changing Experience of Childhood: Families and Divorce*, (Cambridge, Polity Press, 2001)

Stacey, Helen, *Postmodernism and Law: Jurisprudence in a Fragmenting World* (Burlington, Ashgate, 2001)

Stone, Lawrence, *The Family, Sex and Marriage in England 1500–1800* (London, Penguin, 1979)

Taylor, Mark C, *Deconstruction in Context: Literature and Philosophy* (Chicago, University of Chicago Press, 1986)

Thompson, Sharon, *Prenuptial Agreements and the Presumption of Free Choice: Issues of Power in Theory and Practice* (Oxford, Hart Publishing, 2015)

Thomson, JM, *Family Law in Scotland*, 7th edn (London, Bloomsbury Professional, 2014)

Torrant, Julie P, *The Material Family* (Rotterdam, Sense, 2011)

Tronto, Joan, *Moral Boundaries: A Political Argument for an Ethic of Care* (New York, Routledge, 1993)

Unger, Roberto, *Knowledge and Politics* (New York, Free Press, 1975)

Vincent, Andrew, *Modern Political Ideologies*, 3rd edn (Chichester, Wiley-Blackwell, 2009)

Wallbank, Julie and Herring, Jonathan (eds), *Vulnerabilities, Care and Family Law* (London, Routledge, 2013)

Weeks, Jeffrey, Heaphy, Brian and Donovan, Catherine, *Same Sex Intimacies: Families of Choice and Other Life Experiences* (London, Routledge, 2001)

White, Robin CA and Ovey, Clare, *Jacobs, White and Ovey: The European Convention on Human Rights*, 5th edn (Oxford, Oxford University Press, 2010)

Wikeley, Nicholas, *Child Support: Law and Policy* (Oxford, Hart Publishing, 2006)

Williams, Fiona, *Rethinking Families* (London, Calouste Gulbenkian Foundation, 2004)

Young, Iris Marion, *Intersecting Voices* (Princeton, Princeton University Press, 1997)

Chapters in Edited Collections

Auchmuty, Rosemary, 'Dissolution or Disillusion: The Unravelling of Civil Partnerships' in Nicola Barker and Daniel Monk (eds), *From Civil Partnership to Same-Sex Marriage: Interdisciplinary Reflections* (Abingdon, Routledge, 2015)

Bainham, Andrew, 'Parentage, Parenthood and Parental Responsibility: Subtle, Elusive, Yet Very Important Distinctions' in Andrew Bainham, Shelley Day Sclater and Martin Richards (eds), *What is a Parent?: A Socio-Legal Analysis* (Oxford, Hart Publishing, 1999)

Bainham, Andrew 'Contact as a Right and Obligation' in Andrew Bainham, Bridget Lindley, Martin Richards and Liz Trinder (eds), *Children and Their Families: Contact, Rights and Welfare* (Oxford, Hart Publishing, 2003)

Andrew Bainham, Shelley Day Sclater and Martin Richards, 'Introduction' in Andrew Bainham, Shelley Day Sclater and Martin Richards (eds), *What is a Parent?: A Socio-Legal Analysis* (Oxford, Hart Publishing, 1999)

Barron, Anne, 'Legal Discourse and the Colonisation of the Self in the Modern State' in Anthony Carty (ed), *Post-Modern Law: Enlightenment, Revolution and the Death of Man* (Edinburgh, Edinburgh University Press, 1990)

Bottomley, Anne and Wong, Simone, 'Shared Households: A New Paradigm for Thinking about the Reform of Domestic Property Relations' in Alison Diduck and Katherine O'Donovan (eds), *Feminist Perspectives on Family Law* (Abingdon, Routledge-Cavendish, 2006)

Boyd, Susan, 'Challenging the Public/Private Divide: An Overview' in Susan Boyd (ed), *Challenging the Public/Private Divide: Feminism, Law and Public Policy* (Toronto, Toronto University Press, 1997)

Bridgeman, Jo, 'Parental Responsibility, Responsible Parenting and Legal Regulation' in Jo Bridgeman, Craig Lind and Helen M Keating (eds), *Responsibility, Law and the Family* (Aldershot, Ashgate, 2008)

Bridgeman, Jo, 'Relational Vulnerability, Care and Dependency' in Julie Wallbank and Jonathan Herring (eds), *Vulnerabilities, Care and Family Law* (London, Routledge, 2013)

Collier, Richard, 'Anxious Parenthood, the Vulnerable Child and the "Good Father": Reflections on the Legal Regulation of the Relationship between Men and Children' in Jo Bridgeman and Daniel Monk (eds), *Feminist Perspectives on Child Law* (London, Routledge-Cavendish, 2000)

Collins, Jennifer, 'The Contours of "Vulnerability"' in Julie Wallbank and Jonathan Herring (eds), *Vulnerabilities, Care and Family Law* (London, Routledge, 2013)

Cook, Rachel, 'Donating Parenthood: Perspectives on Parenthood from Surrogacy and Gamete Donation' in Andrew Bainham, Shelley Day Sclater and Martin Richards (eds), *What is a Parent?: A Socio-Legal Analysis* (Oxford, Hart Publishing, 1999)

Derham, DP, 'Theories of Legal Personality' in Leicester Webb (ed), *Legal Personality and Political Pluralism* (Carlton, Melbourne University Press, 1958)

Diduck, Alison, 'Autonomy and Vulnerability in Family Law' in Julie Wallbank and Jonathan Herring (eds), *Vulnerabilities, Care and Family Law* (Abingdon, Routledge, 2013)

Fineman, Martha, 'Responsibility, Family and the Limits of Equality: An American Perspective' in Craig Lind, Heather Keating and Jo Bridgeman (eds), *Taking Responsibility, Law and the Changing Family* (Aldershot, Ashgate, 2011)

Freeman, Michael, 'Feminism and Child Law' in Jo Bridgeman and Daniel Monk (eds), *Feminist Perspectives on Child Law* (London, Routledge-Cavendish, 2000)

Gilmore, Stephen, Herring, Jonathan and Probert, Rebecca, 'Introduction: Parental Responsibility – Law, Issues and Themes' in Rebecca Probert, Stephen Gilmore and Jonathan Herring (eds), *Responsible Parents and Parental Responsibility* (Oxford, Hart Publishing, 2009)

Golombok, Susan, 'Lesbian Mother Families' in Andrew Bainham, Shelley Day Sclater and Martin Richards (eds), *What is a Parent?: A Socio-Legal Analysis* (Oxford, Hart Publishing, 1999)

Gough, Kathleen E, 'Is the Family Universal? – The Nayar Case' in Norman W. Bell and Ezra F. Vogel (eds), *A Modern Introduction to The Family*, Revised edition (New York, Free Press, 1968)

Jackson, Emily, 'What is a Parent?' in Alison Diduck and Katherine O'Donovan (eds), *Feminist Perspectives on Family Law* (Abingdon, Routledge-Cavendish, 2006)

Jones, Caroline, 'Parents in Law: Subjective Impacts and Status Implications around the Use of Licensed Donor Insemination' in Alison Diduck and Katherine O'Donovan (eds), *Feminist Perspectives on Family Law* (Abingdon, Routledge-Cavendish, 2006)

Lacey, Nicola, '"Philosophical Foundations of the Common Law": Social not Metaphysical' in Jeremy Horder (ed), *Oxford Essays in Jurisprudence*, 4th series (Oxford, Oxford University Press, 2000)

Laster, Kathy and Ranan, Padma, 'Law for One and One for All? An Intersectional Legal Subject', in Ngaire Naffine and Rosemary J Owens (eds), *Sexing the Subject of Law* (North Ryde, LBC Information Services, 1997)

Linton, Ralph, 'The Natural History of the Family' in Ruth Nanda Anshen (eds), *The Family: Its Function and Destiny*, Revised edition (New York, Harper and Brothers, 1959)

Mackenzie, Catriona, Rogers, Wendy and Dodds, Susan, 'Introduction' in Catriona Mackenzie, Wendy Rogers and Susan Dodds (eds), *Vulnerability: New Essays in Ethics and Feminist Philosophy* (Oxford, Oxford University Press, 2014)

Mackenzie, Catriona and Stoljar, Natalie, 'Introduction' in Catriona Mackenzie and Natalie Stoljar (eds), *Relational Autonomy: Feminist Essays on Autonomy, Agency and Social Self* (New York, Oxford University Press, 2000)

Midgley, Mary and Hughes, Judith, 'Are Families Out of Date?' in Hilde Lindemann Nelson (ed), *Feminism and Families* (New York, Routledge, 1997)

Muncie, John and Sapsford, Roger, 'Issues in the Study of "The Family"' in John Muncie, et all (eds), *Understanding the Family*, 2nd edn (London, SAGE, 1997)

Murdock, George P, 'The Universality of the Nuclear Family' in Norman W Bell and Ezra F Vogel (eds), *A Modern Introduction to The Family*, Revised edition (New York, Free Press, 1968)

Naffine, Ngaire, 'Can Women Be Legal Persons?' in Susan James and Stephanie Palmer (eds), *Visible Women: Essays on Feminist Legal Theory and Political Philosophy* (Oxford, Hart Publishing, 2002)

Naffine, Ngaire and Owens, Rosemary J, 'Introduction: Sexing Law' in Ngaire Naffine and Rosemary J Owens (eds), *Sexing the Subject of Law* (North Ryde, LBC Information Services, 1997)

Nicholson, Linda, 'The Myth of the Traditional Family', in Hilde Lindemann Nelson (ed), *Feminism and Families* (New York, Routledge, 1997)

O'Donovan, Katherine, 'With Sense, Consent, or Just a Con?: Legal Subjects in the Discourse of Autonomy', in Ngaire Naffine and Rosemary J Owens (eds), *Sexing the Subject of Law* (North Ryde, LBC Information Services, 1997)

O'Donovan, Katherine, 'Constructions of Maternity and Motherhood in Stories of Lost Children' in Jo Bridgeman and Daniel Monk (eds), *Feminist Perspectives on Child Law* (London, Routledge-Cavendish, 2000)

O'Donovan, Katherine and Marshall, Jill, 'After Birth: Decisions about Becoming a Mother' in Alison Diduck and Katherine O'Donovan (eds), *Feminist Perspectives on Family Law* (Abingdon, Routledge-Cavendish, 2006)

Rawson, Beryl, 'The Roman Family' in Beryl Rawson (ed), *The Family in Ancient Rome: New Perspectives* (London, Croom Helm, 1986)

Reece, Helen, 'The Degradation of Parental Responsibility' in Rebecca Probert, Stephen Gilmore and Jonathan Herring (eds), *Responsible Parents and Parental Responsibility* (Oxford, Hart Publishing, 2009)

Sellers, Mortimer, 'An Introduction to the Value of Autonomy in Law' in Mortimer Sellers (ed), *Autonomy in the Law* (Aa Dordrecht, Springer, 2007)

Silva, Elizabeth B and Smart, Carol, 'The "New" Practices and Politics of Family Life' in Elizabeth B Silva and Carol Smart (eds), *The New Family?* (London, SAGE, 1999)

Simpson, Bob, Jessop, Julie A and McCarthy, Peter, 'Fathers After Divorce' in Andrew Bainham, Bridget Lindley, Martin Richards and Liz Trinder (eds), *Children and Their Families: Contact, Rights and Welfare* (Oxford, Hart Publishing, 2003)

Smart, Carol, 'The New Parenthood: Fathers and Mothers after Divorce' in Elizabeth B Silva and Carol Smart (eds), *The New Family?* (London, SAGE, 1999)

Smart, Carol, 'The Ethic of Justice Strikes Back: Changing Narratives of Fatherhood' in Alison Diduck and Katherine O'Donovan (eds), *Feminist Perspectives on Family Law* (Abingdon, Routledge-Cavendish, 2006)

Stoddard, Thomas B, 'Why Gay People Should Seek the Right to Marry' in Mark Blasius and Shane Phelan (eds), *We Are Everywhere: A Historical Sourcebook of Gay and Lesbian Politics* (New York, Routledge, 1997)

Stychin, Carl, 'Family Friendly? Rights, Responsibilities and Relationship Recognition?' in Alison Diduck and Katherine O'Donovan (eds), *Feminist Perspectives on Family Law* (Abingdon, Routledge-Cavendish, 2006)

Sugarman, David and Rubin, GR, 'Introduction: Towards a New History of Law and Material Society in England 1750–1914' in GR Rubin and David Sugarman (eds), *Law, Economy and Society, 1750–1914: Essays in the History of English Law* (Abingdon, Professional Books, 1984)

Trinder, Liz, 'Introduction' in Andrew Bainham, Bridget Lindley, Martin Richards and Liz Trinder (eds), *Children and Their Families: Contact, Rights and Welfare* (Oxford, Hart Publishing, 2003)

Tronto, Joan, 'Women and Caring: What Can Feminists Learn about Morality from Caring?' in Alison Jaggar and Susan Bordo (eds), *Gender/Body/Knowledge: Feminist Reconstructions of Being and Knowing* (New Brunswick, Rutgers University Press, 1989)

Tur, Richard, 'The "Person" in Law' in Arthur Peacocke and Grant Gillett (eds), *Persons and Personality in Contemporary Inquiry* (Oxford, Basil Blackwell, 1987)

Wallbank, Julie and Herring, Jonathan, 'Introduction' in 'Autonomy and Vulnerability in Family Law' in Julie Wallbank and Jonathan Herring (eds), *Vulnerabilities, Care and Family Law* (Abingdon, Routledge, 2013)

Weeks, Jeffrey, Donovan, Catherine and Heaphy, Brian, 'Everyday Experiments: Narratives of Non-Heterosexual Relationships' in Elizabeth B Silva and Carol Smart (eds), *The New Family?* (London, SAGE, 1999)

Journal Articles

Abdalla, H, Shenfield, F and Latarche, E, 'Statutory Information for the Children Born of Oocyte Donation in the UK: What Will They Be Told in 2008?' [1998] 13(4) *Human Reproduction* 1106

Ahuja, K, Simons, E, Mostyn, B and Bowen-Simpkins, P, 'An Assessment of the Motives and Morals of Egg Share Donors: Policy of "Payments" to Egg Donors Requires a Fair Review' [1998] 13(10) *Human Reproduction* 2671

Alghrani, Amel and Griffiths, Danielle, 'The Regulation of Surrogacy in the United Kingdom: The Case for Reform' [2017] 29(2) *Child and Family Law Quarterly* 165

Almack, Kathryn, 'Seeking Sperm: Accounts of Lesbian Couples' Reproductive Decision-Making and Understandings of the Needs of the Child' (2006) 20(1) *International Journal of Law, Policy and the Family* 1

Amato, Paul and Gilbreth, Joan, 'Nonresident Fathers and Children's Well-Being: A Meta-Analysis' (1999) 61(3) *Journal of Marriage and the Family* 557

Auchmuty, Rosemary, 'What's So Special About Marriage? The Impact of Wilkinson v Kitzinger' [2008] 20(4) *Child and Family Law Quarterly* 475

Auchmuty, Rosemary, 'Beyond Couples' (2009) 17(2) *Feminist Legal Studies* 205

Auchmuty, Rosemary, 'Law and the Power of Feminism: How Marriage Lost its Power to Oppress Women' (2012) 20(2) *Feminist Legal Studies* 71

Auchmuty, Rosemary, 'The Experience of Civil Partnership Dissolution: Not "Just Like Divorce"' (2016) 38(2) *Journal of Social Welfare and Family Law* 152

Bainham, Andrew, 'Arguments About Parentage' (2008) 67(2) *Cambridge Law Journal* 322

Bainham, Andrew, 'Rowing Back from *Re G*? Natural Parents in the Supreme Court' [2010] 40(4) *Fam Law* 394
Bamforth, Nicholas, '"The Benefits of Marriage in all but Name"? Same-Sex Couples and the Civil Partnership Act 2004' [2007] 19(2) *Child and Family Law Quarterly* 133
Barker, Nicola, 'Sex and the Civil Partnership Act: The Future of (Non) Conjugality' (2006) 14(2) *Feminist Legal Studies* 241
Barlow, Anne, 'Cohabitation Law Reform – Messages from Research' (2006) 14(2) *Feminist Legal Studies* 167
Barlow, Anne, 'Solidarity, Autonomy and Equality: Mixed Messages for the Family?' [2015] 27(3) *Child and Family Law Quarterly* 223
Barlow, Anne and James, Grace, 'Regulating Marriage and Cohabitation in 21st Century Britain' (2004) 67(2) *Modern Law Review* 143
Barnett, Adrienne, 'The Welfare of the Child Re-Visited: In Whose Best Interests? Part 1' [2009] 39(1) *Fam Law* 50
Barnett, Adrienne, 'The Welfare of the Child Re-Visited: In Whose Best Interests? Part 2' [2009] 39(2) *Fam Law* 135
Bendall, Charlotte, 'A Break Away from the (Hetero)norm?: *Lawrence v Gallagher* [2012] 1 FCR 557; [2012] EWCA Civ 394' (2013) 21(3) *Feminist Legal Studies* 303
Beresford, Sarah, 'Get Over Your (Legal) "Self": A Brief History of Lesbians, Motherhood and the Law' (2008) 30(2) *Journal of Social Welfare and Family Law* 95
Bevan, Chris, 'Self-Represented Litigants: The Overlooked and Unintended Consequence of Legal Aid Reform' (2013) 35(1) *Journal of Social Welfare and Family Law* 43
Bottomley, Anne, 'From Mrs Burns to Mrs Oxley: Do Co-Habiting Women (Still) Need Marriage Law' (2006) 14(2) *Feminist Legal Studies* 181
Boyd, Susan, 'What is a "Normal" Family? *C v C (A Minor) (Custody: Appeal)*' (1992) 55(2) *Modern Law Review* 269
Boyd, Susan, 'Gendering Legal Parenthood: Bio-Genetic Ties, Intentionality and Responsibility' (2007) 25 *Windsor Yearbook of Access to Justice* 63
Boyd, Susan, 'Autonomy for Mothers' (2010) 18(2) *Feminist Legal Studies* 137
Bremner, Philip, 'Collaborative Co-Parenting and Heteronormativity: Recognising the Interests of Gay Fathers' [2017] 27(4) *Child and Family Law Quarterly* 293
Bremner, Philip, 'Surrogacy and Single Parents Following *Re Z*' (2017) 21(2) *Edinburgh Law Review* 281
Bridgeman, Jo, 'Accountability, Support or Relationship? Conceptions of Parental Responsibility' (2007) 58(3) *Northern Ireland Legal Quarterly* 307
Brook, Heather, 'Zombie Law: Conjugality, Annulment and the (Married) Living Dead' (2014) 22(1) *Feminist Legal Studies* 49
Brown, Alan, 'Re G; Re Z (Children: Sperm Donors: Leave to Apply for Children Act Orders): Essential "Biological Fathers" and Invisible "Legal Parents"' [2014] 26(2) *Child and Family Law Quarterly* 237
Brown, Alan, 'Two Means Two, but Must Does Not Mean Must: An Analysis of Recent Decisions on the Conditions for Parental Orders in Surrogacy' [2018] 30(1) *Child and Family Law Quarterly* 23
Brown, Kate, '"Vulnerability": Handle with Care' (2011) 5(3) *Ethics and Social Welfare* 313
Butler-Sloss, Elizabeth, 'Ethical Considerations in Family Law' (2006) *Web Journal of Current Legal Issues* 4
Callus, Therese, 'First "Designer Babies", Now à La Carte Parents' [2008] 38(2) *Fam Law* 143
Callus, Therese, 'A New Parenthood Paradigm for Twenty-First Century Family Law in England and Wales?' (2012) 32(3) *Legal Studies* 347
Chan, Winnie, 'Cohabitation, Civil Partnership, Marriage and the Equal Sharing Principle' (2013) 33(1) *Legal Studies* 46
Clarke, Victoria, 'Lesbian and Gay Marriage: Transformation or Normalisation?' (2003) 13(4) *Feminism and Psychology* 519
Clough, Beverley, 'What About Us? A Case for Legal Recognition of Interdependence in Informal Care Relationships' (2014) 36(2) *Journal of Social Welfare and Family Law* 129

Cobb, Stephen, 'Legal Aid Reform: Its Impact on Family Law' (2013) 35(1) *Journal of Social Welfare and Family Law* 3

Collier, Richard, 'A Hard Time to Be a Father?: Reassessing the Relationship Between Law, Policy, and Family (Practices)' (2001) 28(4) *Journal of Law and Society* 520

Conaghan, Joanne and Grabham, Emily, 'Sexuality and the Citizen Carer' (2007) 58(3) *Northern Ireland Legal Quarterly* 325

Crawford, Claire, Goodman, Alissa, Greaves, Ellen and Joyce, Rob, 'Cohabitation, Marriage and Child Outcomes: An Empirical Analysis of the Relationship between Marital Status and Child Outcomes in the UK using the Millennium Cohort Study' [2012] 24(2) *Child and Family Law Quarterly* 176

Crawshaw, Marilyn, Blyth, Eric and van den Akker, Olga, 'The Changing Profile of Surrogacy in the UK – Implications for National and International Policy and Practice' (2012) 34(3) *Journal of Social Welfare and Family Law* 267

Cretney, Stephen M. and Reynolds, FMB, 'Limits of the Judicial Function' (2000) 116 (Apr) *Law Quarterly Review* 181

Crompton, Lucy, 'Where's the Sex in Same-Sex Marriage?' [2013] 43(5) *Fam Law* 564

Cullen, Deborah, 'Adoption – a (Fairly) New Approach' [2005] 17(4) *Child and Family Law Quarterly* 475

Dawson, John, 'The Changing Legal Status of Mentally Disabled People' (1994) 2 *Journal of Law and Medicine* 38

Deech, Baroness Ruth, 'Sisters Sisters – And Other Family Members' [2010] 40(4) *Fam Law* 375

Dewar, John, 'The Normal Chaos of Family Law' (1998) 61(4) *Modern Law Review* 467

Diduck, Alison, 'Shifting Familiarity' (2005) 58(1) *Current Legal Problems* 235

Diduck, Alison, 'If Only we can Find the Appropriate Terms to Use the Issue Will Be Solved: Law, Identity and Parenthood' [2007] 19(4) *Child and Family Law Quarterly* 458

Diduck, Alison, 'What is Family Law For?' (2011) 64(1) *Current Legal Problems* 287

Dietz, Mary, 'Context is All: Feminism and Theories of Citizenship' (1987) 116(4) *Daedalus* 1

Donovan, Catherine, 'Who Needs a Father? Negotiating Biological Fatherhood in British Lesbian Families Using Self-Insemination' (2000) 3(2) *Sexualities* 149

Donovan, Catherine, 'Genetics, Fathers and Families: Exploring the Implications of Changing the Law in Favour of Identifying Sperm Donors' (2006) 15(4) *Social and Legal Studies* 494

Douglas, Gillian, 'Assisted Conception and the Welfare of the Child' (1993) 46 *Current Legal Problems* 53

Douglas, Gillian, 'The Intention to Be a Parent and the Making of Mothers' (1994) 57(4) *Modern Law Review* 636

Draper, Helen and Ives, Jonathan, 'Paternity Testing: A Poor Test of Fatherhood' (2009) 31(4) *Journal of Social Welfare and Family Law* 407

Dunn, Judy, Cheng, Helen, O'Connor, Thomas G and Bridges, Laura, 'Children's Perspectives on their Relationships with their Nonresident Fathers: Influences, Outcomes and Implications' (2004) 45(3) *Journal of Child Psychology and Psychiatry* 55

Dunne, Gillian, 'Opting into Motherhood: Lesbians Blurring the Boundaries and Transforming the Meaning of Parenthood and Kinship' (2000) 14(1) *Gender and Society* 11

Eekelaar, John, 'Rethinking Parental Responsibility' [2001] 31(6) *Fam Law* 426

Eekelaar, John, 'Beyond the Welfare Principle' [2002] 14(3) *Child and Family Law Quarterly* 237

Eekelaar, John, 'Then and Now – Family Law's Direction of Travel' (2013) 35(4) *Journal of Social Welfare and Family Law* 415

Eekelaar, John and MacLean, Mavis, 'Marriage and the Moral Bases of Personal Responsibility' (2004) 31(4) *Journal of Law and Society* 510

Emmerson, David and Platt, John, 'Legal Aid, Sentencing and Punishment of Offenders Act 2012: LASPO Reviewed' [2014] 44(4) *Fam Law* 515

Everett, Kim and Yeatman, Lucy, 'Are Some Parents More Natural Than Others?' [2010] 22(3) *Child and Family Law Quarterly* 290

Featherstone, Brid, 'Taking Fathers Seriously' (2003) 33(2) *British Journal of Social Work* 239

Fenton, Rachel, Heenan, Susan and Rees, Jane, 'Finally Fit For Purpose? The Human Fertilization and Embryology Act 2008' (2010) 32(3) *Journal of Social Welfare and Family Law* 275
Fenton-Glynn, Claire, 'The Regulation and Recognition of Surrogacy Under English Law: An Overview of the Case-Law' [2015] 27(1) *Child and Family Law Quarterly* 83
Fenton-Glynn, Claire, 'Outsourcing Ethical Dilemmas: Regulating International Surrogacy Arrangements' (2016) 24(1) *Medical Review Law* 59
Fineman, Martha, '"Elderly" as Vulnerable: Rethinking the Nature of Individual and Societal Responsibility' (2012) 20(1) *Elder Law Journal* 71
Fortin, Jane, 'Children's Right to Know Their Origins – Too Far, Too Fast?' [2009] 21(3) *Child and Family Law Quarterly* 336
Fox, Marie, 'The Human Fertilisation and Embryology Act 2008: Tinkering at the Margins' (2009) 17(3) *Feminist Legal Studies* 333
French, Peter, 'The Corporation as a Moral Person' (1979) 16(3) *American Philosophical Quarterly* 207
Gabb, Jacqui, 'Lesbian M/Otherhood: Strategies of Familial-linguistic Management in Lesbian Parent Families' (2005) 39(4) *Sociology* 585
Gaffney-Rhys, Ruth, 'Same-sex Marriage but not Mixed-sex Partnerships: Should the Civil Partnership Act 2004 be Extended to Opposite-sex Couples?' [2014] 26(2) *Child and Family Law Quarterly* 173
Gaffney-Rhys, Ruth, 'EU Directive on Freedom of Movement' (2006) *International Family Law* 65
Gardiner, Michael, 'Alterity and Ethics: A Dialogical Perspective' (1996) 13(2) *Theory, Culture & Society* 121
Gilmore, Stephen, '*Bellinger v Bellinger* – Not Quite Between the Ears and Between the Legs – Transsexualism and Marriage in the Lords' [2003] 15(3) *Child and Family Law Quarterly* 295
Gilmore, Stephen, 'Contact/Shared Residence and Child Well-Being: Research Evidence and its Implications for Legal Decision-Making' (2006) 20(3) *International Journal of Law, Policy and the Family* 344
Gilmore, Stephen, 'Disputing Contact: Challenging Some Assumptions' [2008] 20(3) *Child and Family Law Quarterly* 285
Glennon, Lisa, '*Fitzpatrick v Sterling Housing Association Ltd* – An Endorsement of the Functional Family?' (2000) 14(3) *International Journal of Law, Policy and the Family* 226
Glennon, Lisa, 'Displacing the "Conjugal Family" in Legal Policy – A Progressive Move' [2005] 17(2) *Child and Family Law Quarterly* 141
Golombok, S, Braeways, A, Giavazzi, MT, Guerra, D, MacCallum, F and Rust, J, 'The European Study of Assisted Reproduction Families: The Transition to Adolescence' [2002] 17(3) *Human Reproduction* 830
Golombok, S, Murray, C, Jadva, V, Lycett, E, MacCallum, F and Rust, J, 'Non-Genetic and Non-Gestational Parenthood: Consequences for Parent-Child Relationships and the Psychological Well-Being of Mothers, Fathers and Children at Age 3' [2006] 21(7) *Human Reproduction* 1918
Grossi, Renata, 'The Meaning of Love in the Debate for Legal Recognition of Same-Sex Marriage in Australia' (2012) 8(4) *International Journal of Law in Context* 487
Hale, Brenda, 'Equality and Autonomy in Family Law' (2011) 33(1) *Journal of Social Welfare and Family Law* 3
Hale, Rt Hon Mrs Justice, 'Private Lives and Public Duties: What is Family Law For?' (1998) 20(2) *Journal of Social Welfare and Family Law* 125
Harding, Rosie, 'Sir Mark Potter and the Protection of the Traditional Family: Why Same Sex Marriage is (Still) a Feminist Issue' (2007) 15(2) *Feminist Legal Studies* 223
Harding, Rosie, 'Recognising (and Resisting) Regulation: Attitudes to the Introduction of Civil Partnership' (2008) 11(6) *Sexualities* 740
Harding, Rosie, 'Legal Constructions of Dementia: Discourses of Autonomy at the Margins of Capacity' (2012) 34(4) *Journal of Social Welfare and Family Law* 425
Harris, Peter G and George, Robert H, 'Parental Responsibility and Shared Residence Orders: Parliamentary Intentions and Judicial Interpretation' [2010] 22(2) *Child and Family Law Quarterly* 151

Herring, Jonathan, 'Where are the Carers in Healthcare Law and Ethics?' (2007) 27(1) *Legal Studies* 51
Herring, Jonathan, 'The Legal Duties of Carers' (2010) 18(2) *Medical Law Review* 248
Herring, Jonathan, 'The Disability Critique of Care' (2014) 8 *Elder Law Review* 1
Herring, Jonathan, 'The Welfare Principle and the Children Act: Presumably it's About Welfare?' (2014) 36(1) *Journal of Social Welfare and Family Law* 14
Herring, Jonathan and Foster, Charles, 'Welfare Means Relationality, Virtue and Altruism' (2012) 32(3) *Legal Studies* 480
Herring, Jonathan and Powell, Oliver, 'The Rise and Fall of Presumptions Surrounding the Welfare Principle' [2013] 43(5) *Fam Law* 553
Hibbs, Mary, Barton, Chris and Beswick, Joanne, 'Why Marry? – Perceptions of the Affianced' [2001] 31(3) *Fam Law* 197
Horsey, Kirsty, 'Challenging Presumptions: Legal Parenthood and Surrogacy Arrangements' [2010] 22(4) *Child and Family Law Quarterly* 449
Horsey, Kirsty, 'Fraying at the Edges: UK Surrogacy Law in 2015' (2016) 24(4) *Medical Law Review* 608
Horsey, Kirsty and Sheldon, Sally, 'Still Hazy After All These Years: The Law Regulating Surrogacy' (2012) 20(1) *Medical Law Review* 67
Jackson, Emily, 'Conception and the Irrelevance of the Welfare Principle' (2002) 65(2) *Modern Law Review* 176
Jadva, Vasanti, Murray, Clare, Lycett, Emma, MacCallum, Fiona and Golombok, Susan, 'Surrogacy: The Experiences of Surrogate Mothers' [2003] 18(10) *Human Reproduction* 2196
James, Nicholas, 'Separate Legal Personality: Legal Reality and Metaphor' (1993) 5(2) *Bond Law Review* 217
Kaganas, Felicity, 'Regulating Emotion: Judging Contact Disputes' [2011] 23(1) *Child and Family Law Quarterly* 63
Kaganas, Felicity, 'A Presumption that "Involvement" of Both Parents is Best: Deciphering Law's Messages' [2013] 25(3) *Child and Family Law Quarterly* 270
Kaganas, Felicity and Day Sclater, Shelley, 'Contact and Domestic Violence – The Winds of Change?' [2000] 30(9) *Fam Law* 630
Kaganas, Felicity and Day Sclater, Shelley, 'Contact Disputes: Narrative Constructions of "Good" Parents' (2004) 12(1) *Feminist Legal Studies* 1
Kaganas, Felicity and Diduck, Alison, 'Incomplete Citizens: Changing Images of Post-Separation Children' (2004) 67(6) *Modern Law Review* 959
Kan, Man Yee, Sullivan, Oriel and Gershuny, Jonathan, 'Gender Convergence in Domestic Work: Discerning the Effects of Interactional and Institutional Barriers from Large-Scale Data' (2011) 45(2) *Sociology* 234
Kelly, Fiona, 'Nuclear Norms or Fluid Families? Incorporating Lesbian and Gay Parents and Their Children into Canadian Family Law' (2004) 21(1) *Canadian Journal of Family Law* 133
Kelly, Fiona, '(Re)Forming Parenthood: The Assignment of Legal Parentage Within Planned Lesbian Families' (2009) 40(2) *Ottawa Law Review* 185
Kelly, Fiona, 'Autonomous from the Start: Single Mothers by Choice in the Canadian Legal System' [2012] 24(3) *Child and Family Law Quarterly* 257
Kielty, S, 'Similarities and Differences in the Experiences of Non-Resident Mothers and Non-Resident Fathers' (2006) 20(1) *International Journal of Law Policy and the Family* 74
Lawson, FH, 'The Creative Use of Legal Concepts' (1957) 32(5) *New York University Law Review* 909
Leckey, Robert, 'Law Reform, Lesbian Parenting, and the Reflective Claim' (2011) 20(3) *Social and Legal Studies* 331
Leckey, Robert, 'Marriage and the Data on Same-Sex Couples' (2013) 35(2) *Journal of Social Welfare and Family Law* 179
Leckey, Robert, 'Must Equal Mean Identical? Same-sex Couples and Marriage' (2014) 10(1) *International Journal of Law in Context* 5
Lewis, Jane, 'Adoption: The Nature of Policy Shifts in England and Wales 1972–2002' (2004) 18(2) *International Journal of Law, Policy and the Family* 235

Lind, Craig and Hewitt, Tom, 'Law and the Complexities of Parenting: Parental Status and Parental Function' (2009) 31(4) *Journal of Social Welfare and Family Law* 391

Lyonette, Clare and Crompton, Rosemary, 'Sharing the Load? Partners Relative Earnings and the Division of Domestic Labour' (2015) 29(1) *Work, Employment and Society* 23

MacCallum, Fiona, Lycett, Emma, Murray, Clare, Jadva, Vasanti and Golombok, Susan, 'Surrogacy: The Experience of Commissioning Couples' [2003] 18(6) *Human Reproduction* 1334

MacFarlane, Alan, 'Review of Stone' (1979) 18(1) *History and Theory* 103

MacKay, Kirsteen, 'A Plea from Scotland: Preserving Access to Courts in Private Law Child Contact Disputes' [2013] 25(3) *Child and Family Law Quarterly* 294

McAvoy, Sharon, 'Modern Family: Parenthood' [2013] *Fam Law* 1421

McCandless, Julie and Sheldon, Sally, 'The Human Fertilisation and Embryology Act (2008) and the Tenacity of the Sexual Family Form' (2010) 73(2) *Modern Law Review* 175

McGlynn, Clare, 'The Europeanisation of Family Law' [2001] 13(1) *Child and Family Law Quarterly* 35

Miles, Jo, Wasoff, Fran and Mordaunt, Enid, 'Reforming Family Law – The Case of Cohabitation: "Things May Not Work Out as You Expect"' (2012) 34(2) *Journal of Social Welfare and Family Law* 167

Millbank, Jenni, 'The Limits of Functional Family: Lesbian Mother Litigation in the Era of the Eternal Biological Family' (2008) 22(2) *International Journal of Law, Policy and the Family* 149

Mnookin, Robert, 'Child-Custody Adjudication: Judicial Functions in the Face of Indeterminancy' (1975) 39(3) *Law and Contemporary Problems* 226

Montgomery, Jonathan, 'Rhetoric and "Welfare"' (1989) 9(3) *Oxford Journal of Legal Studies* 395

Munby, Sir James, 'Years of Change: Family Law in 1987, 2012 and 2037' [2013] 43(3) *Fam Law* 278

Naffine, Ngaire, 'Who are Law's Persons: From Cheshire Cats to Responsible Subjects' (2003) 66(3) *Modern Law Review* 346

Norrie, Kenneth, 'English and Scottish Adoption Orders and British Parental Orders After Surrogacy: Welfare, Competence and Judicial Legislation' [2017] 29(2) *Child and Family Law Quarterly* 93

O'Donovan, Katherine, 'A Right to Know One's Parentage' (1988) 2(1) *International Journal of Law and the Family* 27

Parker, Stephen, 'The Best Interests of the Child – Principles and Problems' (1994) 8(1) *International Journal of Law and the Family* 26

Piper, Christine, 'Assumptions about Children's Best Interests' (2000) 22(3) *Journal of Social Welfare and Family Law* 261

Poulter, Sebastian, 'The Definition of Marriage in English Law' (1979) 42(4) *Modern Law Review* 40

Pritchard-Jones, Laura, 'The Good, the Bad and the "Vulnerable Older Adult"' (2016) 38(1) *Journal of Social Welfare and Family Law* 51

Probert, Rebecca, 'Cohabitation in Twentieth Century England and Wales: Law and Policy' (2004) 26(1) *Law and Policy* 13

Probert, Rebecca, 'Families, Assisted Reproduction and the Law' [2004] 16(3) *Child and Family Law Quarterly* 271

Probert, Rebecca, 'Hyde v Hyde: Defining or Defending Marriage?' [2007] 19(3) *Child and Family Law Quarterly* 322

Probert, Rebecca, 'Common-law Marriage: Myths and Misunderstandings' [2008] 20(1) *Child and Family Law Quarterly* 1

Probert, Rebecca, 'The Evolving Concept of Non-Marriage' [2013] 25(3) *Child and Family Law Quarterly* 314

Reece, Helen, 'The Paramountcy Principle: Consensus or Construct?' (1996) 49(1) *Current Legal Problems* 267

Reece, Helen, 'Divorcing Responsibly' (2002) 8(1) *Feminist Legal Studies* 65

Reinders, Hans S, 'The Power of Inclusion and Friendship' (2011) 15(4) *Journal of Religion, Disability and Health* 431

Rogers, Wendy, Mackenzie, Catriona, and Dodds, Susan, 'Why Bioethics Needs a Concept of Vulnerability' (2012) 5 *International Journal of Feminist Approaches to Bioethics* 11

Sandland, Ralph, 'Not "Social Justice": The Housing Association, The Judges, The Tenant and His Lover' (2000) 8(2) *Feminist Legal Studies* 227

Sevenhuijsen, Selma, 'Caring and the Third Way: the Relation Between Obligation, Responsibility and Care in Third Way Discourse' (2000) 20(1) *Critical Social Policy* 5

Sheldon, Sally, 'Evans v Amicus Healthcare; Hadley v Midland Fertility Services – Revealing Cracks in the "Twin Pillars"?' [2004] 16(4) *Child and Family Law Quarterly* 437

Sheldon, Sally, 'Gender Equality and Reproductive Decision-Making' (2004) 12(3) *Feminist Legal Studies* 303

Sheldon, Sally, 'Fragmenting Fatherhood: The Regulation of Reproductive Technologies' (2005) 68(4) *Modern Law Review* 523

Sheldon, Sally, 'From "Absent Objects of Blame" to "Fathers who Want to Take Responsibility": Reforming Birth Registration Law' (2009) 31(4) *Journal of Social Welfare and Family Law* 373

Smart, Carol, 'Losing the Struggle for Another Voice: The Case for Family Law' (1995) 18(2) *Dalhousie Law Journal* 173

Smart, Carol, 'Family Secrets: Law and Understandings of Openness in Everyday Relationships' (2009) 38(4) *Journal of Social Policy* 551

Smart, Carol, 'Law and Family Life: Insights from 25 Years of Empirical Research' [2014] 26(1) *Child and Family Law Quarterly* 14

Smith, Bryant, 'Legal Personality' (1928) 37(3) *Yale Law Journal* 283

Smith, Leanne, 'Is Three a Crowd? Lesbian Mothers Perspectives on Parental Status in Law' [2006] 18(2) *Child and Family Law Quarterly* 231

Smith, Leanne, 'Clashing Symbols? Reconciling Support for Fathers and Fatherless Families After the Human Fertilisation and Embryology Act 2008' [2010] 22(1) *Child and Family Law Quarterly* 46

Smith, Leanne, 'Tangling the Web of Legal Parenthood: Legal Responses to the Use of Known Donors in Lesbian Parenting Arrangements' (2013) 33(3) *Legal Studies* 355

Stafford, Helen, 'Concepts of Family Under EU Law – Lessons from the ECHR' (2002) 16(3) *International Journal of Law Policy and the Family* 410

Stewart, Ann, 'From Family to Personal Responsibility: The Challenges for Care of the Elderly in England' (2012) 34(2) *Journal of Social Welfare and Family Law* 179

Stychin, Carl, 'Not (Quite) a Horse and Carriage' (2006) 14(1) *Feminist Legal Studies* 79

Stychin, Carl, 'The Vulnerable Subject of Negligence Law' (2012) 8(3) *International Journal of Law in Context* 337

Thomson, Joseph, 'Whither the "Right" of Access?' 1989 *Scots Law Times (News)* 109

Trinder, Liz, 'Climate Change? The Multiple Trajectories of Shared Care Law, Policy and Social Practices' [2014] 26(1) *Child and Family Law Quarterly* 30

Waaldijk, Kees, 'Standard Sequences in the Legal Recognition of Homosexuality – Europe's Past, Present and Future' (1994) 4 *Australasian Gay and Lesbian Law Journal* 50

Wallbank, Julie, 'Castigating Mothers: The Judicial Response to "Wilful" Women in Disputes over Paternal Contact in English Law' (1998) 20(4) *Journal of Social Welfare and Family Law* 357

Wallbank, Julie, 'Too Many Mothers? Surrogacy, Kinship and the Welfare of the Child' (2002) 10(3) *Medical Law Review* 271

Wallbank, Julie, 'Reconstructing the HFEA 1990: Is Blood Really Thicker Than Water?' [2004] 16(4) *Child and Family Law Quarterly* 387

Wallbank, Julie, 'The Role of Rights and Utility in Instituting a Child's Right to Know Her Genetic History' (2004) 13(2) *Social and Legal Studies* 245

Wallbank, Julie, 'Getting Tough on Mothers: Regulating Contact and Residence' (2007) 15(2) *Feminist Legal Studies* 189

Wallbank, Julie, 'Channelling the Messiness of Diverse Family Lives: Resisting the Calls to Order and De-Centring the Hetero-Normative Family' (2010) 32(4) *Journal of Social Welfare and Family Law* 353

Wallbank, Julie and Dietz, Chris, 'Lesbian Mothers, Fathers and Other Animals: Is the Political Personal in Multiple Parent Families?' [2013] 25(4) *Child and Family Law Quarterly* 451

Welstead, Mary, 'Surrogacy: One More Nail in the Coffin' [2014] *Fam Law* 1637
Welstead, Mary, 'The Parenthood War: Biological Fathers, Lesbian Mothers and the Best Interests of Their Children' [2015] *Fam Law* 431
Westwood, Sue, '"My Friends are my Family": An Argument about the Limitations of Contemporary Law's Recognition of Relationships in Later Life' (2013) 35(3) *Journal of Social Welfare and Family Law* 347
Whitney, Shiloh, 'Dependency Relations: Corporeal Vulnerability and Norms of Personhood in Hobbes and Kittay' (2011) 26 *Hypatia* 554
Wikeley, Nick, '*Fitzpatrick v Sterling Housing Association Ltd*: Same-Sex Partners and Succession to Rent Act Tenancies' [1998] 10(2) *Child and Family Law Quarterly* 191
Wilson, Graeme, 'The Non-Resident Parental Role for Separated Fathers: A Review' (2006) 20(3) *International Journal of Law, Policy and the* Family 286
Woodcraft, Elizabeth, '*Re G*: A Missed Opportunity' [2007] 37(1) *Fam Law* 53
Woods, Lorna, 'Family Rights in the EU – Disadvantaging the Disadvantaged?' [1999] 11(1) *Child and Family Law Quarterly* 17
Wong, Simone 'Cohabitation and The Law Commission's Project' (2006) 14(2) *Feminist Legal Studies* 145
Wong, Simone, 'Shared Commitment, Interdependency and Property Relations: A Socio-Legal Project for Cohabitation' [2012] 24(1) *Child and Family Law Quarterly* 60
Yeatman, Lucy, 'Lesbian Co-Parents: Still Not Real Mothers' [2013] *Fam Law* 1581
Zanghellini, Aleardo, '*A v B and C* [2012] EWCA Civ 285 – Heteronormativity, Poly-Parenting, and the Homo-Nuclear Family' [2012] 24(4) *Child and Family Law Quarterly* 47

Reports

Adoption Policy Review Group, 'Adoption: Better Choices for Our Children' (June 2005)
Barlow, Anne, Burgoyne, Carole, Clerly, Elizabeth and Smithson, Janet, 'Cohabitation and the Law: Myths, Money and the Media', *British Social Attitudes Survey* 24 (SAGE, 2008)
Canadian Law Commission, 'Beyond Conjugality: Recognising and Supporting Close Adult Personal Relationships' (December 2001)
Crompton, Rosemary and Lyonette, Clare, 'Who Does the Housework? The Division of Labour within the Home', *British Social Attitudes Survey* 24 (SAGE, 2008)
Department for Children, Schools and Families, 'Support for All: The Families and Relationships Green Paper' (January 2010)
Department for Education, 'Positive for Youth: A New Approach to Cross-Government Policy for Young People Aged 13 to 19' (February 2010)
Department for Education, 'Supporting Families in the Foundation Years' (October 2011)
Department for Education and Ministry of Justice Consultation, 'Co-operative Parenting Following Family Separation: Proposed Legislation on the Involvement of Both Parents in a Child's Life' (July 2012)
Department of Health, 'Adoption: A New Approach' (December 2000)
Department of Health, 'Review of the Human Fertilisation and Embryology Act' (December 2006)
Department of Health, 'Surrogacy: Review for Health Ministers Current Arrangements for Payments and Regulation' (October 1998)
Department of Health and Social Security, 'Report of the Committee of Inquiry into Human Fertilisation and Embryology' (July 1984)
Department for International Development, 'The Future Operation of Civil Partnership: Gathering Further Information' (May 2018)
Deputy Minister for Justice, Hugh Henry, 'Response to Justice 1 Committee Stage 1 Report' (August 2005)

Equal Opportunities Commission, 'Fathers: Balancing Work and Family' (March 2003)
Family Justice Review, 'Final Report' (November 2011)
Harding, Maebh and Newnham, Annika, 'How Do County Courts Share the Care of Children Between Parents?' (Nuffield Foundation, July 2015)
HM Government, 'The Coalition: Our Programme for Government' (May 2010)
HM Government, 'Equal Marriage: The Government's Response' (December 2012)
Home Office, 'Supporting Families: A Consultation Document' (December 1998)
Horsey, Kirsty, 'Surrogacy in the UK: Myth Busting and Reform' (Report of the Surrogacy UK Working Group on Surrogacy Law Reform, November 2015)
Hunt, Joan and MacLeod, Alison, 'Outcomes of Applications to Court for Contact Orders After Parental Separation or Divorce' (Ministry of Justice, September 2008)
Hunt, Joan with Roberts, Ceridwen, 'Family Policy Briefing 3: Child Contact with Non-Resident Parents' (University of Oxford, 2004)
Joint Committee on the Human Tissue and Embryology (Draft) Bill, 'Human Tissue and Embryos (Draft) Bill, Volume I: Report', HL Paper 169, HC Paper 630 (August 2007)
Law Commission, 'Cohabitation: The Financial Consequences of Relationship Breakdown', Law Com No 307, (July 2007)
Law Commission, 'Thirteenth Programme of Law Reform', Law Com No 377 (December 2017)
Minister of State for Health, Philip Dunne, 'Human Fertilisation and Embryology Act 2008: Remedial Order: Written Statement' (29 November 2017, HCWS282)
Ministry of Justice, 'Judicial and Court Statistics 2011' (June 2012)
Ministry of Justice and Department for Education, 'The Government Response to the Family Justice Review: A System with Families and Children at its Heart' (February 2012)
National Records of Scotland, 'Divorces Time Series Data' (March 2013)
National Records of Scotland, 'Marriage and Civil Partnership Time Series Data' (August 2017)
National Records of Scotland, 'Vital Events Reference Tables 2014, Section 2: Adoption and Re-Registrations' (August 2015)
Nuffield Council on Bioethics, 'Novel Techniques for the Prevention of Mitochondrial DNA Disorders: An Ethical Review' (June 2012)
O'Brien, Margaret, 'Shared Caring: Bringing Fathers into the Frame' (Equal Opportunities Commission, 2005)
Office for National Statistics (ONS), 'Time Use Survey 2005' (July 2006)
ONS, 'Social Trends: Households and Families' (No 41, February 2011)
ONS, 'Short Report: Cohabitation in the UK, 2012' (November 2012)
ONS, 'Women in the Labour Market' (September 2013)
ONS, 'Divorces in England and Wales, 2012' (February 2014)
ONS, 'Marriages in England and Wales (Provisional), 2012' (June 2014)
ONS, 'Divorces in England and Wales: 2016' (October 2017)
ONS, 'Families and Households: 2017' (November 2017)
ONS, 'Marriages in England and Wales: 2015' (February 2018)
Parliamentary Under-Secretary of State, Ministry of Justice, Jonathan Djanogly (6 September 2011, Hansard HC Col 16WS)
Park, Alison and Rhead, Rebecca, 'Personal Relationships: Changing Attitudes Towards Sex, Marriage and Parenthood', *British Social Attitudes Survey* 30 (2013)
Registrar General for Scotland, 'Scotland's Population 2011 – The Registrar General's Annual Review of Demographic Trends 157th edition' (August 2012)
Registrar General for Scotland, 'Scotland's Population 2013 – The Registrar General's Annual Review of Demographic Trends 159th edition' (August 2014)
Scott, Jacqueline, 'Family and Gender Roles: How Attitudes are Changing?' (GeNet Working Paper, No 21, 2006)
Scott, Jacqueline and Clery, Elizabeth, 'Gender Roles: An Incomplete Revolution?' *British Social Attitudes Survey* 30, (2013)

Scottish Government, 'Review of Civil Partnership: Scottish Government Response to the Consultation' (November 2017)
Scottish Law Commission, 'Report on Family Law' (No 135, May 1992)
Scottish Law Commission, 'Tenth Programme of Law Reform' (No 250, February 2018)
The Scottish Office, 'Scotland's Children: Proposals for Child Care Policy and Law' (August 1993)
Wasoff, Fran and Martin, Claudia, 'Scottish Social Attitudes Survey 2004: Family Module Report' (August 2005)

Newspaper Articles

Dutta, Kunal, 'Masculinity in Crisis: "There is a Battle Going on Inside Us That is Never Discussed"' (*The Independent*, London, 19 May 2013)
Hope, Christopher, 'We Will Legalise Gay Marriage by 2015, says David Cameron' (*Daily Telegraph*, London, 24 July 2012)
Poole, Glen 'How Tackling the "Crisis of Masculinity" Creates a Crisis for Feminism' (*The Guardian*, London, 15 May 2013)

Internet Resources

'Book of Common Prayer: The Form of Solemnization of Matrimony': www.churchofengland.org/prayer-worship/worship/book-of-common-prayer/the-form-of-solemnization-of-matrimony.aspx
Childlessness Overcome Through Surrogacy: www.surrogacy.org.uk/
'HM Government – Childcare Choices': www.childcarechoices.gov.uk/
'Modern Fatherhood: Fathers, Work and Families in the 21st Century': www.modernfatherhood.org/themes/fathers-and-work/?view=key-facts-and-figures
'The NHS Choice Framework': www.gov.uk/government/publications/the-nhs-choice-framework
'Trends in Fathers Work-Family Arrangements and Fathers Working Hours (2001–2011)': www.modernfatherhood.org/wp-content/uploads/2014/01/Nuffield-PRESENTATION-FATHERS-FINAL-2.pdf
'What Do We Know about Nonresident Fathers?': www.modernfatherhood.org/wp-content/uploads/2013/11/Briefing-paper-Non-resident-fathers.pdf

INDEX